ARLOTT

The Authorised Biography

ARLOTT

The Authorised Biography

DAVID RAYVERN ALLEN

HarperCollins*Publishers*

HarperCollins*Publishers*
77–85 Fulham Palace Road,
Hammersmith, London W6 8JB

Published by HarperCollins*Publishers* 1994
1 3 5 7 9 8 6 4 2

A catalogue record for this book is
available from the British Library

ISBN 0 246 13825 4

Photoset in Linotron Janson by
Rowland Phototypesetting Ltd
Bury St Edmunds, Suffolk

Printed and bound in Great Britain by
HarperCollinsManufacturing Glasgow

To Rosemary, Lindsay and Briony,
who gave me room and knew when to leave

Contents

List of Illustrations

Acknowledgements

The making of some books can render the author almost incidental to the process, and this biography fits into that category. A great many people gave freely of their time, hospitality and thoughts during its long gestation, and mere thanks seem a poor reward. I shall be forever grateful.

I was very reliant on the enormous help and support given by John Arlott's wife Pat, his sons Tim and Robert, Dawn and Donald Barrington, Christopher Fielden, Richard France, David Frith, Leslie and Norma Gutteridge, Leo and Joan Harrison, Joe Molloy and Dennis Stevens. Part of their assistance is apparent in the body of the book.

Jack Bannister, Mike Brearley, Jack Donovan – sadly no longer with us – Patrick Eagar, Bill Frindall, Geoffrey Whitelock and John Wilkes also provided invaluable aid, as did the staff at the BBC Written Archives Centre in Caversham, where Gwyniver Jones, Christina Harris, Jeff Walden, John Davy and Guy Delauney were endlessly patient with my queries, realising that, in the last resort, John was most famous as a *radio* broadcaster, and that it was vital to demonstrate, reveal and recall how unforgettably he illuminated the art.

Many others are deserving of an individual eulogy which space denies. They know what they did, and so do I, and my thanks are none the less: Norman Ackroyd, Penny Ackroyd, Michael Aireton, Rex Alston, Kingsley Amis, Arthur Appleton, Arthur Attwood, Trevor Bailey, Frank Baker, Molly Baldwin, Mike Barnard, Peter Baxter, Staff at BBC Sound Archives, Gramophone Library and Reference Library, Richie Benaud, Barbara Benton, John Bodnar, Ian Botham, Chris Brasher, Chris Breeze, John Bridges, Dorothy and Alan Brisbane, Staff at British Newspaper Library at Colindale, Michael Broadbent, E.K. Brown, Jasmin Butt, Staff at Cambridge University Library, Diana Cappleman, Dennis Castle, Marjorie and Vincent Chapman, Denis Compton, Dick Corbett, Alan Curtis, Count André D'Aquino, Archie Davies, Patric Dickinson, Peter Dobereiner, Basil D'Oliveira, Marjorie Donovan, Michael Down, David Downs, Bert Duffin, Annabel Eagar, Hazel Edelston, Adrian Edwards, Matthew Engel, Lord (David) Ennals, Godfrey Evans, Ann Fielden, Paul Fitzpatrick, Joan Foa, David Foot, Lord (John) Foot, Debbie Frith, John Gatrell, Alan Gibson, Harold Goldblatt, Alf Gover, Tom Graveney, Stephen Green, Nigel Griffiths, Lord (Jo) Grimond, Hampshire County Police, Robert Harragan, Janet Hart, Reg Hayter, Jackie Hendriks, Eric Hill, Julian Holland, Justine Hopkins, Lord (Denis) Howell, Robert Hudson, Colin Ingleby-Mackenzie, Geoffrey Irving, David Jacobs, Evelyn James, Neil Jenkinson, Brian Johnston, Mark Jones, Frank Keating, Alister Kershaw, Charles Knott, Tony Laughton, Tony Lewis, David Lloyd, Preston Lockwood, Derek Lodge, Trevor McDonald, Alan McGilvray, John McKenzie, Ian McLoughlin,

Joyce Malcolm, Christopher Martin-Jenkins, Ron Mattison, Carol May, Michael Melford, Keith Miller, Tony Mitchener, Geoffrey Moorhouse, Jim and Stephie Morgan, Arthur Morris, Roy Nash, Mavis Nicholson, Bill O'Reilly, Kathy Parker-Allen, Staff at Park Prewett Hospital, Ray Parkin, Michael Parkinson, Tony Pawson, Clive Porter, Staff at Public Record Office and Somerset House, Alain Querre, Barry Reed, Geoffrey Rennard, Georgina Rice-Oxley, Marcus Robertson, Neville Rogers, David Roper, John Samuel, Bonny Sartin, Doris 'Mingo' Saunders, Don Shepherd, Gillian and Peter Sleight, Rachel Smith, Philip Snow, Karen Spink, Helen Steven, Eric Stokes, E.W. 'Jim' Swanton, John Thicknesse, Rt. Hon. Jeremy Thorpe, Ted Tillen, Bryan Timms, Isabella Todd, Frank Tyson, Betty Usher, Richard Walsh, Andrea Watson, Crawford White, Glenys Williams, John Woodcock, Ian Wooldridge, Wilfred Wooller, Derek Wren, Graeme Wright.

I would like to thank the following for permission to reproduce copyright material: the BBC for quotations from letters and memoranda; David Higham Associates Ltd for extracts from *Dylan Thomas: The Collected Letters*, edited by Paul Ferris (Dent, 1985); Alister Kershaw, literary executor to Richard Aldington, for three letters by Richard Aldington, © Catherine Aldington-Guillaume; Channel Four Television for the extract from *Arlott in Conversation with Mike Brearley* (Hodder & Stoughton in association with Channel Four Television, 1986: the programme of the same title was produced by Cheerleader Productions for Channel Four Television Company Limited; Quartet Books for the extract from *A Particular Kind of Fool*, by Noel Whitcomb (Quartet Books, 1990); Desmond Elliott, administrator of The Estate of Sir John Betjeman, for the version of 'Autumn 1964 (To Karen)', by John Betjeman. Also to Wally Fawkes and Peter Pugh-Cook for illustrations. While every effort has been made to contact the owners of copyright material, in some cases this has proved impossible. If the owners of such material contact the publishers, any omissions can be made good in future editions of the book.

I am grateful as well to John Pawsey for his encouragement, to Richard Johnson, Robert Lacey and Caroline Hotblack at HarperCollins for their equanimity, to John Bright-Holmes for his sympathetic guidance and dedication to the calendar, to Janet Reeve for her miraculous keyboard skills, and to my daughter Briony for her methodical indexing.

Finally, I should like to doff my hat to John Arlott himself. It was he who really started all this, and who is, unhappily, not able to see the result. The ready involvement of those above reflects the esteem in which he is held.

Preface

At first sight, it might be thought unnecessary to write a biography of a man who, a year before his own death in 1991, produced 'The Autobiography', as it is described on the title page of *Basingstoke Boy*. Yet those who have read that book will know to the contrary. John Arlott's fundamental humility made the writing of his autobiography no easy task. His adoption throughout of the third person as a literary tool reflected not only his feelings towards the project, but also his feelings about himself. In the end, the device became a method and a challenge to summon his own interest, and a shield for his reticence.

Although broad arrows never identified a convict more clearly than his own voice identified John, he was, basically, a private person. By placing himself at one remove from the narrative he in effect maintained that mental separation, and felt he kept a certain inbuilt objectivity. Essentially, though, he did not really wish to write an autobiography, and he would not have done so had the financial inducements not been too tempting to refuse. By the time he came to put it together, physical frailty had taken him past the stage where he could deliver a book that matched his stature.

Importantly, also, John's autobiography is unfinished. A second volume, entrusted to his son Tim, was sensibly transformed into a personal memoir which, by its very nature, does not deal in depth with many of the public events of his father's life.

When I proposed this biography to John he was totally supportive. 'There is no one else in the world I would rather have do it than you,' he wrote to me in a letter. Having been a close friend for over twenty years, I knew well the contours of his life. Apart from countless social occasions, we had spent much time working together in broadcasting and recording studios, and involved with literary collaborations. On my next visit to Alderney I told John that I intended to record interviews with those who had known him professionally and personally – a mirror from the other side. He opened his address book: 'So and so could tell you something about me,' he said, turning over a page. 'And he knows me well.'

'This cannot be hagiography,' I warned. 'There are going to be comments you will not like.'

'People will say what they have to say,' he replied. 'And so will you.' A pause, and then jocularly, 'That is, if there *is* anything to say.'

That knowingly mock-modest remark does not wholly conceal John's difficulty in accepting that anything he had done or taken part in would be of interest to anyone else. He was therefore prone to dramatise some of the events that had surrounded him, and to heighten his feelings in relation to them, ready to serve on cue to interviewers and audiences alike. Doing so was part of an emotional impulse, and is the reason, of course, why he was so adept at letting loose the imagination of his listeners. His intellect, though, was never clouded by passion.

John was a creature of extreme contrasts and bewildering complexities: at times scathingly critical of the faults of others (although never in print), indulgent and generous to a fault, gregarious and reclusive, self-effacing yet needing to be the centre of attention, overtly emotional yet full of calm reasoning and wisdom. Nevertheless, his public and private fronts were one. He was never anything other than himself in any situation.

The process of gathering material was long: visits far and wide, taped and telephone conversations, much researching and reading, forays into every corner that reasonably could be explored. During the course of the preparation, John died, which, however much one pretends otherwise, is bound to alter to some degree the tenor of the text. Even so, interviewees were just as forthcoming before and after his passing. The high level of direct quotation reflects both these conversations and those with John – casually over the years and on a more semi-formal basis for anthologies of his work and this book in particular. Most word-for-word is attributed in the text; but sometimes, when that might have interrupted the narrative, it has been left implied.

Although biography can impose certain constraints, it is impossible for me to refer to John Arlott in any other way than 'John', and so, in the main, the term is used throughout. All his friends called him that, and it is what he would have wished.

ARLOTT

The Authorised Biography

1

A Boy in Basingstoke

The sturdy yellow Trislander was sitting on the runway at Eastleigh, warming its engines. The journey to Alderney – a distance of some eighty miles – would take roughly forty minutes. Everybody in the waiting group carried their sadness lightly, but shared a single thought.

It was Wednesday 18 December 1991. The previous Friday night, John Arlott had lain in bed talking to his two sons. Tim and Robert had made their way to Alderney separately, one from France, the other from England. In recent years there had been many sightings of death, but this time, surely, there could be no escape. The local doctor, Struan Robertson, had confided in Pat, John's wife, and Geoffrey Rennard, a family friend, both of whom had been maintaining a vigil. 'He's fooled me before, but I don't think he will this time. One lung is just about solid.'

More than one plane carried passengers to the funeral that day in the beautiful parish church in Victoria Street, St Anne's. An abundance of friends, some relatives, a number of acquaintances and yet more friends. A truly eclectic mix that mirrored the man they had come to mourn: the famous, once-famous, nearly-known and unknown, their status irrelevant except to the hovering television camera.

The Revd. Stephen Ingham, vicar of Alderney, took the service; rarely had the church been so full. The address was given by John's oldest surviving friend, Jack Donovan. Jovial Jack, of Friar Tuck proportions, was exactly the right choice. A natural if unsophisticated public speaker, he delivered his thoughts with straightforward sincerity, recalling John's affection for Hampshire and Alderney and his great love of companionship: 'One was never bored or thirsty in his company . . . I didn't know John because he was famous. I knew John because he was my friend, since the time we both wore short trousers and sat next to one another at school. He was eleven and I was twelve, nearly seventy years ago . . .'

Basingstoke in 1914 was an unexceptional medium-sized country market town in northern Hampshire, 'waiting, not very impatiently, to be dragged into the twentieth century'. There was no remaining evidence to support the preacher John Wesley's view that he 'found the inhabitants put him in mind of the wild beasts of Ephesus'. In fact the town had sedate Nonconformist and Quaker connections, historical links with the corn and woollen trades, was an important railway junction, and a trading centre for engineering firms such as Thorneycrofts and Wallis & Steevens, who between them manufactured everything from steamrollers to military vehicles. Like hundreds of similarly-sized towns around the country, in which everyone seemed to know everyone else, it had a Church Street, Market Square and Potters Lane – and two 'gaffs', as the cinemas were known. The population in 1914 was around eleven thousand, and not until much later did it start to grow at twice the national average, when, along with such places as Stevenage, it became one of the 'dormitories' for London's overspill.

John Arlott, christened Leslie Thomas John, was born on 25 February 1914 in the old Cemetery Lodge on Chapel Hill, a long boundary throw from the railway station in the centre of the town. The cemetery was where his grandfather 'Old John' registered interments.

The Lodge was, and still is, a strikingly unusual building, with semblances of a medieval East European castle and an up-market Swiss chalet. Two turrets, separated by impressive wrought-iron gates and an elevated footbridge, form the entrance to the grounds. Once inside the gates, a steep incline with a sharp fork to the right takes the visitor to the crumbling arches of an ancient ruin – the thirteenth-century Chapel of the Holy Ghost: some of its Latin inscriptions are now barely decipherable. A pathway half-left leads to the middle of the cemetery. On the right is a small strath of unused green – unused for burial purposes, that is – which is surrounded by hollies and yew.

John arrived a few months before World War I, and it was during those years of turmoil and then revendication that he played his first games on home territory. Not all of them were with bat and ball. 'Young Jack', as he was known throughout his childhood and early manhood, was the archetypal mischievous boy. His cousin Molly, seven years his junior, who lived in the Arlott household with her mother Edie Baldwin, remembers him as 'a little horror'. A recurrent vexation for her was when John took it upon himself to shut and lock the various cemetery gates at night. He would take Molly along for the walk and then leave her inside, pleading to be let out.

He would also offer to push Molly's pram for her mother, and as they approached the brow of a slope, let go of it without warning. With the pram gathering pace and the little girl strapped in and screaming, John would make a last-second dash to stop it just before the road was reached.

As she grew older, Molly's tribulations eased to the extent of being allowed to participate – as a fielder only – in games of cricket with John and his chums in one of the few open spaces in the cemetery.

Another favourite trick of John's was to hide the key of the chapel just as a funeral cortège arrived at the gates. Amidst barely restrained panic, the key would suddenly materialise from beneath the stair carpet. These were the pranks of any spirited schoolboy, and this one, according to his parents, was a 'lazy little devil' who liked to lie in bed.

John's father, William John, also called Jack, had been born in Victoria Street, Basingstoke, on 2 July 1883. For most of the 1914–18 war he served as a fitter with the Royal Army Service Corps in Mesopotamia and India, repairing Thorneycroft lorries, just as he had done at home. The 'funeral business', as the family referred to it, continued to be conducted by 'Old John' from a sitting-room in the lodge. John's grandfather was 'a short, lean, physically hard man' who drove himself relentlessly and was often violent in his responses, particularly when training animals. His birthplace was Silchester, in a simple thatched cottage with a yew tree, or 'Hampshire weed', shading the front door. Silchester was where Hampshire's first 'new town' had been built by the Romans. From there to Basingstoke is only eight miles, and it is a straight road. But 'Old John' did not take the straight road. He went to sea.

In years to come, when seated around the converted Italian oak refectory table at which every meal took place, whether at the Old Sun in Alresford or at The Vines on Alderney, John Arlott would tell his guests the story of how that was supposed to have come about.

As a youngster, 'Old John' worked for a baker in Aldershot. On Saturday mornings he was required to be at the bakehouse by 3.30 a.m., in order to load the cart for the extra-long delivery round. Not surprisingly, he sometimes overslept. The baker, who paid for his delivery boy's lodgings, warned the landlady that if she did not rouse him in time, he would transfer him to the premises of somebody who would. The landlady – an elderly widow who could ill afford to lose the income – duly passed the buck to the boy: 'If you're not in by half-past eight on Friday nights, you'll be locked out.'

Inevitably, one January night a few weeks later, the boy was late, and she kept her word. His banging on the door and pleas for clemency only reinforced her uncompromising stance. 'You can stay outside and go straight to work from there,' she cried out. 'I'm not letting you in – perhaps now you'll learn a lesson.'

The boy – who was not only very tired but extremely cold – changed his tactics: 'If you don't let me in, I'll throw myself down the well.'

Silence.

'I will!'

Further silence.

Desperation lent him strength, and he managed to lift the boulder off the well cover. The splash as it hit the water far below sounded authentic enough. A lit candle in the bedroom, a scamper by the boy to hide in the shadows behind the door, clomping footsteps coming down the staircase, the unbolting of the door and, as the landlady rushed across to the well, he skipped into the house and secured the lock behind him.

'Now stay outside yourself, and see how you like it!' he yelled.

The old lady was too proud to beg for re-admittance. The boy only intended her to experience the nocturnal freeze for a few minutes, but unfortunately the combination of fatigue and a warm fire led him to fall asleep. He awoke with a start some hours later and immediately scuttled out into the yard. The figure in the woodshed was wearing only a night-gown. She was icy cold, and decidedly dead.

'So that was why he ran away to sea,' recounted his grandson.

John loved to tell stories. A lot of them were true, or only slightly varnished. That tale about his grandfather was usually accompanied by a chuckle and a shake of the head as a sort of rider. When pursuing the family pedigree further back, he would trudge to one of the shelves of the adjoining Long Room which housed his book collections, and return with the *Annual Register for the Year 1773* as evidence:

Winchester, March 20. This day Robert Arlett, for robbing and threatening to murder Mr D. Chase, near Basingstoke, was executed here pursuant to his sentence. He confessed the fact. His father and grandfather were both hanged here for offences of the like nature; his mother was transported; his brother is now here under sentence of transportation; and he himself was tried at Reading, on four indictments, two years ago.

There are Arletts in Basingstoke's Worting Road cemetery, and even on official documents variable spelling was a common occurrence in the eighteenth century. Surnames originated from nicknames, a practice adopted by the Anglo-Saxons. The name 'Arlett' referred to a young lad, or a vagabond or rogue.

In October 1919 John's father finally came back from the war, to find himself unemployed. Not that work was uppermost in his mind when his troop train pulled in to Basingstoke station. First there was the emotional family reunion and refamiliarisation with domestic life to be enjoyed, but soon his thoughts turned to finding a way to earn a living. With the end of hostilities demand had slackened, and his old employers Thorneycrofts had a surfeit of unsold lorries and components in their yard. The firm was looking to lay off rather than re-engage staff, and many returned servicemen had stronger cases than Jack Arlott for being re-employed, as they had worked for 'Thorneys' for longer before the war.

The manager was apologetic but adamant: there was nothing he could offer. As he walked back up the hill to the lodge, John's father reflected bitterly. By repairing the TCVs (troop carrying vehicles) so competently on foreign shores, he had helped put himself out of a job at home. Fortunately for his family's future, the solution to his problem lay just outside his own doorstep.

'Old John' was looking after two Basingstoke cemeteries, the one by Chapel Hill and another in the Worting Road, which nowadays lies alongside part of the circuitous traffic flow system Ringway West. 'Be my assistant,' said the old man to his son. 'We need a chap at the Old Lodge: take on there.' And so he did, for the rest of his working life.

John's mother, Nellie, was a daughter of Thomas Clarke from Brockenhurst in the New Forest, who had worked on the land. Later in his life Clarke, who was known as 'a bit of a roamer', had been employed as a foreman by dam builders in the Scottish Highlands, and while sleeping in a tent in damp and cold conditions he contracted rheumatic fever, which led to a heart condition. He semi-retired to Eastbourne with his Worcestershire-born wife Elizabeth, and as a part-time job helped maintain the public gardens for the Duke of Devonshire. It was in Eastbourne that his daughter Ellen – 'Nellie', one of twelve children – met and married John's father.

Jack Arlott had gravitated to the south coast via Coventry and Wolverhampton, where he had worked as a metalworker, and Harrods' hardware department in Knightsbridge, London, where he had 'attended to' damaged goods. The chance in 1910 of joining a colleague called Parker, who was opening an ironmonger's in Meads Village, Eastbourne, and 'being able to serve behind the counter' was too good to resist.

Unfortunately, the denizens of Eastbourne did not frequent Parker's Store frequently enough, for just before Nellie and Jack were to be married in April 1912, the shop door shut, never to be reopened. With Parker bankrupt, the newlyweds moved to Basingstoke, where Jack felt he might find work. And sure enough, he was soon 'fitting' at Thorneycrofts, and did so until war intervened.

The imminence of international conflict, and Nellie's pregnancy with John, persuaded the couple to accept an offer from Jack's father to move from the tiny terraced cottage in a Basingstoke backwater where they had been living to a likely long-term haven in the Cemetery Lodge, which was now lying empty. Crucially, too, the rent was cheaper. With the ground rapidly filling up, the council had moved 'Old John' and his wife Katherine (shortened to Kate) – who came from Blackrock, Dublin – to a lodge at the newly acquired cemetery in Worting Road.

Once the war started and Jack had joined up, Nellie invited his sister Edie Baldwin to come and live with her at the Old Lodge: her husband Bill was also away serving his country. After the war the reunited Baldwins moved to the New Lodge to look after 'Old John' when Grandma Arlott, as Katherine was known to the younger generation, died in 1921.

Despite her initial misgivings about Jack having taken on the job at the Old Lodge – she was worried he would be under her feet all day – Nellie was content. Tall, fair-haired, blue-eyed and rosy-cheeked, she was a good cook and a sinew of the local Women's Liberal Association. Her political stance had been inherited from her father, a devotee of Gladstone, to whom he bore a marked physical resemblance. That is not to say she was not an independent thinker. Very much the dominant partner in the marriage she brought up John, whom she called 'Les', with warmth, humour and 'the right values'. And those values included many of the tenets of Liberalism. Through his mother's connection with the party John, at an impressionable age, came to meet David Lloyd George, and her untiring efforts on behalf of local Liberal candidates – in particular Reginald Fletcher in the 1920s and John, now Lord, Foot in the 1930s – were widely admired. Even today, sixty years later, Foot remembers Nellie as 'a tower of strength who gave over four whole weeks to tramping the streets at the by-election of 1934'. From her John inherited Liberalism naturally, at first-hand and through the national press – the *Daily Chronicle* (later the *News Chronicle*) was the Arlotts' newspaper.

The family was materially poor, but in their way of life spiritually rich. Nellie baked and decorated; Aunt Edie, a seamstress, made most of John's clothes; and Jack – 'Dad' – dug the allotment and produced cabbages, potatoes, broad beans and Brussels sprouts. He also bricked, plumbed, fitted, repaired and carpentered, and in his so-called spare time played the euphonium and other instruments that were temporarily at a loss for a player in the North Hants Ironworks Band.

John could do none of these things, nor did he wish to. His interests were more conceptual, and he was a born bibliomaniac. With his mother's help he had learned to read by the age of four. As a small boy he used to spend his pocket money on 'twopenny bloods', which he stowed in strict date order in a large margarine box under his bed. He took to reading by candlelight on wild winter nights when he was supposed to be asleep. Having rushed home from school and had his tea – dripping toast was his favourite – he would skimp his homework and settle down in his bedroom with a tale of derring-do and a cup of cocoa. After a scalding sip the cocoa would usually be forgotten and would go cold while he was transported to a world where anything was possible and everything seemed to happen. In time, tiredness would take over, his eyes would droop, and conscious unreality would slip into the unconscious reality of dreams.

Needing somewhere to store a series of booklets which the *Rover* comic had begun to give away, John cut the top off a cardboard boot-box and put it on his dressing-table. His father took the hint, and built him a long grainy-wood wall-shelf, on to which Nellie tacked a shallow cloth fringe. The collection grew, and so did John's desire for more books and magazines. Jules Verne, Dickens, Scott, *The Strand* – they were all devoured ravenously, again and again, although he never had any difficulty in remembering the stories.

From this came John's first takeover bid – for his father's bookcase. Three months of negotiation with both parents eventually secured the deal. Jack made way for John. Apparently, he did not mind too much. According to John, 'He was a man who read books – usually in the old classics series – but then had no further interest in them, except to lend them or give them to his friends – or to me.'

Such powers of persuasion as John practised upon his parents were not always so effective at school. He started at Fairfields Infants in 1920, and moved on to the Senior Boys a year later. Shortly after this, he failed dismally in his attempts to dissuade a red-headed schoolmistress from Cornwall from wanting to see a slow-worm, or grass snake, he had secreted in his pocket. The resulting visit to the headmaster's study brought predictable chastisement. John felt betrayed. The teacher had demanded to see it. He had not wanted to show it to her. And then, when he had done so, she sent him for the very punishment threatened if he continued to disobey. It was his first taste of adult duplicity.

There were other, less hurtful, lessons available in town. Amidst the broad Shire and Percheron carthorses drawing the railway drays, and the Suffolk Punches pulling the farm carts, were the local traction engines and the odd lordly London motor snorting past on the road to the South-West. Just as interesting to John were the cattle auction and the boys scraping horse manure into buckets in the wake of privately-owned pony-traps, and the local characters to be seen at every turn: 'Porky' Clark, deep-chested in straw hat and blue-and-white striped apron, his huge butcher's knife expertly dividing boiling chitterlings; 'Punch' Avery wheeling his handcart with its paraffin tank from door to door; 'Happy Bob' Hutchings selling herrings a penny each, 'You takes 'em whether they'm hard or soft roe'; Canon Boustead making his way from the vicarage on the other side of the fire station, in a flat black hat and with the rolling gait of an old salt, his fingers perpetually playing a non-existent piano, at his side the gaunt verger Brown and Ansty, the blind organist; and on market day the hucksters of flawed china and the quacks offering medicines for any ailment.

Then there were the shops; they all had their special smells. The new bread freshly baked in the peel-ovens at the bakery; the pulse and bran at the corn merchants, Hopkins & Beasley's; the tangy new leather at Bottings the cobblers; and a sight that never ceased to engage John, the coin balls rolling unerringly along the aerial wire to and from the cashier's box at Lanham's palace of riches, where piles of material were sold to the wives of the gentry – 'That will be three and three-three, moddom'. He also caught tantalising glimpses of an exclusively adult domain as the pub doors swung open revealing a smoky haze, bursts of ribald laughter and a row of different-coloured bottles suspended upside down behind the bartender. 'Forty pubs in the town,' his Dad had told him, from the Angel and the Feathers to the Anchor and the Barge Inn: 'Nobody ever goes thirsty.'

John was aware of all this and more as a separate part of his boyhood , as he walked towards one seedy side-street where a faded but still jauntily-coloured pole announced the barber's shop. Here, in raffish surroundings, he was raised up on the high stool by a wooden box to have his ears pinned back. The low-ceilinged, yellow-gaslit basement room, with a window camouflaged by giant dummy cigarette-packets, was, in a way, redolent of the opium dens he had read about in his 'twopenny bloods'. A den it certainly was, but for local scandal and for gossip about horses that 'didn't try'. The hissing of the gaslight did not entirely cover the illicit book-making which was conducted with much muttering, scribbling and clinking in the distant corner by the till.

'I can see that little room now,' recalled John in an article for the *Evening News* thirty years later, 'with its two round-backed chairs with ratchet headrests, the twisting involved frames of the tall mirrors with their blobs and stains, one of which looked like a map of Africa and another like an old woman's head. On the shelves in front of the glass, huge lather-brushes stood in floral-patterned mugs and, below, the white basins swelled out and hair stood in swept-up mountains on the dark brown linoleum.

'At the end of the room there was a wheel – like the wheel of a mangle

– and at a shout the barber's boy would put down the broom against which he leant daylong looking into space, and turn the handle. From it a driving belt ran to a smaller wheel close against the ceiling which, when the belt turned it, revolved in its turn a bar that ran the length of the shop. Two more wheels stood along the bar, one immediately above each chair, and the barber would throw over them as they turned a rubber belt which would stretch to any position while it turned a huge cylindrical brush to give the customer's hair "a good brush-out".

'One day, after my haircut was finished, the barber called to the boy, threw the rubber belt over the wheel and, taking the brush by the two handles at its end, he drew it, spinning, through my hair. It was then that I knew I was a grown-up.'

Well, not quite. He was still wearing short trousers, though only just. And there was the grammar school to be reached and overcome.

2

Battles and Beatings

Queen Mary's School, Basingstoke, known locally as 'Basingstoke Grammar', traced its origin to an ancient religious guild, the 'Fraternitas Sancti Spiritus' (Guild of the Holy Ghost), for which a solitary priest exercised educational as well as devotional duties. Just how much secular instruction took place in the period up to 1527 is not clear, but from that date at least a schoolmaster was being paid by the Crown. During Edward VI's reign the guild was suppressed – though surprisingly the scholastic side of its activities survived – but in 1556 Queen Mary restored its full status, and gave the school her name.

Halfway through the seventeenth century Basingstoke Corporation annexed the guild's properties and administration, leading to prolonged disputes and litigation between the town's elders and subsequent school-masters over emoluments and use of revenues. In fact, not until the 1850s was a degree of harmony restored, when a move was made from the half-timbered schoolroom that had been erected above the foundations of the western tower of the original chapel (in ruins since the Civil War) to a new building in the Worting Road.

This was the building which John Arlott, aged eleven, entered as a Double Scholarship boy in Michaelmas Term of 1925. He had gained the County Scholarship (at the second attempt), and also the Aldworth Charity, which bestowed an extra pound a year specifically for the purchase of books. For the Aldworth he had had to undertake an examination in religious knowledge, including an inquisition from the Bishop of Winchester's chaplain. John's retentive memory was apparent when he answered most questions immediately and accurately, identifying a passage from a commination denouncing God's anger and His Judgements against Sinners. During the course of the *viva*, the man of the cloth disarmingly admitted that he too did not understand all of the Revelations. With this mutual recognition, John was 'highly commended', the first time any candidate had been as highly placed in nearly a quarter of a century.

Any newness in the school at Worting Road had long disappeared by

John's time. Possibly it had always looked old. The building, constructed 'in the duller period of Gothic revival', had not one iota of architectural elegance. The inside had become terribly dilapidated, and was icy cold in winter and airless in summer. The classrooms were lit, inefficiently, by gas, and constituted in such a way as to be a fearful fire risk. A result of one official inspection was the installation of boxes with rope ladders inside the windows of the upstairs apartments. Fire drill then exposed a number of boys as too plump to get through the windows, a cause of considerable merriment to their schoolmates.

Sharing a decidedly battered and penknife-hacked double desk with John was another John known as Jack – Jack Donovan. Donovan, who was to become a close friend of John's and a hugely entertaining companion, later held a succession of appointments with British Rail – in Birmingham, Exeter, Plymouth, Bristol, Paddington – and during his career was Principal Industrial Relations Manager, Railways Board and General Administration Manager for the National Freight Corporation. He served in the Second World War with the Irish Guards and was taken prisoner at the Anzio landings in 1943.

Jack had come from Dublin as a youngster and, living near Bramley, ten miles from Basingstoke, represented one of the three parts rural to one part urban community that made up the 130-strong grammar school. He remembers John in those days as 'a very chatty, outgoing kind of kid – articulate, argumentative, extremely likeable, great sense of humour – and . . . just a nice bloke.

'We sat next to each other virtually throughout our time at the school. I was struck by his friendliness. He was quite a sensitive boy, courageous, very intelligent, an enquirer after the truth. He was always after facts, seeking knowledge, tremendously alive, active and kind – if you were a friend of John's you had a very loyal friend indeed.

'He led a fairly chequered school life. I was an average kid who discovered early on that if you defied the authorities too much you wouldn't win. Now, this might not be a very courageous attitude to life, but it was one adopted by most kids. John took the view a) that masters and teachers were not infallible and b) that one should enquire of them if in doubt or uncertainty about any aspect of your education. So he was well known as a character who would deal with masters almost as if they were equals.

'Looking back from our present day that doesn't seem unreasonable, but in the early 1920s much of the Victorian attitude to children still persisted and John was clearly not one of those little boys made to be seen and not heard. He was argumentative with the powers-that-be and this led him into a lot of trouble. In his own mind, it served – to some extent – to colour his period at school. Indeed, his experiences evoked the sympathy of his friends. He became, I think, the most caned kid of my time at school' (*chuckle*).

In those days, of course, the cane was often the first method by which school authorities imposed discipline.

'The Queen's School at Basingstoke was full of sturdy individualists, so discipline was essential,' Jack Donovan went on. 'It was unfortunate that John became cross-buffered – to use a railway phrase – with the headmaster, C.W. Percivall, Esquire, Master of Arts. He got into the position – quite wrongly in many cases – where he was known as a trouble-maker. He wasn't a troublemaker, he was just an enquirer after the truth who sometimes overstepped the proper relationship in those days between a schoolboy and a master. Percivall spent quite a bit of time looking at the Arlott trouser-seat and delivering to it some fairly hefty blows. Percivall was a disciplinarian who lacked a sense of humour and he became irrational, I think, in his relationship with J.A. He couldn't see that here was a boy who was a little different from the rest perhaps, and who couldn't be dealt with in the same way as he could deal with the majority of us.

'He made the terrible adult mistake of personalising a dislike, and he caned him frequently. And, I regret to say, though not a cruel man, in the broad sense of the term, he seemed – not to enjoy, perhaps, that would be overstating it – but he didn't seem to mind caning Arlott very much. And John didn't help himself. We all knew the masters weren't infallible, but we had a fairly clear idea of how far we could go in demonstrating that, but John seemed to lack a bit of tact in his approach. He was physically and, indeed, must have been mentally, fearless. He never gave Percivall the pleasure, the gratification, of seeing any fear, or evidence of pain or that he was getting to him at all.'

Even if Charles Wilhelm Percivall was not exactly Attila the Hun, his Prussian-sounding middle name fostered that image. He came from a military family, and was a direct descendant of Sir John Percivall, Lord Mayor of London in 1498. The headmaster had arrived at Queen Mary's by way of Ipswich School, Jesus College, Cambridge, the University of Paris and Magnus Grammar School, Newark-on-Trent. He was a competent gymnast and rower, and an excellent mathematician.

John, on the other hand, was adequate enough at sums, but hardly an excellent mathematician. 'I spent hours on arithmetic. I was taught – and I have forgotten – to work out how long it takes two trains, travelling in opposite directions at different speeds, to pass one another. I was also taught how to calculate the time taken to fill a cistern from one pipe pouring in water, at so-many-gallons-an-hour while another emptied it at a different so-many-gallons-an-hour. This, unless one has the common sense to turn off the pipe which is emptying it, is no easy calculation.'

Percivall himself often sounded like a pipe starved of water. He suffered from asthma, and when it was bad other people suffered too. The audibility of his wheezing, together with the decibel level of the glass-pane door as it slammed between the headmaster's house and the central washbasins, was a kind of geiger-counter for the state of his temper. The basins were where 'vim' was used on posteriors as well as on porcelain, and the fact that Percivall was the first headmaster at Queen Mary's not to be a Clerk in Holy Orders did not inhibit him from feeling that, as Bishop Fulton J. Sheen said, 'Every child should have an occasional pat on the back – as long as it is applied low enough and hard enough.'

Said Jack Donovan: 'I remember John asking the physics teacher, "Why, sir, when your eyes are closed, do you get spots which appear to move?" The master, instead of playing it down the middle, said, "That's typical of you, Arlott. You're just trying to talk me into spending time on the question. I'm not falling for that. You go and stand by the basins." Now that, to me, was a terrible miscarriage of justice, because he had asked a perfectly legitimate question.'

On one occasion, Donovan himself had been in trouble for inattention. He had been drawing up a list of the football team when Lee, the physics teacher, had come up behind him unawares and thumped him on the head. The propelling pencil clenched in his hand at the time left a trickle of blood running down Jack's forehead. According to Jack, the wound looked far worse than it was, but solicitous as ever for his friend, John sprang to his feet and demanded that an apology be made. Surprisingly, it was immediately forthcoming.

The young Arlott was obviously not slow in coming forward, and on 25 November 1927 he volunteered to be a stand-in speaker at the School Debating Society, supporting the motion 'That this house considers that corporal chastisement as a punishment is to be deplored.' He spoke with feeling, and the motion was carried narrowly by twenty-four votes to twenty-two.

There were other debates during his years at Queen Mary's. That old chestnut the future of the Channel Tunnel attracted the attention of the Literary and Scientific Society, and on another occasion John eloquently defended cyclists who, now that more and more cars were coming on to the roads, were considered a curse. The school magazine notes that Arlott spoke eight times; the most anyone else managed was three. Many years later W.G. 'Boney' Pearce, who taught English, remarked that 'Arlott suffered from verbal diarrhoea.' Maybe Pearce did not like bikes.

Several of the Literary and Scientific Society's debates were on sporting themes. John Carter, another of John's close friends, supported the motion that professionalism was a bane of sport. 'Arlott and Donovan took a contrary stance, feeling that amateurs were often quite as unsporting as professionals.' Their arguments swayed the majority.

On 4 October 1929, a packed house heard John trace 'the development of cricket from its original games' and give 'interesting accounts of old cricket matches'. So, at the age of fifteen he was already versed in the lore and laws of bat and ball. Did he, one wonders, sense his power to communicate? Feel a thrill at being able to transmit to an audience his love of his subject? Whether or not that was the case, as a member of the fifth form he was invited to write a short piece for the 1930 Lent issue of the school magazine on 'Early Football at Queen Mary's':

In the year 1879 Association Football was just beginning to become popular in North Hants and, with the idea of further establishing the game in Hampshire, Colonel Robert May offered a challenge cup to be competed for by football clubs in the county. Such clubs as Bournemouth, Basingstoke, Aldershot and Winchester competed.

In the semi-final Queen Mary's School, Basingstoke, beat Basingstoke by 3 goals to nil before a crowd of 300 people on Basingstoke Common. In the final the School met Fordingbridge Turks before a record Hampshire football crowd of 500 people. The game was very fast and even, marked by terrific kicking by the School backs. Ten minutes from time Fordingbridge Turks scored and won by one goal to nil. The Turks wasted a great chance of making the game more popular in Hampshire by refusing to put the cup up for further competition.

The School's feat in reaching the final is all the more praiseworthy for the fact that (as an Old Boy assures me) as late as 1875, if not later, the only football the School played was Rugby football between the boys, no outside matches being played.

When John put on football kit himself he found a position as a long-kicking full-back, before moving upfield to a more attacking role. 'He was,' said Jack Donovan, 'a very fast centre-forward over twenty-five yards. His one ambition was to break the back of the net – if possible with the goalkeeper still clutching the ball to his midriff. He was a very good finisher if you gave him a through ball where he could run on to it; a direct challenger who could hit the ball really hard. He had a reputation for being unnecessarily rough. He wasn't dirty or a deliberate fouler, but a fast, rampaging, rootin'-tootin' kind of centre-forward on the lines of a Ted Drake.'

The centre-forwards John himself had in mind were such nationally-known strikers as George Camsell of Middlesbrough and 'Dixie' Dean of Everton, whose methods he discussed at length with Ron Prickett, another close friend and teenage soccer strategist, who was an effervescent outside-left in school matches.

The 'through ball' mentioned by Jack Donovan was usually laid on by Jack himself at centre-half. Jack's skills embraced scheming as well as stopping, for he was adept at spotting weak links in the opposition. Both at house and school level John prospered because of Jack, a hat-trick for 'A' house in a game in 1929 being just one example. Queen Mary's pitch for football – and indeed cricket – was tufty and uneven, and sloped quite sharply. A goal kick from the top end more often than not ended up in the bottom penalty area. In the middle of the field was a perpetually waterlogged yard-wide hole known as 'Billimore's blockhole', a real ankle-twister for the unwary, though nobody seemed to know how it got its name or indeed anything about the mysterious Billimore.

The fives court, which had been erected in 1874, was 'lonely and cold and, in some queer way, always isolated even when it was crowded'. John was above average at fives and handball, and was also quite a good swim-mer, if not as impressive in the water as his father, who practised what he called 'a trudgeon stroke'. He was very much a team man who would try his hand at any sport to get points for his house, although, as Jack Donovan remembered, when it came to cross-country running they were both reluctant volunteers: 'On a five-and-a-half-mile course we would go out with apples and oranges and walk most of the way arguing about literature. We knew where masters and prefects were placed and then we would run. Once out of sight we'd slow down. We used to break into a trot now and then. The odd gallop. About a mile from home we would accelerate. After we reached the school gates we'd shoot towards the finish like a couple of tanks. We nearly always got a point – about thirty-second and thirty-third. Honour had been satisfied.'

As far as cricket was concerned, John was not only steeping himself in the history of the game, but in the statistics as well. An early self-appointed task was to fill an old school exercise book with an analysis of all the Glamorgan scores from the time they became a first-class county in 1921. As the Cinderella club in the Championship, and underdogs in all their matches, John felt a natural sympathy, and gave fervent support from afar. His love of the game had sprung from a sense of wonderment when, as a child, he had watched the 'portly outfitter-alderman' Mr Chesterfield

and the 'limping mighty-shouldered tobacconist' Mr Crate of Basingstoke
C.C. practising their strokes in the nets at May's Bounty, which was next
to Fairfields, his first school. Bert Butler, the local professional and for
fifty years the club groundsman, whom John described as having a 'short,
lean, berry-cheeked and bird-eyed figure', had not discouraged him from
putting on plimsolls and acting as outfielder, and when a Hampshire side
played Basingstoke in 1921 and the captain, Lionel (Lord) Tennyson,
cleared the boundary rope with a mighty hit that travelled up to the Castle
football pitch beyond, a small stocky figure in grey pullover and short
trousers could be seen straining every muscle as he chased after the ball.

Practice at home against Dad's underarm and a hard compo ball helped
to complete his captivation, and from then on his dreams of heaven were
peopled by white-clad figures against a background of greensward and
blue skies. Wearing clinging flannels, his uncle Frank's dirty white shoes
and a single pad, John would rush to a nearby field of vetches to improvise
drives with a cut-down bat, while in the indoor net at school he would
defend his wicket determinedly as the ball came speedily off the matting
stretched over a wooden floor.

'John was a capable non-strokemaker,' recalled Jack Donovan. 'He
specialised in the front foot. A very large left leg encased in a very large
pad would come a foot or two outside the crease accompanied by a bat.
He scored runs but he scored them very slowly – mostly confined to glides
and pushes. His bat was close to the pad, very rarely did he open his quite
broad shoulders. He had a theory that, while adopting this practice, he
was unbowlable. To some extent he was right. You had to get the ball
very much in the right place to get him to make a false stroke in order
to hit the stumps. He was a useful if limited number six or seven, capable
of staying there. A stonewaller, basically. He was also a good fielder,* but
as a bowler he had very little control at speed. He was better at off-breaks
– and very interested in the technique of off-spin bowling. He would more
often tie himself up in knots, though, than the batsman. A couple of times
a season he would bowl a virtually unplayable ball.' An afterthought struck
Jack: 'But twice a year was a good year,' he chuckled.

'Mind you, you could bet your bottom dollar that, if you had J.A. in
your team, you would get 110 per cent effort, because he was extremely
dedicated and would break his neck to do well and get a result. He was
also very talented at telling skippers where they were going wrong. "You
should put so and so on and do this and do that." He was free with advice

---

* John himself always maintained that he was clumsy.

because he was so immersed in the game that he wanted everything to go right. He sometimes ignored the fact that a lot of captains didn't really appreciate being told what to do.'

The cockiness and certainty that the youthful John Arlott displayed outwardly disguised other dispositions. 'Even contemporaries – friends and enemies – who were with him a lot didn't realise how sensitive he was,' Jack Donovan observed. 'He showed a tough face to the world, a very tough exterior, but John always wanted to have friends around him, and he wanted to like people and in turn to be liked. I suppose that's a characteristic we all share. A lot of people at school – boys and teaching staff – were impatient with him because of his lack of tact, but I got to know him really well, and appreciated the depth of his character.

'I liked both his parents, too. His father was a small, terribly active, do-it-yourself man. He appeared at suppers and smokers [smoking concerts] to do a turn. He would do an Irish jig and sing "Phil the Fluter's Ball" with great clarity and a by no means imperfect Irish accent which he managed to put on.

'Mrs Arlott no doubt spoilt John – he was an only child. She was a nice, friendly kind of person with a heart as big as a London bus, and gave a little of it to her son's friends who were always welcome at the Arlott household. We would play cricket and she would call for us to come in and feed us blackcurrant pie or mince tart. It was a happy childhood. She usually found threepence or sixpence when we wanted to do something together.'

At home John was indulged. For the first five years of his life he had the undivided attention of his mother and aunt, and even when his father returned from the war there was no brother or sister to discourage the expectancy of getting his own way. That expectancy never really left him throughout his life.

If it is not a contradiction, John was a teenager with troubles, rather than a troubled teenager. He was, as he has admitted, 'a bit of a rebel'. Though not in search of himself, he was in search of an acceptable way of expressing himself. He wanted others to share his convictions, but did not go the right way about convincing them, misunderstanding and feeling misunderstood. There was a feeling amongst the teaching staff at Queen Mary's that he was 'beyond the pale', and most of them treated him with a fair amount of suspicion. The young Arlott was thought to have a large chip on his shoulder, and he was known to be the ringleader of a coterie of classmates who admired his defiant attitude to authority. A new teacher on his first morning at the school was stopped by a colleague on his way to the classroom. 'Where are you going now?' he asked.

'To the fifth form.'

'Well, I warn you, there's a boy in that class called Arlott, who will set out to give as much trouble as possible. Don't put up with it. Send him to the headmaster straight away.'

At that time there was little use of psychology in the teaching profession. 'They' decided what had to be taught and the pace of learning. Scant notice was taken of a burgeoning mind, of an intelligence that constantly needed feeding with further information. This did not apply to Pete Ballard, however. Ballard taught Latin at Queen Mary's, and was one of those teachers who taught well if the pupil was keen to learn; if he was not keen, he was told to keep quiet. John, though good at languages, did not pay much attention to a dead tongue that he decided was principally for the delectation of Roman Catholics; nevertheless Ballard, who liked sport too, allowed him to pursue more important studies such as looking up the latest cricket averages. The master, though more introspective by nature than John, may have recognised similar paradoxes between them. Years later, the pupil went to no end of trouble to contact his erstwhile tutor, then in failing health, and he was with him when he died.

In the chemistry laboratory John liked to experiment. On one occasion he was diligently engaged – to the accompaniment, as he later recalled, 'of completely spurious indications of nausea from my dear schoolfellows' – in manufacturing a gas called sulphuretted hydrogen from iron pyrites and hydrochloric acid. His efforts were abruptly terminated by a monumental box on the ears from the burly but olfactorily sensitive chemistry master.

Music lessons were given by a Mr Garrett, who 'looked like a musical comedy Frenchman' and was determinedly arty. One morning he went in search of *bel canto* and did not find it, at least not with John, whose rendering of 'Onward Christian Soldiers' was neither. Immediate ejection to the handwriting class. Ever afterwards John proclaimed he was tone deaf. Fifty years later I took issue with him over this, saying that very few people are completely without a sense of pitch, and inviting an impromptu performance of 'Three Blind Mice'. Much laughter, but to no avail. When it came to school musical evenings John stuck to numbers like 'The Grand Old Duke of York' which could be delivered virtually in a monotone.

Jack Donovan, similarly evicted from Mr Garrett's class a week later, was sent to the other penitentiary department, the physics lab, to manufacture ink. Having brewed the powder he would go round the classrooms filling inkwells: 'If you had enemies you made sure they had enough ink to sink a battleship. What emerged from our boyhood is that I learnt how to make the ink – John learnt how to use it.'

The English teacher, 'Boney' Pearce, did not share this view. Jack Donovan admitted that, in his own essays, he was always prepared to use fifteen words when two would do – 'dressed things up with a flowery style, over-egging' – whereas John wrote graphically and economically. But on one occasion, after receiving essays from each of them, Pearce enthused, 'A superb effort, Donovan. You one day will earn your living with your pen. As for yours, Arlott, I shouldn't bother too much about it, there's nothing there.' Amusing to relate now, but wounding to be told then.

There were other wounds that did not heal, and in the end they led John to leave Queen Mary's. A football match against Peter Symonds School of Winchester during the Lent term of 1930 was the linchpin. The Basingstoke boys were outmatched in size, and were heavily outscored. Jack Donovan had left the school by this time and John, at centre-forward, was starved of the through balls that he had come to expect, and was forced to resort to despairing rushes after long, aimless punts. As the game wore on he grew increasingly frustrated and tired. The opposing goalkeeper began to taunt him by bouncing the ball tantalisingly close before smartly sidestepping to clear it to the centre circle. All of a sudden there was a fifty-fifty ball. John charged at full pelt, and for once the goalkeeper did not get out of the way. He was upended in the goalmouth, and the ball rolled into the back of the net. The referee blew for a foul, disallowing the goal, and gave a free kick.

The next morning the headmaster, Percivall, who had been watching the match, sent for John. He declared that because of what he considered his ruffianly conduct towards the goalkeeper, Arlott would never again play for the school at football or cricket. John could not have been dealt a more devastating blow. He was inordinately proud of representing his school, and the anger he felt was fuelled by the sympathy of his team-mates and by the injustice, which they all acknowledged, of his punishment.

How could he best express his defiance? All right, if the school, through its headmaster, did not want him, he did not need the school. He would leave of his own accord. He had had enough.

His parents tried desperately to dissuade him. It was his School Certificate year. Much better to stay on, take the exams and prove a point by getting high marks. But sweet reason from mature heads was no antidote for a resentment that refused to be bottled up. John was adamant. He would not go back to the school. Irrational? Impetuous? Wilful? Most certainly. But then, John had a temperament that was easily riled, and once he had decided on a course of action, nothing could deter him.

At about this time the Yorkshire and England opening batsman Herbert Sutcliffe came to Queen Mary's to give a talk. 'Cricket,' he said, 'is a game which helps to bring out all that is best in a man. It is a contest calling for courage, skill, strategy and self-control. It is a contest of temper, a trial of honour, and a revealer of character.' All of these attributes and factors had been present or absent in the feud between the young Arlott and the middle-aged Percivall. It was a battle of wills that should never have been allowed to continue, and Percivall's single-gear response to an audacious and, at times, hard-to-control lad was, at best, unintelligent. The school already had a long-standing record for the excessive use of the cane (an assistant headteacher had been warned after complaints by parents in 1869, and eight years later a famous test case was taken against a master and monitor), although Percivall was certainly not thinking of the past when beating Arlott two or three times a month. 'He had piggy eyes,' recalled John with venom fifty years later, 'and after three or four strokes the pain was excruciating. Percivall was a sadist who enjoyed whacking little boys. He used to carry a heavy three-foot-long bamboo cane, which was as thick as his thumb, inside the hem of his gown. The weals would last a fortnight.'

According to Ted Tillen, who was at Queen Mary's at the time and later became editor of the *Basingstoke Gazette*, Percivall used to soak his canes in oils to keep them pliant. He remembers John being paraded in front of the whole school. 'Percivall whacked him really hard. With one of the strokes the cane broke off John's back trouser button. There was a loud crack and it flew through the air.'

John never fully exorcised the unhealthy effect Percivall had on him. Perhaps if he had yielded to tears at the time, his hurt and anger would have dissipated sooner. Astonishingly, he managed revenge of a sort some thirty years after leaving the school. This therapy called for a fair degree of courage, and an ever-present sense of dramatisation.

The Committee of the Old Boys' Association had asked him to propose a toast to Percivall at their annual dinner. Quite what their motive was in asking John, of all people, to do this is not clear. He was a regular speaker at their functions, but this invitation would seem to have been prompted either by mischief-making or by a total lack of awareness. At any rate, after John had reminded them of his less than charitable feelings towards his former headmaster, they still insisted he go ahead. By all means, they said, speak your mind. Don't forget, you'll be speaking for us as well.

The dinner was held at the Swan Inn at Sherborne St John near Basingstoke. It was a crowded occasion, with about 150 people present. Percivall, who had asked to be invited, had travelled from Brighton, where he was living in retirement. First, John responded to the toast to the Association, then continued with some affectionate recollections of his schooldays before finally coming to the *coup de grâce*. He did not dwell on his own experiences, but on those of other boys. He records his words in his autobiography *Basingstoke Boy:*

Gentlemen, many of you will remember personally the subject of this toast; for them, no description is necessary. For others, the purpose of this speech is simply, with the knowledge of your committee, to recall a single incident in his life. One day in 1929, this speaker was sent out to the basins to await the inevitable. He did not relish the prospect. He was to play for his house in a soccer match that afternoon and, as some of you will recall, the disciplinary tattoo made football impossible. He therefore, in cowardly but, surely, wise fashion, hid behind the coats hanging in the lobby by the basins. After a few minutes, the door of the upper third opened, and out came a frail, timid, twelve-year-old named Woodcock. It was clearly his first time at the basins and he shifted uneasily on his feet, obviously wishing he could fade into the wall. Presently the old, familiar, asthmatic wheezing could be heard, and the glass in the door to the headmaster's house shook in its frame as he slammed it shut.

He saw Woodcock and said, 'What are you doing here?'

'Mr Pearce sent me out, sir.'

'What for?'

'Talking, sir.'

'Then we shall have to teach you not to talk, shan't we, Woodcock?'

No reply.

Then, loudly, 'Eh, Woodcock?'

'Yes, sir.'

'Get down, Woodcock.'

The boy got down; the headmaster whisked up his coat tails, gave the cane a few preliminary swishes and brought it down. As he did so, Woodcock stood up and the cane hit him across the back of the legs.

'That doesn't count, Woodcock; get down again.'

He got down; again it swished down and, this time, landed squarely across the ass.

Another stroke across the behind.

As the third stroke came down the wisp of a boy straightened up again, took it across the back of the legs and fell over. He lay on the ground weeping.

'Stand up. I've told you once already, Woodcock, that doesn't count. Get down again.'

He got down. The third 'counting' stroke landed and he fell on his face, sobbing. Percivall turned him over, gently enough, with his foot. 'Get up, Woodcock, you fool.'

The headmaster looked down on him for a moment and strode off into the fifth form.

That, gentlemen, is an accurate, eye-witness account of a happening which until now neither of the people concerned realised was seen by anyone else. This cowardly witness was unseen and, after the custom, unseen meant unpunished; he played for the house that afternoon.

That may remind you, gentlemen, of the headmaster whose toast is now proposed: Charles W. Percivall.

'It was an unfortunate occasion,' Jack Donovan remembered. 'He got applause – a bit muted – because people didn't know quite how to react. They weren't expecting it. They were a bit taken aback by this sudden diatribe. But John had warned the committee that he would tell home truths, and to their everlasting regret they didn't pay any attention.

'Percivall was very quiet. He had made his speech. He didn't have a chance to make another one in rebuttal, so to speak, but he took it all right. All in all, the atmosphere was a bit taut – nevertheless quite friendly. Percivall left quickly. It shook him, I don't think there's any doubt about that. It shook him considerably. He never came again to an Old Boys' dinner.'

John had thought long and uneasily before delivering such a public impugnment. There were several moments during the course of it when he wished he had not begun. Yet afterwards he felt he had struck a blow for those who had suffered such indiscriminate punishment. The school motto was '*Spiritum nolite extinguere*' – 'Quench not the spirit'. Percivall must have realised that at least he had one pupil whose spirit he had not quenched.

In 1951 John had composed a piece for the school magazine on 'The Old Place', of which he was, perhaps, the best-known ex-pupil, with due recognition to Gilbert White, author of *The Natural History of Selborne*; a Poet Laureate, Thomas Wharton; and Lord (George) Wigg. He wrote:

I cannot pass it, even now – that old place on the Worting Road – without disturbing the echoes in my mind of its disasters and triumphs, their extremes so much further apart than any adult sense of proportion allows.

Yet if you were there . . . you may still hear it and smell and see it today, wherever you are. You may hear the rumble of voices, the hustle of heavy boots and shoes on the hollow wooden floors, the sudden fierce roar of a form let out, the harsh babble of break. You may smell the chestnut leaves rotting in the November rains, the scythed grass dying in its swathes by the hedge, the choking fumes which 'Beaver' Harris's stoking produced from those ancient, messy, chilly stoves . . . you may see the chestnuts as they stood in their irregular row where the gravel ran to the edge of the half-disciplined grass . . . the school field, its rank turf falling away past the crudely timbered 'pav', between the limes and the hedges to the distant ditch.

Most of all, you may hear and smell and see the passage on a rainy day – that passage between the dark cavern leading to the Staff Room and the cane-echoing coldness of the 'Basins'. The smell came from a huddle of humanity and a dense, steamy mass of wet coats and mackintoshes hanging six deep against the wall. The noise was that of argument, laughter, hurried 'last checks' on prep, incompletely committed to memory and imperious hushing from those who feared their own particular activity being marred by the noise of others drawing a banishing master from the Staff Room; shoe-studs grated on the rectangular-headed nails from which so many footsteps had worn back the surrounding floor-timbers. You may see faces which have grown older now, some of them are dead faces; others, again, have no names; another evokes a memory of an old friendship and the realisation that face and friendship had been forgotten these twenty years.

Romanticise or condemn it, recall or push it into the background of the mind, but, if you were there, the 'Old Place' is with you all your days.

3

First Test and First Jobs

John's parents had reluctantly conceded defeat in their battle to get him to return to school, but they insisted he took the forthcoming School Certificate – part of the Cambridge syllabus – externally. John himself realised he had been stupid to leave school so early, and in *Basingstoke Boy* he recalls his attitude at the time, referring to himself in the third person: 'fool again, estimating that he had done enough to pass the geography examination in the first hour (he was relying on arithmetic and geography to take him through the maths and science group) he walked out to watch Reading's Cup tie. Of course, he was failed in geography, not for lack of knowledge, but for what had to be seen as a bad-mannered gesture. Neither would he take it again.'

John's failure in the maths and science group cancelled out his efforts in his better subjects – English, History and French. But how could he have walked out to watch a cup tie? The School Certificate examinations were held in July, one of the months in which no domestic football was played. Other schools did have a re-run at Christmas, but not Queen Mary's, where John is likely to have sat, albeit as an ex-pupil. In 1930 Reading, then in the Second Division, had lost 5–1 to Aston Villa in the third round of the F.A. Cup in January, away. The previous year they had also lost to Aston Villa, this time in February, at home. It would appear that John conflated different events – perhaps he walked out of some other examination while he was still at school.

In the weeks after John left Queen Mary's and before he took a job, there was a glorious flutter with freedom. The relief of not being told what to do for so much of virtually every day was intense. Framing his own timetable, in which extensive reading was ever-present, was total joy. Jerome K. Jerome, Harrison Ainsworth, Wilkie Collins and Captain Marryat rotated with John Buchan, Jeffrey Farnol, Robert Graves and Joseph Conrad, and their way with words was eagerly retained. His father had opened the doors of his bookcase, which contained many of the Nelson's Classics series, and some were read twice; indeed, a number were

read more often than that. His fellow bookworm John Carter, a friend
from schooldays, shared evenings of hushed companionship and provided
supper. He also shared days of talkative cricket-watching in the season,
and some of John's lunch. L.J. Carter was a modest, studious young man.
A bachelor all his life, he became a schoolmaster at Fairfields. He was far
more reserved than John, but they were both passionate about literature
and sport, particularly cricket.

John had watched his first important cricket match four years earlier,
in 1926, when he was twelve and on holiday in London with his parents.
Staying at the flat of his uncle Frank (his mother's brother) near Victoria
Station, he had seized an opportunity. They had already performed some
of the tourist rituals: the Tower of London, the Natural History Museum,
the Changing of the Guard and Maskelyne & Devant's Theatre of Magic,
and after all this, his parents fancied a quiet day, with possibly a visit to
the cinema. So when young John realised that Kennington Oval, where
England was playing Australia in the Fifth Test, was only a tram ride
away, a mixture of eloquence and relentless repetition – 'Please! *Please!*'
– together with two pairs of aching feet, did the trick. He found himself
in the queue with a mac over his arm – 'You must take it in case it rains,'
his mother had said – sandwiches she had provided in his left hand, a
book of sepia portraits of the two teams purchased on the way in his right,
and four shillings and fourpence in his pocket. He experienced a few
moments of suspense wondering if the gates would close before he could
get through. Fortunately they did not, although he nearly dropped his
two-bob bit in his anxiety.

The bare details of the sides were on the 'card o' the match'. That cost
twopence. A glass of warm lemonade cost sixpence. Hobbs and Sutcliffe
cost nothing – well, a minuscule part of the admission fee. During that
first day of the Test match John saw the revered England opening pair
put on 53 in less than an hour before Hobbs was bowled for 37. Woolley
and Hendren were dismissed cheaply, and lunch was taken at 108 for
three. Afterwards the new England captain, Percy Chapman, tried to hit
Arthur Mailey, the leg-spin and googly bowler, off his length before the
last six wickets fell for 91 runs, Mailey 6 for 138. The day finished with
Australia on 60 for 4, including two wickets to Larwood, 220 runs behind.

Even more than the progress of the game, it was the personalities that
focused John's attention. To an impressionable youngster they were real
and unreal at the same time; chimerical names before, now charismatic
flesh and blood. He was hooked inescapably. He now knew what he wanted
to do. He wanted to watch cricket, but the circumstances in which he
would be able to do so were not even a distant dream. Radio broadcasting

was still in its infancy, and the first attempt at cricket commentary in England was a year away, although it had already happened in Australia. John saw no more of the match, but he read the newspaper reports avidly. How Herbie Collins and Jack Gregory restored Australia's position; how Hobbs and Sutcliffe both scored masterly centuries on a rain-affected pitch for their seventh three-figure partnership against the old rivals; how the bowling of the elderly Wilfred Rhodes and the youthful Harold Larwood, and flawless fielding, led to an Australian collapse and England's regaining the Ashes before an animated crowd.

The game was so alive to him that afterwards he convinced himself he had been there for all of it, writing and talking about it as if he were giving a commentary. E.M. Wellings and Harold Lake were also at the match: the didactic Wellings, with whom John was to become a colleague at the *Evening News* a quarter of a century later, was also watching his first Test match; Lake, whose real name was John Marchant, was so galvanised by the struggle that he rang a director of the publishing house of Faber & Gwyer's and persuaded him, there and then, to commission a book on just that one Test. Eleven days later the manuscript of *The Greatest Test Match* was delivered.

John had started by watching the best cricket on offer, and perhaps he was fortunate in that he was unable to see any other top-level game soon afterwards. The excitement, the intensity, the drama and the size of the crowd would have been less, and the sense of anti-climax disappointing. As it was, he remained intoxicated by what he had seen, and started to compile a cricket scrapbook of match reports, portraits and cartoons.

The scrapbook kept him amused throughout the winter, but it was not until a year later, in August 1927, that John saw his first full county game. The holiday period again offered a week away, and this time it was spent with Grandmother Clarke at Eastbourne. Sussex were entertaining Lancashire at the Saffrons, and the Red Rose batsmen that season 'had taken runs ... like nuts in a copse'; it looked as if before long the Championship pennant would be flying at Old Trafford.

John watched all of the match, mostly with one eye. Dissatisfied with a sideways-on position, he moved to the vacant area behind the sightscreen and squinted around the edge. From there he watched Maurice Tate and the Revd. F.B.R. Browne pulverise Lancashire into submission, without any pronounced assistance from the pitch. Francis Browne kept a school behind John's grandmother's home at nearby Meads Village, and as he came in to bowl John remembered she had told him that Browne's uncle had died suddenly because he shot a cuckoo. Although he was a man of the cloth, Browne looked fierce enough to have shot a cuckoo too, although he was called 'Tishy', after a racehorse. He bowled in-swingers off a loping run, whereas Tate bowled in-swingers, as well as much else, without loping. Years later, John described Tate's action and effect in an essay, *Packing My Cricket Bag*:

[Tate] was an amiable, rolling, splay-footed man of untidy shamble and airy conversation as he walked back to his bowling mark. But as he began to run he seemed to gather his limbs into a unity. At the moment before he bowled, the big feet of the cartoonist, the shoulders which could look over-heavy, the long arms and the wide hips, were merged in a peak of balance, a focus of energy. His left arm, straight as a lance, pointed high above the far sightscreen, the propelling right arm was drawn right back, against the impelling swing, and his left foot was poised for the lunge which would lever body, shoulders and arm, round and over. His delivery was high and straight and the ball was flung down onto the pitch so that it leapt again from it and at the wicket with new power. His swing was late, so late that, unless you had a line by which to gauge it, the eye could miss it altogether. Then, as the ball pitched, 'cut' or the angle of seam would turn the ball sharply either way. Above all, Tate's fierce pace from the pitch threatened that the ball should always hit the bat and never bat strike the ball. Again and again, in that match and many times since, I have seen the batsman's bat struck by a ball from Tate as if the laws of pace of ball from pitch and, indeed, of all normal timing, were suspended. In fact the batsman had always to suspend his reflexes and time Tate's bowling apart from all other. 'Forward to him,' the old pros said, 'forward to Maurice Tate, and don't try to play back to him until you've thirty or so on the board or he'll get you. You can't time him.' That night a ball from Tate rose like a partridge at Hallows, and Hallows retired hurt. Before the day was over Tate had shot away the main battlements of the Lancashire defence.

The statistics of the game reveal that Sussex beat Lancashire by an innings and 196 runs, after a remarkable eighth-wicket partnership between R.L. Holdsworth and Arthur Gilligan had added 188 runs in two and a half hours, but John had moved on from statistics alone. This time his exercise book was used to write an account of the match. Without John's realising it then, Maurice Tate had become one of the two cricketers who were to personify to him what the game was all about.

Tate bowled, just as one man will shave a lawn earth-close and silk-smooth with a scythe, or another deliver a cow of a calf with a touch of master-sympathy that the qualified obstetrician can never attain. Cricket is a country craft. In an age which lacks roots and traditions, cricket, where the strain is pure, may, like furniture-making, or like masonry in the days of the building of the cathedrals, seem like an art. The craft is in the fingers; catching or spinning a ball can be controlled by an extra and infallible sense like the touch and grain-sensitivity of the perfect stonemason. Practice can produce a superficially similar effect on a basis of fitness, physique and enthusiasm, but the element of greatness in cricket is not compellable.

Over the next two years John watched another couple of 'big' matches. The first was closer to home, at Southampton in 1928, when Learie Constantine excelled for the West Indies against Hampshire and, to the delight of the crowd, performed his trick of catching a hard-thrown return behind his back without looking. After that there was another game at Eastbourne before John ventured, in tandem with John Carter, to matches further afield. From 1930, his cricket-watching was for some years to be restricted to Bank Holidays and annual leave from work.

John's father had managed to get him a job soon after he left school. Basingstoke Borough Council had acquired a former 'gentleman's residence' called Goldings, and in a single room at the top of the stairs on the first floor was the Town Planning Office. In residence there was Yorkshire-born George Paget, Basingstoke's Town Planning Officer, a preservationist as well as a pragmatist. He was also a kind man.

Paget did not really need a typist. And he could have brewed his own coffee and fetched his 'Rhodesian' cigarettes from the shop in London Road. People would ring again if he was out of the office. But he did like company. So John learnt to type after a fashion, and he also learnt what to say on the telephone. That, for him, was not difficult.

Strangely, at about this time John's former headmaster, Percivall, was reporting to Queen Mary's Trustees that the school had started the year 'with an excellent fifth form of fifteen or sixteen boys. The Basingstoke Town Clerk, however, had robbed him of three of the best. He had posts to offer them, and they went, for it was not easy to place a boy, even if he had a School Certificate with which to back himself.' Surely, in his mind, John was not one of the three?

In nearly six months working for the borough council, John was to earn £14, a whole pound of which was a bashful thank-you from George Paget after John had told him he was leaving. But more valuable than cash was a kind of superior home-spun philosophy, containing much common sense and good humour, which Paget imparted to John.

Although they had left school, Jack Donovan, John Arlott and John Carter continued to play as well as watch cricket together. More often Jack and John would play rather than watch, either for the same or opposing sides, and more often John and John would watch rather than play, but occasionally all three did both. In company, and remembering that John Arlott was also called Jack, they were conveniently identified by their initials – J.A., J.C. and J.D.

Jack Donovan recalled one particular game at Beaurepaire Park in Bramley when he was playing for Bramley Village and John was playing for Old St Michaels, a side loosely attached to the parish church at Basingstoke, and for which both he and John used to turn out. 'I was bowling fairly quickish – left-arm round – and John had been in for about an hour and was rapidly approaching double figures,' Jack said, chuckling all the while. 'Like a lot of young bowlers, I was trying to bowl too fast and I slung one down, fairly full length, which pitched outside leg stump and in its trajectory was going even further to leg. John gave a kind of sneer as if it was not even worth hitting – you know, the ball was so bad he would ignore it. I don't know what happened – it may have hit a ridge, possibly the imprint of a cow's hoof – village cricket lends itself to extraordinary happenings. Anyway, leg stump practically flew into the hands of second slip. He was bowled comprehensively. I can still see his reproachful look as he proceeded to the pavilion.'

The Old St Michaels ground was behind the Rising Sun pub just opposite the Old Cemetery where John was born, though he was now living with his parents at the New Lodge of the Worting Road Cemetery, where his father had taken over when 'Old Jack' retired. The pitch was only marginally less bumpy than the remainder of the field. As for the changing facilities, they consisted of a dingy room in the pub commandeered for the purpose. Consequently Old St Michaels tried to secure away fixtures with other clubs in North Hampshire. Nobody minded – it was more comfortable all round and the cricket less precarious. The side enjoyed their matches to the extent that they did not play beyond six o'clock, when the pubs opened. Old St Michaels' boast was that if they had not won by five o'clock, they made very sure they had lost by a quarter to six, even if it meant running each other out.

John also played on a couple of occasions for Queen Mary's Old Boys, as well as for any other eleven that for whatever reason could muster only ten men. For all his lack of boundaries, his love of cricket was limitless, as was made apparent by his interest in a job as 'diet clerk' at Park Prewett Mental Hospital, just off Basingstoke's Aldermaston Road. The advertisement in the *Hants and Berks Gazette* caught his eye because he knew the hospital fielded a good cricket side. There was another attraction as well: fifteen shillings a week was a fifty per cent increase on his salary at the Planning Office, and if all went well, in two years' time his annual salary would expand to £82. The interview was successful and the job was gratefully accepted. On 4 December 1930, John began work at the hospital, which had been established just before the First World War as a 'madhouse unit with lock-up padded cells'.

Being a 'diet clerk' at Park Prewett before the days of pocket calculators called for an aptitude for mental arithmetic. Three hours' work with figures each morning fully stretched John's capacity for multiplication and division. Provisions – or 'nourishment', as one patient referred to it – had to be assessed and ordered. The local butcher and baker soon got to know the personable young man who hurried round each day restlessly making sure of the 'right amount'. For John the diet sheets assumed a nightmarish importance. He dared not make a mistake. 'The sack' carried a stigma and the management, who had responsibility for so much disturbed humanity, came close to adopting an inhuman intolerance of error. On more than one occasion it looked to John as if Damocles' sword was hovering above the exit door. Food could not be kept: too much meat or too many loaves and fishes meant waste, and that did not reap biblical forgiveness. Warnings were given, the buck could not be passed.

Even so, the life was engaging. There was cricket and snooker and badminton and squash and bridge and country walks with nice girls who wore 'two pairs of extremely tight knickers'. And surrounding all this were the inmates, or rather patients. 'They were not out of their minds or insane,' said John, 'they were just different.' Different to the accepted and expected norms of human behaviour, that is. Some would be raging convulsively one moment, ululating the next and *sourdine*, or mute, soon after. Others appeared to be emotionally empty, and no cipher could penetrate their estrangement from the world. A large number were 'normal' for most of the time, and today they would probably be seen wandering the streets or huddling in bus shelters and railway stations.

All of them, in their varying degrees of oddity, needed the security and protection of an enlightened institution which could give freedom of expression without stress. In a television conversation with Mike Brearley fifty years later, John recalled a handbook definition of insanity which he had read at the time: 'Such disability of the leading functions, thought, feeling or will, as should disable a person from thinking the thoughts, feeling the feelings, or performing the duty of that branch of society to which he or she belongs.'

At Park Prewett there was much to discover. The young doctors were cheerfully informative about lust and the young nurses equally helpful with love – or was it sometimes the other way round? Medical matters, too, were on the agenda – intermittently. Human mortality was ever-present. So too were the playing fields, where John could happily escape and practise tactics at football and cricket.

But within the limited horizons of any office, thwarted ambition and petty jealousy can conspire against the plans of juniors. 'We chose our holidays in that office in order of seniority,' John wrote in an article for Oswell Blakiston's book *Holidays and Happy Days*. 'Unnecessarily, and purely sadistically, it was decreed that no two men could ever be on holiday – called "annual" – at the same time. Six men (two of them took a month's holiday and four of them three weeks each) chose their holidays before me. With the cunning of those who knew the ropes they would add on a bank holiday or an overtime leave, running a day into another weekend, leaving only the jagged-ended periods for me. I always managed, however, to get my fortnight's holiday, or most of it, during the cricket season. Once, silently, I saved three days so that I might add them to my holiday in the following year – while there was cricket to be seen. The very day those three days were overdue I was told that I had forfeited them: my seniors were childishly delighted.'

The cricket which John did manage to see left a lasting impression: the First Test at Lord's against the West Indies in 1933, where Walter Robins bowled a googly to Da Costa that 'made for his wicket like a pecking gull' (reminiscent of the metaphor he later used to describe Duleepsinjhi's handling of Larwood and Voce during a match at Eastbourne in 1929, when he 'treated their bowling as a rifleman treats clay pigeons fired from a trap'); and Essex playing Nottinghamshire at Leyton in 1932, where, on a slow wicket, Jim Cutmore and Denys Wilcox treated Larwood's short-pitched deliveries as mere long-hops and scored freely. John and John Carter, sitting on incommodious grey ammunition boxes and trying to remain oblivious to the irritating chant of the ice-cream vendor crying 'Oosezaniceice Wallses?' puzzled long over Larwood's tactic. Their discussion continued during the bus journey through the clotted streets of London's East End back to Cambridge Circus, and even after they had returned to their shabby bed-and-breakfast accommodation near Russell Square. Naturally they did not recognise an early experiment in 'bodyline' for the forthcoming tour of Australia. That night, at least, they were too late to catch an Aldwych farce or a seat at the Metropole. Nevertheless, the order of the day and evening on those holiday excursions was invariable. An immoderate cooked breakfast, a weighty assessment of the morning papers, the journey to the cricket ground – for two energetic young men Southend, Tunbridge Wells, Canterbury, Hastings and Hove were not too far away by train if the match was attractive enough – hours of concentrated watching, followed by a dash for the theatre, and then a half-pint in a pub to slake the thirst and help a staid supper slither down the gullet at a Lyons' Corner House. Cheap 'digs', hopefully cracking good cricket, and cheerful entertainment – an ideal holiday.

They even made one daring pilgrimage across the Severn to Cardiff to see Glamorgan play Notts, and to watch Maurice Turnbull in particular. The fearless, hard-hitting Turnbull, one of the gods of John's youth, was to be killed in the Second World War, and retained that near-mythological status given to those who depart before their time. Besides Turnbull, an added attraction was to try and discover more about that strange bowling tactic used at Leyton.

There was also a holiday at a Folkestone Festival where J.A. and J.C. enlarged the Brotherhood of Cheerful Sparrows, apparently a casual group of cricket-lovers who enjoyed watching the game together in a convivial atmosphere. The Sparrows had their own marquee and beer stall, and spectators on the opposite side of the ground could easily have mistaken their gritted teeth, as they sat in the face of a howling gale, for smiles. The cost of membership gave little protection against the elements; nonetheless the two adventurers were happy enough when they chanced to meet some of the players.

Not all the cricketing gods were on the county circuit. One early 'giant' worked a far less prominent round which, apart from cucumber and cress sandwiches, dough cake and scalding tea, had little in common with the world of the professional cricketer. Dick, a lean and stringy farm labourer, would 'pepper the rash' of village greens and country-house meadow on the local club circuit in Hampshire and Surrey for season after season. His gear was collarless shirts of indeterminate colour with a snake-fastener belt holding up drainpipe flannels – rather like the bottom half of the Teddy Boy uniform of a later generation. Dick's bowling was reminiscent of a machine from a different age. With combine harvester-like precision he would take a stack of wickets, keeping it 'there or thereabouts', just short of a length, at a pace rapidly approaching slow-medium. Frustrated batsmen would in the end more or less dismiss themselves as they tried to loosen the straitjacket. John was fascinated by Dick's technique, and just a little nervous of his taciturn manner. One hot Saturday afternoon he plucked up enough courage to turn to Dick in the slips and say, 'I suppose really good cricket is an art.' Dick, who had a real Hampshire voice that Hardy would have known and loved, replied, 'Huh, get away with ye.' A long pause, and then, after the next ball was bowled, he slowly straightened from his crouch, looked at John and said, 'But it's a damn fine game, or I wouldn't waste my Saturday afternoons at it.'

But the holidays were all too infrequent. Nor were there enough high days of cricket to compensate for the restraints of Park Prewett. John, after almost four years, wanted a change. But to what? His father, who knew what it was like to be out of work involuntarily, preached the value of security. Again he found himself telling his son not to be too impetuous: find a different job by all means, but first make sure it was one with a pension, some security of tenure, and prospects of promotion.

The idea of joining the police really came from John's desire not to be incarcerated in another office. Friends in the force recommended it as a 'manly' job. There would, at least, be fresh air, a certain amount of freedom when on the beat, and the chance of some excitement. Again cricket was a catalyst. John felt it important to find a place where the first-class game was not far away, where there was a good side within the local force, and where there were other forms of entertainment to be enjoyed. London and the Metropolitan Police was considered too large and impersonal. The protective instincts of both his parents were aroused. 'All manner of things go on in London,' they countered mysteriously. There were drawbacks too with the other extreme: a country post would meet only some of the requirements, would be too parochial, and the incumbent was always on duty. What about somewhere middling, like Brighton, or Bristol, or Southampton?

'Now, there's a thought,' said Nellie. 'Wouldn't be too far to come home on days off and have Mum feed you up.' The thought of his mother treating him to Grimsby herrings from Happy Bob's barrow in Wote Street, or a Sunday roast with loganberry pie to follow, made the idea even more attractive.

The applications had to be timed so as to fit a possible interview into one of John's days of annual leave. Secrecy was essential, for if those in charge at Park Prewett knew John was seeking alternative employment, they might give him even more time off work than he needed. Because of that, the offer of an interview at Brighton disqualified itself – on the date they proposed he would be at Park Prewett – but those from Bristol and Southampton fell conveniently into his period of vacation.

In the event, both forces accepted him. The choice was not difficult. Southampton it was. A letter of resignation to the mental home, unemotional goodbyes – four years was obviously not long enough – extensive packing, fond farewells from parents and friends, and, as the train pulled out of Basingstoke station, a feeling of apprehension overlaid with excitement. It was 31 August 1934. He was in his twenty-first year. A new life was beginning. Yet it was not as if he was going to some far distant land. He would still be in his own county.

4

PC 94

Southampton looked or, more accurately, felt, different. John had been there a number of times, but only as a visitor. Now it was to be his home.

At the outset of his new job John was a bright young copper with shiny boots, a notebook, a truncheon, standard handcuffs and a number by which he would be known: PC 94. The landlady at his first digs in Silverdale Road was the aptly named Mrs Warden. She knew all about the habits of puppy policemen: never to expect them when they had told her they would be there, and never to be surprised if they turned up after they had told her they would not be there; indeed, never to expect them at all, for they were hardly ever there. She had a nephew in the CID – he was not there either.

John was happy enough with his lodgings. The Dell, home ground of Southampton FC, was almost opposite, and Hampshire County Cricket Club at Banister's Park was just along the next road, Northlands. He was happy enough too with his wages. Including allowances, £3 9s.6d. a week could go quite a long way in 1934. But John quickly discovered that new boots – including ones that had been 'boned' on the outside for high polish – needed breaking-in, and caused a considerable amount of discomfort when pavement-bashing. A beat on Portswood Division, where he had been deployed, and which was just out from the centre of town, might start at Portswood Park, go through to Shaftesbury Avenue, across to Swaythling Road and back down to the River Itchen and St Denys' Station, roughly two square miles. Another would take in the Bevois Valley, through to Lodge Road and then Archers Road before turning northwards towards the Common, which was notorious as a place where certain inside jobs were performed outside.

After a fortnight trailing senior PCs on their rounds, basic training started in earnest. Not in Southampton but at Digbeth, in Birmingham. The Police School there was no holiday camp – the shock to the system and to the self-esteem was intense. The initiation period in any of the services, military or civil, is deliberately minatory. On arrival, the recruits were required to sit on benches and then handed copies of Moriarty's *Police Law*, from which were drawn 106 legal definitions. The first five had to be recited word-perfect by the next morning: Law, Common Law, Statute Law, Crime, and Felonies. And more still for the day after. The stilted legal phraseology was not easy for the newcomers to retain, even after they had written it down longhand. Their minds were in a whirl as interpretations of affray and aggravated assault were followed by those for sedition and felonious homicide. Concentration was essential. Somebody whispered. The instructor exploded. Absolute silence.

After a couple of weeks Austin Malia, one of the recruits on John's course, who actually enjoyed law, was heard to mutter that he felt he must have committed the abominable offence of buggery with mankind or animal, as it attracted the punishment of penal servitude for life.

All the trainees helped one another out, and when necessary combined their various strengths to crib or 'fake'. John would assist the less intellectually-minded in the written dictation and arithmetic, and those who were more gymnastically adept or better swimmers would cover his weaknesses in rope-climbing and lifesaving.

Early on the agenda was the haircut. Many felt they did not need one, but whatever their feelings, they all got one: peeled-off hair down the centre until totally shorn. Depersonalisation with a few snips. Joe Molloy, later to be a colleague of John's at Southampton, remembers: 'It made you look like a convict. With all your hair off, it dissuaded you from going out in the evening, skylarking and suchlike. Everybody knew you were a policeman. You'd buy hats to try and disguise the baldness. Then, when you went to the cinema and they played the National Anthem, you'd have to take 'em off. So you nipped out before "God Save the King". If you weren't quick enough you just lifted your hat three inches off your head.'

The training term lasted thirteen weeks. The routine was regimented, with the emphasis on all-round fitness, discipline and first-aid. Running on the spot, touching toes, formation gym, early morning parades, drill, swimming and boxing. John's previous fighting had been confined to the school playground, and after one bout in the ring, he needed a second's aid. A haymaker which started from behind his opponent's back sent him sprawling. 'Larry' Gaines, who delivered the punch, had obviously tried to live up to his professional near-namesake.* He stood by apologetically as John tried to recover from the effects of a bloody and broken nose. Ever after, John could raise a smile by grimacing and moving his nose to the right with his left hand. His other party trick was to twist his jaw to

---

* The heavyweight Larry Gains.

make a cracking noise, an effect more easily accomplished in wet weather.

Most of the Police School staff came from within the force, but one of the physical training instructors, Bulstridge, was a civilian of mid-European extraction. He was shorter than most of his colleagues, but extremely muscular, with coarse features and a thick neck. Bulstridge was a bully, and enjoyed taunting young policemen who were not robust in build, although he was careful not to incite those who looked capable of taking care of themselves. He would invite the other instructors to the Saturday-morning sparring sessions, then set out to provoke the inexperienced recruits half his age. They would soon be flat on their backs, having been made to look ungainly and stupid. The next stage was to goad the probationary policemen into 'knocking the living daylights out of one another'. 'On my course,' said Joe Molloy, 'five army chaps refused to take it. They just packed up on the Monday morning and walked out.' John not only stayed, but finished first in the final examination.

There was, of course, motive in the method. The stringent training was a hardening process which aimed to teach self-reliance and remove physical fear. Not that John experienced any lack of dismay when, back in Southampton, he was sent to deal with some trouble in a fish and chip shop just off East Street in the docks area of the town. An Irish labourer called Michael Tierney, who had a considerable reputation for being violent and uncontrollable when 'tipping the elbow' and who had been known to take on six men at a time, was putting himself about a bit. When John tried to intervene, Tierney, looking frighteningly ferocious with his grotesque jutting jaw and huge hunched shoulders, grabbed hold of his hair and threatened to throw him into the chip pan. Quite suddenly, and sensibly, John decided he was not feeling hungry and discreetly withdrew, just as the squad car arrived to take over.

Southampton housed a number of aggressive characters, not all of them male. The Common provided a shelter of sorts for some of the ladies of the town. A plainclothes night patroller, a former constable called Fletcher who had retired on health grounds, together with a man in uniform, might be attracted by a small fire. On investigation they would be likely to find either Nellie Tate or ''alf-nose Annie' sleeping in a hollowed-out bush. Both were prostitutes who operated in and around the Horse and Groom down in the town, servicing sailors on shore leave. Annie had lost the lower part of her nose, so it was said, through it being eaten away by some dreadful disease; Nellie, who was tattooed all over her body, would strip off and fight any man at the drop of a bottle. If it were two bottles the response would be even more spirited.

Another of the prostitutes had a daughter who was a nun in a convent on Jersey, which ostensibly had no connection at all with an inebriated and rather aristocratic-looking lady whom John brought in to be charged one evening. Apparently she had been rowdy and revealing, the more noticeably for wearing an expensive fur coat and jewellery, and nothing else. Once inside the police station, she flung open her coat and screeched, 'He only brought me in for a look!' To John's surprise the desk sergeant looked embarrassed, made placatory noises and sent her on her way without taking any further action. When John asked why, he was told in a whisper that the woman was the illegitimate daughter of 'Jersey Lily' – Lillie Langtry – and Prince Louis of Battenberg, nephew-in-law of Edward VII, and advised 'Do be careful, boy, who you arrest in future.' Or did the sergeant say she was the daughter of the illegitimate daughter? John could never remember.

Patric Dickinson, a Cambridge golf blue, poet, author and one-time BBC producer, for whom John was to work in his early days in broadcasting, knew him during his time on the beat. 'Southampton's Common was open and wildish, beside a main road which ran straight down and through the town to the Bargate, north to south,' he remembered. 'This road had a tramway. Oswald Mosley [leader of the British Union of Fascists] was in spate – holding a meeting on the Common which John was deputed to oversee. It got out of hand and hostile. John decided it was time to get Oswald out. Oswald didn't want to go, but was a small man and John seized him and hailed a (luckily) passing tram and thrust him through to the driver and in that voice you knew commanded "Drive straight to the Bargate and DON'T STOP." The police station was just through the Bargate, so the tram accelerated to its full four miles per hour, and gradually brickbats stopped busting the windows and the cowering passengers were resigned to fate. It is the only rescue by tram I know of.'

John quickly adapted to the routines of a copper's life, which did not normally include rescuing Oswald Mosley. 'Early Turns' – 6 p.m. to 2 a.m. for two weeks; 'Second Relief' – 2 a.m. to 10 a.m. for another two weeks; and 'Nights' – 10 a.m. to 6 p.m. for two weeks. There were six beats on the semi-urban Portswood Division, and each would be covered for a fortnight. In that way every policeman got to know the whole division. The uniform was a light-blue serge suit with white piping and a white flat cap for summer, a heavy Melton cloth tunic for autumn, and an additional overcoat in winter. Helmets were not worn until after the Second World War.

An eight-hour tour of night duty could be solitary and unnerving for a young policeman on parts of Portswood's territory. Mysterious shadows, strange sounds and distorted shapes can alarm the least imaginative. In a thinly disguised autobiographical essay for *St Martin's Review*, the magazine of St Martin-in-the-Fields church in London, published in 1946, John gives a vivid impression of the experience:

> The rain beat down in grey lines, just out of the vertical. The street-lamps were alight but nothing moved except a ripped awning outside a greengrocer's shop, flapping under the storm and slowly tearing further. The lamplight shone in every shade of yellow and blue across the drenched roadway and was thrown back again and again, beyond counting, by the shop-windows. Nothing moved. Why should it at a quarter to three on a filthy morning in a provincial manufacturing town?
>
> But there was life in the street. If you were walking home at that hour you would rather expect to meet a policeman. Sometimes, in fact, after a long and lonely walk home from the station and the last train, you have said, in a rather aggrieved tone, 'I walked right across the town and never met a single policeman.' But, I wonder how many policemen saw you as you went? I wonder how many policemen were standing back in shop doorways, back in the shadow, so that they saw you but you never saw them? The night-patrol policeman's job is to see what goes on, not to parade.

'D' Division, as the Portswood Division was known in the force, was a little away from the main activities of the town, relatively quiet, a spread-eagled mix of different-standard dwellings and every level of income, from prosperous to poor. Crime was regular rather than rife, unexceptional to most but those who suffered directly, and centred on larceny, road accidents, domestic disputes and drunken behaviour. There was the occasional murder and the odd instance of indecent exposure. Many a copper thought that he himself must be odd to face the indecent exposure to the elements. John's account goes on:

> There was life in our street at a quarter to three on that wet night. At the back of the row of show-cases that lead to the door of Budge's Drapery Store there was a policeman. He was twenty-three and his name, which is of no importance, was Charles Williams. In fact he was more often known, in this strange town to which he had come as a policeman, as One-Five-Seven. His immediate colleagues, all older than himself, called him 'you' or 'youngster' or 'hi there' for they did not know him, he had served with them for only four months, they were still weighing him up. 'Old copper, old fool,' said

the older men ironically, even bitterly, and they lay low, talked little and suspected much, far too much.

With a gingerly twist, One-Five-Seven eased his big toe away from his sock and the boot that pressed upon it. He had learned to smear soap on the outside of his socks where the boots blistered him – three patches on the left foot, two on the right. But he had not learned, until tonight, that if you walk in pouring rain for four hours, walk in it until it runs down your neck, and under your clothes into your boots, the soap will be washed away and the wet socks will chafe more than ever. Tonight he learned also that a cloth cape and the lower, uncovered part of a police greatcoat can hold their own weight of water so that the shoulders that support them cry out in pain and strain.

He felt lonely, but not completely neglected. He knew that if at ten minutes past the hour he flashed his night-duty lamp down the street towards the Cross or, at thirty-five minutes past the hour, flashed it up the street towards the Barracks, there would be an answering flash. Then, if he walked towards the other lamp, there would be an 'old-hand' from the neighbouring beat to answer his questions with a fatherly or contemptuous air.

By now, however, he did not need to ask so many questions. He knew all the places on his beat where people worked at night behind closed doors. He knew, too, those houses from which he might hear the sudden flare of roaring, foul-mouthed argument which would as suddenly die with no harm done, though the listener might think it betokened murder. He knew, too, some less officially-approved items of local importance – bakehouses where tea and buns could be had at night, hotel-porters only too glad of company over a cup of tea and a smoke in their cubby-holes.

Every policeman also knew that he had to 'make a point' at every hour during the night. Contact might be made by a telephone call from the station or, as in Charles Williams's case, a visit from a senior officer.

He was waiting for the sergeant. From five minutes before the hour to five minutes after it, he must wait for him here. A little early, he could 'hang up' for twenty minutes out of the rain. Last night it had been five minutes either side of the half-hour, the night before five minutes either side of the quarter-past. It was a little confusing sometimes but there was no excuse for mixing point times – no excuse in official eyes at least. The sergeant might come from any direction, might come on foot or cycle. He might, in fact, be standing back in a doorway a little way away, without showing himself. In that case One-Five-Seven would know nothing about it until later in the morning when the sergeant would say 'I logged you at Budge's at two-forty-five – early on the point, weren't you?' Two minutes to the hour. The lamp on the sergeant's bicycle showed dimly as he rode up from the Barracks. 'All correct, sergeant.' 'All correct.' The sergeant propped his bicycle carefully inside Budge's doorway, stepped into shelter himself and, bending with a gasp, took off his trouser-clips. 'Dirty night.' 'Yes, sergeant.' The sergeant sucked at his moustache: there was nothing to talk to these youngsters about: even if you knew you could trust them there was nothing they knew anything about – particularly this one, he was a clerk before he joined the force. The police would make a man of him though. These bad nights were harder on the young ones than on the older men who knew enough to keep dry – but you dare not tell a kid a thing like that, he might repeat it, then where would the sergeant be? He was taking this weather well though. 'Ah, well,' he said, 'better be getting along – log you Budge's at three – s'long Williams – what's yer other name?' 'Charles, sergeant.' 'Course it is – s'long Charlie,' said the sergeant a little awkwardly. Slowly the red lamp of the bicycle shimmered away in the blue-wet road.

'Decent of the old boy,' thought One-Five-Seven. He knew the sergeant talked with the older men on their points, often smoked a pipe with them or walked on with them round part of their beat. That would come; he felt a friendly warmth towards the sergeant; a thing like that put heart in a chap . . .

He braced his wet and aching shoulders and walked round to the back of the shops. There would be greater merit in catching a burglar on a night like this when some men would be taking shelter. As he walked along the rough lane which ran along the back entrances to the shops he stepped into a pot-hole filled with water to more than the depth of his boots. The muddy water flooded through the boots and squirted out as he stepped hard on the ash road-surface. But he hardly noticed, he was already wet through.

John's wetness behind the ears soon dried; more experienced colleagues made sure of that. He was shown the vulnerable points of shops on his night-duty beat, the places of concealment, the methods of getting into and out of property, which first storeys were residences and which were businesses. He learned also how to remember appearances, to be able to give an estimate of height, weight and build, to describe features, mannerisms and apparel.

'Making a point' every hour taxed the invention of every policeman on the beat. 'The point' could be at a telephone kiosk on the perimeter of the beat of a fellow copper who *might*, in a friendly gesture, dislodge the receiver as he was passing, thereby giving his mate a few extra minutes down the road at the home of the dear old lady who had invited him in for a peg of whisky because she was lonely and her old man who was a captain on one of the boats was away at sea and . . .

An engaged or out-of-order telephone was an excuse that could be used, but only rarely. It was more plausible to see something suspicious, investigate, and be delayed. 'Don't forget, Joe,' John would say to his friend and colleague Joe Molloy, 'you saw me down so and so at such and such a time.' 'Fair enough, Jack,' replied PC Molloy. 'I'll do the same for you,' continued PC Arlott.

Nothing could really be proved against the beat copper who adapted his schedule if he remained unseen. And who was to say that a PC having a quiet smoke in a shop doorway wasn't just as likely to see something he wasn't meant to see as if he was sticking rigidly to his schedule?

Some of the sergeants who rode around on their bikes to check the duty patrol had a sense of humour and were fairly accommodating. They remembered their own nights on the beat, when they had bent the rules by calling in at friends' houses or 'looked in at the local or kipped in cars'. After all, they reasoned, if the weather was bad, statistics proved that crime was low. Others, however, were inflexible.

One senior sergeant in particular, called 'Tiny' because he was large, made life as difficult as he could for young recruits; and with a preponderance of older men in the division, and only one or two youngsters, the available choices for victimisation were as limited as his own intellect. He was extremely keen to browbeat John who, apart from having seed-time on his side, had committed the cardinal sin of finishing top at Digbeth. 'Tiny' gave John the equivalent of Army 'jankers' – the longest beat, Bassett and Swaythling – which was a *month* of night duty in winter, with no bike. A month of nights gave plenty of time to think up ways to retaliate. A convenient excavation in an unlit road with a crescent at one end, which meant there was no through traffic, provided the means. Extinguishing warning lanterns and removing protective barriers just prior to 'Tiny's' expected arrival on his bicycle signalled the way. Now all that was required was for the detested sergeant to take that way and descend into the means. His preparations made, John lay in wait, but unfortunately, or perhaps fortunately, the fall guy did not co-operate. 'Tiny' did not turn up. Result: one empty hole, and a rankle unwrinkled.

Upholders of the law are, of course, supposed to be immune to temptation. One day John and a colleague found that some bottles of milk had been left uncollected outside the door of a house in Alma Road. Nobody had seen the owner for some time. On breaking open the door they found him dead in bed. In various cupboards were wads of pound notes held together by elastic bands – at a quick estimate something in the region of £40,000 or £50,000. A little of it, surely, would not be missed. Both of them dismissed the thought without much difficulty.

All the constables had to make enquiries in their own time, when they were off-duty. Often these were of a mundane nature, such as taking statements from witnesses of a traffic accident. A few enquiries could build up an appreciable number of hours, which were taken as compensatory leave. Naturally, none of the PCs was slow to take any advantage that could be gained. On one parade the inspector asked John how many hours' leave he had to come. 'Thirty, sir,' he replied imperturbably. The immaculately turned-out Sergeant Brown, who was accompanying the inspector and who had been involved in the rostering, went white with anger. As he had Anglo-Indian features and hue, the effect was quite alarming. 'How can you possibly have thirty?' he exploded. John explained that a significant proportion of the hours had accrued because he had to go right to the outskirts of the Portswood Division to make enquiries, and that as the people there were never in, he had to go back time and time again. The discussion continued after the parade finished, and in the end John's notion of the extra hours he had worked was drastically reduced by Sergeant Brown.

There was another occasion when a fatal accident happened on John's beat. The noise of a skidding vehicle and the resulting crash could be heard distinctly a couple of streets away in the pub where he was on duty making sure the landlord was pouring the right measures. It was not done to be seen coming out of the front door of a pub, however, so by the time John managed to reach the scene of the accident via the back door, garden shed and passage wall, another constable had taken care of practically everything that needed to be taken care of. 'It's all right, it's on my beat. I'll deal with it,' said John confidently. He proceeded to write an elaborate and detailed report on why and how the accident took place, and its aftermath. A few weeks later at the coroner's hearing he was highly commended, not only for the coherence of his statement but for his quick action.

In 1936 the arrival at the station of a new young constable, John

Creighton, proved invigorating for John. They not only liked one another immediately, they were instant soul-mates. Of about the same age, they shared many of the same interests. Being young, energetic and fit, they tried to cram as much activity and enjoyment into any day or night as could be managed: football and cricket for the division; swimming at the Lido – encouraged by police chiefs, as thefts from cubicles were always taking place; badminton, including coaching the team of the Royal South Hants Hospital; drinking to all hours at pubs and clubs – mostly only beer and barley wine, but frowned on officially; and dancing, solely because of the opportunities for meeting girls, or 'wenching' as they preferred to call it. John himself said that he had a hectic sex life as a young copper, but that he was very careful indeed. Sleep as such was in short supply. This seemingly carefree attitude to life drew some critical comment from a few of the older men who, feeling the weight of their family responsibilities, were no doubt a little envious.

Nevertheless, when there was a need for speedy apprehension, their youthful vigour was in demand. For some time several streets in South-ampton had been treated to the spectacle of a young man exposing himself to public view. Despite numbers of complaints and numerous sightings, no policeman had been fast enough to catch him. It was getting to the state where 'the priapic flasher' had a sizeable reputation to protect, whereas the police were worrying not so much about the size of their reputations, but more about the lack of service they seemed to be providing. Added to which, there was a novelty in the man's approach which captured wide-spread attention. It was time to put Arlott and Creighton on the job.

The flasher's method was ingenious. Having chosen the back of a row of houses that had matchboard strip fencing or iron railings, he would ride rapidly on a bicycle from one end to the other. At the same time he would attract viewing figures – never had so many curtains twitched at once, and there was no competition from television, which had yet to reach the home – by rattling a walking-stick along the strips as he rode; the noise was like a crazy drummer. His *pièce de résistance* was to hold in his other hand a switched-on torch which cast light on his erect penis.

All this caused much hilarity, though not all of the houses' occupants were amused. In general the police found it funny too, even if they did not appreciate the raillery. After one non-start, when the flasher had ridden the rows during a supper break, it came to a showdown.

It was in the bleak early winter, and on this particular night Arlott and Creighton were enjoying coffee and a fire in a friend's sitting-room. They were, of course, meant to be keeping a discreet watch in the street, but surely, they reasoned, it was too cold outside even for a proud man. Suddenly a loud drum-roll proved it was not.

They had been left at the post. By the time they had leaped on to their bicycles he was three-quarters of the road away. Their frantic pedalling was spurred on by guilty consciences as much as by a desire to catch their quarry. The chase was hazardous – down a steep hill, across a major intersection, up an incline, and left towards a busy junction. A tram screeched to a halt, and bodies and bikes parted company over its front bumper. Fortunately no one was hurt – not even the culprit, who turned out to be half-witted. No awkward questions were asked, and proper acknowledgement was given to the two constables for getting their man. When in due course John went to visit the youth's mother, she remarked: 'It's a terrible shame. There's many a woman down that street who would give her right arm for what Billy's got.'

These reflections of life in the night and day of Constable Arlott should not give the impression that he took his job carelessly. Quite the opposite. He took his job very seriously indeed, although he was not solemn in his approach to it. He had a capacity for enjoying all that was going on and for keeping his work in perspective. Conversely, his capacity for work, and his ability to allow enjoyment to be part of it, helped the accomplishment.

The police knew what John did best. They recognised a young man who liked to go his own way, but had character and was open. Most folk took to him instantly, so they put this to use. With his wide circle of contacts in Southampton, John was an obvious choice to sell tickets for the periodic Police Band concerts at the Mayflower Theatre in the Commercial Road. For three weeks he would be lost to the office – skiving, teased his mates – as he cycled around town inveigling those who were only mildly interested in selections from Gilbert and Sullivan into going along. Free from his fetters grim, for a time at least, that particular policeman's lot was quite an 'appy one.

John himself always considered that he was not a very good policeman. Some of his mates did not disagree. 'His interests weren't really in the police,' remarked Joe Molloy. He went no further, but there is no doubt that the rigidities, conformities and hierarchical code of a provincial police force were irksome to a young man of zest and capability. But John cared all right. About people. Far too much, perhaps, to be hard enough when it was needed. He dramatised the problem in another article for *St Martin's Review* which appeared after the Second World War:

He likes you to think of him as 'tough'. That is how he thinks of himself. He wears his cheap cap on one side, blows Woodbine-smoke down his nostrils with more bravado than pleasure, and is perpetually conscious of his walk, which he varies from a jaunty swagger to a mock-muscle-bound slouch. He is just sixteen years old.

Six years ago his father joined the Army; about eight months later, a private soldier's allowance being too little to maintain the family, his mother went to work in the canteen of an aircraft factory. Since then he has had all the streets round his home for a playground, for five years blacked-out streets.

Blitzed houses gave the eleven, twelve, thirteen-year-old boy a magnificent playground, rails wrenched out from balustrades made perfect tommy-guns with which to snipe his pals in their gangster battles.

Eighteen months ago at the Juvenile Court he was found guilty on two charges of store-breaking. Face clean and shining, hair smeared down with water and wearing his Sunday suit and a clean collar he faced four kindly magistrates. His mother, frightened, anxious and completely out of her element, stood beside him. Brokenly and honestly she protested, justifying herself: his father away, she herself working shifts: of the son she did not know she said he was a 'good boy'. He, brazen, wide-eyed but with tongue in cheek, promised to 'be a good boy'. The magistrates hoped against their common sense, sent him away with a caution. He winked at his friends waiting their turn outside the pleasant, informal court-room and next day, at school, he boasted how he had 'fooled the old ginks'. The policeman responsible for his case knew that the boy's determined lying concealed his guilt in other cases of which there was no proof.

Again, eight months later, two months after he started work as an errand-boy, he was brought before the court. This time the charges were of store-breaking and stealing a bicycle. The magistrates debated: he was 'bound over' to be of good behaviour for twelve months. The probation officer visited his home, spoke to him and found him apparently milder, more well-behaved than any reasonable person dare expect a healthy lad of fifteen to be. Nevertheless, the probation officer found him a job in a factory: his foreman found him 'idle and a young liar, but not much worse than a good few others'.

Today he is before the court again. Proved against him and another lad are two particularly daring cases, one of shop-breaking, one of housebreaking.

What is to be done with him?

In the article John went on to weigh up the alternatives: 'I know him. I know him in three hundred editions.' Should he, once more, be 'bound over'? He would think he had got away scot-free. What about the birch? An effective deterrent, but how does it affect the man who administers the birching? The physical aspect too. The recipient often loses control of his bodily functions. The results are impressive when successful, but the depths of its failures are unplumbable. Then he should go to Borstal? The influence of like-minded lads might be lastingly formative.

John, aware of the charitable idealist in himself, felt there was no *right* answer, only one that might be expedient. He recognised the arrogant virility of adolescence – not altogether absent when he was that age in his own make-up. If only that strength, laudable in wartime, could be canalised into the emulation of somebody or something worthwhile. To let the boy feel himself a man. The thought was accepted as at best a part-cure, not a root-prevention.

In a pamphlet called 'Attention', John recalled the first case of any real complexity that he handled. At one point he was utterly bemused:

After every possible enquiry, the taking – and re-taking – of detailed statements, I went sadly to the sergeant. 'Either I've made an awful mess of this case or someone – or everyone – is telling lies, skipper,' I said. The sergeant read through the statements and grinned. He went into the next room and came back with a book.

'You're a great one for believing what you read in books,' he said. 'Read that.'

The book was Hans Gross's *Criminal Investigation* and he pointed to two sentences: 'The witnesses, however anxious they may undoubtedly be to tell the truth, have told different stories while, if they had observed accurately, they should all have given absolutely identical accounts ... No one in the world is by nature an exact observer and, if he has not noticed a particular detail, all the questions in the world are worthless.'

The contradictions in that case were at least half my fault. The witnesses had told me what they saw – or rather what they *thought* they saw – and those original stories, some slight, some more substantial, differed very little. But, when I began to ask questions, their minds played tricks, they found themselves 'remembering' things out of imagination, and the associations of ideas – perhaps even 'remembering' things they thought I wanted them to remember.

Who would be a copper?

5

Of Period and Place

The Second World War, which broke out in September 1939, was eventually to bring John Arlott a new job, although it was not the one he and John Creighton had in mind when they attempted to leave the police.

At the outset of the war Johnny 'Sailor' Malan, who later became a legendary pilot in the Battle of Britain, was a fourth officer on a Union Castle boat that sailed between England and South Africa. He had met John at Mrs Warden's lodgings when he was dating her daughter Mary. One day in a pub he mentioned to the two Johns that the Royal Air Force was offering short-service commissions which carried a far better wage than they were ever likely to get in the police.

The prospect was too good to resist, and all three set off for the local recruiting office. Having filled in forms which required details of present occupation, they settled down to wait. Very soon 'Sailor' Malan was sent into another room to take a medical. Suddenly, Arlott and Creighton became aware of the looming figure of the duty inspector from police headquarters, who had been informed of their intentions by a telephone call from the recruiting officer. The inspector advised them that they were in 'restricted employment', and were now under arrest. Back at the station he continued the lecture and told them not to be 'so damned daft' again.

Through his coaching of the Royal South Hants Hospital badminton team at St Mary's Drill Hall, John had met a nurse, Dawn Rees. His visits to the hospital had mostly been of a sombre nature on police duty, interviewing those who had attempted to commit suicide, which was then still a criminal offence. However, apart from such nights at the bedsides of patients, his skill at badminton – which had led him to play a County trial – was no hindrance either in helping him to play with the nurses.

'He was very good-looking,' says Dawn, 'and he took out one nurse after another, so initially I refused to go out. I thought, "You fancy yourself, boy." Anyway, I eventually did.'

Before the 'eventually did' actually happened, John had waved down the car in which Dawn was travelling with a young doctor. There is nothing like a uniform to help hide a pretext or give an unfair advantage, and very soon, for Dawn, there was nothing like the man in the uniform.

The bright and bubbly girl had been born in Poplar, in the East End of London, and brought up in Ireland. Her Welsh father, who came from the Brecon Beacons, had emigrated to Toronto and joined the 1st Canadian Battalion as a dispatch rider. Her mother was the daughter of a director of Dewhurst the butchers in the south of England. Dawn had Celtic colouring and was exceedingly attractive, with dark hair, sparkling blue eyes, dimples and a winning smile. John called her 'Pippin' because of her rosy cheeks. She was not short of suitors; however, John saw off all rivals.

They were married on 18 May 1940 by Father Caesar in a High Church wedding at St Luke's, Southampton. Dawn's mother could not bring herself to be there; instead she sent a telegram expressing regret that her daughter had married beneath her. It was the time of the fall of France, and the town was full of French sailors. Police leave was hard to get, but eventually Dawn and John managed a slightly belated honeymoon at 'a posh hotel in Ilfracombe' where, extraordinarily, they met 'the only two Arlotts in the London phone directory. Charming but quite old – over forty.'

A month after they were married, Southampton suffered its first air raid. It was a mere foretaste of what was to come, for in the ensuing weeks the town was to receive regular visits from Goering's pilots. A lot of other cities and towns did too, of course, not least Portsmouth and Plymouth, but Southampton bore more than most. The 'V' between the Test and Itchen rivers provided an unmistakable bearing for the Luftwaffe, and the considerable tonnage of shipping that sailed in and out of the docks, and its strategic importance, made the port a prime target.

In November 1940 came the great Blitz. At one juncture, after an intensive onslaught on four out of five nights, the town was close to being evacuated. Surely an irruption was imminent? The two succeeding nights brought a temporary respite and much-needed rest for jangling nerves.

But then on 23 November there was a monstrous assault. The raid lasted five hours, during which seventy-seven people were killed and 311 were injured; 358 properties were either totally or partially demolished and over three thousand were damaged to varying degrees. The Germans' tactic was to drop flares, shortly followed by incendiary and then high explosive bombs; there were direct hits on the police block in the Civic Centre, and fourteen members of the force were among the casualties.

On 30 November and 1 December police headquarters were again extensively ravaged, the resulting fires being fought with stirrup-pumps, sand, earth and dustbin lids. Temporarily the HQ had to transfer to the Polygon Hotel. In *Southampton: The English Gateway* (1951), Bernard Knowles describes the scene: 'The sky was illuminated by a thousand floating flares, in whose incandescent glare the sprawling white mass of the Civic Centre took on the ghostly semblance of a winding sheet ... Even as the ghostly festoons of light were flickering out, the sky began to empty itself of a terrible arsenal. It was like the earthquake, the tornado, the waterspout, and the thunderbolt combined.'

During these raids one sergeant and two constables were killed, including George Brown, son of the Hampshire and England cricketer of the same name, who was in the mobile unit. Only seconds before a bomb exploded on his car, he had been engaged in a brief conversation with John. 'Lucky chap. Enjoy it,' had been John's parting sally as Brown set off to drive a nervous chief constable to a quieter part of town.

A pleasant flat in Howard Road, on the periphery of the Freemantle and Shirley districts of Southampton, was where John and Dawn first set up home. The dwelling was close to the docks, and they were fortunate not to receive a direct hit – an indirect one was bad enough. Luckily, at the time the bomb fell, both were on night duty; Dawn now as a sister at the Southampton Children's Hospital and John on air raid standby. There was a certain amount of relief when they found the furniture and household effects intact, but shards of shattered glass were everywhere; trying to perch on the edge of the settee produced a sharp reminder.

At least they were unhurt, but where were they to live? Friends of an aunt of Dawn's came to the rescue, and within hours they evacuated to a house in Chandler's Ford some miles north of Southampton, joining several other couples who had also been bombed out. For six weeks their lives revolved around one room with a camp bed on the floor and much cycling to and from the city through freezing snow in the dark. Their one comfort was to compare tales of woe with those suffering similarly.

But this could only be a short-term solution. Apart from the inconvenience of the distance, the accommodation was far too cramped, and so John and Dawn moved back to Southampton, to share a modern semi-detached property in Bassett Green Road with Herbert Bumby and his wife Doll. 'Bumble', as he was known, worked in the Southampton Library and knew John well, since John spent as much time as he could foraging among the shelves.

At the beginning of 1941 a War Emergency Department was set up, and the fact that John's personal file showed he could speak schoolboy French, and had learned how to use more than two fingers on a typewriter while working for George Paget in Basingstoke, impressed those in authority who could not. He was moved to join the unit at the Southampton police headquarters at the Civic Centre. Drill on official parades and the 'boning' of boots to a high gloss – John was always the first to discover the latest polish, whether for boots or buttons, that promised a greater shine for less effort – now receded to occasional aggravations. His mind was engaged by broader concerns.

The new job, as a detective constable with Special Branch, involved writing situation reports, summarising new legislation and screening aliens. This last involved occasional forays into a twilight world. Lists of ships' personnel and civilians about to embark or disembark ended up on John's desk. His command of written and spoken English, and his growing knowledge not only of French, but also of Italian, German and Norwegian was essential in this part of his job. Dutch, too. He wished, though, that he knew a little more of that language when a Netherlander arrived by light aircraft and put up at the Polygon Hotel. He was the first man whom John was deputed to tail.

While the man was at dinner John went to his room to see if he could find anything incriminating. 'Did you change the lightbulb before you left?' asked Dawn afterwards. 'Because he would know somebody had been there if he felt it and it was still warm.' 'No, Pippin, I didn't do that,' John admitted. 'I had to be out of there ready to follow him. He was going up to London.'

In due course the man emerged from the hotel and John tagged along behind. Within ten minutes he had lost sight of him completely. As Dawn said, 'If you've been on the beat, it's not easy to follow somebody who wants to lose themselves. John was not one of those little men in grey mackintoshes.'

Dawn was not the only one who had to tell the would-be sleuth how to cover his tracks. 'Someone wanted to know something about someone,' wrote John for a pamphlet in the *Take Home* series, 'and I went with the first someone to search the second someone's room. We found something – which might have been significant or might not. I replaced everything and we were about to leave the room when the first someone stood a moment, his back to the door, and then began to readjust the things I had "replaced". "Did you notice when we came in," he said, "that the edge of the pyjamas on the pillow, the dressing gown on the bottom of the bed, the suitcase on the floor and the notecase on the dressing table were all in a straight line from the edge of the door, so that he would see if anyone had disturbed them?"'

Although operating now in plainclothes, John still had to attend mandatory pistol practice at the converted old cinema in French Street, where an ability to 'do the business' with a 45 Colt revolver had to be demonstrated. There were still other enemies around, such as the IRA, who could have caused havoc at the aircraft factories in the vicinity, not least the Supermarine Works, once the home of the Spitfire.

One day John was sent to detain Joe Beckett, a former British heavy-weight boxing champion who, married to a German wife, was reported to have said he would become the Gauleiter of the City if the Allies lost the war.

'I was shivering in my boots when I approached this huge man in his camelhair coat,' said John to the sports reporter Neil Allen years later. '"Are you going to arrest me?" asked Beckett. "I'm afraid I am. You've been a silly chap," I said, and awaited the onslaught. Beckett stared at me, and then said: "I'll tell your father of you." You see, he came from Basingstoke too.'

An advantage of John's job in the Emergency Department was that he could legitimately be out of the office pursuing enquiries. These enquiries could, and did, take him to the local library or the reading room at the Art Gallery if he needed to research some obscure point. The fact that he was unsupervised allowed him to read and digest much that had little to do with his official duties, such as the works of Hilaire Belloc and George Bernard Shaw. Fortunately his chief constable, Frederick Tarry, for whom he acted as a kind of unofficial amanuensis, was an understand-ing man. Tarry, newly arrived from the West Country, had been quick to see John's capabilities and gave him free rein. He knew where he was likely to find his 'booksy boy' as he called him, when he was not at his desk. A phone call to the library, a quick transfer to the reference section extension, and when Herbert Bumby answered, 'If you happen to see Detective Constable Arlott, please tell him the chief constable wants him'.

John read voraciously, particularly during air-raid standby, when he was required to stay at police HQ every other night. The alert often remained on through the small hours and, with sleep not permitted, becoming engrossed in a book was an escape from the uncertain realities outside and the crawling clock on the wall. He even snatched opportunities to dip into chapters while in the office during the day. Archie Davies, who as a detective ran the Criminal Record Office before becoming a CID administrator after retirement, remembers John sitting at a desk. 'He would have the drawer open with the book he was reading balanced just inside. Immediately somebody came in he would shut the drawer smartly.'

One of John's new duties was to interview conscientious objectors, and even in the custodial cell books were not forgotten. Lawrence Thackray, an objector remanded in Southampton in 1942, wrote in the *Guardian* many years later:

A young man in civilian clothes visited me, and we engaged in a long discussion on conscientious objection – why I held these views, what had influenced me, my reading. The young man was courteous, shrewd, fair. The conversation ranged widely – it seemed to go on for an hour or two. Somehow at one stage it centred on Elizabethan poetry and this unusual police officer (for so I assumed he was) . . . took me to my medical which, not to his surprise, I refused. Back in my cell he gave me a parting gift of *The Good Soldier Schweik* and twenty Weights [cigarettes]. Many years later I . . . realised that my interrogator had been John Arlott.

John had only recently discovered poetry himself. At school, in common with most boys of his age, he had only been interested in 'dirty' doggerel, and it was ten years after he left before he opened a book of poems, to find 'it said more to me as a human being than anything else did'. Perhaps in 1940 prose could not fully reflect his powers of observation, which had been sharpened during his police duties. For him the image needed to be important in itself, and not just as 'orchestral colour' in another form of composition. He started to experiment in verse form.

Despite the ordered auxiliary response during heavy bombing raids, the turmoil in Southampton was indescribable. Helping to extinguish the fires after waves of incendiary attacks brought John face on with the detritus and the tragedies of human existence. However inured he may have been to seeing cadavers during his days at Park Prewett, this was something else. The shock and barely controllable nausea at finding a burnt and dismembered corpse amidst smoking rubble – and perhaps, lying alongside, a cracked sepia photograph of the dead person's loved one – was hard to dispel. Their countenances stayed with him for days. His expressions in verse were cathartic.

Snow Scene: Blitzed Church

> Itself the night-fired sacrifice,
> Coolly palled by gentle drifts
> That, cloaking, dignify its scars,
> Humbly, tirelessly it lifts
> Across the grey-veiled winter sun
> Scorched twin-turrets' silent pain:
> Two dead and pleading arms for pardon
> Of the wreckers and the slain.

Twisting girders rigor-fixed
In agony of iron and rust
Are softened whitely into garlands
Blooming in the altar's dust.

In mystic cloud of flurried snow
The window bars are slim and pale
That curve like harpists' arms to play
The anthem of the north-east gale.

(Semaphore, 1946)

Life continued in a haphazard and surreal way. To survive in wartime it was sometimes necessary for the mind to be switched to auto-pilot and for the body to function mechanically. Enforced blackout, a shaft of light from behind carelessly-drawn curtains, the hammer of a door-knocker and a shouted instruction from a nightwatchman to the people inside, bicycle tyres swishing almost silently over wet roads, the low hum of invisible aircraft, shadowy figures scurrying to shelter, sudden searchlights pricking the night sky, the erratic boom of coastal defence artillery and a flare of explosives as a bomb-cluster found a target. Any night might be the same, any day might be different, but in the long, dark space of winter, distinctions were blurred and sensations transparent. Always, though, in the beginning and at the end, there was the dreaded siren, like a demented clarinettist practising the opening of 'Rhapsody in Blue'.

The Other Fear

Awake and tense in my island bed,
I heard our night-planes overhead,
Felt their growing roaring hurled
To flood my little curtained world,
And, once again, in plane-racked night
Fear hung for me in sound of flight.
Not now the fear of pain and death
To make me check my trembling breath,
But guilty fear for friends who fly,
Simply to do a job or die.

Youth heard the challenge of its times,
And, blind to statesmen's tricks and crimes,
Youth went, to high adventure thrilling,
Not pausing now to weigh the killing –
Flying and fighting in our name –

If blame there be, we share that blame –
Blame not purged by praise of nations
But only by those generations
Who, not needing passports, fly
Unchallenged over common sky.

(Of Period and Place, 1944)

By 1942, John's literary tastes were leading him beyond the town library and district bookshops. An introduction to Southampton University Library by two friends on the staff, Harry Howell, a physicist, and Reg Loader, a lecturer in Classics, allowed him to pursue an interest in Russian history up to the Bolshevik Revolution. As always with John, any new enthusiasm was all-consuming. Before long, and with the assistance of John Parker, head of the university's Extra-Mural Department, he found himself under their ambit giving lectures on the subject – with all its military implications – to service education officers and then Workers' Educational Classes. For a provincial policeman the additional income – an average of over eight pounds a week – was very welcome.

As he was educating others he was also educating himself, and cultivating friendships with writers and reviewers. He became obsessed with learning for its own sake and for the pleasure it gave. In this process of ripening into a fully-informed man he tested views and defended principles in conversation with well-stocked minds. One such protagonist, and one of John's closest friends, was Terry Delaney, an Irishman and an author who spent time in prison during the war for his pacifist views. Delaney was described by Julian Holland, one-time editor of Radio 4's *Today* programme, as 'a perfectionist. He was like a clerk in the civil service who is always rewriting the first sentence of his great novel, polishing it again and again, and is never going to write the second sentence until he has chiselled that first sentence to his own satisfaction, and, of course, he never does. Enormous talent, small output.' Delaney too was to work for the BBC, on such programmes as *Radio Newsreel* and *World at One*.

There were also Douglas Goldring and Tommy Earp, both of whom had been impecunious poets, who were infinitely capable of broadening John's mental horizons. Goldring liked to write about the Mediterranean, and Earp had a particular interest in the histories of London and Paris. John would be fascinated when Goldring reminisced about meetings with D.H. Lawrence, Richard Aldington and Robert Graves.

With so much 'normality' crumbling all around, the sanity of the printed page was instantly therapeutic for John. He enjoyed the civilising and pervading influence of books. His collection grew and grew, stretching the spacial resources of everywhere he lived. Both Joe Molloy and Frank Baker, a police sergeant at the time, recall John's love affair with literature. 'He was setting up a library at Shaftesbury Avenue,'* remarked Joe. 'He would take every opportunity to pop into a bookshop.' Frank Baker concurs: 'He was an affable, happy-go-lucky, non-aggressive bookworm. Extremely able at writing reports. He gave me a copy of *Seven Pillars of Wisdom* after I told him how I had met T.E. Lawrence. I was on afternoon shift and went into Munn & Underwood's garage in Southampton and saw this magnificent Brough Superior motorbike. I was sitting on it talking to the mechanic when Lawrence came in. As I got off I was very ill-at-ease, so for something to say I said, "some bicycle this is." "I've done a hundred miles an hour on it," he said. "Why don't you get a car?" I asked. "I'm a friend of Brough's," he replied tersely, got on the bike and rode off.'

Baker continued: 'John had masses of books in Lodge Road – secondhand, first editions . . .' 114 Lodge Road, in the Bevois Town area of Southampton, was the house where Dawn and John eventually moved in 1943 on a short lease with an option to purchase. As John wrote in his autobiography *Basingstoke Boy*: 'Then followed a period of driving off to Basingstoke in borrowed, clapped-out vans, begging small items from his parents; buying larger items in sales and junk shops.'

Nobody can pinpoint, other than for themselves, the exact and crucial moment when the creative juices start to flow. But certainly, in retrospect, it would appear that John's life in the early 1940s helped shape much of the remainder of it. The poetic muse, the prose style, the wide vocabulary were, in a sense, innate, yet they now found expression as he put pen to paper. He was fortunate that his abilities matched his desires, and that he had always sought to discover where they might lead. The learning curve steepened as outlets were found. The time of preparation, unrecognised as such, was nearly over. How did the connections come to be made? The answer is ordinary and obvious. Dawn explained: 'He got to know literary people by reading their novels – he would buy first editions and then get people to make vast parcels and he would write to X, Y or Z with points related to sections of the books and say "Would you mind signing for me?" Often this led to continued correspondence.'

In a comparatively short time, John was exchanging letters and parcels with significant writers, poets and artists – Richard Aldington, Edmund Blunden, John Betjeman, Clifford Bax, Cyril Connolly, Walter de la Mare, T.S. Eliot, Osbert Lancaster, George Holbrook Jackson, John Piper and Vita Sackville-West. 'God, how I remember those parcels,' said Dawn

* Where he had lived after moving on from Mrs Warden's.

with a laugh. 'He had a friend, Clem the chemist, and we were on this tram and to my horror John stopped the tram and said, "Just a minute" – having been on the beat he knew everybody – and went over to Clem's chemist shop with a huge load of books and kept the tram waiting there while this man made up the parcels for him to post. I was so embarrassed. Eventually I made up the parcels myself.'

The artist John Piper became involved in one such exchange in July 1942, when he was living at Fawley Bottom near Henley-on-Thames. 'I have been negligent about important things such as your parcel,' he wrote, and with the returned books he enclosed 'a proof of an aquatint for Brunswick Square which I prepared as a spare illustration for the hand-coloured edition (of *Brighton Aquatints*) in case anything went wrong with any of the plates during printing. Nothing did go wrong, so this illustration does not ordinarily appear . . . with, once again, many thanks for your kindly appreciation, and good wishes to yourself, and for the future of your library.'

To enter a bookshop with John was an experience one did not forget. He would go through the door quickly and, as the clang of the bell diminuendo-ed through the disturbed dust, stand silent and still. Then a deep breath and an appreciative sniff as the familiar smell of ribbed morocco and tattered page aroused his acquisitive instincts. His head would not move, though his eyes would seem to look in five directions at once. Suddenly, with supreme certainty, he would go straight to the shelf or corner where everyone else would have gone if they had known where to look. He never, ever, came out of a bookshop empty-handed, always choosing a piece that was well done or extremely rare.

A Second-Hand Bookshop

The sunlight filters through the panes
Of bookshop windows, pockmarked grey
By years of grimy city rains,
And falls in mild, dust-laden ray
Across the stock, in shelf and stack,
Of this old bookshop-man who brought,
To a shabby shop in a cul-de-sac,
Three hundred years of print and thought.

Like a cloak hangs the bookshop smell,
Soothing, unique and reminding:
The book-collector knows its spell,
Subtle hints of books and binding –

In the fine, black bookshop dust
Paper, printer's-ink and leather,
Binder's-glue and paper-rust
And time, all mixed together.

'Blake's Poems, sir – ah, yes, I know,
Bohn did it in the old black binding,
In '83.' Then shuffles slow
To scan his shelves, intent on finding
This book of songs he has not heard,
With that deaf searcher's hopeful frown
Who knows the nightingale a bird
With feathers grey and reddish-brown.

John gathered friends with his collection – the authors and the books became indivisible. Years later, in the *Guardian*, he wrote:

What kind of man is it who does not collect the works of his friends? After all, they contain much of the character of the man who became a friend. It was, too, for many years, habit to have those friends sign their books . . . To live among books, known books, lived books, is a condition of life some people find infinitely rewarding and others no more than investment – which ruins the point of the exercise, and should only be considered as a side issue – wallpaper, or even a fire risk. The one thing a book collector learns, apart – wicked word in this context – from what he reads inside the books, is that he is no more than a tenant, one who lives in and with his books only to pass them on to another generation.

John's custodianship of his books was generous to a fault. He would never deny a book to a friend, and would positively encourage foraging among his shelves. He would enjoy, too, moving sections of his collection to different parts of the library. Books for him were a living thing, and never a decoration. They were to be cherished, and also used.

In 1942 the idea came to him to make an anthology of topographical verse. He wrote to John Betjeman asking if he would collaborate, but the future Poet Laureate was already committed to a not dissimilar undertaking, and regretfully declined. John then got in touch with George Rostrevor Hamilton, a poet, writer and civil servant who held a succession of senior positions in the Inland Revenue. Hamilton had already edited an acclaimed anthology of verse translations from the Greek, and at their first meeting he presented John with a seventy-two-page manuscript of his translations of French epigrams and madrigals. After some to-ing and fro-ing between publishing houses, Cambridge University Press – influenced by Hamilton's involvement – agreed to bring out the collection.

Landmarks, a picture of England and Wales seen through the eyes of 180 writers of English verse and edited by George Rostrevor Hamilton and John Arlott was published in 1943. The writers represented included Shakespeare, Byron, Clare, Hood, Housman, Crabbe, Drayton, Rose Macaulay, Thomas Tickell, Hamilton himself and, making his debut within the covers of a book, John Arlott. The plan had been to cover each county, going round the country in a more or less clockwise progression. As the cover blurb says, 'there are odd, out-of-the-way places, fine prospects, grimy and beloved towns ... here and there will surely leap out some name that strikes a special personal note. "Yes, I remember Adlestrop –". To forty million this may mean little; but to those who live in High Street, Adlestrop, it comes as a touch of immortality.'

Just before the deadline for the delivery of the typescript, disappointment had struck. Worcestershire was inadequately represented. Permission to reproduce a poem by the Poet Laureate, John Masefield, was refused, and John was told not to approach the great man personally. A little piqued by this rebuff, and with Hamilton's blessing, he got to work himself to fill the gap. He showed the result to his police colleague Frank Baker, who thought it very good. George Rostrevor Hamilton also thought it very good – he made a few minor amendments – and so too did the distinguished editor of *Horizon*, Cyril Connolly, who had been sent a copy by Hamilton and who printed it in the magazine as well.

Cricket at Worcester, 1938

Dozing in deck-chair's gentle curve,
Through half-closed eyes I watched the cricket,
Knowing the sporting press would say
'Perks bowled well on a perfect wicket.'

Fierce mid-day sun upon the ground;
Through heat-haze came the hollow sound
Of wary bat on ball, to pound
The devil from it, quell its bound.

Sunburned fieldsmen, flannelled cream,
Looked, though urgent, scarce alive,
Swooped, like swallows of a dream,
On skimming fly, the hard-hit drive.

Beyond the score-box, through the trees
Gleamed Severn, blue and wide,
Where oarsmen 'feathered' with polished ease
And passed in gentle glide.

The back-cloth, setting off the setting,
Peter's cathedral soared,
Rich of shade and fine of fretting
Like cut and painted board.

To the cathedral close for shelter,
Huddled houses, bent and slim,
Some tall, some short, all helter-skelter,
Like a sky-line drawn for Grimm.

This the fanciful engraver might
In his creative dream have seen,
Here, framed by summer's glaring light,
Grey stone, majestic over green.

Closer, the bowler's arm swept down,
The ball swung, swerved and darted,
Stump and bail flashed and flew;
The batsman pensively departed.

Like rattle of dry seeds in pods
The warm crowd faintly clapped,
The boys who came to watch their gods,
The tired old men who napped.

The members sat in their strong deck-chairs
And sometimes glanced at the play,
They smoked and talked of stocks and shares,
And the bar stayed open all day.

There were four other poems by John in the anthology – 'Brighton' and 'Southampton' under his own name, and 'Basingstoke' and 'Isle of Wight' under the nom-de-plume 'Leslie Thomas' – but it was 'Cricket at Worcester' that made a lasting impression. As Connolly remarked, 'When I was a boy my uncle used to take me to watch county cricket, and it was exactly like that, and that is why I published the poem.'

It was at Worcester that John had made his solitary appearance in first-class cricket. While still on the beat in Southampton, he had taken to going into the Hampshire county ground in Northlands Road close to his lodgings and standing behind the nets while the players practised. He would spend hours watching, totally engrossed. If on night duty, he would snatch a couple of hours' sleep and then make his way to the ground, and whenever possible would also support the team when they were playing away. Soon he got to know the players well. Leo Harrison, the able and affable wicket-keeper who made his debut in 1939, was to become a life-long friend. 'The first time I saw John he was in police uniform, standing behind the nets watching me bat [laugh]. I don't think it did much good for his own batting, though.'

Whenever John was free from police duties he used to hang around the dressing-rooms at Hampshire games, almost as a sort of unofficial supernumerary. And so it came to pass – the lovely cathedral overlooking the county ground at Worcester encourages biblical beginnings – that the twelfth or thirteenth man found himself on the field in early August 1938, in the size-and-a-half-too-big crepes of 'Lofty' Herman, the opening bowler, and somebody else's flannels.

'I was fielding mid-on and third man,' he told Mike Brearley almost fifty years later, during their Channel Four television conversation in 1986, 'which is about all I was fit for. The Nawab of Pataudi made, as far as I can recall, 180,* and at third man, if I was fine he played it square, if I was square he played it fine, and he had me running backwards and forwards like a dog on a string.

'Eventually he played one hard to the pavilion gate, and I had a long way to go. I knew I was never going to get round this ball. I don't know why it occurred to me, the least athletic of men, but I remembered Learie Constantine running over the ball, bending and picking it up between his legs as he went and throwing it in. So I did this. I got down to it all right and I got it in my hands. But I was going very very fast and there was all that water weed from the flooding in front of the Worcester pavilion. I felt my feet start to go.

'Now, my second appalling delusion was that I could turn a complete somersault, land on my shoulderblades and get up the other side, gangly and clumsy as I was. I did even succeed in that, but I shut my eyes with fear, drew my arm back and, as I opened my eyes, I saw the crowd in front of the Worcester pavilion parting like the Red Sea before the children of Israel: I was about to throw it in through the pavilion window! When I turned round to throw it the right way, Neil McCorkell, the wicket-keeper, was on his back with mirth, along with two other people, and they

* It may have seemed like 180, but actually it was 121 not out.

ran three from what should have been one to third man. At least I saved
one. It wasn't a four.'

There were plenty of other strokes that were, though, before Worcestershire finally declared at 413 for 3. Rain ensured that the match
ended in a draw, and perhaps the downpour interfered with press lines,
for one paper reported that P.C. Harlot had fielded for Hampshire.

Cricket was not forgotten during the war years – as if it ever could be.
Although he was not a good enough player to represent the full Southampton Police side, John did man the public address system at their games,
to persuade people to pick a pocket or two for charity. The Southampton
team contained a number of ex-professionals, and could match the Metropolitan Police XI, which had many times the personnel strength from
which to select their side.

It was on a train journey to London that Sergeant Frank Baker remembers John displaying his love and knowledge of cricket. The two of them
had been sent to the capital on a job, and at a stop on the way to Waterloo
a soldier got into their compartment. For the rest of the trip the squaddie
was held enthralled by stories of cricket from someone who, unbeknown
to any of them, was rehearsing his future career.

That someone did know that he had no future career as a player. 'I
was an extremely poor player . . . an intense, nervous player . . . an
enthusiastic bad player . . . The only thing I could do was to try and keep
the ball out of my wicket with anxiety and determination.' He had taken
part in a limited-time division match and, irrespective of the fact that he
was more suited to be a dogged opening bat, had found himself facing
the last over with four runs required for victory. Lloyd Budd of Hampshire, but then in the police, was bowling. Three times John tried to cut
Budd. Three times he missed. Budd also missed the wicket – but only
twice. John was bowled middle stump. On his return to the pavilion he
declared he would never play again, and straight away auctioned off all
his gear.

'Terrible innings that was,' he told Norman Harris of the *Sunday Times*
thirty years later. 'I lost the match. I had this silly idea in my mind to cut
Lloyd. I was pretty stupid. It was the end of my competitive cricket. It
was an agonising moment. But I thought, you know, I'd better make it
. . . a bit extravagant. If you say, for *God's* sake, this is the thing I've
wanted to do for all these years, *hell* I'm not going to quit . . . Admit it,
face it, you're a Bad Player.'

Renting the house in Lodge Road meant that John and Dawn now
had room to entertain, and a number of writers and artists enjoyed their
hospitality. James Laver, whose *œuvre* included a book on Nostradamus

and another on the history of costume, came to stay, and complained he did not have enough blankets. J.B. Leishman, translator of German literature and noted for his eccentricities, was a regular visitor who apparently had plenty of blankets but very few teeth. One day he left his pipe in a shop in Winchester, and insisted on cycling the fourteen miles to retrieve it. He was rewarded on his return with lettuce and cress sandwiches without the crusts, so as not to hurt his gums. The handsome glass engraver Laurence Whistler, then in the Rifle Brigade, who had tragically lost his wife, the actress Jill Furse, in childbirth, found some comfort and much warmth. Other visitors included George Rostrevor Hamilton and his wife Marion, and, frequently, John Betjeman.

Betjeman and his wife Penelope often returned the Arlotts' hospitality at their home in Wantage, but whereas Dawn was a splendid cook, Penelope was less domestically adept. 'Food is beyond me,' she would say, wearing a skirt stained with cow dung and serving uncut grapefruit with her eyes fixed on distant horizons. On one visit, the horizon was no further than the end of the garden. Obviously having exhausted her husband's lack of ability as a handyman, she seized the opportunity of a good-looking, athletic young male in the offing. 'Just the man I want to move my henhouses,' she ordered cheerfully, knowing that John could not refuse.

John's own poetry has been thought to be in the Betjeman mould. Kingsley Amis, a friend for many years, said when asked to allocate John a position on the poets' pyramid: 'I suppose you'd put him at the top of the second division. Some of his output was a little sub-Betjeman.' However, Cyril Connolly, who had a reputation as a pungent critic, placed him higher, writing in May 1944:

> Dear Arlott,
>   These poems are a great improvement. You are getting right away from John Betjeman. You are, in fact, original now, with a growing talent for getting crowds, groups of people, *collectiveness* into poetry. This is very rare. And your Hampshire local colour is delicious. What about a poem on Southampton? or Eastleigh? . . .
>   The Winchester, I think is the best.

Following his collaboration with Hamilton, John had been sending his verses to Connolly and to the editors of a number of other periodicals: the *Fortnightly*, the *Spectator*, *Writing Today*, *English* and *Time and Tide*. His canon had grown. Two of his poems appeared in collections: *The Little Review Anthology* and Reginald Moore's *Modern Reading*.

It was an encouraging time for young poets. Despite wartime shortages, verse was well represented in the output of publishing houses and in 1944 Jonathan Cape agreed to produce twenty-five of John's poems in a slim volume entitled *Of Period and Place*. 'What this poet sees,' wrote the publishers on the dustjacket, 'he can bring before the reader's eyes, what he feels is more subtly conveyed, though without recourse to exotic symbolism. Scenes of a country fair, of a cricket match, of Brighton beach, of fog-enshrouded Southampton Water, of a parched field, sights and sounds of human activities – these contrast with period pieces and interiors, a lodging in the London of the yellow nineties, a Victorian house where life goes sedately on in spite of "blasted" windows, a Sickert-like music hall. The subjects are interesting and their content immediately apprehensible' – like, for example, John's description of a pub round the corner:

Invitation to the Local

Swing-doors, dark-curtained, will let you in
To the heat and light and merging din
Of laughter sprung from broad-based humour,
And gossip out of slight-based rumour,
Then weighted pause for the point of a joke
Till sudden roars ride the waves of smoke
To drown the whisper of racing tips
And crackle of bags of potato-chips.

Old women with Guinness and beaver coats,
Scrub-wrinkled fingers and beads at their throats,
Tap gently with tired, black-booted feet
To faded piano's nostalgic beat.

Catch the reflection of beer-engine's brass
In the wealthy brown of a full pint-glass,
Haunting and sad is the smell of spilt beer,
If beer is best, then what heaven is here.

The barmaid twists in her tight satin frock
To look at the pale-faced, oracle clock;
Then shouts and jostling for the night's last drink,
The till-bell rings and the glasses clink.

Now shuffle of boots on the splintery floor,
Warm-breathing crush in the wide-open door,
And the night-wind strikes with cheek-chilling stroke
To carve a deep cleft in the banks of smoke –

They're turning them out at the old 'Black Bull'
For both the till and its fillers are full.

(Of Period and Place, 1944)

The poem 'A Little Guide to Winchester', which Cyril Connolly had commended, made a reference to King Alfred wearing the crown of Wessex, a tangential reminder of John's retort in later years to those who commented on the distinctiveness of his voice: 'I speak the King's English – the one that came from Winchester!'

Of Period and Place was well received: 'Mechanically considered, it is the function of the poet to "set" an emotion or an experience as an entomologist sets a beautiful butterfly. The poet, however, must take care to hide the pins and varnish. This Mr Arlott does with no little success. His mechanics do not obtrude in either verse or rhyme,' went the report in one local paper. 'Already knowing life, he avoids the "precious" which plagues so many young verse-makers. Nor does he tax belief with a too self-conscious straining after the popular modern "realistic" note. His reality, though, can be more than a backcloth, as readers will see when they have read "Slum". For the rest, the periods and places, chosen for attention, are all on the human level.'

More cautionary notes were sounded by E.H.W. Meyerstein in *English*: 'Mr Arlott has a clear vision of what he means to do ... His is the eye of a realistic painter ... his "Back to the Fair" is the stuff of an early Dame Laura Knight ... no ecstasy but concentrated precision of phrase ... the humour of e.g. Mr John Betjeman is absent ... he must learn to pass from the thing seen to the thing felt, but he apprehends the way.' A reviewer in another provincial paper summed up the collection with: 'this volume will be welcomed by those who dip hopefully into the work of so many young poets without finding much which lies between Faerie and flapdoodle'.

John had received advice on his poetic expression from the one-time canon of Chichester Cathedral, Andrew Young. Young is often placed among the rural company of parson poets, but he probably deserves a higher billing. He never ceased to seek the spare phrase, polishing words, as John put it, 'like a lapidarist'. Nor was he beyond seeking guidance himself, so his and John's was a mutually supportive friendship. Writing in 1944 from The Vicarage, Stonegate, near Tunbridge Wells, he thanked John for sending a copy of *Of Period and Place*: 'You need not worry about "Prayer for an Immortal Line", that poem should always appear in anthologies. I am rather sorry "Brighton" has been altered, on the whole the poems seem better in a book, as a painted canvas does in a frame.

Somehow I don't remember reading "Southampton Water" in the proofs; I should do so, as it is very good indeed . . .'

When Young first responded to some poems sent by John, he had told him: '"Cricket at Worcester" was the one I enjoyed most. I don't think sounds often get expressed in verse, except in Pope's cheap way of making the sound echo the sense. I was immediately struck by the way you reproduce two sounds in verse: "the hollow sound/Of wary bat on ball", and "Like rattle of dry seeds in pods/The warm crowd faintly clapped". Anyone who has been to a cricket match will recognise these sounds. This seems to me an unusual gift you should cultivate. But you give the whole picture very well, action and spectators and setting. It's a delightful poem.'

Six years later, in 1950, Jonathan Cape was to do for Andrew Young what they had done for John Arlott. They produced his *Collected Poems*, with illustrations by Joan Hassall. John heralded the event in the Autumn 1948 number of *Now and Then*, the Cape in-house journal:

> I was walking one day with Andrew Young across the field behind his Sussex vicarage. The country fell away before us into the valley and then climbed again to Robertsbridge. There was a farm to our left, a farm ahead and beyond that, houses only on the distant ridge. I was finding the going hard – for all that he is thirty years my senior, Andrew Young walks still with the speed and endurance of the Highlander. Conversation was checked by my breathlessness and my friend's concentration – his eyes miss nothing in the grass or the hedges. Then he said suddenly, 'You know I shall never live in a town again.' 'Oh,' I said weakly, 'why not?' 'It's too dull. Nothing ever happens there – but here – here there's always something happening.' One of the characteristics of Andrew Young's poetry is the excitement of the man for whom there is always something happening in the quietest field. Few people have seen so many of the British wild flowers as he has done – and he has travelled all over Britain to see them – to see, not to pick or dissect or preserve them. Those travels have originated his poems in almost every part of the country. Another influence in his work is the exhaustive reading of the poets which has perfected his technique and made him so severe a self-critic that his forthcoming *Collected Poems* by constant pruning and writing, is almost a distillation of his poetry.

The influence of Young's work on John was profound, as is mirrored on the page.

To Andrew Young
on reading his poems

Behind these limpid words I find
Reflections, in a crystal mind,
Of images so sharp and clear
That I can almost see and hear
The subjects of your calm delight.
The spider-webs of which you write
Are not more accurate, more fine,
More integral, more light of line,
Nor spun by wisdom more innate
Than are these lines where you create
With living eye, with living hand,
Your real and visionary land:
So clear you see these timeless things
That, like a bird, the vision sings.

Andrew Young and John spent much time in one another's houses, and across the generation gap developed a firm friendship. Young was delighted when John and Dawn asked him to christen their first child, James Andrew, born on 4 December 1944. The occasion was a kind of metrical reunion, as one of the godparents was George Rostrevor Hamilton.

One of the other 'literary' people whom John met in 1943 was Michael Ayrton, a co-member of the ENSA Brains Trusts which were formed to give entertainment and enlightenment to service audiences. John had been recruited onto the panel following his successful service lectures. According to John, Ayrton was seven years his junior, but 'certainly his intellectual superior'. He was extremely articulate on a wide range of subjects, and appeared to be a man of daunting certainty, yet in a letter to John he wrote, 'I am very ambitious and self-confident, but suffer grave doubts most of the time.' At that stage of his life, perhaps much the same could be said of the recipient.

Ayrton and his partner Joan Walsh, who took his surname by deed poll after her husband refused a divorce, stayed on a number of occasions with the Arlotts at Lodge Road. Joan remembers going into the kitchen and making 'a rude remark about the peanut butter Dawn was using', which drew a laugh in response. Michael and John became boon companions and collaborated on *Clausentum*, a book about Bitterne Manor House in Southampton which stood on the site of the Roman

Clausentum. Michael provided six lithographs, John a twelve-part sequence of sonnets.

Bitterne Manor, at one time a residence of the Bishops of Winchester, had been damaged by fire and bomb-blast, and now stood empty, probably for the first time in over a thousand years. In its state of dilapidation it showed, in startling depth, Norman, Elizabethan, Georgian and Victorian stages of building and extension. It was, as can be seen in John and Michael's joint preface, very much a shared experience.

> Clausentum is clenched in a twist of the tidal river Itchen at South-ampton, its southern boundary now the main Southampton–Portsmouth road instead of the old fosse. There is good reason to believe that it has been in human occupation for over two thousand years, that it was the site of an ancient British encampment and, later, a Roman landing-station and the galley-fleet headquarters of the usurper-emperor Carasius, Count of the Saxon Shore.
>
> When we saw Clausentum for the first time we felt an air of peace and isolation almost incredible in a place pent in by the industries of a modern port. We went there again, many times; once late on a still summer night. Every visit brought some fresh revelation . . . Part of the grounds has been made into allotments, the front of the house has been used as a rifle-range and hooligans have defaced the walls and torn away the woodwork. Even in the few months that covered our visits to Clausentum we saw tragic and irreparable dam-age done to the house. Without expectation we record the hope that some steps may be taken to preserve this parcel of land, its trees, its buildings and that rare character which became our familiar.

On one occasion the two collaborators decided to extend their occupa-tion by staying overnight at the Manor – or even better, just outside the Manor, by the river's edge. They took waterproof sheets and blankets, plus a goodly supply of food and drink, and got to work:

By Night (III)

> The south-west wind goes down before the night
> And soundlessly the river saunters by.
> The crumbling walls are chalked in moonbeams white
> On trees pinned out with stars across the sky.
> A still and sharply-lined grey figure fills
> The glassless window of a floorless room,

And creeper on a smashed door-pillar spills
Across the hallway's shuttered trap of gloom.
Now with the mask of midnight on its face,
The faithful river mutely toils to force
The bank that bars the long-dry fosse and race
Once more along the old remembered course,
To make again the old full-circle sweep
And, with its body, guard Clausentum's sleep.

Clausentum was published by Jonathan Cape in May 1946. To a certain extent, Arlott and Ayrton's hopes for the house were fulfilled. Eventually, Bitterne Manor became a Grade 2 listed building, and today it is converted into flats.

By 1944, police work in Southampton had once again become mainly routine. German planes had long ceased to rage above their heads, and urgency had given way to something approaching boredom. For John, sitting at his desk, any available moment was spent trying to chisel words into place. Without realising it, he had found the door to a new career.

6

A Hell of a Gamble

The invitation to the padded room with the open microphone had come by chance. A former UK press attaché in Dublin, John Betjeman, had casually mentioned to a former literary editor of the now defunct *Morning Post*, Geoffrey Grigson, that he knew of a policeman who liked – no, was besotted by – poetry. They were sitting in an office in Whiteladies Road in Bristol, one of a great number of rooms that had been converted from residential apartments to form Broadcasting House, West Region. Betjeman, then known, if not yet famous, as a poet, and Grigson, known, yet never to be famous, as a poet, were making a programme together. Betjeman did not press the point.

Grigson, however, did not forget. As a senior talks producer for the BBC he was always on the lookout for new ideas, and new slants on old ideas. He had heard about *Of Period and Place*, and knew that one of the poems in the collection, 'A Second-Hand Bookshop', had been included in producer Edward Sackville-West's programme *New Poems* broadcast earlier that year, in March 1944. He wrote to John Arlott asking if he was prepared to give a talk on being a policeman who had an addiction for poetry. John was not. He wanted to do a broadcast very much indeed, but he did not want to be paraded as a gimmick, as if he was somebody trying to rise above his station, with all the social and intellectual implications that might suggest.

Grigson pondered. All right, there would have to be a trial run to see if he was any good. In other words, an audition.

The passage from Coleridge's *Biographia Literaria* was not easy to read. Grigson, a tall, dark-haired man with piercing blue eyes, listened carefully. He had a reputation for being awkward The seventh son of a canon, he had had the terrible misfortune of losing six brothers either killed in military conflict or in other tragic circumstances. John did his best. In the studied BBC manner of the time (and many later times), Grigson was neutral in his response.

He moved on from the reading. Could Mr Arlott write a script? 'Yes,

I expect so.' 'What I want,' said Grigson, 'is a kind of lay sermon, for one of those Sunday night postscripts.' An onerous undertaking. The spot had regularly been J.B. Priestley's until around the end of the so-called 'phoney war' at the time of Dunkirk. Priestley had then been replaced by a wide range of speakers, after pressure had been put on the BBC by the Ministry of Information, who had disliked his blunt comments on post-war aims and social structures. Later, Priestley had returned on a more sporadic basis.

Initially, Grigson's confidence seemed misplaced. 'I put in four or five scripts but they were absolute rubbish,' John recalled. 'They were no use whatever. A year later, when I started to learn what script writing was about, I could see what rubbish they were – wooden and written and not speakable.'

John had discovered the gulf between words to be read and words to be spoken, the difference between private expression and public communication. The latter should have much of the desired intimacy and informality of the former: in effect, be conversational.

Knowing that Grigson would soon be looking elsewhere, John turned in desperation to a subject dear to his heart – cricket. This time the script was accepted, and so, on 23 October 1944, on the Home Service, John Arlott was heard broadcasting for the first time, as *An Enthusiast on his Enthusiasms*.

It's unfashionable to be fond of cricket nowadays – and unseasonable to talk of cricket in October – except for the enthusiast – and for the enthusiast, his enthusiasm explains and excuses everything.

First, then, what do I mean by cricket? I mean playing cricket, watching cricket, studying cricket, and perhaps best of all, cricket by the fire – cricket in retrospect – that more-than-human game that is always played in rich sunshine, with no sneaking breezes, no threats of rain, with enough deck-chairs for everyone, and enough drinks (and cool drinks at that) to go round, where every innings is a good one and yet the bowlers and fieldsmen also manage to do well . . .

And I ought to say what I *don't* mean – and I *don't* mean 'prize-day speech cricket', that queer game about which old gentlemen used to ramble at our school prize-giving ordeal – a game that was played, so it used to appear to me, by prigs and half-wits, intent on giving away the game to their inferior opponents in a *nauseating* display of over-politeness: thank heaven that that game exists only in the clouded minds of those old gentlemen. Cricket, despite such hypocrites, should be played 'all out' – old 'W.G.', the greatest of them all, would do anything that could be done within the rules to win – and how he gloried in his opponents' discomfiture. I like the cricketer, to watch or play with, who 'lives' the game to the exclusion of everything else while he is playing – the man who curses his own shortcomings no less than the failings of umpires, the flukes of batsmen and the fumblings of fieldsmen – the cricketer, when his side can no longer win a match, who digs in, forgets the scoring of useless runs, and says, in effect, to his opponents – 'Now get me out, and if you can't, you don't deserve to win.' And then he does his best to play out time to deny the other side the win it wasn't good enough to force.

Reading between the lines of Grigson's subsequent report, it would appear that during rehearsal John was too careful and monotonous in his delivery, but that he responded well to a suggestion to speed up and inflect his phrases. When it came to the recording, nervousness and a dry mouth made him slow down once more.

But there is nothing like a taste to whet the appetite, and soon John was providing more from his own back yard:

A hundred and seventy years ago there were giants in Hampshire. If you walk up the road from Hambledon, past Park Gate, towards Clanfield, you will come to an old red-brick and tile inn, bleaching in the sun; across the road from it there is a great bare Hampshire down. Don't walk by without looking at it; it's the home of the giants – the old inn is the Bat and Ball and the down is Broad-halfpenny Down, the ground of the Hambledon Cricket Club, the greatest single club in the history of cricket . . .

To John's great relief, Grigson liked *The Hampshire Giants*, and said as much in a memorandum to the BBC's Assistant Director of Talks, C.V. Salmon, in January 1945:

It seems to me a very much better script than his earlier one, and I feel that he showed with that first script that he was potentially a very good broadcaster indeed . . . Arlott's a slowish speaker with a fairly rich Hampshire voice. He takes production very well, and can be bullied with discretion into style and vigour. I have found him apt to slow down a bit on transmission.

From somebody as cautious and perceptive as Grigson, this was a firm recommendation. Others, too, liked the sound of John's voice.

Before and after the fifteen-minute talk, which was broadcast on 6 May 1945, he was asked to take part in programmes by several producers. Leonard Cottrell of the Features and Drama Department required him to *sing* in a feature for a short series about Air Transport Command in England, Gibraltar, Tunis and Algiers, called *Britain's Our Doorstep*; Patric Dickinson wanted him to read some topographical poetry on the Home Service, and Brigid Maas chose the Hampshire dialect as the English-language subject of *Transatlantic Call – People to People*, for which John delivered his own script. Through sheer bad luck, or rather last minute rescheduling to accommodate world events, all three of these projects were either shortened or cancelled. The singing was the first to go, which, given John's lack of musical ability, is not surprising. He made up for the loss in another feature, though, by standing in at the last moment 'to say three words in a high voice as a maidservant'.

John soon discovered that BBC fees were nearer to parsimony than profligacy: for all these engagements he received only 5 guineas plus £1 subsistence and a third-class return railway voucher. After the postponement of one recording there was little delay before a missive was heading his way from Programme Contracts, requesting the return of 'the 3rd Class railway voucher which you will not now require and which we will want for cancellation'.

The invitation with the greatest brevet, so to speak, came from Francis ('Jack') Dillon. Dillon was a one-time tax inspector with boundless energy and a squeaky voice – what with George Rostrevor Hamilton, John seemed to hold a fascination for ex-employees of the Inland Revenue – and was now the producer of the popular *Country Magazine* which went out at lunchtime on Sundays. He wanted John to compere the seventy-first edition of the programme. John wanted to too, and did so – more than adequately.

There were other calls. An anniversary number of *Country Magazine*; the metaphysical poets for *Book of Verse: Anthology of the Month*, which drew a wry reference from Patric Dickinson to the last sentence of John's script as 'one of the most dramatically involved I have ever read – the mystery of the Trinity is nothing to it!'; and *Tribute to the President*, following the death of Roosevelt in April 1945.

One assignment, for Noni Wright of the Pacific Service, took him out of the studios to a village in Surrey. 'I am very pleased you will be free to go to Ripley next Sunday,' she wrote, 'to do a talk for us on the occasion of the New Zealand–All Services cricket team playing on one of the oldest village greens in England. I am enclosing a letter from the local chemist, where the whole thing started, as you will see – and also some delightful material about Ripley which seems to be right up your street.'

The local chemist at Ripley was Kenneth White. He met John in the pub by the green, where two elderly spinsters, 'with a sense of shock, served me drink'. Without much difficulty, John cleverly wove a historical context into the encounter. The vicar came from his morning service to say grace at lunchtime – just in case – and the likes of Blunt, Badcock and Dempster for New Zealand allowed Sunnucks, Lindo and Jelly, the star performers for Ripley, to beat them by four wickets. No heavenly intervention necessary.

In a regular feature called 'The Spoken Word' the BBC weekly magazine the *Listener* gave space for a talk by John on *Old Lucas* – Richard Lucas, the nineteenth-century Salisbury artist who moved to Chilworth – which was broadcast on the West of England Home Service. This was a tricky talk to research, and its highlight was an anecdote centred on mistaken provenance. 'The great German art critic Bode came upon a wax bust of "Flora" in England, identified it as a work of Leonardo da Vinci and bought it at the cost of £9,250 for the Kaiser Friedrich Museum in Berlin. Soon afterwards, it was established beyond doubt that the actual artist was not Leonardo but Lucas; but the great Bode, having irrevocably pronounced him to be Leonardo, firmly refused the English vendor's offer to take the bust back and refund the money – a magnificent example of German pig-headedness.' No doubt this last comment met with an appreciative response at the time.

A drama-documentary, though it was not called that then, brought John and that versatile actor Deryck Guyler to the music studios at Maida Vale. Arlott and Guyler had been allocated the roles of forward and rear-gunners in a bomber that had been 'shot up' by the 'ghastly Hun'. 'Or was it the other way round?' laughed John as he recalled the occasion. 'Perhaps it was Deryck at the front and me at the back. I do remember that, as supposedly the plane went down in flames, we both had to sing, "We're gonna hang out the washing on the Siegfried line". I think it was accompanied by the whole BBC Symphony Orchestra. Deryck sang sharp, I sang flat – the orchestra got it about right.'

An epic called *Threshold of the New* by Louis MacNeice again employed J. Arlott as an actor. The piece's espousal of a radical cause would have appealed to John: it was 'a dramatic survey of the Nation, taking stock of our resources and our prospects on the first New Year's Eve since the War and involved much declamation and inciting of all and sundry to march on London to strike a blow for the rights of the common people'.

John had the part of John Ball, executed in 1381 as a leader of the Peasants'
Revolt, who appeared to be the chief inciter. Throughout, a kind of Greek
chorus kept chanting 'John Ball hath rungen your bell.'

Another request was for John to provide a talk for the series *From All
Over Britain*, which introduced overseas listeners – in this case those in
the Pacific, Africa and North America – to aspects of British life. Surprisingly the producer, Evelyn Davy, wrote to John: 'I thought you might
talk about haymaking on your father's farm this year – a topic you suggested.' John's father had never owned a farm, although he and 'Old Jack'
had employed men to help scythe down the long grass at the cemeteries
(one of them had recently asked John, 'And what be this 'ere Lunnun talk
you'm puttin' on then?'). Whether or not John was disguising the fact
that his father was a sort of sexton is impossible to say. At any rate, when
it came to writing the script, he used a technique that is now called
'faction'. He interpolated the incident of the schoolmistress and the slow-
worm at his primary school and observations from the pub across the
road from the Cemetery Lodge. As for anyone with imagination, the
embellished and adapted tale becomes the adopted one. Told and retold
as an automatic response to a given cue, it starts to turn into fact. The
following passages give a flavour of John's approach:

> They walked backwards and forwards in front of the window where
> I was eating my breakfast and one field was cut in a morning. For
> three days the house was full of the smell of ripening hay. Then the
> same horse came back with a huge iron rake that dragged up the
> hay and dropped it in heaps as the driver lifted the rake with a handle
> set beside his seat.
>
> A week later I came back – the hay was gone. 'Where is the hay?'
> I asked my father, 'and where is the rick?' 'Oh,' he said, 'it's gone
> – I sell it straightaway now, saves a lot of trouble.'
>
> We smoked quietly for a little while, and then I said 'And where
> are the Merryweathers?' – 'Dead, surely you knew, dead long ago.'
> But you see, I've been away a long time now. 'And the Leadbetters?'
> – 'Dead' – 'And Jim Cook?' – 'Dead.' 'And Ted Blake and old
> Charlie too?' 'Yes – all dead.'
>
> All dead – Jim and Jack Merryweather, Ted and Jack Leadbetter.
> Jim Cook, Ted Blake and even old Charlie – the men who *were*
> haymaking for me. My grandfather's men and my father's men after-
> wards. About the middle of June each year I'd hear my father or my
> grandfather say 'Better get the grass cut, have to go and see the
> men.'

And the next Monday morning they would be there at seven, all the old men – they always seemed very old to me, yet they never seemed to change. They would put their coats and their bottles – bottles of cold tea – under the hedge and get out their scythes and start to sharpen them so that I would wake to the ring of rubbers on scythe blades – the 'rubber' was the whetstone that each of them carried in a slit in his wide leather waistbelt. Then the grass-cutting started. The men worked in a line – and, if you didn't know the work, they seemed to be slow. Have you ever tried to handle a scythe? It has a long curving handle, with two short hand-grips sticking out at the side and an arc of blade a yard long. If you haven't the knack of it you may try for an hour and never cut a single blade of grass. But these men were masters. They worked in a row, each bending slightly forward, each with his hat on, an old bowler, or a cap – Ted Leadbetter in a genuine 'billycock' – none of them wore collars but most of them gathered the shirt at the neck with a stud, and they wore their waistcoats unbuttoned but held in a loose curve by their watchchains: their corduroy or dark-grey trousers were tied just below the knee and they wore great heavy boots of leather that looked as if it could never bend. If you were near them as they worked you heard a note like a tiny bell as they leant on the scythe and the blade seemed to slide through the grass which toppled for a second and then fell slowly in an even swathe. They stopped often to sharpen their scythes, but always seemed to work a little harder when my father or my grandfather was in sight . . .

Those men, the Merryweathers and the Leadbetters, Jim Cook, Ted Blake and old Charlie were my father's and my grandfather's men at haymaking time every year – all the farmers did their haymaking at the same time, so each took the same men every year. They were old men – about sixty, most of them when I first knew them, and Jim Merryweather was eighty-one when he did his last summer's haymaking for my father. Most of them did odd jobs the rest of the year, clipping hedges, lopping trees, digging plots. Always moving so slowly, but, because they never wasted energy, always doing their jobs pretty well and pretty thoroughly.

It was sad to think of those old men being dead, sad, too, to think of their kind dying out. 'Are there any of the old scythe-mowers left?' I asked my father before I left. 'No young ones,' he said, 'but there are some working over at Burdon's Farm.' So I went over to Burdon's and there they were, five old men in dark trousers and waistcoats, swinging their scythes through the grass. I went over to talk to them as they knocked off for dinner, and offered them a pipe of tobacco. The scythe-mowers are dying out, but some of them still remain, wielding their scythes as they and their forefathers have done in England for twelve hundred years.

While all this BBC work was going on, John was still with the police, anxiously trying to manoeuvre his duties so as to allow time off for broadcasting. It was a continuing problem. On 20 May 1945 he wrote to Patric Dickinson about a proposed recording: 'The date is most essential; despite my frantic struggles I have been made a patrol sergeant which makes the booking of leave rather difficult − I really need to know a fortnight in advance of the projected date − and since I imagine that you let the *Radio Times* know then, it should be possible.'

For a time John had been attached to Southampton Police Training School, lecturing to war reserve coppers, mainly on emergency legislation. From there he had been seconded to the Police Instructors' Training School at Peel House, Regency Street, Westminster, as one of a nucleus of potential high-flyers who were to be briefed on the anticipated structure of the police force after the war. There were bound to be vacancies with the departure of reservists, and with service personnel being demobbed and looking for work, it was a unique opportunity for in-house reassessment. Six training schools around the country were doing the same thing. John was one of three members of the Southampton force who were sent to London.

While he was on the course came the offer − no, the command − to represent the police in the broadcast *Tribute to the King* on VE Day. From the Corporation's point of view, having someone with broadcasting experience to do the job was much to be desired. From the police standpoint, given John's known qualifications, it was probably hard to refuse. And there was a sense in which there was an added authenticity in having a policeman of comparatively junior rank to speak on behalf of the whole force. Chief Constable Frederick Tarry, John's boss in Southampton, who had been so supportive of his ventures, was delighted. Here was one of his lads in the limelight. Commander Willis, in charge at Peel House, was not delighted. Why should a provincial policeman take the place of at least a dozen in the metropolis who could do it as well? The police insisted that if Arlott was to speak, they would supply the words. The words they supplied were not exactly suitable for speaking − they were not unlike one of those stilted press handouts asking for help with enquiries after a nasty crime. No matter; with producer Cecil McGivern's connivance the text was changed and the sense retained.

The cast for the tribute assembled in Studio 8, Broadcasting House, on Monday 7 May 1945. It was a false alarm. VE Day was not, in fact, announced until the following day. With victory formally proclaimed, the cast returned to the studio and, just after 8.30 p.m. on the Home Service, an anonymous policeman said:

> I speak for the men and women of the British Police; for those who've taken the ancient oath to serve your Majesty faithfully in the office of constable. The war brought us many new tasks: we've faced them not only as officers of the law, but as the friends and protectors of your Majesty's subjects.
>
> In protecting life and property, we've shared all the battles of the Home Front. Throughout the war we've been privileged to work in close collaboration with the Armed Forces of the Crown and with those of our allies. On other fronts, many of our comrades are fighting in your Majesty's Forces.
>
> We have had the honour of being near your Majesty and the Queen on your journeys among your people, and we know . . .

As John's voice carried on, his mother and father were at home, their ears glued to the wireless. It was a long time since Jack had pieced together their first crystal set, and they had listened to banjo music battling against atmospherics over the ether. Who would have thought their boy would actually be talking to the whole nation?

Chief Constable Tarry was also listening, and a few days later he wrote:

> My dear Arlott,
>
> Please accept my sincere congratulations on the fine contribution which you made to the Tribute to H.M. The King on VE Day. It has been most interesting and pleasing to me to hear many people say that the policeman's homage was excellent, and it has given no end of satisfaction to us in Southampton to know that it was one of our own members who was chosen for the honour. If you still have the script I shall be glad if you will loan it to me, as I would like to quote it in my paragraphs on 'War Commentary' for the next *Police Journal*.
>
> I also listened to your talk on *The Hambledon Giants*, and thought it very good indeed.
>
> I hope you are having a good time on the course.

Whether or not John was having a good time on the course, he certainly did on Victory Night. After an exultant evening on the town, he and his colleagues returned to Peel House to find that austere establishment firmly closed. How four decidedly unsober policemen managed to clamber over a roof from the top of a fire escape and then hang over a parapet to bang with their boots against the window of a sleeping Brummie inspector is not recorded.

Back in Southampton after the course had finished, John did not relish being an acting patrol sergeant. It was promotion, but at a price. Once more he had to don uniform, and the freedom he had enjoyed became severely restricted. Now *he* was the one who had to supervise the young constables. There was little opportunity to lose himself in the libraries, because he had to be on call when on duty. However, he had seen a job advertised in the *Listener*. The post of Assistant (English Programmes) Eastern Services – in effect, Literary Programmes Producer in the BBC's Overseas Service – had fallen vacant. John wanted that job very badly indeed, although he did not expect to get it, as he felt he was scarcely experienced enough.

At Lodge Road, Dawn was looking after the infant James Andrew, now six months old. She was also having to bolster John's confidence. 'I remember the tension before the interview. I had to iron about twenty silk shirts – well, a lot anyway. They cost about twelve and six in those days [laugh]. "Pippin," he said, "I must have another shirt in case I sweat." It was a hot summer. He had never really liked the police. Spying on people wasn't his forte, he said. "Pippin, I don't really want to sit here watching if people put too many gallons in their tanks. It's very boring." "Quite right," I said.'

The two hundred or so applications for the Literary Programmes job were whittled down to a shortlist. The board interview went well. A few days later, John received the good news. 'He was terribly pleased,' said Dawn.

The congratulations of Chief Constable Tarry were genuine. There were Home Office restraints on leaving the police force for reasons other than age or illness, but with typical consideration, Tarry, who later became an Inspector of Constabulary at the Home Office, intimated that a way would be found. He smiled when John offered 'sick of the police force' as a reason for his departure. Whether John's stay in hospital shortly afterwards had any connection with this is open to question. 'I went to the police surgeon and said I am going to a new job. I want to be ready and tidied-up before I go. He replied "All right," and gave me a terrific going-over and said, "These are all the things that need to be put right. They are all minor and none very important, but if that's the way you feel, OK." So, I had four weeks in hospital.'

A farewell dinner at Red Lodge, Bassett was arranged by the Literary Circle of the Southampton Police Force before John left for London. He had been a popular lecturer at the Literary Circle as well as at the Workers' Educational Association, and a superintendent, an inspector, a detective-sergeant, a constable and two policewomen expressed their regret at losing him and wished him every success. So did Chief Constable Tarry, who was in the chair, and who presented John with a copy of 'a standard work on criminal investigation' as a memento – the title was not disclosed. Clarence Firbank-Carr, editor of the *Southern Daily Echo*, paid tribute to John's literary work, especially his poetry. Carr was an engaging character, expert in all manner of unlikely subjects, such as the coastal walkways of Britain, and in John he recognised a fellow polymath. They had met when John called at the *Echo* offices in Spa Road during the war to inspect one of the few complete and freely available sets of *Wisden*. He had encouraged John's literary aspirations after reading some of his early verse, though that support probably did not go as far as putting it into the paper.

John was genuinely touched by all the tributes, and bashfully replied in kind. He had, he said, received much help and good fellowship from his police colleagues. (This was true. Although John hated the constraints of the organisation, he had made a number of good friends whom he would miss.) 'He was particularly grateful,' ran the *Echo* report of the occasion, 'for the great help, encouragement and consideration he had always received from the Chief Constable, whose kindness had done much to help him to success. The fact that he was changing his occupation from police work to literature and broadcasting at the age of thirty-one might seem an admission that his first choice had been ill-made. He would never regret, however, the eleven years he had spent in the Southampton Police Force, where he had made those human contacts which were the ultimate test of experience and happiness. He was grateful for all the kind things which had been said about him, which would help him in the new work he was about to undertake.'

Sergeant Frank Baker thought the step John was about to take extremely courageous. 'It was a hell of a gamble. To leave just after being promoted was very brave. Because there were only 240 men in the Southampton Force, promotion was slow. Normally, it would take twenty years to get where he had. He had done it in half the time.'

John's parents too were worried. He was the youngest police sergeant in the local force, perhaps in the South of England. He could be a chief constable one day. 'The BBC seems a very insecure sort of place to me,' muttered his father gloomily. 'All this gadding about. Why on earth didn't he stay in the police? Much better for him,' Nellie used to laugh years later when John, constantly working as ever, was a nationally known figure.

But though he was 'pension-conscious' – his father never let him forget it – John knew there would be no return. Would he, I asked him once, have gone back to the police force if the BBC job had not worked out. 'I doubt if I could have done,' was his reply. 'I wouldn't have regained my old rank.'

A predecessor at the BBC Eastern Service desk had been Eric Blair, better known as George Orwell. Orwell, whose craggy features looked as if they had been hewn from the side of a cliff, was not cut out to work in a large organisation. He had come to feel stultified by the mass of what he considered irrelevant paperwork, 'bureaucratic bilge', and disillusioned with his broadcasts to the Indian subcontinent, which were mostly listened to by groups of English intellectuals. As a result, he resigned at the end of September 1943. John did meet Orwell, but received little advice. 'I remember he wore one of those Gannex-type raincoats much favoured later on by Harold Wilson. He didn't tell me much, and then quizzed me savagely on my views. I was in complete awe of him – a great respect – but I was never close.'

Between Orwell's departure and John's arrival the job had been carried out in an acting capacity by Sunday Wilshin. Sunday was well used to acting, as before being engaged by the BBC she had trodden the boards of numerous theatres in a variety of roles. She invariably wore trousers and clothes of a masculine cut – very liberated for the time.

John started work for the BBC on 1 September 1945 at 200 Oxford Street, formerly the Co-Op store, which had been converted into offices and studios. His office on the fourth floor was little more than a cubicle, with flimsy walls which reached half way to the ceiling. The surrounding offices were similarly styled – virtually open plan. For the first year his secretary was Sylvia Rotger, who, before she left to become an air hostess, called out to her friend Barbara Forrester in the adjoining enclosure, 'My boss says would you like to take my job when I go?' Barbara, bored with the memo-ridden routines of Programme Planning, was not slow to say yes. And so, for the next four and a half years, she sat face to face with John on opposite sides of a desk. It was an exciting time for her, and even more so for John.

Obviously he could not continue to live in Southampton, and he began looking for affordable property within a reasonable distance of London's West End. About sixty paces from the front door of Broadcasting House was a house occupied by the Ayrtons and the composer-conductor Constant Lambert. No. 4 All Souls Place could not have been more convenient – or more convivial. Michael Ayrton suggested to John that he move in during the week, while he was searching for a new family home. At week-ends he went back to Southampton to see Dawn and baby James, affection-ately referred to as 'young bug'. With Michael and Joan Ayrton away on holiday in Pembrokeshire, and with a bed in the artist's studio with its sloping glass roof – his head no more than a few feet from the organ console of All Saints' Church, and his feet no more than a long header away from the portals of broadcasting – John began a new life.

7

Poetry and the BBC

John's new life was such a transformation as to be positively surreal. The irksome restrictions of the police force had vanished, and the war had ended. There was no real connection between the two, but in John's mind they were linked, as marking the end of a chapter. His new job was a direct extension of what had happened so far in the literary compartment of his life, and now there was an opportunity to connect his study and his love of the subject with the contacts he had made. It was an exhilarating prospect.

The activity in All Souls' Place reflected John's own feelings of freedom and excitement. Once the domicile of the composer Weber, who had completed his opera *Oberon* there in 1826, it now resounded to the strains of animated conversation and the occasional Wagnerian soprano. At the piano would be Constant Lambert, who had moved in the year before John's arrival when he was working with Michael Ayrton on the ballet *Le Festin de l'Araignée* (The Spider's Banquet), which had a score by Roussel. At the age of forty, Lambert had a formidable reputation as conductor, composer and alcoholic. He also suffered from diabetes, and needed drink to dull his hyper-awareness and sensitivity. Also to avoid the desperation of *ennui*. Absinthe helped still the inner clamour – for a while.

Constant had for a number of years been having an intense affair with the ballerina Margot Fonteyn. He had conducted her, notably at Sadler's Wells, and she had danced for him. Rather as Diaghilev was to Massine, Lambert was to Fonteyn. He had played an important part in her mental development and cultural awareness. She had helped calm his emotional instability and extreme nervousness before going on to the podium, and knew that, as she put it, he 'understood ballet as a genuine marriage between music and dance, with music the senior partner'.

In the late summer of 1945, much drinking of double gins took place, mostly at nearby public houses such as the George, known as the Gluepot, or at the Marie Lloyd club which was open during 'closed' hours. In the evening, in search of food, it was but a few steps to Pagani's – or rather its offshoot, as the original had been destroyed in the bombing – or the

Casa Prada, a little further away in the Euston Road. The clientele and décor of both were strong on artistry. Around the table might be found Michael Ayrton, with his pointed shaped beard wagging every time he spoke; Joan Ayrton, who had once worked in the BBC Press office, quietly observant and listening attentively; Constant Lambert, heavily-built and not unlike Randolph Churchill in appearance, the smoke from his large cigar failing to obscure his limericks; the composer and critic Cecil Gray, quick to assert his unconventional views; and the cheerfully intemperate Dylan Thomas, who might have dropped in for what he hoped would be a free meal, but certainly some drink. John, the new boy in town, was simply pleased to be there.

The discourse was wide-ranging, sometimes erudite yet not pretentiously so. On rare occasions Margot Fonteyn could come in late for a coffee, having just left the theatre after a performance. Petite and vivid, expressive hands framing her sentences, she would be drawn to talk about the recent Vic–Wells ballet tour to entertain British forces stationed in Brussels and Paris. Constant would interpose mischievous witticisms and then become lost in thought humming to himself a few bars of what on enquiry turned out to be Hindemith's overture *Cupid and Psyche*, the British première of which he conducted at the Proms. The trenchant Cecil Gray might counterclaim for the music of Peter Warlock, or steer the conversation into the mystic realms of black and white magic and the *mementi mori* of rival exponents Aleister Crowley and Barnet Stross. Dylan, presently engaged with his *Reminiscences of Childhood* for the Welsh Region Children's Hour, would, with his famous 'organ voice' furnished by an uneven supply of wind like a faulty bellows, launch into one of his favourite stories about the man who used to take off his hat and set fire to his hair for no reason that anybody could discover.

And then there was the master of all trades himself. Painter, sculptor, draughtsman, engraver, portraitist, theatre designer, book illustrator, poet, novelist, short-story writer, essayist, critic, art historian, broadcaster, film-maker – what did Michael Ayrton not do? He was never at a loss for things to talk about. At this time he was art critic of the *Spectator*. In conversation his voice was compelling and mellifluous, though some found him intimidating and thought they detected conceit. If so, they missed 'a dry wit (an original imagination) and a wholly beneficent solipsism deriving not from personal vanity but from the indubitable fact that his own experiences, serendipities, and ideas were genuinely of greater creative interest to himself and others than the notions and characters of most other people' – the assessment of T.G. Rosenthal in *The Dictionary of National Biography*. Ayrton had insatiable curiosity and considerable eclecticism. What he did not have was good health. In 1942 he had been invalided out of the RAF due to mysterious and unexplained fevers which were later found to have been caused by a deep-seated throat abscess.

By any standards it was an extraordinary group, and not exclusive to the above-mentioned as, at any time, others such as Frederick Ashton, Nigel Balchin, Robert Donat and William Walton might be part of it. John, however, had little time to get too involved, for he had programmes to make and much to assimilate. He did not realise it at the time, but his whole production career from September 1945 to the beginning of January 1951 was to be based on *Book of Verse*, although this did not preclude him from making other programmes. *Book of Verse*, usually recorded but occasionally live, was transmitted weekly at 3.30 or 4.30 p.m. The programme went out on the Eastern Service, with repeats on other overseas services such as Pacific and North American. From 1948 to 1950 it also claimed a late-evening slot on the Light Programme, the civilian successor to the Forces Programme.

John was in his element in *Book of Verse*, on which the literary lions appeared in force. Daniel George presented the work of Lewis Carroll and Edward Lear; Edmund Blunden the dramas of Shelley; William Plomer the Sitwells; and John's old friend Andrew Young delved into Beaumont and Fletcher (John himself also introduced the work of Andrew Young).

Occasionally, the programme became a little incestuous. Vita Sackville-West and Ruth Pitter would discuss, say, Andrew Marvell and William Collins; and Viola Meynell would look at Vita Sackville-West and Ruth Pitter. But this mattered little, for the range of the series was enormously wide: anonymous seventeenth-century poetry, Rossetti, the Imagists, modern verse, translations from the Chinese, Betjeman, Joyce, Yeats, Ben Jonson, the complete Shakespeare cycle and the sonnets, Lascelles Abercrombie – but not in that order. The people speaking into the microphone were names to conjure with too: Cecil Day-Lewis, Robert Herring, Neville Coghill, V.S. Pritchett, P.H. Newby, J.C. Trewin, Maurice Willson Disher, Laurence Whistler, Allardyce Nicoll, Christopher Hassall, Richard Aldington, Roy Campbell, Stephen Spender, Dylan Thomas.

As always with John, in whatever he was doing, work and socialising overlapped. Julian Holland first met him when he was working in the same building, and was soon to become a producer on *Radio Newsreel*. 'There was a great social atmosphere in 200 Oxford Street, because it was just after the war and the wartime feeling still persisted. There was a huge canteen on the ground floor* where we all used to meet – engineers,

---

* Almost certainly George Orwell's model for *Nineteen Eighty-Four*.

announcers, producers. They'd all be doing programmes and then have a break for an hour or so, automatically go to the canteen and sit round however many tables it was necessary to pull together for them to sit in comfort. It was a kind of fun family and, of course, it was all talk. John's pattern was to work during the day, take a fairly long break and have an early evening meal, then go back upstairs to his office and work throughout the evening. From the moment he started doing cricket commentaries he was writing cricket books and he used to do these too in the office, until late at night.'

The almost casual beginning of John's journey into cricket commentary is a supreme example of how the best-laid plans can come about by accident. Donald Stephenson, Director of Eastern Services at the BBC, and one of the pioneers of foreign-language broadcasting, wanted to cover the first two matches and the three Tests of the Indian cricket tour in 1946, the first full cricket season after the war, for the subcontinent. The matter came up for discussion at a planning meeting a few months before, and names were put forward. Abdul Hamid Sheikh, the Hindustani commentator, was thought not to be right for the role – ironically, his English was felt to be too Indian – and a couple of other suggestions also did not find favour. Stephenson suddenly had an inspired idea. 'Have you ever done a cricket broadcast?' he asked John. 'Yes,' John replied ingenuously, thinking of *The Hampshire Giants* and his outing to Ripley, and knowing full well that match commentary called for a different technique. 'Good,' said Stephenson, pressed for time and not inclined to enquire further. 'Put yourself down for those two matches.'

The matches were played at Worcester and Oxford. All seemed to go well with John's commentary, and on his return to London he received a summons from Donald Stephenson. In Stephenson's hand was a telegram from James Pennethorne Hughes, Director of the BBC's New Delhi Office, and later to become a close friend and a central figure in the course of John's career. It read: 'Cricket broadcasts greatest success yet East Service. Must be continued at all costs – Hughes.'

'Well, you started it,' said Stephenson. 'You'd better go on with it . . . that is, if you can do your own work at the same time. But make sure there's no falling off in the quality of your poetry programmes – that's what you're employed for.'

Of course, it was not quite as straightforward as that. First, Stephenson had to satisfy himself that technical and financial requirements could be met, that the regions would be able to provide adequate facilities at the grounds, that the ninety days' play which was envisaged for the Indian tour could be assimilated and scheduled at such short notice.

The decision to use John was made easier by the fact that he was well ahead with the planning and recording of his poetry programmes, since at one time it had been thought that he would be in India for two months during the summer. An itinerary was planned whereby he would not be away from his desk at Oxford Street for more than a week at a time. Accompanying him were to be Abdul Hamid for the Hindi listeners, and Arthur Russell, who was in charge of actuality programmes at the Overseas Services outpost at Aldenham. Russell suffered from spinal problems which left him terribly stiff and in pain for much of the time, but he was a huge asset in terms of reliability and outside broadcast experience.

Donald Stephenson explained his appointment of John in a memorandum to his Controller, J.B. Clark:

> I was extremely anxious to ensure that whatever commentators we used would be wholly receptive to the necessity of catering for Indian requirements – e.g., the Indian cricket lover can absorb a much greater measure of pure technicalities than would be welcomed by the normal British home listener ... It was agreed in discussion with Service Directors and Outside Broadcast Department at a very early stage that Arlott was the right man to use for the five games originally planned for coverage. You will remember that his first appearance in broadcasting was as the writer of, and narrator in, a number of successful cricket features. He has also himself been a County player [sic!] and with his West Country accent he is a 'natural' in giving a real atmosphere of green fields and white flannels to his commentaries.

The set timetable was five minutes' live commentary in Hindi by Abdul Hamid, from 3.23 to 3.28 p.m. Greenwich Mean Time, followed by five minutes' live English commentary by John from 4.10 to 4.15 p.m. on every day of the important matches. For the three Tests, there would be ten-minute special spots in the programmes in English and in the Hindustani output, with edited extracts of the English commentary for the African and Pacific Services.

A month or so later James Pennethorne Hughes was once more rhapsodising from New Delhi:

> I thought I would say again that I am sure the cricket commentaries are the most popular thing we have ever done in the Eastern Service ... Davenport, newly returned from Bombay, confirms the tremendous interest there ...

I have only heard two dissident comments about the programmes, the first from BORs [British Other Ranks] who complain that when they tune in to England the last thing they want to listen to is about Indians, and the extremist Congress papers ... Neither of these opinions of course matters in the least as against the extraordinary goodwill which the broadcasts are creating.

As for John himself, he could not believe his good fortune. Here he was, being *paid* for watching and talking about cricket.

But however enamoured John was with this new world, Donald Stephenson's proviso could not be forgotten: his poetry programmes still had to come first. Not that John wished otherwise, for cricket and literature were twin passions. In that he was not alone: 'They were interests we had in common, so we got on very well from the start,' said Julian Holland. 'He used to ask me to go and sit in on the poetry programmes when I was free, because he knew I knew my poetry. I'd had a good Eng. Lit. education. So very soon I was going to his house at weekends. It was tremendous, because we'd gather at the house for Sunday lunch, and Dawn didn't seem to mind cooking enormous meals for a lot of people. They'd be local people who were interesting – some bloke who was a schoolmaster who did watercolours, literary people, cricketers, sportswriters like Denys Rowbotham of the *Manchester Guardian*, Bill Bowes, the Yorkshire and England fast bowler who wrote for the *Yorkshire Evening News* and was a great friend of John's – about a dozen at any one time.'

Dawn and John had found a house at 58 Barrington Road, Crouch End – a London district that could be described as a sort of below-stairs Highgate. Ever-present and ever-welcome at the lunch, dinner, supper and breakfast table was the hugely convivial, wonderfully disorganised and usually homeless Irish scriptwriter Harry Craig. Craig brought some of the refreshing anarchy of Dublin to London's more sedate streets, and never failed to be a stimulating companion. The nest of women with whom he was entangled would vouch for that.

John was very much a 'people' person, interested in them for their own sake. He was always generous with his advice. Julian Holland benefited from his suggestions about strategy at job interviews, and John also helped him to get a job as a journalist in Fleet Street. 'For such a workaholic who would seem never to have a moment spare, if a friend had a problem he would take twenty minutes off and think about it very constructively and very well. You'd bump into him and you'd mention something and he'd say, "Yeah, we ought to talk about that. Let's have a drink or come up to the office at such and such a time," and then when you did, he'd say, "It seems to me that what you ought to be doing is this." He was so good. He did it with me a number of times. I owe so much of my career to John.'

He was generous too with his money, particularly where Dylan Thomas was concerned. At one point he was sending Dylan £10 a week. 'Dylan was a scrounger,' commented John's secretary Barbara Forrester. 'He was always borrowing money. He never had money for a taxi or the railway. Once John sent me with Dylan in a cab to Paddington to make sure he got on to the train to South Wales and didn't deviate to a pub.'

Dylan Marlais Thomas did about forty programmes for John, something like two-thirds of all his broadcasts. 'He often and much wanted money,' wrote John. 'He was not covetous of gold for its own sake, nor did he ask for more than would house and feed himself, his wife Caitlin, and their three children, and leave enough to buy drink for himself and the friends he wanted to entertain.

'He was an essentially simple person. He liked cricket, Rugby football and beer, jokes, idleness and other men's poetry. Generous but not extravagant, he was sadly harried by demands for income tax which he never really understood and which in the end drove him near to desperation – without ever penetrating his contempt deeply enough to reach his hate. Yet even when eighty per cent of the first pound of his earnings went to the Inland Revenue, he would never debase for a moment the writing which was the nearest matter in the world to his heart. He could have been one of the most highly-paid hacks in the country. He could have spun stories out of his head at speed and for high fees, but his respect for his craft would not allow that.'

Dylan wrote often to John when he was 'ready to do a bit of booming', as he was on 26 August 1946:

My dear John,
    I tried to get hold of you as soon as I got back from Ireland but you were always out. I don't know if you'd written while I was away, because my letters haven't been forwarded yet: I expect them tomorrow. I should, anyway, have given you my Irish address ... Ireland took all my money in the world – and some of other people's money, too – so I *must* get as much work now as I possibly can. Will you help? Any scripts and/or readings you can manage will be terribly welcome. I'll do you a script in a few days if you can get me one, or can come up to town for a reading at a day's notice – provided

the BBC will pay expenses to and from Wales. I have to spend 10 days or a fortnight here with my mother, who is ill, and after that will go back to Oxford. Do your best for me, please, John: I'm in a real spot and simply must have a lot of work to do. Ireland was grand: I ate myself daft, but have now recovered. When do you go abroad? Hope to hear from you very soon. And *any* work: the bigger, of course, and the higher paid, the better.

John's life, already busy enough, was further complicated by being sucked into Dylan's orbit. A month earlier, Dylan had written from a damp summerhouse on the banks of the Cherwell. The refuge, in which the only running water seeped in through the roof and walls, had been lent to the Thomases by Margaret Taylor, patron of the poet and wife of the historian A.J.P. Taylor, then a Fellow of Magdalen College.

My dear John,

I forgot, last Yeatsday, entirely, to ask you to have lunch with Margaret Taylor, Roy Campbell, & myself – & any young man of Margaret's – on Wednesday of this week, the 24th, at the White Tower, Percy St. It's Margaret's lunch and she's very keen on it. She wants us to meet about a quarter to one in the Wheatsheaf pub next door.

I had to tell Margaret T. that I'd asked you, as she'd been at me to do so for days & days. So, if you can't manage it, will you ask – as a special favour – Sylvia Rotger to wire deep regrets for inconvenience etc to Margaret at Holywell Ford tomorrow, Tuesday.

Sorry to be such a nuisance, but I *had* to tell Margaret I'd asked you & you'd said yes. I've put you in a false position, but it's only a tiny one, I hope. Will you do it for me? That is: either turn up – the lunch will be good – or wire apologies, impossible, sudden call to work etc to Margaret. I hope you can manage it, of course.

I hope you get this note before you go Test-wards. If you do, will you leave all information & details with Sylvia or at the reception-desk on TUESDAY. I'll be in town & I'll ring Sylvia. If there's no reply, I'll call at Oxford St.

But do your best. I'll be seeing you Friday.

Margaret Taylor was inordinately fond of Dylan – with disastrous consequences for her own marriage. When, a year later, Dylan was staying in Florence, he wrote:

My dear Margaret,

You are the best friend that a stout – oh, I'd love some – temporary exile could hope to have and better than I deserve . . . I hear John Arlott's voice every weekend describing cricket matches. He sounds like Uncle Tom Cobleigh reading Neville Cardus to the Indians.

Writing to John on 11 June 1947, by which time John was broadcasting on the South African Tests, Dylan had put it slightly differently:

My dear John,

Thank you for writing. It was very good to hear from you. Though I hear your voice every day: from Trent Bridge, at the moment. You're not only the best cricket commentator – far and away that; but the best sports commentator I've heard, ever: exact, enthusiastic, prejudiced, amazingly visual, authoritative, and friendly. A great pleasure to listen to you: I do look forward to it. Here, in the hills above Florence, I lead the quietest life I ever remember leading: it is sizzling hot, I'm far too limp & lazy to go often into Florence, and I can work only in the early mornings and evenings: never my best time: I'm used to working from after lunch until pub-time, which, in the country used to be about seven. Here, I drink in the garden, alone or with Caitlin: we have no social life: I am a sun vegetable: I live on red wine, cheese, asparagus, artichokes, strawberries, etc. The etc is usually more red wine. We have our own vineyards. The villa is enormous. So, probably, am I, after two months. I'm coming back in August: if the lire last till then. I was given some travelling money by the Authors' Society; otherwise I'd have been back long ago. And I'll be broke when I return, so any bits of booming – I heard Rape of Lucrece today; is Shakespeare over? and what is the next series? – narrating, etc, will be very very welcome. Also, I'd love to write any programme you think I could do: *and, scrupulously, on time.*

Yes, of course I'd love some dollars, but I have, so far, no poem. It would be useless giving you a chunk of the long one I'm twisting and gnarling: it's got to be read as a whole. If I do manage to write any short ones in between, I'll send them to you straightaway.

I can't afford to go to Venice. I've spent some time in Rome, in Genoa, in Sienna, and on the Riviera. But now I can just afford to stay here on my sunburnt behind. I *would* like to go to Venice, though. Perhaps I can seduce your girl [an Army Education Corps

guide who accompanied John during a visit to Austria and Venice –
see p. 194]: or am I the wrong shape?

I'll be ringing you in August. Love to you & your family. Remember me to Val [Dyall], when you see him. My daughter has fallen
in a cactus bush.

It is difficult to visualise the Mr Thomas of the briefcase and homburg
hat which he affected in the vicinity of Broadcasting House; rather more
easy to imagine is Dylan in full flight in his 'roaring boyo from Wales'
role at a King's Road afternoon drinking club, where he could be richly
bawdy and totally unpredictable. His holidays from being a serious artist
were manifested by drunken bouts of relaxed debauchery. They were not
confined to London. 'Despite his appearance,' reported Brendan Gill
in *Here at the New Yorker*, 'he enjoyed considerable sexual success
among suggestible college girls, whom he would approach with the honest
unappealing inquiry, "Can I jump you?"'

'He didn't like being lionised,' observed John in a *Radio Times* profile
of Dylan Thomas in September 1973. 'He was intolerant of bores, but he
was a person it was easy to be fond of. There were people who didn't like
him, as a lot of people don't like me. They included people who wouldn't
have liked poets in any generation. There were other people who would
have done anything for him. I trusted him and I think he trusted me. I
was very fond of him.'

Contrary to much received information, Dylan Thomas was never
drunk when broadcasting – well, perhaps on one occasion, but even then
it was not entirely his fault. Called on to take the green light when deputising at very short notice, he treated his listeners to an 'Ode on Shaint
Sheshilia's Day'. John, however, was voicing the opinion of a number of
producers when he remarked, 'In all the time I worked with him he never
let me down in any way at all. I can only say that he worked for some
five years for me . . . he was never late; he was never drunk; and he never
did a bad job.'

Dylan would sit through rehearsals smoking – mostly from John's
packet of oval-shaped Passing Clouds – and sucking dyspepsia tablets
given to him by Valentine Dyall, a regular reader on *Book of Verse*, in an
effort to combat the excesses of the previous night.

'He took production like a professional actor and, when he stepped up
to the microphone to read, made a happily extravagant figure,' John wrote
in his essay 'Dylan Thomas and Radio'. 'Round, with the roundness of a
Tintoretto urchin-cherub, and in a large, loose tweed jacket, he would
stand, feet apart and head thrown back, a dead cigarette frequently adher-

ing wispily to his lower lip, curls a little tousled and eyes half-closed, barely reading the poetry by eye, but rather understanding his way through it, one arm beating out a sympathetic double rhythm as he read. His voice would be sometimes almost naively young and clearly tenor, while at others, a dynamic throbbing seemed to drive him to an intense rolling depth.'

In the last year of Dylan's life, John was still trying to help him. Dylan wrote on 6 February 1953:

John,

Very many apologies. I've been away, missed your letter until today, and now am ill with flu, bronchitis, etc, croaking and snuffling. Thank you very much for the letter, for thinking about me, for suggesting that piece, & for pushing up the price. I'm awfully sorry I can't do it: not because I don't want to, but because I *daren't* promise that I could turn it out by mid-February: I'm in a tangle of doubts & debts, as well as shored to the eyebrows with frogs' catarrh, and am disastrously behind in two commissioned jobs. But thanks a *great* deal for the offer of the job, which I'd like to do, & the money, which, dear, I'd simply adore.

Did I ever thank you for that bit of practical help you sent along so kind & so quick? If not, I should have, very much indeed; and if so, I do it again.

Dylan died in New York on 9 November 1953. John's moving obituary appeared in the *Spectator*:

He died in a country to which, had England heart for poets, he would never have gone. He was, perhaps, most hurt of all when Wales did not understand the man who wrote with Wales at the heart of his imagination and understanding. He was himself a very generous and very Welsh Welshman ... He lived to live and to write: there his integrity was absolute.

Because his roots were in the folk-literature of the Welsh, birth, love and death were constant in his thought: the concept of death had, for him, awe but not terror. I can hear now his voice, bugle stop, drumming under, as he came to the measured last line of his own poem – 'And the coins on my eyelids sang like shells'.

One evening in 1950 Barbara Forrester and her sister had gone to the Lyric Theatre, Hammersmith, to see Christopher Fry's play *The Boy with a Cart.* Next morning, she enthused to John. 'Oh, I saw a marvellous play last night. There was a wonderful actor in it, he had a lovely voice – he'd make a really good poetry reader.'

'Oh, would he? Well, why don't you ask him to come along, I'll give him an audition.'

The phone call to the theatre's stage door had no direct response, as the actors were not due until half an hour before curtain-up. Barbara left a message for the actor to ring John's office. Thirty minutes later the phone rang. Would he be interested in coming in for an audition for poetry reading? Yes, certainly. Good. Date, time and studio were fixed.

'Having booked a studio for 10 o'clock on a Tuesday,' remembered Barbara, 'I met him at the reception and took him down to the bowels of the earth in 200 Oxford Street and sat him down. We waited and waited – no John. 10.15 came and went. I was getting rather embarrassed, having asked him to come. I plied him with coffee and eventually about half-past ten John came in, having been tied up in the traffic in his old Alvis in the Archway Road. Anyway, he was so taken with Richard Burton's voice that he used him quite a lot. You can imagine how he and Dylan Thomas reading poetry together made a good pair.'

Many of the *Book of Verse* programmes were narrated by John Whitty or David Jacobs. With a half-smile David says, 'I was asked to do it for the simple reason I was the only one who would walk up all these stairs from the basement to get the coffee. It used to be laced with whatever tipple was thought to be suitable for Mr Burton or Mr Thomas – maybe rum, maybe brandy.

'One of the things John taught me was how to get a story told in thirty seconds or a minute with a beginning, a middle and an end. He had me looking out of the window of his room overlooking Oxford Street and said, "Righto, here's a watch. I want you to tell me what's happening in that street. You have to start when I tell you to and when it comes to be thirty seconds you've got to be halfway through and knowing you've got thirty seconds to finish and at the minute you've got to have finished. Not a minute and one second, a minute." He had me doing that for quite a time, which I found very attractive for two reasons. One, that he should take the trouble to do it, and two, that he was concerned that I should learn. Ever since, it's been very useful, because if somebody says "Will you give me thirty seconds," I can count in my head and do it. People say I never overrun, and why should I? If a clock can be seen it's very easy, but if it can't you have to count in your head. That's what John taught me.'

If John had chanced to tell David Jacobs to look out of a window on the Great Portland Street side of 200 Oxford Street, he might well have found himself describing the immensely wealthy industrialist Nubar Gulbenkian and his beard coming out of the Anglo-Iranian Oil Company offices and getting into his custom-built wickerwork taxi. It was one of the more curious sights of London at the time.

David had been a newsreader before working on *Book of Verse*. When he left the staff to freelance, John gave him another couple of tips. 'He was very patient. He said, "I want you to stop being a newsreader and become a narrator. Hold a pencil in your hand. Fiddle with it. Don't hold up the script, leave that on the table, but fiddle with the pencil because that will relax you. And before you get to a fresh paragraph say to yourself – but not out loud – the word 'now', so that if, for example, the paragraph began: 'The works of John Donne were so and so and so and so', if you say 'now' quietly to yourself, the inflection is quite different." It's amazing, that little word that he taught me . . .

'There were some wonderful radio voices on *Book of Verse* – Robin Holmes, Laidman Browne, Carleton Hobbs – mostly men, very seldom women, I don't know why.'

True, although the actress Marjorie Westbury, a prominent member of the BBC's Drama Repertory Company, was allowed equal access. Possibly, John felt, men had more timbres available within their voices. In any case, in those days the prevailing thought was that men brought greater weight and authority to whatever was being said or read. Undoubtedly, too, John would have been more comfortable directing men, more certain of their reaction. He was, predominantly, a man's man.

Ruth Pitter he regarded as a poet's poet. John had first met her during the war in her deliberately simple blacked-out house in Old Church Street, Chelsea, after corresponding on literary matters. The clumping of guns and bombs was dispelled not by the words she spoke, but by the *sound* of her voice. That sound stayed with John – 'cool, level, yet sensitively modulated, firm, clear, reassuring'.

She read from the manuscript her recently finished poem 'But for Lust'. John reacted impulsively. Could he take away a copy? Might he be allowed to have it printed? Ruth did not think the poem good enough for that, but John was insistent. 'The war-time restrictions (which still applied) made the result physically meagre, a small, single fold in a cream card cover bearing the title: but the printing was clear and sympathetic. Fifty copies were struck off, and numbered and signed by the poet. One (copyright copy) was duly sent to the British Museum and we shared the remainder, using them later as Christmas cards which evoked a quite remarkable response from those who received them. That remains my solitary excursion into publishing: I do not hope ever to improve upon it.'

Another encounter in a writer's den had a less satisfactory outcome. (Not that any apartment in the exclusive Albany off London's Piccadilly could be described as a den.) Clifford Bax, brother of Sir Arnold, Master of the King's Musick, and a literary cricketer of repute, had bought what purported to be an unknown portrait of Shakespeare through the good offices of one Harry Jonas. Enquiries about the provenance of the picture inevitably led to grapevine gossip. 'Excitement began to ripple outward,' Bax wrote in a 1946 issue of the *New English Review*:

One afternoon John Arlott, the cricketer-poet, came to Albany on his way to Broadcasting House, where he was to give in his pleasant Hampshire brogue a talk about cricket; but no sooner had he seen Shakespeare plain than he determined that he would tell the world of our discovery. He rushed hatless along the Rope Walk, and in strolled Sir John Squire, who came, saw, and was conquered; nor had he been gone for more than a few minutes when Eric Gillett appeared, bringing with him a well-known publisher. They were still comparing favourably the bone-structure in the Droeshout picture and in our portrait when a mournful and infuriated Arlott reappeared. The Broadcasting Corporation, he told us, would not allow him to speak about the picture unless it had received the blessing of some art official of high standing, and Arlott, all his detective instincts now scenting the quarry, had taxied pell-mell to a famous art gallery, where he had burst in upon the custodian, no less a personage than the celebrated Dr Perito. 'Well, and what did he say?' we asked. '"Oh," he said,' groaned Arlott, '"it cannot be Shakespeare. There can only be the Droeshout engraving and the Stratford bust. You will never find anything else."' To this Arlott cried boldly, 'But you won't even look at it, Doctor?' and Perito stated authoritatively: 'Shakespeare was not important enough to be painted. Thank you. Good afternoon.' But then, not wholly quenched, Arlott, with burning eyes, pelted to the House of Commons, found Mr Tom Driberg, the Independent Member,* lent him a photograph of the portrait, and came back to us with an assurance that Mr Driberg would write upon the subject (as he did) in *Reynolds' News*. When I reported this development. to Harry Jonas he shrank again into a

---

* Driberg was an Independent Member of Parliament from 1942 to 1945, after which ᴉe became Labour Member for Maldon.

man who, since he had once brilliantly discovered a hidden Holbein, now had a reputation to lose. 'Remember,' he murmured, 'a saint in the act of blessing might without much difficulty be transformed into a poet with poised quill in the act of soliloquising.' However, a week later the X-ray negatives put all his qualms to rest and he became 'the head and front' of our offensive. Moreover, Eric Gillett's publisher had been so well impressed that, catching something of John Arlott's enthusiasm, he said: 'Perito, with whom I was at school, must, I think, be induced to glance at so remarkable a find. Perhaps I will remind him that he was once my fag.'

'That,' said I mercilessly, 'should bring him to heel'; and, true enough, the telephone announced on the morrow that Dr Perito had consented to call upon me before the week was out.'

Perito came, but was not conquered. He remained unconvinced, saying that Bax had got hold of an imaginary, idealised portrait, 'a representation of how some eighteenth-century artist supposed that a poet should look ... Quite interesting.'

Both Bax and Arlott were determinedly unconvinced by this lack of conviction, but there was little more that could be done, and so a thwarted broadcaster, denied his story, channelled his enthusiasm into presenting programmes for other BBC departments. A talk about the newly re-opened Theatre Royal at the other Stratford in the East End of London, interviews with cricketers in the news, and a report on how the National Health Service was supposed to work were all part of a divergent mix. The mix was in fact becoming a little too divergent for the guardians of the West Region programmes when, for their local consumption only, John related his impressions of Dublin. 'Good talk,' they said, 'but wrong subject.'

John was also heard as Cobbett in readings from *Rural Rides* in a Home Service feature, *New Judgement on William Cobbett*. The narrator was the Dorset farmer and *Any Questions?* panellist Ralph Wightman. Martin Armstrong in the *Listener* was much impressed: 'Wightman and Arlott make a perfect combination. Both have a warmth of tone and accent and a way of modulating their speech so that their English sounds like a recital on the cello rather than, like so much polite speech nowadays, a performance on the typewriter.'

Nowadays it is easy to forget how constricted the BBC was with the spoken word during the 1930s, 1940s and early 1950s. Indeed, it was not until the new-wave loosening of the 1960s that regional voices were heard in any great numbers on the national networks. Even in the regional services they were not exactly common. Could it have been that the Corporation, influentially peopled from the ranks of Oxbridge and the English eccentric, deemed them 'not proper like'? Not really. What happened was an unconscious aping of a social climate that was based inherently on the class structure. There was an unspoken school of thought that ignorantly linked accent or dialect with lack of education and cultural awareness. There were, however, notable exceptions who made their mark by being just themselves. They not only enhanced broadcasting, but held open the door for others.

John was one of them. C.H. Middleton, the gardener, had paved the way in the 1930s, and later came the West Country farmers Ralph Wightman and A.G. Street. Also Wilfred Pickles. During the war Pickles had read the news, and his Yorkshire 'Good neet' raised a few eyebrows and opened many mouths. The experiment was not prolonged.

Until they hear a recording, most people are totally unaware of how their voice really sounds. When John first heard his own, he did not recognise it. This is hardly surprising, perhaps, because it was half past five in the morning, and the *Country Magazine* programme he had compered for Jack Dillon was being repeated on the Overseas Service. He got out of bed and switched on the wireless. 'Oh no,' he said to Dawn, 'they've cut me out. That's my script, but they've brought in a country chap to read it.'

Many of John's *Book of Verse* programmes featured Robin Holmes, a newsreader with a light tenorish voice, and Valentine Dyall, whose sepulchral *basso profundo* had made him well known as 'The Man in Black' who introduced ghost and horror stories on the air. These two provided a wonderful vocal contrast, and were instantly receptive to timbre. During a rehearsal one Thursday, when John was filling in a part (to save on programme budget,) Val Dyall noticed that he was trying to adopt standard Southern English. 'Why are you altering your voice?' he demanded. 'The part doesn't call for it.' John's doubtful reply to the effect that everybody in the BBC spoke like that met a withering response. 'I'll personally cut out your tongue if you carry on. Only you can speak the way you do. Stick to it.'

Whether this happened before or after the famous comment by the 6'7" Head of Outside Broadcasts, S.J. de Lotbinière, that John had 'a vulgar voice, but an interesting mind' would be interesting to know. 'Lobby' was not being unkind, just appraising. Such remarks could, however, reinforce uncertainties in those who were still finding their way; not so much socially – the BBC in those days was very much a welcoming club, and a number of its members came from ordinary backgrounds – but intellectually, for there was perhaps no greater concentration of diverse achievement and well-stocked minds per square yard anywhere else in Britain.

Notwithstanding the fact that he had lectured for ENSA and had been a member of their Brains Trusts, John was still unsure of himself in this new world. 'He was not sophisticated, just a straightforward country chap,' said the actor Preston Lockwood, who worked on many programmes with John. 'I took him to see England versus Scotland at Wembley and it was the first time he had been there. He was staggered by the size of the crowd.'

John, though, was soon cutting his own cloth. More programmes with a cricket theme and the narration for a Technicolor documentary film financed by the Ministry of Information called *Make Rich the Land* helped to give him experience. And his horizons had been further widened during the autumn of 1946 by short trips to Rome, Vienna and Paris. In Vienna he had lectured to the occupying forces, and in Paris and Rome he gathered material for programmes.

One of his most demanding undertakings as a producer was to mount a memorial feature on Mahatma Gandhi just after his assassination in January 1948. He had just over an hour in which to prepare a one-hour programme. He managed it by announcing, narrating and acting himself, with the assistance of two readers, three books of Gandhi's aphorisms and a record of the Gujerati prayer-hymn of the bells. 'Every time I ran out of ideas, we put the disc on,' he told me. Gandhi was the man John would have most liked to have met: 'To take on the whole British Empire and win – without raising a hand in anger – to change the course of history. Fantastic.' Unfortunately, John only ever visited Delhi on a brief stopover in 1954 on his way to Australia, too late to join the throng in front of the Birla House as Gandhiji came out each morning to say his prayers on the lawn.

Whatever else he was doing, John still had to fit in his weekly production for the subcontinent. What sort of audience listened to *Book of Verse* in India? That is hard to establish. In the main it was likely to be university students – perhaps no more than a few hundred of them. And what they thought of some of the programme's more esoteric forays into English literature can only be imagined. There was never much feedback.

One programme, however, that went beyond the confines of India – to Burma and Malaya as well – was the monthly book review by E.M. Forster. Forster was fastidious in preparation and totally objective in his comments. As far as it can ever honestly be said of anyone that they required no production, it could be said of him. 'Forster is no work at all,

but don't try to alter him,' George Orwell had warned John, in one of
the few pieces of advice he had given.

Among the paradoxes of the war effort had been Orwell's broadcasts
to India. There he was, meant to be representing the official voice of
Britain to a land in which his own works, such as *The Lion and the Unicorn*,
were thought too seditious to distribute. The subtle counter-propaganda
effort expected by the government, and the 'switch censor' by which
bureaucratic hands could silence unsanctioned comment, aroused Orwell's
natural antipathy. It made him feel, he said, 'like an orange that's been
trodden on by a very dirty boot'. Cultural imperialism of that kind was
bound to truncate Orwell's tenure behind the microphone, though he
never doubted the fundamental integrity of the BBC. Nor did Forster,
who was himself constantly on the alert against the forces of reaction. In
John's words, 'He was the one contributor the programme *had* to have if
it was to command respect in India . . . He was as eager as *A Passage to
India* would suggest to establish understanding, trust, and affection
between Indians and people like himself.'

Forster would arrive at the studio wearing an aged ankle-length overcoat that looked as if it served as a tent. Around his neck would be a heavy
woollen scarf fixed firmly by a safety-pin. John would attempt to help him
off with this protection against the winter chill; the studio, after all, was
warm. But Forster did not want to be helped off. His mother had pinned
him up, and he was doubtful that anyone else could do so if he became
unpinned. Soon after her death at the age of ninety, Forster received
notice to quit the family home, West Hackhurst at Abinger Hammer,
which was rented. His dismay surfaces in a letter to John:

> It's a horrid business here. We have been in this house for seventy
> years, my father was the architect, and I am being turned out by
> 'family friends', and losing a garden which I shall miss even more
> than the house. I shan't go in for roots any more, but propose, for
> the years that remain, to be one of those graceful floating wobbly
> objects that occasionally sting.

As far as John's own roots went, they were still, and would always be,
inextricably Hampshire. That did not stop him from enjoying all that
London had on offer – pubs, clubs, theatre, cinema, and primarily people.
'He loved literary people and they loved him,' said Dawn. 'We had all
sorts round the house – Charles Madge, one of the *New Verse* poets;
Christopher Hassall, who was a neighbour; Stella Gibbons, the author of
Cold Comfort Farm; Rupert Hart-Davis, the publisher, a very nice man;

Robert Frost; Margot Randeburg, who had a lovely voice; Esmé Percy, who was rather mannered; Anthony Quayle. We'd go to the theatre all the time – he took his work so seriously – he'd go to see this actor or that. "What d'you think of that boy?" he would ask me. He never stopped.'

One visitor to the Arlotts' household was Alister Kershaw, an Australian writer who found living in his native land isolating and claustrophobic. He came to Europe and eventually became a kind of personal secretary and assistant to the novelist Richard Aldington in the south of France. He relieved Aldington of the chore he detested most – answering mail. Even those letters marked 'to be opened by Mr Aldington only – private and personal' were delegated to Kershaw. 'Christ, those are the very ones I don't want to see!' Aldington would say.

Kershaw stayed at Barrington Road for some time. When not tripping with Dawn to an expensive charcuterie in Soho for Portuguese sardines, French cheeses and calvados, he was, on Aldington's behalf, having discussions with the publisher Allen Lane about the Penguin paperbacks of the author's work. In the late 1940s Aldington, whose novel *Death of a Hero* was regarded by John and many others as one of the finest in the English language, was in the throes of preparing his biography of D.H. Lawrence, *Portrait of a Genius, But* . . . In the correspondence between John and Aldington, comparisons and complaints would be aired about conditions in each other's territory, a not unusual subject when one letter-writer is an expatriate. On 30 November 1949, Aldington wrote:

> We seem to be at rather useless cross-purposes – for after all you have to live in England and I don't, and so we both have nothing to grouse about! Do coppers grouse as much as Tommies? I believe I got the habit in the army! You can't dislike the British middle and upper class more than I do, with whose arrogance, insolence and brutality I am well acquainted; as well as with their custom of buying themselves a reputation in the arts by patronage of more or less venal writers. In English art and literary circles it is even now much more valuable for a writer to own the compensation money for former coal royalties than to have real literary gifts. An aptitude for intrigue still out-weighs a life-time of service to the arts. You will see all that illustrated in my *Life of Lawrence*.
>
> I have been reluctant to tell you about the Lawrence plans, for after all you are on the BBC and share their confidence, and they are part of the jolly little open and above board British efforts to discredit me. The *Listener* and the 'Literary' Supplement of the London *Times* go hand in hand there. (They won't and don't

succeed, but that's no reason why I should have any truck with
them and their friends;) In the past I have found it useful to conceal
publication plans until as late as possible.

But I believe you to be my friend and an honest man, and therefore tell you what is brewing in the certainty that you will not use
the information to my disadvantage . . .

Aldington then went on to give intricate details of publishing arrangements and the extra labour he had undertaken for the Heinemann
and Penguin reprints of D.H. Lawrence's books to commemorate the
twentieth anniversary of his death in 1930:

> All this has meant a great deal of concentrated work, for my introduc-
> tions are not just airy opinion and pub philosophy, but full of exact
> information. I don't grudge one moment of it or regret my present
> feeling of slight weariness – I am doing nothing but amuse myself
> and rest – for I know the work is honest and thorough and a real
> monument to the last great English writer – the only real genius I
> think who has come right out of the English industrial working class.
> And, my dear lad, I don't give a snap of the fingers what the Beery
> little Buggers of the BBC say or do or don't do or say about it. They
> can't stop it.

Even though Aldington had confided in John, he was amusedly
exasperated by what he regarded as John's conventional BBC liberalism
– membership of a kind of shadow establishment. 'Naturally, he is liberal
– aren't they all?' Aldington remarked to Alister Kershaw. For Aldington,
John's views were too pat. 'Richard in completely anarchic mood would
have welcomed somebody who was all for slavery and who loved eating
babies for breakfast,' laughed Alister.

In 1955 a book by Aldington on the other Lawrence – *Lawrence of
Arabia: A Biographical Enquiry* – made him some powerful enemies among
Lawrence's admirers, including Basil Liddell Hart, Robert Graves and
Winston Churchill. Expecting to write about a great soldier and scholar,
Aldington had discovered evidence that cast doubt on much of the legend.
According to Alister Kershaw, when the book was published Aldington
was 'denigrated, misrepresented, spoken of as a surly curmudgeon and so
on. Not true. He was a delightful man and jovial companion and most
generous. It was a squalid campaign that reduced him to penury. All doors
were shut, all openings closed, no work forthcoming, all references in the

British press insulting. He was belittled as suffering the occupational disease of all writers – persecution mania.'*

All of which would seem to have little to do with John Arlott; even so, John had twice given Aldington broadcasting work, presenting *Book of Verse* programmes on the Imagist Poets and *Macbeth*. In spring 1948 Dawn and John had gone to stay with Aldington, his wife Netta and their young daughter Catha at their home at the Villa Aucassin at St Clair, Le Lavandou, in the South of France. Alister Kershaw, who was there with some Australian friends, had mixed feelings about John. 'Everybody liked him, he was a sympathetic character and all that, but Richard and myself found him a bit much on occasions. I remember one evening Dawn, who was very pretty and vivacious and who had been sitting there quietly while John was going on about something, suddenly broke in, 'Oh, Jack, for Christ's sake stop being so fucking pompous.' We all sort of rallied round. Dawn's comment endeared her to us all. He *was* being pompous. He did have a tendency to talk about things he didn't know all that well, though he did listen a lot which was a good thing. He had a lot to learn, as had I, obviously. We both knew that, but the difference was that I openly listened whereas John wanted to conceal the fact that he had a lot to learn by talking – perhaps out of shyness, out of nervousness. He certainly did learn a lot from Richard. John was very English, of course. Richard, who was a very English Englishman, was at the same time very cosmopolitan and essentially French . . .

'The English provincial accent irks me for some reason, and I think that probably was one of the things that separated me from John. My second wife had a slight English provincial accent and I think that is why it exasperated me at the time. I'm well aware an Australian accent is enough to make anybody cringe – I don't mind, in the least, an English upper-class accent.

'I somehow had the feeling that he wished he hadn't been a copper because that made him looked down on by the people he wanted to know and frequent, but I may be wrong, it was just a feeling. To his credit he did make the breakthrough. In Britain, you had your place in life at that time and he was trying to break through a social stratum which was very hard.'

Alister Kershaw recognised John's determination to make a career, which was another factor in their incompatibility. 'The difference between him and my friends and myself was that we wanted to drink a lot of

---

* In 1985 an expedition led by Captain Charles Blackmore to retrace Lawrence's trails in Jordan supported Aldington's findings.

wine and make love and write and paint whereas John worked on making something of himself. It created a lack of understanding and sympathy between us. John's interests weren't really mine except for literature and wine, about which he subsequently knew a great deal more than I did. There was just not a chemistry between us. I found him rather solid, good old English. Didn't happen to be me.' In his autobiography John acknowledged his 'English small townness' at this stage of his life, and he came back from France determined to adopt a wider outlook and greater tolerance. The stay had obviously touched some feelings of insecurity in himself.

'As a producer he was extremely professional and very competent indeed,' continued Kershaw. 'He was generous to me in London when I needed the money and gave me work reading scripts. He was a kind producer, which isn't always the case. When you did something wrong, he'd tell you it wasn't what he wanted. But he did it the right way, so you didn't think you were being put down. He didn't need to give me work, but he did. I remember that with gratitude.'

During the 1948 visit to Le Lavandou by the Arlotts, Alister Kershaw went out one night to see a girlfriend in the village. "'I'll be back pretty late," I said to Richard. "You'd better leave the door unlocked." "Oh, don't worry about that," interrupted John. "As an ex-policeman, I'm accustomed to waking up just like that" – snapping his fingers together to illustrate his point. "The merest tap on the door and I'll be awake."

'Well, I came back at three or four in the morning. The door was locked. I hammered on it for about five minutes. Finally, it was Richard who opened that door. John had not stirred in his sleep.'

John's feelings about Alister were not quite so mixed. He thought him brash, dissolute and charming. As for Alister's feelings about Dawn – they were not mixed at all. 'Dawn was a great addition to that gathering in the South of France, you know. Everyone really did love her. She was an exceptional person. I remember her to this day with real delight. She was lovely – beautiful to look at, relaxed and happy. I was in love with her.

'Richard used to say, "Why can't we keep Dawn here forever and let John go back to England?" He was a lucky man to have met and married her.'

John was supportive of Aldington after he had been ostracised because of his T.E. Lawrence book. Aldington never really returned to favour in Britain, although his work remained popular in America and, strangely enough, was revered in the Soviet Union. In October 1949 he wrote to John: 'We had rather *too* many people calling in this year, and I don't mind telling you that Netta and I would gladly have swopped many of them for you and Dawn. On 16 December 1950 he was felicitous over the arrival of Timothy Mark, John and Dawn's second child:

> All congratulations to Dawn and yourself on the happy outcome of what at one time must have looked rather grim! How very fortunate the oxygen was at hand! But why the very Scriptural names, I wonder? He sounds like a cross-section of evangelists and apostles. All good luck to him in this bomb-happy world.
>
> Before I forget – do you think Jimmy is too old for the Babar books? Or has he got them? I think Catha will now relinquish them, and if you'll let me know I'll send them along – not perhaps in time for Xmas but as soon after as possible.
>
> I hope your newspaper contract comes off with the *Evening News* [see Chapter 11]. You deserve to have a time of not being over-worked. It doesn't pay to overwork, first because honesty, industry and merit are not rewarded (time-serving and kow-towing to the right people are what pay in England) and then over-work leads to breakdown. I've had two – one in 1922 after three years incessant work to try and get on my feet after war, and a series in the past year or so. I believe I can't now work more than 5–6 hrs a day and more than 6 days a week. In America, and part of the time here, I have had spells of 10–14 hrs a day for 7 days a week for 3 or 4 months. In the end one conks.
>
> Talking of which, I used to do rather well with short feature articles, literary bits and short stories before 1939. Do you know of any editors who would consider such stuff from me now, and to whom you could mention me? I don't mean a regular job, just free-lancing. I don't see why I shouldn't shoot off my prejudices in print like anybody else. Advise me.

Which John undoubtedly did, though not after Netta Aldington left her husband and came to stay with Dawn and John for a long period some time later, which effectively brought the friendship with Richard to an end.

Aldington's experiences in the First World War and just after had left a vein of vitriol in him. He sometimes chastised bitterly those he cared about most deeply – a quality born of a striving for perfection and a distaste for the second-rate.

It may be an anachronism to say that John enjoyed 'networking', but his contacts in all his fields acknowledged not only his ambition to set out his stall, but also his enthusiasm for folk. He enjoyed the company of people who mattered because they might matter to him. He enjoyed their company for itself as well, because of who they were and not what they were. He also enjoyed the company of people who had not been noticed outside their own immediate circle.

John met many of the 'poets of the thirties', some whose best work was behind them, some whose flowering was yet to come: a combination or grouping from *New Verse* and *Twentieth Century Verse*, including the Welsh nationalist Keidrych Rhys, the anarchist poet and critic Herbert Read, Herbert Mallalieu, Roy Fuller, Ruthven Todd, Gavin Ewart, W.H. Auden and Stephen Spender.

The gatherings of two, three or four were often as not in town: the Salisbury in St Martin's Lane, or Bertorelli's in Charlotte Street, or possibly the Admiral Nelson in Chelsea or the Helvetia in Soho. A generally shared feeling was that 'poetry should strive for the greatest possible intellectual clarity'. A poem that did not reach the understanding of a sensitive reader had failed. That definition might tend to exclude an irrationalist poet like Dylan Thomas, but his overwhelming talent was recognised as outweighing a normal disqualification.

On his way to Victoria one morning, John bumped into the stooped figure of the lone-wolf publisher Caton, for whom a surname somehow seemed sufficient. Caton led a somewhat secluded life in his basement – or dust-hole – in the Buckingham Palace Road, from where were produced the first books of a number of writers who were to become celebrated, notably Cecil Day-Lewis and Philip Larkin. Callers would find him, as John did, 'humourlessly lurking in a state of perpetual nervousness', a condition brought on by the fear of a visit from the police. For in that basement, the offerings from soon-to-be known names lay alongside recycled semi-pornography by names that never wanted to be known. Caton would calm his nerves by smoking incessantly, and every so often treating himself to a potency pill from the Damaroids bottle on the shelf. These were presumably intended to counteract any feelings of inadequacy from reading his brown-paper-covered collection. While they were talking in the street, Caton floated an idea for a poetry anthology to John, but it was left floating, as it were, and never came to ground.

Others from the fringe publishing circuit were in touch with John in what they liked to think of as their offices. The 'office' could be the Café Royal one day and a coffee-bar in Kilburn the next, depending on their cash-flow and outlook. In temporary residence might be the exiled Russian Stefan Schimanski with *World Review*; Wrey Gardiner, who included experimental work in his *Poetry Quarterly*; Tambimuttu, a Tamil from what was then Ceylon, who collated *Poetry London*; and several more. On the one hand, they were on the lookout for new poems and reviewers, while on the other they would be seeking an outlet for their protégés' latest work on *Book of Verse* and other specialist programmes – a mixture of altruism and conscience. Although many avant-garde writers regarded *Book of Verse* as having a mandarin image, John did, in the last two months of 1947 produce ten programmes in which modern poetry was chosen by contemporary literary editors, Philip Tomlinson, Michael Goodwin, Robert Herring, John Lehmann, L.A.G. Strong and G.W. Stonier among them.

The fluctuating habits of literary 'meet' spread beyond what is now known as the media mile. For some, the bohemian existence of a bunk in Bloomsbury quickly palled, and as greater affluence took a few further north, and lack of it an even greater few further south, so did new circles begin. Nevertheless, a Fitzrovian phalanx might break cover and slum westwards to East Marylebone and the Wheatsheaf in Rathbone Place, or the Marquis of Granby round the corner, or the Yorkshire Grey, or the George, or the Stag's Head, all within shouting distance of Broadcasting House. There the worlds of writing and wireless were indivisible.

Around the bar could be BBC producers like Geoffrey Bridson, Robert Kemp, Cecil McGivern, Louis MacNeice, Laurence Gilliam and 'Jack' Dillon, who when on song was wont to cultivate the exclusive use of the 'f' expletive. They formed a sort of advance party from the Features Department, and most of them would be talking at the same time. Another group coming on later or on another day or at a different pub might include Stephen Potter, the BBC producer Reggie Smith, Douglas Cleverdon, Rayner Heppenstall, Terence Tiller and John Bridges. Bridges, who had been in the Grenadier Guards and had gone temporarily blind after treading on a mine in the North African desert during the battle of Mareth, got a job in Features after walking uninvited into Laurence Gilliam's office, standing stiffly to attention with his eyes fixed firmly on a point six inches above the head of the Head of BBC Features Department, and offering to work for six months without pay. The offer was accepted, although Bridges did get paid, which was how he was able to buy his round at the bar. Again, everyone would talk simultaneously, yet everyone would also be listening at the same time, having an adrenaline-lit discussion in which it was impossible to withhold thought for a second. There were no cliques – members from any grouping were interchangeable.

Joining them at any moment, and certainly soon after opening time if he was in London, would be Dylan Thomas and, likely as not, Roy Campbell. The South African-born Campbell had led a fantastic life and yet lived to fantasise – a man of action as well as a dedicated romantic. Before becoming a radio producer Campbell had fought for Franco in Spain – right-wing Catholicism was the root of his support – and had stayed there to hunt down German spies for the British. He was a fine horseman and an *aficionado* of the bullring. Posters of bullfights in Seville decorated his office in the Langham, which had been London's largest hotel before being taken over by the BBC at the end of the Second World War.* John's secretary, Barbara Forrester, remembers the posters from the times she went there to collect scripts. She also remembers that the office had no central heating or coal, and was freezing cold. Roy Campbell thought fires were sissy.

John believed that Campbell had many of the qualities of the Eliza-bethans: 'There is power in the man. There is power, too, in his verse. His satires are boiling, scourging utterances but his less topical writing has a richness which sits well with his strength.' The two argued feroci-ously, but liked one another none the less. Campbell half-convinced John of the legitimacy of bullfighting, but although he admired the skill and bravery of the matador and the beauty of the ritualistic dance of death, he shuddered at the savagery. The writer George Woodcock related in his autobiography *A Letter to the Past* how one evening a drunken Campbell 'danced in the middle of Piccadilly Circus, making veronicas with his trenchcoat at the taxis as if they were bulls and he a matador in one of the corridas of his youth'.

When drinking, Campbell was not above escalating violent argument inside into fisticuffs on the pavement outside. He and Stephen Spender once parted company in such a fashion, though Campbell relied on purely oral assault when it came to deflating Aleister Crowley, the necromancer and self-proclaimed 'Beast from the Book of Revelation', during an evening encounter in the Fitzroy pub in Charlotte Street. John also met Crowley briefly – which was probably the best way, though within the tippling circle on that occasion 'the wickedest man in the world' had looked a broken wreck of his former self.

Surprising as it may seem, John did not enjoy being perched on a stool in a public bar. The drinking schools from BBC Features and literary London would find him in their midst with a half-pint of beer or a sherry, but he seldom stayed long. Apart from having so much to do, his boredom threshold could not tolerate those who liked to tell the longest stories in their loudest voice.

When John came to make a selection of over 150 contemporary poems

* It was reconverted to its original glory as a hotel in 1991.

for *First Time in America*, an anthology of poems that had never before appeared in the USA, published in New York in 1948, he inevitably included the work of many of his friends. How could he not? He had acquired a sympathy with poets – he was, after all, one of them. He tried, however, to aim at a collection formed 'by a taste which dare not admit of personal bias', and 'solely by the "feeling" of poetry'. On a copy of the book that he gave to me he wrote: 'This did not pay for the paper it was typed on, but it was fun to do.'

By January 1951, when he moved to a different department within the BBC, as an instructor in the Staff Training Unit, John had become one with another world. The commentary of cricket, and the company of cricketers, had been assiduously pursued and enjoyed during the same years he had been producing *Book of Verse*. Working continuously, on both sides of the microphone, he was in danger of becoming too versatile even for a Renaissance man. But something had to give, and strangely it was the very thing that had first taken him into the broadcasting world. Poets and poetry did not receive a farewell wave; they just gradually receded from the foreground of John's life, as the clamour and demands of public performance trampled upon his time.

'The ability to write poetry left me,' he told me once. 'I don't know why. I just couldn't do it any more.' The reasons are, perhaps, not hard to find. He was not having to work in the medium, as he was no longer a producer. And the writing of poetry surely needs repose, which John did not have, nor give himself. By the early 1950s he not only had his new job as a Training Unit instructor, he was writing nearly every day for the *Evening News* on cricket, football and topical affairs; he was broadcasting, commentating, penning articles, compiling books, delivering speeches, travelling, attending meetings, sorting out this and doing that – all of it dictated by deadlines, deadlines, deadlines. When could he stop?

But there was one special date he had to honour – the seventieth birthday of Jack Hobbs on 16 December 1952. At various times John has given conflicting timescales for the composition of his ode to Hobbs, but whether it took seven weeks or five months is unimportant. In fact, it would probably be more accurate to say it had been nurturing in his subconscious for over twenty-five years, since that day when, as a schoolboy, he had first seen Hobbs bat in the Oval Test in 1926. Over the years his feelings had intensified, particularly after meeting his hero and becoming aware of the quality and character of the private man. Because he cared so much for Jack, and wanted so desperately (John's favourite adjective) to get the poem right, he suffered a kind of mental obstruction. He almost despaired of ever being able to finish it.

However, his determination won through. 'Jack Hobbs was the best man I ever knew in my life,' he said many times. 'I would say this even if he never made a run. There was something incredibly Christ-like about Jack, there really was . . . I had terrible problems and difficulties, probably because I'm not a very good poet. There was one verse in the middle I couldn't get right . . . it took me three months to get that one verse right . . . and looking back on it, I didn't write all that many, about forty or fifty poems at the most, between 1942 and until Jack was seventy . . . and when I'd finished it, it was the best poem or piece of verse that I'd ever written.

'It was not good, but it was the best I could ever write: it said what I wanted to say as well as I could say it – and I knew I could never write another piece of verse, and I never have.'

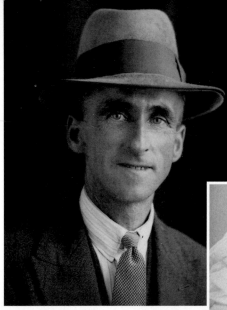

William John Arlott, John's father: 'Jack' of all trades.

Lying 'prophetically idle' – early evidence that there was no difference between John's public and private fronts.

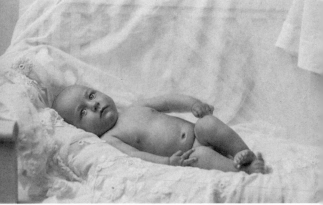

Sitting tall with mother Nellie.

August 1917. With Dad away at war, a young soldier on home guard.

Above: The Old Cemetery Lodge, Basingstoke, where John was born, and *(below)* the New Cemetery Lodge, the residence from the mid-1920s, when his grandfather retired.

Christmas 1935: a well-groomed twenty-one-year-old.

Southampton Police, 30 November 1941. The annual parade in front of the pavilion at Hampshire CCC's ground. Chief Constable Frederick Tarry *(front row, 7th from left)* and the two likely lads, John Creighton and J.A. *(4th and 5th from left, 2nd row from back)*, looking decidedly sullen, having failed to find an excuse to miss the proceedings.

Left to right: Harold Wells, John Creighton, J.A. and Joe Molloy: four coppers, barely disguised in Jantzen swimwear, at Southampton Lido, looking out for pilfering from cubicles.

Dawn, John's first wife. Early 1940s.

Dawn with sons James and Timothy.

Tim and Jimmy, at around five and eleven years of age respectively.

Eric Hill, Somerset's opening batsman, and Arthur Wellard, of six-hit fame, with John at Swansea during a game against Glamorgan in May 1948.

Left to right: Len Hutton, Alec Bedser, J.A., Cliff Gladwin and Roley Jenkins sharing a microphone during the MCC tour of South Africa, 1948-49.

July 1949. Finding out the players' point of view in the dressing-room at Bristol during Gloucestershire's match against the New Zealand touring side. The visitors won by seven wickets. Padded-up, a youthful and pensive Tom Graveney.

Concentrating hard with his 'lipper' microphone during the same match.

The game's over, but the really important work has just begun. John recalled walking along a little street near Waterloo one day when some boys came up to him. 'Can you tell me the right time?' asked one. He told him, and as he did so they tilted their heads to one side with an air of critical judgement. 'There,' said the leader. 'I told you it was 'im.'

Daniel Querre, John's mentor, recognising that God made water but man made wine.

Château Monbousquet – for John a life-enhancing experience.

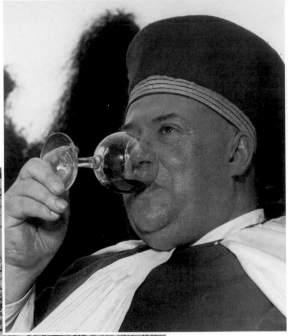

To John Berry Hobbs
on his Seventieth Birthday
16 December 1952

THE MASTER

There falls across this one December day
The light remembered from those suns of June,
That you reflected in the summer play
Of perfect strokes across the afternoon.

No yeoman ever walked his household land
More sure of step or more secure of lease
Than you, accustomed and unhurried, trod
Your small yet mighty manor of the crease.

The game the Wealden rustics handed down,
Through growing skill became, in you, a part
Of sense, and ripened to a style that showed
Their country sport matured to balanced art.

There was a wisdom so informed your bat
To understanding of the bowler's trade
That each resource of strength or skill he used
Seemed but the context of the stroke you played.

The Master: records prove the title good:
Yet figures fail you, they cannot say
How many men whose names you never knew
Were proud to tell their sons they saw you play.

They share the sunlight of your summer day
Of thirty years; and they, with you, recall
How, through those well-wrought centuries, your hand
Reshaped the history of bat and ball.

8

Gone to the Cricket

Traditionally, the signal for the start of any English cricket season is steady rain. The year 1946 was no exception. John booked into the Diglis Hotel, Worcester on 3 May, the day before the match was due to start. He wanted to be fully prepared, to familiarise himself with the geography of the commentary position and the telephone links, to establish access to the dressing-rooms, and to get to know the Indian touring team. He had met most of them briefly when they booked in to their London hotel on their arrival in England. There he had commiserated with their manager, Pankaj Gupta, who seemed to have some prescience that the next four months were not going to be easy.

'In the hall of the hotel was a small man ("Gupta Sahib"), wearing a blue trilby hat so soft as to change its shape and significance with each of the varied emotions that racked him,' wrote John in his account of the tour, *Indian Summer*, which was published in 1947. 'He had discovered that the telephone bore him a grudge, that airborne cricketers are for ever announced but never arrive, and that, as T.S. Eliot had discovered before him, "April is the cruellest month". He had tickets for the Association Football cup-final but no team to take to the match, limousines to command but no one to fill them, words to utter but no ears to receive them . . .'

Poor Pankaj. John was often in his company in the ensuing weeks, and he noted that the manager's trilby never did attain a final shape.

Worcester was cold and damp. Even so, having been starved of formal first-class cricket for six seasons, eight thousand people turned up on the first day of the match, wrapped in overcoats and mackintoshes, stoically prepared to put up with a bitter north-easter. It was the sort of morning for mulled wine, but John had to content himself with a flask of coffee and the thickness of his tweed suit. He was keen to begin. Six sharpened pencils and a new notebook, which remained unopened throughout the entire tour, were his only props.

A moment of panic as the Indians came on to the field. How was he to tell one player from another? Seven of them – in a circle from gully to short leg – had their backs to the commentary position. They were all wearing similar caps and three sweaters, the top one long-sleeved and bulkily shapeless. At that distance all of them looked identical.

His police training came to the rescue. Observe and sift the evidence. The wicket-keeper was easy to identify, and at the end of the first over, one of the group went on to bowl. The two in consultation with the bowler had to be the captain and vice-captain, Pataudi and Merchant. Bowed legs, head held at a certain angle, shirtsleeves showing beneath the sweater, distinguished three more, and very soon John was able to put a name to ten of the eleven, and by elimination the eleventh as well – Shinde, the leg-spinner.

His professional powers of observation were to become an integral part of John's commentary. He would instinctively be aware of the slightly furtive movement by which a bowler would attempt to dry his nervously perspiring hand on the side of his trousers, the batsman fidgeting with the bat at the crease, the quick moistening of lips with the tongue, the constant touching of the tip of the cap – all reflecting players' inner tension and stress. And then, that awareness would be shared as an image within his commentary. His sharply-etched aural refractions eventually built up a reputation, and then an expectancy from his listeners. When describing a bowler with a crab-like run and bent knees approaching the wicket 'like Groucho Marx chasing a pretty waitress', or an umpire signalling a bye 'with the air of a weary stork', John would be drawing a picture that all of his listeners could visualise in their own minds – the essence of communication on radio.

In his 1959 pamphlet *Attention* John wrote of sitting next to a cartoonist who was watching for the first time a cricketer who was making headlines. 'He watched him for over an hour and then turned to me and said, "This is the first time I have ever seen a man without a single feature, from hair to bootlaces, that will give me a recognisable twist: but I *will* find one." He did – in the last hour of the day's play, as the sun dropped low, the young cricketer produced and donned a cap of vivid stripes, creased from his pocket into odd lines. The cartoonist heaved a deep sigh of relief and reached for his pencil and sketching pad.'

John used to maintain that, for himself, the descriptive device was purely surface observation. 'I talk about what I see. A lot of commentators tend to talk about what they are thinking rather than what they are watching.' And yet, John was more interested in finding out what his *subjects* might be thinking. He would try to interpret their thoughts from their actions, and their personality from their characteristics – a study at a distance of what is now called body language. In that same pamphlet, *Attention*, he noted: 'If, as is certainly true, much of the unhappiness in life is caused by failure to understand other people, we cannot escape the conclusion that if we really *observe* other people, we are less likely to misunderstand them. Looking can so often be the first step to understanding a person's behaviour.' Therefore, by implication, John's so-called surface observation could merge, almost, with psychology.

Commentating at Worcester had been thrilling for John. Both teams had overcome the unkind conditions and provided entertaining cricket in an even match. The tourists had not arrived at their hotel until nearly 3 a.m. on the first day, as their coach driver had lost his way. What with that, the strange surroundings and little time to acclimatise – one net practice at Lord's the previous day – it was remarkable that they lost by only 16 runs. Singleton, Howorth and Perks for Worcestershire and Mankad, Modi and Shinde for India had all made outstanding contributions. John had experienced few problems with his commentary. His main difficulty had been timing his hand-back to the studio, encapsulating what had happened and the current situation in a few minutes, all of it governed by the stopwatch, but this was essentially a matter of practice and experience, and would soon become second nature.

Rex Alston, who was then the BBC's staff commentator, had heard about a young man who had been asked to cover matches for the Overseas Service and who had played for Hampshire. This had puzzled him. He could find no record in *Wisden* of an Arlott playing for Hampshire, and so he had rung Ronald Aird, Assistant Secretary of the MCC and a former player for the county. Aird was equally baffled. Nobody seemed to have heard of him. But at last the mystery was solved. Said Alston: 'I was deputed to go to Worcester. I walked across the ground and a chap with his hair all over the place – a young man – came rushing up to me. "I'm John Arlott," and he thrust into my hand a book of poems. I registered that this was the one who had played for Hampshire and we found out the truth about his sole appearance – it's a good story, he didn't mind being laughed at.

'It was obvious there was something there, though it needed training. He got very excited in the early days – rushed away with his talk about things – a lot of it inaccurate but enthusiastic. It was the enthusiasm that came over.'

That enthusiasm was nearly lost for the listeners during the Indians' game at The Parks in Oxford, where the New Zealander Martin Donnelly played two commanding innings – 177 runs for once out. The 'synchronisation' of Donnelly's strokeplay convinced John that he had been watching one of the best left-hand batsmen in the world. He was also much intrigued by Donnelly's cap, which looked 'as if it may have been worn, schoolboy fashion, with birds'-eggs or cakes stored in its crown'. But John's most lasting memories had been his visits to Oxford's bookshops when the first day's play had been washed out by rain, the conviviality of his stay with Dylan Thomas in his borrowed boathouse, and, crucially, his close call in getting to the commentary position on the second afternoon. In soporific sunshine, he had been sitting in a bomb crater on the edge of The Parks, idly chatting and sipping with Dylan, Louis MacNeice and Cecil Day-Lewis – a poets' tea party, though it was not tea that was being drunk. In such circumstances time seems to stand still. Suddenly, John glanced at his watch, which showed seven minutes past four. At ten past he was due to broadcast live for five minutes up to the tea interval. The engineer could be seen in the doorway of the van on the opposite side of the ground, peering anxiously in all directions. John ran and ran as if his job was on the line – which it may well have been – and got there with seconds to spare. The first two minutes of commentary were delivered at a pitch verging on falsetto, with much use of pregnant pause against a background of heavy breathing. Apparently, nobody noticed anything amiss.

During a Test match at The Oval some years later, John again reached the microphone with only seconds to spare. This time somebody did notice. The engineer on duty complained that there was nobody ready to begin broadcasting at under a minute to eleven o'clock, the scheduled start. This led to considerable anxiety both at the broadcast point and in the studio. John was called to explain. He said that he had looked into the box five minutes earlier, although the engineer had obviously not seen him, that it was advantageous to his broadcast to assimilate the atmosphere and crowd talk around the ground for as long as possible, and that anyway he disliked waiting and twiddling his thumbs in a confined space for a moment longer than was necessary. He emphasised that he had never, ever been late for a broadcast. The defence was thought to have won on points – narrowly.

At another match during another season John lost on points – decisively. Rex Alston did not need any reminding that 'occasionally John wasn't a very good timekeeper. I was the senior commentator, in charge of it all. "Jim" Swanton summarised and did bits of commentary as well. I used to work out the batting order of when the commentators did their twenty minutes and John was number one on a particular morning and he didn't turn up. So we carried on and I got rather angry when he did arrive and I said, "OK, buzz off – we'll bring you back in the afternoon," and he had to go away' (*laugh*). 'Swanton and I coped with it up to lunch.'

Considering his action-packed life, it was perhaps not surprising that John was constantly chasing the second hand. There were, however, moments of relative tranquillity, even in the company of Dylan Thomas. For a Forces programme called *Day Out* the two drinking companions journeyed from Oxford down the Thames on the pleasure-boat the *Golden Eagle*, together with Michael Ayrton and Hugh Metcalfe, the manager of the Crazy Gang. (John was on good terms with the six members of the Gang – Flanagan and Allen, Naughton and Gold, and Nervo and Knox, all of whom dined at his home at one time or another.) On this particular Jeromish jaunt, such copious quantities of wine accompanied a seafood platter that someone remarked that there was more liquid inside the boat than in the river. The day was remembered long after the broadcast, and some of the party were out for most of it. Ayrton's charcoal sketch of Dylan contentedly awash adorned John's wall for ever after.

Some time later there was another excursion with Dylan, to a club in Tiger Bay, Cardiff. The pair were struck by the talent and potential of a young girl singer, and they told her so. Her name was Shirley Bassey.

That summer of 1946 passed for John in a haze of activity: new friends, fresh fields, dawning knowledge, different hotels; the only thing that remained constant was travel. John was discovering places for the first time. A town or a city that before had just been a mark on a map now had a feel, a perception and an identity.

From the vast Oval in the grimy streets of Kennington – where John experienced a feeling of unease at his back similar to that 'when a neighbour (who knew I stole his apples) was watching me from his window as I went down the road', and where Banerjee and Sarwate had their record-breaking last-wicket partnership of 249 against Surrey – to Cambridge, Leicester, and Scotland – where rice, curry and fruit crowned the finest hospitality of the tour, and where a hat-trick was greeted with anxiety or phlegm, depending on whether you were a solitary commentator whose attention had been distracted or a Scots scorer whose had not. And then back down south to Lord's, and a dress rehearsal for the First Test in the match against MCC. Although John's short commentaries for Overseas were not very arduous, he felt totally involved, for close at hand, sharing BBC domestic coverage over the season, were Rex Alston, E.W. Swanton, Arthur Gilligan, Percy Fender and C.B. Fry. Not expecting his foray into commentary to last longer than the one season, John envied their position.

Early in the tour, the Indians were either drawing or winning their matches convincingly. Most of the team had adapted to English conditions remarkably well. In London, John brought them to a basement studio at

200 Oxford Street to record messages for their families and friends back home, and then back at his own home fed Mankad, Merchant and Hazare rice, potatoes and tea, after belatedly realising that meat, poultry, fish and alcohol were, by the tenets of strict Hinduism, regarded as 'ritual pollution', though in fact the tiger-hunting Hazare was a practising Christian.

In Wales for Whitsun, John enjoyed the lack of barrier between 'pavilion and bob-bench'. He did not appreciate quite so much the dryness of the Sabbath and 'the cult of a bottle in the bedroom which made a glass of beer seem a furtive, dirty thing'. As he watched Emrys Davies and Arnold Dyson leave the pavilion to open the Glamorgan innings in response to a substantial Indian total, John was reminded of 'two artisans going out to dig a well or thatch a house'. The match qualified for an entry in the cricketing curiosity columns when the Glamorgan number eleven, Peter Judge, was twice bowled for a duck within a minute by Sarwate. The home side followed on, and John Clay, the captain, had reversed the batting order and dispensed with the ten-minute interval between innings in order to give the large crowd as much cricket as possible after delays from rain.

This game also saw the start of a forthright friendship between John and the Glamorgan all-rounder Wilfred Wooller. He expanded on the encounter in his book of the tour, *Indian Summer*:

> Wooller bowled medium-paced swingers. Already the idol of Wales as a rugby player, he will be a cricket personality – and may yet be a better player than most of the prophets admit. Wooller, still not fully recovered from his spell as a prisoner-of-war of the Japanese, is yet a promising medium-pacer who occasionally hurries off the pitch, a brilliant field close to the wicket and a batsman who promises intermittent delight to spectators. It seems certain that he will succeed John Clay as captain of Glamorgan. If he does, he will be as popular even as Clay is: and since he has a longer head than his cheery ease might at first indicate, he will learn the game.

Wooller, who did succeed John Clay in 1947, has his own opinion about who was wearing the L-plates. 'I introduced John to the players and to the atmosphere of the dressing-room – we were very hospitable – and so he was meeting them and talking and asking things about the cricket. He was a pretty good learner. Although he always gave the illusion that he was up to his ears in first-class cricket, he wasn't really. He did hide his real background in cricket, which was natural anyway. It was a process of growing up. Technically his knowledge was limited, and speaking as a cricketer on the circuit, it was a great help for him to be associated with me in particular and the Glamorgan team. So that when he became a commentator for domestic programmes during the following seasons we saw him from time to time at allocated games – always on a very friendly basis. The extraordinary part about it was that, by the time he had been involved with the cricket circuit for several years, he had acquired the knowledge and way to talk about things – at least superficially.

'He then had such confidence in himself that he would come into the Glamorgan dressing-room and say, "You know, the way to beat these chaps is to so and so and so and so, and I'd play such and such a bowling such and such a way," and so on, and I'd look at my professors – the county team, the regular players there – and I'd see them staring up at the ceiling and wonder whether they were going to be rude, because one thing a professional cricketer doesn't like is someone who can't play the game coming in telling him what to do. But it never worried John. He always did, and we laughed and out he went. No one resented it too much. Although there was a bit of press waggery going on about John's ability as a player, he was such a pleasant, good-tempered fellow about everything, they accepted and recognised his talents as a commentator.'

The Glamorgan dressing-room was not the only one to benefit from a visit from the impetuous young commentator. Rex Alston recalls: 'He was full of enthusiasm, so much so that he infiltrated a lot of dressing-rooms and talked to the cricketers, and that's where he got all his background knowledge. I don't think anyone else had tried it. I didn't go. I was rather shy about going into the dressing-rooms and so on. I didn't think they'd want a snooper in there. But he managed to do it, because he made himself one of them. He saw a great deal of them – even having drinks with the players afterwards, that sort of thing. He also learnt a great deal because of his playing about in the Hampshire nets in between matches – he was always there – very keen.'

Wilfred Wooller continues: 'I always think his great virtue was that he could impart a mystique into all his commentary. Great county cricketers, great bowlers in Test cricket – they deliver a ball, fast, medium, so they know whether they're pitching it on the seam or where they're about to pitch it. But they can't guarantee – can't *know* that a particular ball is going to do anything other than what they hope it will do. But John had a marvellous way of explaining how this had been planned in the mind and produced on the ground and deceived the batsman and the reason. So he built almost a parable story about the delivery and the wicket that was taken, which endeared him to the listeners. It gave a panoramic picture of a game in a most extraordinary way which people lived with, and with his curious Hampshire accent it became a characteristic of cricket.'

In later years, John recognised that the amount of commentary he was able to do in that first year and after gave him the chance to make every mistake there was to be made, at least twice. 'The poor Indians were too frightened to complain in case the broadcasts were stopped and they failed to get the score at home.'

Rex Alston recognised John's 'misconstructions' at the time. 'He would make a comment about the pitch and how a bowler was doing this or that. I remember that at Valentines Park, Ilford, Tom Pearce, the captain of Essex, had been listening to what John was saying before going in to bat. It wasn't a very easy wicket and as Tom walked out he said to a fielder, "I don't know whether I'm going to live or not. This is a *terrible* pitch, isn't it?" Of course, it wasn't that bad, but John had built it up so that it was jolly good listening, but was of dubious authenticity. He sounded very authoritative, you see.

'There was also an occasion at Headingley when I was sitting next to George Duckworth, "Ducky", the wicket-keeper, whom we used and he was a damn good talker. John was enlarging on this and that. George whispered to me, "What can I do? It's all wrong." So I said, "Oh, well, you just put another point of view. That's all you can do – you can't say it's all wrong because that's letting him down and letting the BBC down." And he did it jolly well.

'After that John had to be hauled over the coals and told, "Look here – you've got a lot of ability and that sort of thing, but you've got to be careful about this and that and you've got to tidy it up and so forth," and, bless his heart, gradually he did so.'

It would seem that those initial excesses were fairly quickly moderated. Alston went on to say: 'As he got more and more confident he was, at times, really frightfully funny. Particularly if there was nothing exciting happening. I can remember a Test match against the Australians, 1948, I think, again at Headingley, and the commentary position was behind one of the stands and the windows were open when John came to do his stint. I can't remember the details – it doesn't really matter – but he was very entertaining about Bill Edrich slinging the ball down, fastish stuff, almost as if he was going to throw his arm off. Also for about a quarter of an hour he spoke about Bill Johnston, the Australian number eleven, who was a bit of an ass in the field. The whole stand was laughing, because they could hear everything he was saying. That was typical of him. If we had a very dull patch, he was the chap we hoped would take us through it, because in some way or other he would enlarge the scene.

'One of his lovely phrases was when Len Hutton was batting at Bramall Lane and John said something like, "And he walks out of his crease and touches the pitch with the end of his bat, but doesn't damage it at all, because it's *sacred ground*." That was Arlott at his best. And then when Middlesex were playing the South Africans in 1947 and "Tufty" Mann was bowling to George Mann, "Mann's inhumanity to Mann" – wonderful phrase.'

That charming, witty raconteur, the actor Dennis Castle, was another who had a professional interest in John's commentary technique: 'Had he had time he should have been employed to update children's pantomime scripts. His gift of observation was fantastic simply because he described the scene unselfconsciously. Too many commentators are being themselves. Arlott staged the scenes convincingly, anticipating the comments of the ordinary listener. Impossible in a book to infuse his cadences, the rise of surprise, quite genuine, the fall of a possible explanation rarely designed personally . . .'

Dennis Castle also remembered the younger Arlott, 'in his sometimes misunderstood go-getter days. He was not, as many thought at the time, pushy but a sheer enthusiast.' But some thought him pushy *and* a sheer enthusiast. And also chippy. During his first visit to Lord's as a commentator in 1946, John felt unwelcome. The upper-crust environs of cricket's headquarters were not his natural habitat. He saw the headquarters of cricket as the seat of an autocracy where snobbery and class distinction held sway. His liberal, egalitarian instincts would be put on hold, which led to a state of unease. As he wrote, 'Some of his colleagues did not disguise their opinion of this down-market interloper.'

It was not at Lord's that he clashed with Jim Swanton, but at Trent Bridge. Whether it was in 1946 or 1947 – conflicting dates have been given – is not important. Apparently there was a difference of opinion over who had booked the commentary box. John told me: 'I was in there doing a recording, and not understanding or caring who I was he came in and told me to get out. So I stood up, shut the microphone off and said, "If you don't go away I'll throw you off the top of this pavilion." There were no adjectives interspersed – I was too much of a copper for that.'

'It was a silly thing, really,' recalled Jim some forty years later. 'I much regret that it ever happened. I was wanting to make a recording and it was over who had the rights of the box. It was the only altercation we ever had. I wouldn't say we were blood brothers, but I think we respected one another.'

Both were innately too sensible and too professional to let a feud

develop. They had, after all, to work together. John was stretching himself
– perhaps over-stretching himself – in so many directions that any obstacle
could cause him to succumb to tiredness and temper. Around this time
he had actually thrown somebody who riled him down the stairs at 200
Oxford Street, so it was no idle threat. Nevertheless, as he admitted, he
could hardly have lifted Swanton off his feet, even allowing for the fact
that Jim must still have been in a weakened state following his period as
a PoW of the Japanese.

The locking of horns led John to pen a somewhat unworthy squib
which went the round of the press-box:

> Stately is my manner and Swanton is my name,
> and in the *Daily Telegraph*, I write about the game.
> I was never at Oxford or Cambridge,
> But I think that my accent will pass;
> and I've got a check suit and deer Michael,
> and that's in the Bullingdon class.
> I've dined out with all the best people,
> and I thought I made quite a hit;
> So why should mere cricket reporters
> declare I'm just a big journalist?

Each of the two, in his own uncopyable way, was to help make the
broadcasting of cricket a national institution; Arlott with his commentaries
and Swanton with his summaries, though Swanton also gave extensive
commentaries in his time. Was there anything finer than Jim's masterly
coverage of the day's events, when it seemed that everything possible had
already been said many times over? With very little time at his disposal,
he would, off the cuff, assess the game in its overall context, putting it in
a different perspective in that wonderfully comforting brown, treacly
voice. It is easy to see now how, in delivery and sound, one voice so
perfectly complemented the other, and how two such disparate personalities from such dissimilar backgrounds could only extend the range for the
listener. But at the moment of confrontation they could have been seen
as potential rivals, though Jim, having been writing and broadcasting since
before the war, had a head start on John. He was already established and
working for the national press.

'My first impression of John was that he was different,' Jim Swanton
told me. 'There was no Arlott prototype, so to speak. You can imagine
Alston, the schoolmaster, the steady orthodox performer. John was not
orthodox – as it seemed at that time. The thing about him, of course, was

that he produced a personal idiosyncrasy of style – if not idiosyncratic, a very natural style of talking. He was a very good reporter with a gift for colour ... was "quick on the ball" to spot anything off or on the field, any quirk of a fielder, that sort of thing. He was unconventional in that way, I think ... You must realise, of course, that there hadn't been all that much running commentary in broadcasting until 1946. In 1946, it took a different form altogether ... I suppose he thought I was very much an establishment figure, but I think he may have revised that opinion after my attitude to the South African question which, of course, happened years later.'

Jim Swanton is absolutely right. The South African question did not happen – for English cricket – until *much* later, for in 1947 a South African team toured England with no political controversies in evidence. 1947 was to be a vintage summer in many respects. For John, looking back to the previous year when he felt as if he were on a stolen excursion, rather like 'a long and glorious spell of truancy with no fear of recriminations', it held high hope. He had missed very few of the Indians' matches, fitting in his production work by setting off from around Britain by sleeper train on Saturday nights, recording in the London studios on Sunday, and returning by another sleeper that evening or very early on Monday morning. His secretary, Barbara Forrester, helped to make it all possible. A routine was established which took care of the irregularities of John's life – a routine, or rather the acceptance that nothing was routine, which was to hold good for the next few years. The voluminous paperwork, the booking of and correspondence with artists, the typing of scripts and now, as well, the typing of books. John had started to write on cricket to supplement his income and also, as Rex Alston says, because he 'really wanted to be in the game somewhere, somehow'. It had always been part of him, now he wanted to be part of it.

Barbara, whom John called 'Bob' for short, was to type 'about eight books' for her boss during the time she was with him. 'I think it was eight because it felt like it, but it may have been one or two less.' In fact it may have been one or two more.

After *Indian Summer*, his account of the Indian tour, which came out in 1947, he assembled and edited some of 'the classics of cricket' into one volume for the following year, *From Hambledon to Lord's*. Also in 1948 came *Gone to the Cricket*, a description of the previous year's South African tour of England; *How to Watch Cricket* for Sporting Handbooks and the poetry anthology *First Time in America*. In 1949 there was a new edition of *How to Watch Cricket* containing a review of cricket books published during the previous year; *The Middle Ages of Cricket*, another assembly of nineteenth-century cricket writing; *Concerning Cricket*, a collection of essays, some of which had previously appeared in periodicals; *Gone to the Test Match*, an account of the Australian tour of England in 1948; and *Wickets, Tries and Goals*, about play and players in modern cricket, rugby and football of which John was co-author with Wilfred Wooller and Maurice Edelston. The next year, 1950, he introduced and edited studies by various authors of first-class counties in action entitled *Cricket in the Counties*, and brought out an account of both the MCC tour of South Africa in 1948–49 and the New Zealand visit to England in 1949, *Gone with the Cricketers*. Interspersed with these were several booklets on the game as well.

Barbara Forrester would stay late at the office, clicketty-clacketting on her typewriter, until around 10 p.m., when she would catch a tube back to her home in Acton: 'I'd do it with impunity, because you didn't have to worry then about being mugged or raped.' An annual present to her from John was tickets for Wimbledon. John was not overly interested in tennis. He had worked with the tennis commentator Dan Maskell, and indeed helped him in the art of broadcasting, and when Joanna Spicer, then in Programme Planning and later to be a seminal influence on the growth of British television, gave him tickets for the Centre Court each summer he was not about to turn them down. 'Joanna had a soft spot for John,' said Barbara, 'and when he passed on the tickets to me, he used to say, "Don't let Joanna know."'

A sport that had more appeal to him was boxing, although John was not sure that it could strictly be defined as sport, or indeed whether it was right to enjoy it.

He gave voice to his thoughts over the air on 22 April 1947, on the weekly Eastern Service series *One Man's Horizon* apropos the world heavyweight championship contest at Harringay between Bruce Woodcock and Joe Baksi. Why, he asked, did eleven thousand people pay £43,000 to see the fight?

> Well, I went because I've boxed a little, enough to know that I can't box, and to acquire a broken nose in the process. I went because I like to see anyone playing his part well, and because I like to fancy that I recognise the touch of genius when I see it; and I also went to see it because it was a great event.
>
> Why did the other people go, I wonder? Many of them, there's no doubt at all, went because they were so very anxious to see Bruce Woodcock, an English boxer, make a real challenge for the championship of the world; others went because it was a social

occasion – oh yes, there were tail coats and ermine in the ringside seats; there were film stars there and famous boxers of the past, and famous cricketers; three or four peers of the realm and all the gentlemen who rank high in the aristocracy of boxing; some of them went because it was a social occasion, then; others for partisan reasons; others to see some good boxing; and others just because the seats were expensive and difficult to get.

I don't believe that many people went there in the hope of seeing someone hurt; you're far more likely to see a man violently hurt in a street fight than you are in a boxing match because good boxing isn't fighting, it's a science.

After some preliminary bouts, including one in which a future world champion, Randolph Turpin, knocked out his opponent in under two rounds, there came the big fight, preceded by 'a certain amount of ballyhoo which left rather a bad taste in my mouth' involving a portrait of Joe Louis, and Uncle Sam and John Bull respectively carrying the Stars and Stripes and the Union Jack.

Everyone was waiting very anxiously for the gong. The big sign over the arc lights came up with the names in red, of Woodcock and Baksi. The gong went and the fight was on. Well, the fight proper didn't last more than ten or twenty seconds. Woodcock opened in the manner amateurs always adopt – the manner I always adopted, which was to keep well out of reach for the first ten or twenty seconds while pawing the air a little and taking a thorough look at one's opponent to see that he wasn't armed with a bludgeon or a revolver. But while Woodcock was doing this Baksi came up very close to him and hit him on the jaw, and Woodcock went down, not as if he was knocked down but as if he'd been thrown down. The power behind that punch, which only moved a few inches, was immense.

You knew as soon as you saw Baksi that he was a genuinely strong man. This terrific curve of the shoulders was a typical miner's physique. It seemed as if he couldn't raise his arms above shoulder level for the sheer weight of dropping shoulder muscle, which made a semi-circle not only vertically but also horizontally round the shoulder blades. He was just one mass of muscle. I thought it was rather a pleasant face. He looked a bit puzzled about most of the ballyhoo that had gone on before. I think he thought that boxing was the business and that was what he wanted to get on with. It wasn't a particularly brutal face, though no doubt many of the people who don't approve of boxing would like to think so; it seemed a kind face with a slightly puzzled frown, and the frown didn't wear off until the fourth round.

He pursued Woodcock round the ring and hit him several times more and eventually Woodcock was carried to his corner by his seconds. And at that time some of the experts thought the fight ought to have been ended; you know only too well from the newspapers that it continued into the seventh round, with Woodcock's face a rather unfortunate mess and Baksi winning very easily. Woodcock took a great amount of punishment and I'm inclined to blame most of it on the training. I think it is something to blame. I don't think there's a great deal of room to talk glibly about bravery, because, quite frankly, what seems to me to have happened to Woodcock is that he was so badly concussed in the first round that he was never fully conscious afterwards, and those of us who played any sort of game at all know how often people do carry on, half unconscious, after they've been concussed. He carried on in that way because of his training. The man who used to attempt to train me used to tell me that the idea of training was so that you could play yourself completely out. If you weren't trained, he said, you could only use part of your strength; complete training – and you could point proudly to the Boat Race crews who end up being violently ill and in a state of collapse – complete training will enable you to play your strength completely out; in other words give every ounce of what's in you; and to be quite honest that's what happened to Woodcock that night: concussed, he carried on, took all the punishment a man could possibly take, and was still on his feet at the end.

I don't think very many people in that hall relished seeing him take the punishment, you know. In those opening rounds, that opening round in fact, when the really damaging blows were landed, and Baksi's fist was landing right to the stroke of doom, in that early round there was dead silence right through the hall; it was the silence of horror. I think that was the most impressive example of mass emotion that I've ever encountered in my life. There was certainly the loss of hope that an English champion was going to make an important challenge for the world championship. There was something more than that; so many people in that hall had identified themselves with Woodcock that every blow seemed to land on them. Believe me, I don't believe there was any glorying in what was happening, except by one spiv character just down in front of me, who at the peak of one of the most impressive hushes, got to his feet and begged Mr Baksi to knock the living daylight out of his opponent. He wasn't a very popular character; he did, I think, relieve the tension a little in a number of people who wished they could have started a fight with him. It wasn't a very pleasant exhibition but it did rather show that mass feeling wasn't in favour of seeing a carve-up in either direction.

It was a rather tragic business; it had a funny postscript, four days afterwards, when Covent Garden early in the morning was full of the story that Bruce Woodcock was dead, and that story obviously originated from the fact that the night before Benny Leonard had died in New York; one of the wise boxers, a man who did his boxing and got out – got out intact, a retired, undefeated champion of the world. Too few of them have done that; too many have stayed, taken a punishment they couldn't stand for economic reasons or for sheer conceit, and have gone the uncomfortable way that the punch-drunk boxer does go, down to complete obscurity. Leonard was wise; we hope that some of the others, having made their little fortunes, will go before they who have been idols become something which their supporters, their friends, their followers, really regret. But most of all let's hope that the people who make wry faces at the very mention of the name of boxing will one day come to understand that it's a skilful game; it's a game of tactics, and that when a man's hurt it may not always be boxing or a man's own ideas that really cause serious damage.

Having expiated his lingering guilt with that defence of boxing, John found batting gloves fitted more comfortably. It was late April, and rain was in the air.

9

Season of High Hope

The season of high hope for John now fully materialised. It was to be one of the most rewarding cricket summers of his life, as is witnessed by the book he wrote twenty years later, *Vintage Summer 1947*. Even though his Indian tour commentaries in 1946 had been greeted so warmly, he had not presumed to be asked again. But he was – and this time his commentaries were to be heard throughout the four and a half months, on overseas and domestic regional and national radio networks.

A complicated itinerary was made of travel, hotels and, not least important in what was to be a very hot summer, laundry journeys. A stockpile of recordings of his own productions was prepared, as far as was possible. Then, on 29 April he had a haircut, packed a dispatch case, got on a train, and booked in once more at the Diglis at Worcester.

For the second year running he had forgotten to bring an overcoat. The wind whistled up the Severn by the Diglis Lock and rattled the bar-room windows so much that it seemed to make any thoughts on the tourists' opening match, and cricket in general, redundant. John was one of a group that included Worcestershire's veteran seamer Reg Perks, who had played two Tests for England in 1939. Perks put down his glass and said, 'We might all be surprised; this could be a much better season than we think – even without Wally' (Wally Hammond had retired after a relatively poor tour of Australia in 1946–47). English cricket was still regrouping after the ravages of war, and hardly anyone else around the table shared Perks's optimism. However, six months later, in his book *Gone to the Cricket*, which was dedicated to his father 'who knows nothing about cricket and cares less but who *wos wery* good to me', John was able to testify:

> It has been a year of happy cricket, and I cherish many memories of it – of Tremlett hitting sixes out of the Taunton ground and Wellard coming in to join him and to re-establish his own reputation by hitting a six even farther out of the ground than any of Tremlett's.

Andy Wilson, the stocky little Gloucester wicket-keeper, in the game
against Essex, ran, pads, gloves, and all, to the extreme long-leg
boundary and fielded the ball almost on the line. In the same match
Ray Smith made fifty runs in twenty minutes in a style which placed
him on one of those pinnacles of greatness which every good, whole-
hearted cricketer attains at a few moments of his career. I remember
Carey of Sussex, at the end of a day in the field which had been six
hours and more than four hundred runs long, running up to the
wicket for twenty yards, bowling furiously, and then walking back
at a speed which approached a trot to bowl again – and all this on
a wicket which was a bowler's graveyard. I recall the furious
onslaught of Pope and Copson at, of all places, Trent Bridge, which
shot out a strong Notts batting side – all but Jepson, who doubled
the score in a stirring innings only marred, for Jepson, by the fact
that Harold Butler was not playing – to admire and pay. And never
let any man who saw or heard of it forget George Heath's record
innings of an hour and twenty minutes on three consecutive days at
Bournemouth, an innings which grew slower and slower, until it
stopped altogether when George had attained double figures.

Added to which, Gloucestershire, thanks largely to the dangerous slow
bowling of the forty-seven-year-old Tom Goddard, pushed Middlesex all
the way to the title, notwithstanding the record-breaking Middlesex twins
Denis Compton and Bill Edrich, who had a galvanic effect on practically
every game in which they played. The South Africans, though beaten 3–
o in the five Tests, provided wonderful entertainment as well and the
crowds, hitherto starved of cricket and sun, finally basked in both. In fact,
the welcome but sweltering heat at the Oval Test led 'some young men
on the popular side to dispense with their shirts and one lady guest to
cast off sufficient raiment to draw some appreciative – and some critical
– eyes away from the less lively spells of play'.

Above all, it was a season in which John really made his mark. At home
and in South Africa, the press was adulatory, with the *Pretoria News* voicing
the opinions of many other journals:

Will readers join in in founding the S.M.J.A.H.U.N., the Society
for Making John Arlott an Honorary Union National, for there is
no doubt but that never was a 'foreign' commentator so friendly to
South Africa as John Arlott . . . South Africa played badly in the
Fourth Test [but] there was John Arlott last night, doing his best
for them, still cheerful, still trying to give the impression that things

were not as bad as the figures showed. For they are bad. For this is by no means a first-class England side and yet they have defeated the South Africans so easily . . . I hope that he [John Arlott] comes to South Africa with the next MCC team. There may yet be an opportunity of formally giving the Honorary Union Nationality to Jan Arlott.

Not every paper or listener was quite sure of the commentator's name or how he looked. In the *Natal Daily News* he was referred to as Mr John *Arnott*, and envisaged as an 'oldish man, slightly wrinkled with fair hair, a trifle bald perhaps'.

A listener who wrote to the Durban *Sunday Times* Sports Editor was obviously not a student of acoustics:

Sir,
   I would like to congratulate the BBC on their selection of George Arlott as cricket commentator on the Springbok tour.
   He is not only thoroughly conversant with the game but he has a delightful sense of humour peculiarly his own which frequently covers up dull and uninteresting play, thus retaining the interest of listeners.
   I sincerely hope it can be arranged that Arlott comes over with the MCC on their next visit to South Africa.
   E. Montgomery

This correspondent's better-known namesake, of El Alamein, said to John years later at Portsmouth, 'Of course, you are an Australian.' No remark could have been more guaranteed to offend, as John disliked the 'Ocker' generally, for what he felt was their ability to deride others and their inability to laugh at themselves. He would have much preferred to have been told he had a Yorkshire accent – as he often was by strangers to British shores.

By the end of the 1947 season, John had distilled the essentials of commentary into what was to become, eventually, almost his own art form. These essentials had been handed down to all commentary teams like tablets of stone by the imposing 'Lobby' (de Lotbinière, Head of Outside Broadcasts). First, the basic facts – the score, wickets to have fallen and so on; then the overall picture and the commentators' place within it; an introduction of associative material, whether historical, expository or personal; other elements – subjective description, significance of the event, and human interest and suspense ingredients. *Never, never*, miss the action.

John assimilated these intrinsic requirements quickly. But knowledge of the rules did not mean they were always put into practice. He liked to find his own format, and this identified him as a 'personality commentator'. There was still the odd aberration. He often forgot to give the score, and with all the exuberant confidence of a young man, he occasionally failed to remember that the only certainty we have is that of doubt itself. A categorical appraisal of a cricket situation could still cause experienced practitioners to pause and shake their heads. But this happened more rarely. Fame had uncovered one of its own with frightening speed. John had become part of the public awareness. Radio was in its pomp, and its performers carried as much charisma as television's would in the years to come. Its only popular rival – and that perhaps once a week – was the cinema. And John was part of radio, in all sorts of programmes, though primarily cricket. His voice was unmistakable. More than that, his voice sounded quite different to all the others. It was made to be heard.

John remained remarkably unbewildered by all that had happened. Two years before, he had been an unknown policeman. Now he was a household name. The fan-mail had swollen enormously. But he remained level-headed. He felt – no, he *knew* – that he had slipped in through the side door while others had barely returned from the front line. What he did not appreciate at the time was that he would not have lasted long if he had not had something different to offer. He was still learning, and hungry for experience.

One day, early in 1948, he had a lesson in how not to deal with another household name – the didactic and brilliant C.B. Fry. Fry, the complete all-round sportsman, scholar, politician and journalist, was a gold-medal-standard social dancer who 'was inclined to take such long and imperious strides that his partners found it very hard on stockings'. In conversation, or more likely monologue, he was inclined to be just as imperious in maintaining his reputation as a free-thinking rebel. And he enjoyed expressing his bold opinions over the airwaves. Although this was entertaining for much of the time, many a producer must have had moments when they felt tempted to put a stocking over Fry's head, because his self-deprecation did not entirely camouflage his conviction that, in his own words, he could 'talk a lot of rot and be listened to'.

John had asked the seventy-five-year-old Captain Fry, RNR, to do a talk at short notice for the Eastern Service 'On Round and About Physical Prowess'. During the talk the recording was jammed. Fry was not pleased.

In fact, he was incensed. The cause of contention was his reference to 'the American darkie athlete Jessie Owens'.

'Just think,' wrote C.B. afterwards in an angry letter to John, 'the proper name particularises a man known the world over as a negro.' The substitute term had been suggested by James Pennethorne Hughes, who, having returned from his Indian posting, was now John's boss. John had rung him to query Fry's usage of 'darkie', and had been told that 'negro' would be preferable. Both were anxious not to offend any listeners.

Fry was not appeased. He had put himself out in order 'to advance the recording' by nearly a week. He had sent in the script four and a half days beforehand, in plenty of time, he felt, for 'censoring'. He denied that John had asked him to reconsider the description before the recording because 'it might be tactless'. In a written complaint to Pennethorne Hughes he asserted that no one could be offended by the word 'darkie', and that 'negro' was much worse because it sounded so like 'nigger'. The interruption was, in his view, idiotic, ignorant and impudent. Moreover, it could be damaging to his reputation in India.

John was distressed by the incident. He was aware of Fry's tyrannical manner. He was also aware that the great man did not expect his chosen words to be 'improved' by young producers, however well-known. It had been a difficult situation. Much the best thing would have been simply to take the word out. But once Fry decided his dignity had been trodden on, any suggestion would have met resistance.

Outwardly, their relationship was unimpaired. Fry continued to do programmes for John, and they met at commentary positions and on social occasions. John often spoke and wrote with admiration of C.B.'s unique career. Fry, in his turn, praised John's talks on cricket. But did a lingering canker stay with the erstwhile Corinthian? During the Headingley Test of 1953 between England and Australia, he sent a trenchant telegram to Rex Alston: 'Please restrain Arlott from quacking nonsense.'

In July 1948, for the centenary of the birth of W.G. Grace, John wrote and narrated the longest and most elaborate feature that the BBC had ever devoted to any cricketer. Fry, who had opened the innings for England with Grace, provided historical verisimilitude. He also helped coach the actor Preston Lockwood in getting the pitch and accent of Grace's voice. 'The legend of Grace's "high-pitched" voice might easily have given rise to a voice-quality which would have been inimical to those who knew Grace personally,' John wrote in an introductory note to the portrait which he included as a chapter in his book of the following year *Concerning Cricket*, 'therefore our debt to Captain Fry is a most considerable one.'

The tribute to Grace featured actors playing C.T. Studd, Tom Emmett and Ranjitsinhji, among others. Alan McGilvray, the Australian radio cricket commentator, delivered four sentences in the 'strine' of W.L. Murdoch, and the cast included W.S.A. Brown, Jack Hobbs, Charles Kortright, C.J. Barnett and Arthur Paish as themselves. Sadly, Paish, the old Gloucestershire left-arm bowler who had played under Grace, died shortly after the broadcast. Also involved in the tribute was C.B. Fry, naturally playing C.B. Fry.

In an expansive mood over a magnum with a journalist years later, John extolled the achievements of C.B.: 'A most remarkable man, Charlie. You know, he was in his late seventies when he took out a bird I knew, took her to a night club and gave her a magnificent dinner, and danced with her afterwards, enthusiastically – modern dancing – and she said to me, "And do you know, he's seventy-eight and he didn't have a piss for five hours!"' By now, John's shoulders were shaking with laughter. 'Terribly observant of the girl.'

During the visit of the all-conquering Australian team of 1948, English cricket was yearning for the return of past heroes. As country and counties were given a lesson in all departments of the game, John was busy seeking to glean what he could of the Antipodean trade secrets. Bill O'Reilly, the Australian bowler who had attained almost mythical status in the 1930s, was in England on a press ticket. He remembered how John haunted the Charing Cross Hotel for two or three days when the tourists were staying there. 'Whenever you went in or out of the foyer you'd run across Arlott. He'd pick on fellers who knew about different sections of the game. He went to Ray Lindwall and asked questions about types of bowling he wanted to know more about. And then after a bit he'd switch to someone else for another skill. He cottoned on to me and used to give me a lift around the counties in his old car – Humber, Armstrong-Siddeley, A.C. Tourer or something, I forget which. I know it was fashionable at the time. He was into sherry then. My plebeian tastes never went above beer. He was a know-all regarding cricket,' O'Reilly chuckled. 'Really, he was an apt pupil. He'd had no real training in the game. His unusual accent was attractive and though we were never close friends we knew each other pretty well. I liked him.'

Arthur Morris, the left-handed Australian opening batsman whose composure, magnificent footwork and classy strokes brought him an aggregate of nearly 700 runs in the Test series – more than anyone else, including Bradman – confirms O'Reilly's view. 'He was a bit new to the business then, as far as the players were concerned, and sometimes we doubted him when he came on. But he talked a lot with the players and got to know what happens on a cricket field. Not that you can always tell. A commentator would see two batsmen talking in the middle and say, "They're chatting about how to handle this attack." They're more likely saying, "Have you seen this blonde in the third row at square leg? Jeez, have a good look at her." As he went on John gained a great knowledge of the game. And of course, there was that superb voice and wonderful accent. He was popular with the fellows, too. They liked to have a drink with him and talk to him.'

One of the Australians with whom John felt a close affinity was Keith Miller, then generally accepted as the finest all-rounder in the world. John and Keith had first met in Southampton during the war over a game of cricket. 'John was still a copper,' says Miller, 'and afterwards we went to this skittle alley and knocked down a few pins. It was a rough old runway and rough cider – I got pissed.' Despite this handicap, or perhaps because of it, Miller predicted that he would hit the single skittle standing at the end of the alley – and did so. 'You've got a good eye,' said John. 'No, I haven't,' replied Keith, 'but if you give me any more of this stuff I'll be able to bowl straighter.'

In a sketch of Miller for *Gone to the Test Match*, John wrote:

Keith Miller, finding himself a public figure, shrugs his shoulders and continues to be Keith Miller.

The Keith Miller he continues to be is a happy, comradely and often humorous man. He had discovered that the world is his oyster, and he proposes to swallow it without caring a damn what anyone thinks. Before the oyster can be swallowed, however, it has to be opened – Keith Miller likes to open his oysters for himself – and, if he has to do so with his bare hands, then that is exactly the sort of challenge he relishes.

He is the gayest and most stimulating of company – with an ease of manner which puts his companions at ease. He is, too, generous – in a gentler fashion than those might suspect who know him only at long range. As to what the critics say of him, what the crowd thinks of him, or what the averages declare to be his value, he cares nothing at all. He is rather annoyed that his freedom to do anything he wants to do should be complicated by being a famous cricketer. Of all the members of the Australian party he was the most uncomplicated – if his character was unusual, it was, nevertheless, almost entirely without contradictions. Keith Miller decided long ago how he wanted to live, and everything he does is consistent with that decision.

During the 1948 tour John invited Miller, who he thought was 'as human as the man in the next hospital bed', and some of the other Australians to dinner at his home. After any convivial evening at the Arlotts', John was always anxious to find a reasonably sober person to chauffeur his guests home. Miller, however, was one who knew how to hold his drink.

The commentaries that John did during this season are the earliest of his still to be found in the BBC archives. Mostly they have been kept with an eye to recording some dramatic happening, and the effect is rather like the close-of-play edited highlights on television nowadays. There is little sense of match continuity, and obviously the moments surrounding the fall of a wicket, the reaching of a hundred or the breaking of a record do not always correspond to the best passages of commentary. To replay these excerpts one after the other is to reel like a boxer after a flurry of knockout punches. There is much hitting the canvas, but not much painting of it. John was often at his best when apparently little was taking place, or when a situation was evolving. He could then enlarge. For that, space is needed.

During the Fourth Test at Headingley, Lindwall was bowling to Hutton, John was at the microphone, and the new ball was due (this season it became due after fifty-five overs):

> Just to indicate that he's about to take it. Shows it with a warning and paternal air to Hutton and . . . he's just going to bowl with the new ball now from the Grandstand end. Goes through the usual Lindwall bout of physical jerks. The shirt is now comfortably loose and it fills with wind as he comes up now from the Grandstand end, bowls the first ball to Hutton [*voice rises in pitch with excitement*] – a magnificent outswinger [*pulsating applause*] – hit for four. [*Waits for applause to die away.*]
>   Now that was hit on the half-volley by Hutton for four and a difficult ball it was to cope with. Over its last two yards it went eight inches – it went off the line of the middle and off, clean outside the off stump and Hutton, right over it, hit it firmly past the somnolent Toshack at point . . . And now here comes Lindwall again to Hutton . . . and [*muted applause – voice rises*] . . . that was a magnificent in-swinger that bowled him off his pads. [*Prolonged applause as Hutton returns to the pavilion.*] Well, that was another magnificent ball. It's got rid of Hutton and he is out . . . bowled Lindwall . . . ? [*Pauses for confirmation of score. Scorer's voice: 'Eighty-one.'*] Eighty-one. Hutton, bowled Lindwall, 81. England are 168 for one.

When it came to Australia's turn to bat, England did not possess the high pace with control to match fire with fire. However, they did try:

One of these days I am convinced Edrich will burst on the way to the crease. As it is, he merely explodes when he gets there. It's an amazing action; he leans forward, goes up on to tiptoes and gradually with a heel-swung gallop he flings that one down at Bradman and it moved in the air. It was overpitched but Bradman had to come late down on it to play it. Very late indeed. It's quite fast, it's not by any means as fast as Lindwall and it's a slingy action and it's completely out of the normal traditions of fast bowling but it certainly propels a ball very fast indeed from one set of wickets in the general direction of the other.

[*Applause.*] There's another one, that's short and Bradman's hooked it for four [*applause continues*]. And that is fielded by a gentleman in a grey suit, whose return to the wicket is not at all accurate. And at this juncture, Edrich decides that perhaps, at least, a forward short-leg is something of a luxury and waves him back as deep as the umpire where he's forced to borrow Pollard's cap – that's Cranston. Pollard remains short – Cranston can't get Pollard's cap on. Edrich bowls to Bradman, he hooks him for another four [*applause*]. Four to square-leg. Two hooks for four off consecutive balls and they're Bradman hooks, they're not lifted, he rolls the wrists as he plays the stroke and the ball goes out there like a flash all along the ground.

And Edrich comes up now and bowls again to Bradman. A full-toss on his hips [*a ripple of applause*], glided away on the leg side, they take one, they take two – and it's bounced out of Hutton's hands over the boundary for four, giving Bradman three fours off this Edrich over.

In those commentaries there is nothing exceptional, but they are a concentration of what was happening on the field, relayed as a story to the listener. It is impossible to convey in print the rise and fall of the voice, the inflections, the pauses which heightened what had been said before and what was said after, and the dryness of the moments of self-contained humour. But they are all there, and those will appreciate it best who can most accurately recall the *sounds* his voice actually made.

When 'the Don' walked to his wicket at The Oval for his last Test innings, Rex Alston had been commentating. As the crowd's ovation and the three cheers called for by the England captain Norman Yardley gave way to an expectant buzz, Alston prepared to hand over the microphone:

Alston: The crowd settle down again – they've got forty minutes – forty minutes more left for play and Bradman is now taking guard, Hollies is going to bowl at him and John Arlott shall describe the first ball, so come in, John.

Arlott: Well, I don't think I'm as deadly as you are, Rex; I don't expect to get a wicket. But it's rather good to be here when Don Bradman comes in to bat in his last Test. And now, here's Hollies to bowl to him from the Vauxhall End. He bowls, Bradman goes back across his wicket and pushes the ball gently in the direction of the Houses of Parliament which are out beyond mid-off. It doesn't go that far, it merely goes to Watkins at silly mid-off. No run, still 117 for one. Two slips, a silly mid-off, and a forward short-leg, close to him, as Hollies pitches the ball up slowly [*voice rises*] and [*sudden applause*] – he's bowled.' [*Applause continues. Several comments off-mike. Applause dies.*]

[*Slowly and distinctly*] Bradman, bowled Hollies, nought. Bowled Hollies, nought. And – what do you say under those circumstances? I wonder if you see a ball very clearly in your last Test in England on a ground where you've played out some of the biggest cricket of your life, and where the opposing team have just stood round you and given you three cheers and the crowd has clapped you all the way to the wicket. I wonder if you really see the ball at all.

Once more the human factor is apparent, with John trying to probe beneath the surface of the contest to empathise with the feelings that he thought were being felt. What he did not know was that in the coming months, the human factor was to become a major issue in his own life, on a far bigger scale.

10

Any Questions? *on South Africa*

The 1948–49 MCC tour to South Africa had been on John Arlott's mind for months before he left. Melville's 1947 team in England had aroused his interest in cricket in that part of the world in a way that could only be satisfied by going there. John was still incredulous at the thought of being paid for doing what he did. He had started to get used to the idea of being a *known* person, yet he never ceased to wonder at what he thought of as his amazing good fortune. His pleasure at Glamorgan's first Championship success in 1948 had capped an exciting summer, even though England had been overwhelmed by the powerful Australians.

But before John could enjoy the relaxations of the twelve-day voyage on the Castle Line, a mountain of work had to be ascended. There were books to be written – yes, plural not singular – articles to compose (both of these activities often started at 10 p.m. and were not completed until 4 a.m.), programmes to complete, broadcasts to make, meetings to attend, letters to dictate, speeches to be given, trips to go on, and entertaining to be done: in other words, even more of what had become the usual pattern. Life on any one of John's days was hectic, yet it rarely seemed so. Why? In part this was because the measured speed of his speech patterns was deceptive. His thoughts and reactions were always three laps ahead of his words and his body actions. Those who were fooled into believing that John thought as slowly as he spoke were often surprised or left floundering. This gave him quite an advantage. Admittedly, in his younger days he spoke less deliberately and for far longer, and moved more quickly, but, relatively, the differential remained. His friend Kingsley Amis once commented, 'He had a very direct gaze behind which one eventually realised he was thinking about his next story. He always listened to what you were saying, though.'

Another reason why, although so much was going on it seldom felt that way, was John's inbuilt immunity to flap or panic. Others might agitate on his behalf, anxious for him to be moving to this or that, because they were aware of his schedule. But he hardly ever did, wanting to spend more time with the people he was with at that moment or, simply and sometimes stubbornly, refusing to be pressured.

The adrenaline on which he had been operating barely had time to settle before he reached Cape Town. With the sun on his back, he could revel in the unexpected adulation of the South African public. Both Denis Compton and Godfrey Evans testify that, because of his commentaries, John was fêted in the Union. 'He had a crowd following him wherever he went,' said Denis. 'He was hugely popular,' said Godfrey, 'and better known than most of the players.'

A two-page illustrated article in *Spotlight*, the self-proclaimed 'Brightest National Weekly for All', confirms John's status:

> A Sports Bentley and a farm tractor both work the same way, but what a world of difference in the driving pleasure. Many pedestrian characters try to commentate on sport over the radio, but as rare and racy and full of character as a Bentley is John Arlott, the most famous of 'em all . . . A well-seasoned, likeable, individualistic per- sonality is probably rarer on the radio than in any other walk of life. Most radio announcers and commentators are so mealy-mouthed that John Arlott's famous quotation from Lewis Carroll, apropos of the South African opening batsman Eric Rowan – 'he only does it to annoy' – would be just as apposite of them . . . All we can hope is that the rugger missionaries have been doing a bit of evangelising and manage to convert Arlott to the pigskin in time for the Kiwi tour.

That, of course, was as unlikely as it sounds. A collection of rugby books that John once acquired was passed on to the writer Geoffrey Nicholson, no doubt with a sigh of relief, for the oval ball did not bear enough of the artisan's credentials to be well represented on his shelves for long.

Norman Herd in the *Spotlight* profile tried to work out where it all began:

> Listening to this voice, and the sights and scenes it conjures up, you may form a very clear and inaccurate picture of the man who, well, owns it. 'Here's a fellow who is getting on – say, towards the middle fifties. He has spent some forty of his years soaking in cricket. That's his job, of course, but what he does during the English winter when there are no overseas tours, one cannot think. His birthplace – well, anywhere in Britain, south of the Tweed. At some time in his life

he has been to America and there, like the wolf in the well-loved fairy tale, he swallowed a piece of chalk.'

A glance at the picture accompanying this article may surprise you. The picture is recent, and I doubt whether the subject has quite reached his thirty-fifth birthday. As to the voice, it gives authentic index to the country of his ancestry, birth and upbringing. Lovers of Thomas Hardy will recognise in it (now the clue has been supplied) the deliberate pace and the rough burr and snarl of his native Wessex.

When John told Norman Herd that for him commentary was a side-line, the sub-editor of the magazine could not resist tagging the piece, 'Arlott in Wonderland – He Only Does it to Enjoy Because he Knows it Pleases'. Herd however, asserted that John's commentary was no sideline accomplishment, but

an activity which faithfully mirrors the several sides of his genius . . . Almost any student of cricket with a reasonable education and a fair quota of wits could give us a twenty-minute commentary on one of the big games this summer, but it is the essential poet in Arlott that holds us: 'Here is Jenkins . . . little man with a very muscle-bound, bow-legged walk and almost a sideways action.' 'Nourse looking more Napoleonic than ever . . .'

He then summed up what he saw as John Arlott's technique and achievement:

His sentences are put together with a delightful smoothness and a spontaneous obedience to grammatical laws. He sees in pictures. He sees every player freshly and introduces him afresh at every reappearance, no matter how much he may have done so previously. Wisely, he does not credit his listeners with an intimate knowledge of the physical appearance, the mannerisms, functions and capabilities of each player. Consequently he brings a full-orbed and intelligible picture of the game to the man who listens.

His imagery is remarkably consistent. Watkins, he tells us, is squatting 'rabbit-like' on his heels. Later on, Watkins 'scurries' across. Compton is once again walking down and 'doctoring' this almost 'incurable' wicket.

It is easy to listen to, but the expression of it is an elusive gift. There are several excellent cricket commentators, but only one who combines in his person the poetry, the leisured zest and the eye for people and scenes that is bred in the bone – the inheritance of Hampshire earth and the art of Thomas Hardy expressed in a modern key.

John's commentaries on the 1947 South African tour of England had made a deep impression, and his name featured constantly in the country's newspapers. ' "The Voice" Coming for MCC Tour,' trumpeted one head-line. 'As much the voice to cricket-lovers as Sinatra is to the bobby-soxers' read another caption. 'His voice is as familiar as Winston Churchill or General Smuts' was the opinion of a third. 'Warm-bees buzzing Hampshire rumble' was the apt description by another. And so it continued.

In the *Natal Mercury* John's name was used in the pay-off to a silly story about a sweet potato who tries to convince her parents that her fiancé is of the right social standing: 'Who is he, my dear?' asked the mother. 'He is an Englishman, Mother. His name is John Arlott.' 'Oh, heavens, dear! Not John Arlott; he is only a common-tator.'

Another journal invented one Maria Paapenpoel, who was expecting twins. As she was keen to call her offspring after 'de MCC speelers', and was infatuated by Alec and Eric Bedser, she had no difficulty in choosing Christian names. But then she gave birth to triplets. What was she to call the third child? 'Wat I am wanting is something out orf de kommon – someone orl de peoples is torking erbout . . . My Gawd. I got it!' she shouted, sitting up in bed. 'I will kall him Yon Arlott after de famus broadkastinger.' Thereafter, Maria could tell Yon Arlott from the other two babies because 'Wen he is having er blerry good feed he is mumbling someting wat sounds like strate drivings, leg glidings an kover drivings.'

The cartoonists, too, put John into the picture. In one drawing he was seen sitting in a deck-chair, wearing corduroy trousers and no socks, with microphone in one hand and whisky glass in the other. In 'Cooking à l'Arlott' in the *Cape Argus*, the sketch was of a harassed housewife prepar-ing a meal while listening to commentary. 'To three cups of flour and a maiden over from Doug Wright add an egg snicked by Mitchell down the gully. Fold in the batter at the Town end. Pinch a run by Billy Wade and mix with a Chinaman from Denis Compton. Stir the wicket well. Place in the oven for an eight-ball over and serve to ten thousand people at Newlands.'

For John, the tour had a kaleidoscopic effect. Everything he saw and experienced made a vivid impact: the scenery, the people, the overwhelm-ing hospitality, the well-stocked shops, the brightness and space compared to the drabness and claustrophobic feel of much of post-war Britain. He was kindled by new insights.

As always, he was never still, except when dining or sitting behind a microphone. 'He rarely has more than split seconds to spare before a broadcast,' wrote the sports commentator Charles Fortune in the *Post*, 'so, once in the box, a short joke with the engineer, headphones on, time checked, a glance at the score book and just in time for his cue Arlott picks up his "lipper" [the lip-microphone which John preferred and had brought from England], snaps his stop-watch and is on the air.' The cameos were engraved for ever after: the thrilling photo-finish to the First Test, when England's victory came off the last ball and Cliff Gladwin's thigh (no mere chance that John ate leg of lamb that night), and John's remarks 'and if I'd told this story in a book, no one would ever have believed it', and 'any sane man would tell you that England have won by two wickets' being lost live to the domestic audience as the South African Broadcasting Corporation left the match to take the six o'clock news. Minds conditioned by bureaucratic inflexibility failed to adapt to the realisation that the most sensational and important story of the day was the one they were leaving as it reached its conclusion. Fortunately, at John's suggestion his commentary had been recorded, and was soon being replayed endlessly. Within days, a commercial disc of the Test's closing moments was being marketed.

In the Second Test at Johannesburg there was Hutton and Washbrook's record opening stand of 359, and in the Fifth at Port Elizabeth England's exciting run-chase to get 172 in 95 minutes following George Mann's excellent first Test hundred. Matches too at Bloemfontein in the Orange Free State, where Hutton and Jack Crapp helped themselves to centuries and Roley Jenkins bamboozled the opposition with his 'leggies', and at Kimberley, where Washbrook and Compton pulverised Griqualand West.

Reg Hayter, who was in South Africa for Reuters, remembered that during one of the early games John left his commentary position beside Dana Niehaus, who was speaking to Afrikaans listeners, and took the drinks tray from the twelfth man on to the field. 'There was applause from the spectators and laughter from the players. But in the press-box Charles Bray (working for the *Daily Herald*) and Frank Rostron (*Daily Express*) were furious and wanted to make a protest to the BBC in London. They thought John was taking unfair advantage and searching for "scoops".'

The discontent is unlikely to have got further than the next bar, for in London his boss 'Lobby' was delighted with what he was hearing. He sent a telegram to John just before the New Year: 'Congratulations on broadcasts. Good luck with remainder.'

When appraising the tour afterwards, John felt that if Dudley Nourse, who had succeeded Alan Melville as South Africa's skipper, had been as good a captain as he was a batsman, England might not have won the series. At the climax of that fantastic First Test at Durban, 'if Nourse had had the wit to move "Tufty" Mann, who was fielding at short-leg in spectacles that were covered by driving rain, Gladwin might have been run out. "Tufty" couldn't see the ball. As a captain Nourse had a blind, dedicated courage but lacked subtlety. Eric Rowan would have been a better choice, but was an anti-establishment man.'

It was not just the cricket in South Africa that left deep impressions on John. There were social events and entertainments, at which he made new friends and mixed with old acquaintances; an exhausting charity football game in borrowed gear; winning an oyster-eating competition without any ill-effects; blurred visions of the faces in endless queues of autograph-hunters; manning the Tannoy for a game at Beria Park in the Transvaal between a Pretoria side and English sports writers and coaches in aid of charity; bowling in the nets to the MCC side; recording at the studios of the South African Broadcasting Corporation; the exposed commentary box at Ellis Park, Johannesburg, which was at ground level close to the north sightscreen and within a few feet of the crowd – John's face had never been redder from the blazing sun (or was it the chaffing); being made an honorary member of the famous Wanderers Club; Christmas Day with his old friend from Worcestershire Reggie Perks, who was in South Africa on a coaching appointment, and an unforgettable dinner which would have graced a medieval banquet; a visit to Les Payn, the South African slow left-armer, and his plantation with its 'cuddly boa-constrictors'; sharing a room with Godfrey Evans and returning in the wrong direction in a hired car from a meal at an outback restaurant; an inland flight to Cape Town which persuaded him that all future tour travel should be by plane; waiting in the passengers' hall at Durban airport while Allan Watkins, the Glamorgan all-rounder, climbed into the control tower to listen to a St David's Day broadcast by his wife six thousand miles away in Wales – nostalgic not just for Watkins but the whole team; and, most traumatically, a trip to one of the black townships with the wicket-keeper and future Secretary of the MCC, 'Billy' Griffith, where 'a trickle of a stream ran through the middle, they peed into one end and drank from the other'. Both of them were sickened at the sight.

Other things, too, caused disquiet. Walking along Commissioner Street in Johannesburg, on the day when Denis Compton was scoring 300 at

Benoni, and seeing an inoffensive black man being kicked into the gutter by a white Afrikaaner. Then there was a riot in Durban, and the election of a new government, and with it the structuring of official apartheid. How John longed to be able to talk to 'Sailor' Malan, the Battle of Britain ace and old friend from his 'digs' days in Southampton. As John remembered, 'Sailor' held vastly different political views from his distant cousin Dr Daniel Malan, the new Prime Minister of South Africa and the instigator of these 'separatist policies'.

His journeys by train and car had also not helped John's peace of mind. Grotesquely divergent lifestyles cheek by jowl glimpsed through a sheet of glass. Luxurious apartments on one side, tar-barrel hovels on the other. Affluence and effluence too close for comfort. A tinder-box of tensions.

John had met the South African cricket commentator Charles Fortune in England during the 1947 visit. After spending some time at Fortune's home in Grahamstown, he drove his native cook back to her quarters through a thunderstorm. The ferocity of the weather seemed somehow a chilling portent as they reached her squalid habitation. With his emotions heightened, 'shame, hesitation, doubt, guilt, struggled in the mind'. The questions raised were, for him, never satisfactorily answered.

As he was leaving South Africa at the end of the tour, John left blank the section marked 'race' on the departure form. The immigration officer looked at him impatiently. 'What race are you?' he asked. 'Human,' replied John. 'What d'you mean?' the man asked in an aggressive tone. 'I am a member of the human race,' answered John decisively.

Telling the tale years later, John would say he suddenly felt a tremor of fear. The eyeball-to-eyeball confrontation seemed to go on for ages. It ran through his mind that he was not out of the country yet, and still within their jurisdiction. The immigration officer glowered. At last, between gritted teeth, he said 'Get out.' John did not wait to be told twice.

Almost immediately on his return to Britain, John was asked to give his impressions of South Africa for *Meet the Commonwealth* on the General Overseas Services. His talk is interesting, if partly for what he did not say:

I am fully conscious that I've just toured South Africa under the most luxurious conditions a man could possibly enjoy, as a member of the party that accompanied the English cricket team through the Union.

We were extremely lucky, every facility that could possibly be offered us was offered us, and I owe debts of gratitude that I shall probably never be able to repay to many people up and down South

Africa. Well, it's difficult, obviously, to generalise about South Africa and Rhodesia; in fact only two generalisations possibly occur to me. One is that after many years of austerity in England the country seemed extremely rich, so that when a businessman in Johannesburg spoke of a slump, one who remembers Jarrow in the pre-war years was inclined to smile a little.

Johannesburg seemed, and there were the dumps from the gold mines eternally to remind one of it, a centre of immense wealth, and the shops were a wonderful sight after the shops of England, with almost everything and anything available. The other generalisation I would say, and this I got chiefly because I tried often to leave the side and the official functions and to meet people and talk with them, an impression one got was of their change of values as compared with European ones. Here in England, with the countries of Europe on top of us, and America seeming so close by virtue of the long-distance plane, we've come to regard world politics as important as our own, whereas in South Africa, with vast oceans and deserts separating them from the other countries of the world, the people seemed by European standards rather preoccupied with local affairs to the exclusion of those world affairs which may settle the fate of South Africa together with other nations . . .

As one went from province to province inside South Africa, it seemed so often like going to a completely different country. We found the grapes and the magnificent scenery of Cape Town and the wine industry along to Durban, where so much centred on sugar, up to Johannesburg and the immense wealth of the Rand, to Kimberley and the Great Hole, and perpetually, one was finding these different standards throughout the Union, so that it was difficult to lump it together as a single unit. Again, I was interested in getting away from the side, to observe some of the South African schools and the magnificent outdoor facilities which are there breeding such a magnificent type of schoolboy. The studies one thought perhaps a little meagre with several boys to a study, as compared with the English method of one boy, one study, until one realised that these lads could, except in their sleeping and eating time, be outdoors practically all day with magnificent playing fields and magnificent swimming pools. And then coming from Cape Province, to go north and into Rhodesia to find the Matabeles and the Mshanas there, being educated in building, carpentry, agriculture, so that they could go back to their own people as experts in building, and in an attempt to revive the agriculture of South Africa.

And in that connection, one couldn't help feeling rather sad as one passed over river after river in the Union absolutely opaque with brown mud, as it bore away the topsoil of the Union, and bore away, perhaps, much of the agricultural wealth of the country that has that vast agricultural problem to solve.

It was difficult though, perhaps at times, in that magnificent diet in that wonderful climate, whether it was the bracing windy sunshine of Cape Town or the high arid vital plateau of Johannes-burg – it was difficult to nurture sad thoughts at all. Everyone seemed so very pleased to see us. Everything we saw seemed to have its own special sharpening in that bright and frequently very dry sunshine. The reservation of the Transkei, with the people there in their magnificent beadwork, the fascinating kraals with those huts which looked primitive from the outside, inside shining like the pride of an English housewife. Altogether, it was a thoroughly impressive visit. I'm conscious of the privilege I had in going there and of the extreme generosity and hospitality that I received which enabled me to see so much of the country and of its people.

Is it hindsight that suggests a conscious holding-back; of wanting to be much more assertive, but feeling it was not the time or place to be so? Possibly, but even so this does seem to be one of the few occasions on record where John was not saying exactly what he thought.

That accusation could not be made a year later, when, in March 1950, on an *Any Questions?* radio programme broadcast on the West of England Home Service, he let loose not so much the commonplace cat as the roasted pigeons which, in defiance of the Dutch proverb, did fly into the mouth. What he said was this:

Well, rather to my horror – I speak from personal observation in this matter, of course – the existing government in South Africa is predominantly a Nazi one, and most of the present cabinet there, under Dr Malan, supported Hitler during the past war and objected to anybody who had served in the English forces; and they propose to enlarge their majority in their own House by taking in the former German colonies, who supported Hitler, although they passed from under German rule, during all the war and pre-war, in the doctrine of racial supremacy.

In the Durban riots which took place at just a little earlier than this time last year, when we were out there, more Zulus died than

Indians, although the Zulus were attacking the Indians and the Indians weren't hitting back. The Zulus were shot by the South African police.

Also at the same time, far further north in the Union of South Africa, a man who had a car with no brakes ran down and killed a Bantu and his wife was fined, I think, 25 shillings – but it may have been 27 shillings and sixpence.

Anything can happen to a native in South Africa – any form of violence, carrying through as far as murder, and you may rest assured that the person who kills him or ill-treats him won't suffer in any real way at all.

The present government that is there at the moment is now issuing forms to ascertain everybody's race, and they give you the blanks to fill in – you can fill yourself in as European, African, Asiatic, or other Coloured . . . The greatest credit I can claim for our party is that when asked to fill in our race on leaving the Union we filled in on the relevant line the word 'human'.

I'm sorry, there's just one point I ought to make and it is this – that the present South African policy is one of going backwards . . . The average native there, and the native spokesman, is prepared to say that he is quite willing to accept the white man there as his superior and his guide . . . One of the tragic things is that all his representation is being taken away from him – the representation that he has been given over years, all that advance is now being taken away and there's an attempt to suppress all forms of native representation in the South African government.

About a month went by, and then, on 21 April 1950, came the news that Dr Malan's government was to ban BBC news relays via the South African Broadcasting Corporation from 1 July. The reason: 'Politics,' said Franz Erasmus, the Minister of Posts and Telegraphs. 'South Africa wants to keep politics out of its radio news service, but the BBC is not prepared to do so.' He then quoted, as an example, John Arlott's 'Nazi' comment. 'But, good heavens, that was not in a news broadcast, but a feature programme,' cried members of the opposition. 'It was politics,' declared the Minister. It showed the sort of thing put out by the BBC. He was not going to run the risk of having South Africa's broadcast stations putting out something similar.

The London *Evening Standard*, in a leading article, rushed to the South African Minister's support:

It is quite monstrous that the BBC should allow such attacks to be made on a friendly Dominion ... There will be no disposition in this country to condone the action of Dr Malan in banning the BBC news, for that is an illiberal and intolerant act. But for the BBC to allow such provocation to take place is equally deplorable and can only be regarded with dismay by those who seek to further the unity of the Empire.

Any speaker over the BBC is liable to be regarded as a spokesman of British opinion, if not of the British government. The BBC must set right this wrong at once and should take adequate steps to prevent any similar occurrence taking place in the future.

The *Rand Daily Mail* for 1 May felt there was no case for grovelling, still less for the fettering of criticism, and reacted to the *Standard's* insistence that the BBC 'right this wrong':

We appreciate the desire underlying this demand, which is that nothing shall be done to hinder 'the further unity of the Empire'. At the same time it is as well to remark that the *Evening Standard's* observations, besides proposing a new limitation of the freedom of speech, contain a serious misstatement of fact.

Mr Arlott's observation was made last month. But the South African government's decision to stop relaying the BBC broadcasts was taken nearly two years ago, and was one of the first steps considered by the present government when it came to power. While, then, Mr Arlott's words were quoted by Mr Erasmus last week in support of the government's decision, they cannot be regarded as the cause of it.

As regards the statement itself, of course Mr Arlott went too far. But there are certain features which must be held to mitigate this. It is, for example, a fact that during the war very many Nationalists, including some now in extremely high positions, hoped that Nazi Germany would win. It is a fact that General Poole has been relegated to a position of comparative obscurity because of the distinguished part he played in leading the South African forces to victory against Nazi Germany, and that one of the earliest acts of the government, on its advent to power, was to release a pro-Nazi traitor. It is true that, in the early days of the war, eminent Nationalists drew up a proposed constitution for South Africa which embodied a number of ideas on race, freedom of thought, and other such matters, which were remarkably similar to those previously adopted by Adolf

Hitler. Nor can it be denied that much of our recent legislation savours of dictatorship.

Presumably it was the cumulative impression caused by such events that led Mr Arlott, in the necessary haste of a quiz, to make his unguarded remark. But if he had said that many of the measures of the present government are strongly reminiscent of Nazism, he would have been perfectly right.

Ten days later, the *Johannesburg Star* fuelled the controversy:

Which are the countries that resent criticism to the point of trying to have it suppressed? The answer in almost every case is the totalitarian countries. By appearing, more than once recently, to put itself in this gallery, South Africa has merely helped to reinforce the arguments of the critics.

The disturbing fact about Mr Arlott's broadcast is not that he was wrong on nearly every detail of his indictment, but that broadly speaking what he thought about the Union after a brief visit is what many visitors think. The State Information Office itself admitted in its official report that outside opinion has never been more critical of South Africa. That is the situation that has to be met – and not by gagging the critics.

Three days after that, on Saturday 13 May, the *Durban Daily Dispatch* adopted a conciliatory tone:

During his stay in South Africa Mr Arlott won the admiration and respect of all who heard him – and all who met him. It will be, therefore, a matter of personal regret to thousands of South Africans that Mr Arlott has got himself into the government's bad books and the regret will be, not that he criticised the Nationalist government, but that in doing so he has robbed us of the pleasure of welcoming him once again to the Union . . .

It was probably very naughty of Mr Arlott to tell home listeners to the BBC that the Nationalist government in South Africa was predominantly Nazi and that most of the cabinet ministers supported Hitler during the war – but Mr Arlott spoke no more than the truth. It was probably very naughty to insinuate that 'almost anything can happen to a native in South Africa with impunity'; but our court records will prove that what Mr Arlott said is more or less right. Sentences imposed on Europeans who kill or assault natives are in no way comparable in severity with those imposed on natives who kill or assault Europeans. Finally, Mr Arlott may have been anticipating coming events when he said that native representation was being taken away, that all advance is now denied the native, and that the Union government was pursuing a policy of repression – but can any fair-minded South African deny the truth of Mr Arlott's assertions?

Judging by the letters that were printed, John also had a majority of readers' support both at home and away:
From the *Evening Standard*, 2 May:

If Dr Malan sees fit to take action against the BBC for allowing their speakers to express uncensored opinions with which they do not necessarily agree, it only proves that John Arlott was more justified than I, for one, thought at the time.

Evening Standard, 24 May:

As a British subject of thirty years' residence in South Africa, I entirely agree with John Arlott and admire him for having had the courage to say what he did.

Cape Times, Cape Town, South Africa, 19 May:

Why should Mr Erasmus take exception to Mr Arlott's remarks on South Africa? They appear to be very near the truth however unpalatable . . .

Even a Czechoslovakian Communist newspaper supported John's stand. A. Dicks, however, a correspondent from Plymouth, was not at all concerned about the controversy that had been created. He simply wanted to know when John Arlott had played for England. A few of those who actually had played for England were also annoyed that John had proclaimed his views so publicly. Denis Compton and Godfrey Evans felt, as did others, that it was hypocritical to accept the wonderful hospitality that had been given in South Africa, not to say anything at the time, and then, once safely home, to berate the land which had welcomed them all so readily and in which they had been official guests. Godfrey, who had a great liking for John, laughed ruefully when he said: 'It was tactless and made it awkward for us with our friends over there.' Counsel for the defence would respond by saying that it was not the individual with whom Mr Arlott was at variance, rather the system.

At the weekly conference of the BBC's controllers and heads in Broadcasting House, Arlott's 'outburst', as it had been referred to, was at the top of the agenda. A transcript of the broadcast was to hand; a copy had already been sent to South Africa at the request of their government. It was quickly realised that John, though voicing his opinions powerfully and emotionally, had not said much more than had Lady Violet Bonham-Carter on a previous programme. The Director-General of the BBC, Sir William Haley, listening to the views around the table, was not overly concerned, as he was under the impression that John was no longer a member of BBC staff. But when it was pointed out to him that L.T.J. Arlott was still a full-time productorial employee, with an allocated number – 26655 – Haley wanted to know why he was appearing on a programme where he could express editorial judgement.

Nobody could immediately think of a ready answer to such an obvious question. That did not stop several of them from trying. Obviously Arlott was a splendid broadcaster, instinctive and intelligent, and a valued member of the *Any Questions?* panel, said one. A founder member, emphasised another. Much of the success of the programme was due to his forthright views, argued a third.

Haley listened carefully. Though much indignation had been expressed in the newspapers, there had been a record number (for the programme) of seventy-three letters in John's favour from staunch supporters as far afield as Shetland and Sweden. Finally, it was decided that John should be allowed to appear on any programme for which he was required, including *Any Questions?*, for an amount not less than he had been receiving as a member of staff. In essence, this was pushing the issue aside – a non-solution. Up to now John had been categorised 'Staff, no fee'. In other words, because he was 'salaried personnel' he did not qualify for the separate payments that freelance contributors normally received. But as he was performing duties that clearly fell outside his job description (that of a producer), he was eligible for what was called 'staff contribution'. So, an amount decided by his Head of Department – usually somewhat less than that secured by a non-member of the BBC – would be added to his monthly salary.

The BBC authorities were in a tricky situation. They did not want to be seen bowing to political pressure, nor, God forbid, restricting free speech. It was put to John that it would be in his interests to leave the permanent staff of the BBC and to go freelance – he would almost certainly be better off financially. John wrestled with the idea for some time. Should he take the step? What if all the outside engagements dried up? He was in no position to take monetary risks of that magnitude. It was also pointed out to him that, because he was a member of staff, his views were being accepted in some quarters as those of the BBC. Another furore had been provoked by remarks he made on *Any Questions?* on 31 March 1950, only a few weeks after the programme on which he had made his comments about South Africa. They were reported under a *Sunday Empire News* banner headline, 'Arlott Angers the Scientists':

A member of the public asked why so many scientists appeared to 'lean towards a Communist trend of thought' and Mr Arlott is reported to have referred to a 'Society of Scientific Workers' which had been 'joined by many scientists without knowing that it was part of the Communist party'.

Solicitors acting for the Association of Scientific Workers protested to the broadcasting barons. There was no 'Society' of Scientific Workers, they said, and the ASW vigorously denied any connection with the Communist Party.

At this time, so soon after the Second World War and with McCarthyism rife in the USA, any mention of 'reds under the bed' or fascist thought was emotionally charged. Very few people had escaped entirely unscathed from the events of the recent past. Again, on an *Any Questions?* programme from the Winter Gardens in Bournemouth the previous week, replying to a query on retrospective legislation, John had raised the temperature by remarking that 'Hitler brought in retrospective legislation' and described it as 'a crime against humanity . . . and whether it's done on a large level or a small, it must always be contrary to the interests of honest and equitable law'.

The *Sunday Empire News* reporter concluded his piece: 'A BBC spokesman told me yesterday, "Mr Arlott has a contract which enables him to express his views, which on these occasions were those of a private individual."' As John was an established member of staff, such a contract would have been unusual.

Any Questions? had started as a West of England programme in October 1948, and its success as another form of 'Brains Trust', whose members were not too 'brains conscious', as one newspaper put it, quickly ensured a repeat on the national network. Its appeal was threefold. Firstly, it was lively and unscripted and performed in front of a critically responsive audience; secondly, there was the immediacy of the content, with current issues being argued in a civilised manner; but primarily it was the strong, distinctive characters who made the programme. Opinionated performers like Bob Boothby, Robert Henriques and Mary Stocks, and the ruminative wisdom and common sense of such as Ralph Wightman, Jack Longland and A.G. Street, not forgetting J.A., made compelling listening. They all had a way with words, and having chosen them knew how to maximise their effect. And in the chair, marshalling the jousting with gentle humour, was the urbane Freddie Grisewood, who said neither too little nor too much. Grisewood's weakness was that sometimes he allowed members of the panel to deliver homilies to the nation which had little to do with the question asked.

Any Questions? became a kind of vicarious platform for the people and, with radio still the predominant force in home entertainment, the publicity it engendered was considerable. Eventually, its growing listenership led to an origination on the national Home Service, with a greater concentration on wider matters of moment than those of regional interest. But its fundamental strength had precisely been as a regional programme, distanced from Portland Place and its pall of professional neutrality. There were those who worried that the change to a nationwide broadcast would presage a degree of sanitisation.

Officially, John was still allowed to appear on *Any Questions?* 'if required'. In practice, because of the concern felt over his ambiguous position and his predilection for plain speaking, he was no longer required. His absence was noticed:

Bristol Evening Post, 23 August 1950:

I am perturbed by the growing right wing political bias of the BBC's *Any Questions?* programme. John Arlott was at times the only champion of progressive thought in the programme. Now he has been quietly pushed out. Why?
    Irate Labour listener

Bristol Evening World, 4 September 1950:

I, too, regret the sudden departure of John Arlott from the *Any Questions?* team. Even those who do not share his progressive outlook will agree that his 'sacking' from the team leaves a nasty taste in the mouth. His clear, witty, outspoken comments have been like a breath of fresh air in an otherwise stuffy atmosphere.

In the same paper, on 31 August:

Anyone who listened to John Arlott on the *Any Questions?* programme realised he was a supporter of the Labour Party, and he and others like him were given plenty of scope by the BBC to express their opinions. As far as the BBC favouring the Conservatives, in my opinion, and that of many others, it is the Labour Party they favour.

John continued to be kicked about as if he were political football. Even the programme's producer, Nicholas Crocker, defending *Any Questions?* against accusations of political bias, vouchsafed the opinion 'that John Arlott gave the Labour Party more than a fair crack of the whip'. The *Northampton Chronicle and Echo* joined the *Daily Worker* in thinking that the programme had suffered a slight falling-off in quality soon after it had earned a national hearing, and that the absence of John Arlott had not helped. 'What he thinks, it seems,' wrote the *Echo*, 'has been tinged with a radicalism that not even Lord Craigavon could object to.' *Public Opinion*, in the person of Richard Findlater, asked whether 'the plain man of our time was really a farmer [a reference to Ralph Wightman and A.G. Street]'. He missed John Arlott, 'as a balance to those sturdy and repetitive agriculturists'.

For over three years – between 2 June 1950 and 30 October 1953 – John was not used on the programme at all. This, however, had little effect on the public's awareness of him as a broadcaster. For the moment he may not have been on *Any Questions?*, but he was not kept silent elsewhere, nor was he short of things to do.

11

Bordeaux and the Grape

On leaving South Africa in March 1949, the 'Speedbird' flying boat had the Cape in its wake and Johannesburg in its sights. After an overnight pit-stop it landed on the Zambezi, Lake Victoria and the Nile before reaching Augusta, Sicily.

John was drained, not so much from the flight as from the travel, socialising, work and other activities of the past few months of the England cricket tour; most of it had been enjoyable and rewarding, but it had demanded energy and emotion. He needed a respite for a few days to replenish his reserves, to let the world carry on going round without feeling the need to do the same.

Taormina, on the east coast of Sicily, against the backdrop of Mount Etna, was an ideal spot to stop and relax. And it was during the week he spent there that John 'discovered' the benefits and enjoyment of the grape.

He had drunk wine before, according to his wife Dawn, although in Britain at that time it was a comparative rarity, mostly exclusive to restaurants, and not available in ordinary shops. But now, sitting in the little *albergo* with a carafe to accompany the pasta, John was able to relish wine as if he was experiencing it for the first time. Part of its allure, of course, came from the fact that it was a local wine being drunk in a congenial atmosphere on its own soil. Three days of abstinence following his unremitting consumption of whisky and beer in South Africa heightened the effect of the Muscat. In the following days, a couple of visits to a vineyard in the company of two Americans and a trip to the tavernas of Syracuse (in an undertaker's van with a corpse in the back) cemented the conversion. He had discovered, like Ernest Hemingway before him, that 'wine is one of the most civilised things in the world and one of the natural things of the world that has been brought to the greatest perfection, and it offers a greater range for enjoyment and appreciation than, possibly, any other purely sensory thing'.

As always with John, a new enthusiasm led to a shelf-full of books on the subject within a short time. But in this case it was the practice rather than the theory that was the primary interest. In the years to come, no one was to practise the theory more assiduously.

At first, like most beginners, he drank only sweet white wine. He had not yet developed discernment or taste, not yet found mentors who would happily indulge such a committed student. Richard Aldington advised caution: 'With every glass of wine a glass of water.' But John's spirit was too emboldened to take heed.

More cultivated guidance arrived through a chain of circumstances in the months which followed. John was engaged to provide written commentaries and summaries for the London *Evening News* on the Test matches in the 1950–51 MCC tour of Australia. One day his friend John Marshall, the editor of the paper, came across him drinking what looked very much like champagne. John informed him that it was in fact a sparkling Languedoc, which was bottled in a similar way. Marshall was immediately interested. How could he get hold of some? He was soon to be holding a christening party for his son at which the upper stratum of management was to be present. He could not afford a large quantity of champagne, and this would be an acceptable substitute. John put his editor in touch with the East End importer, and a few cases were obtained at a fraction of the price that the equivalent amount of champagne would have cost. The party went well. As a former political and war correspondent, Marshall was well aware of the advantages of diplomatic oil, and was delighted when his chairman, Lord Rothermere, complimented him on the quality of the champagne and asked for the name of his wine merchant. John then reaped the benefit of his advice when Marshall asked him to write about wine for the paper. The job was not arduous, and required only the occasional article – and much 'compleat imbibing' – in order to recommend wines for his readers. He had no difficulty in meeting the requirements.

Two trips resulted from the appointment: the first, a press tour of vineyards in Bordeaux, triggered the second, a BBC tour of vineyards in Bordeaux. Laurence Gilliam, Head of BBC Features, overheard John enthusing about his journalist's ticket in a Broadcasting House watering hole and asked him to join the party, which included the revered septuagenarian André Simon, author of many scholarly books on wine, the irrepressible broadcaster Wynford Vaughan-Thomas, and Gilliam himself. There was a gap of a month between the two visits.

On the press jaunt was the snappily-dressed *Daily Mirror* correspondent Noel Whitcomb, who had achieved overnight stardom following his discovery of a talking Jack Russell terrier. Apparently, nobody discovered whether its bark was worse than its bite, but the guttural grunts that purported to be words were a seven-day wonder for editors in search of a quirky story. Also on the guest list were Jock Murray, of the publishers John Murray, his young literary-minded wife, who was more interested in Montaigne than Merlot – Montaigne had connections with the area – and Stanley Baron of the *News Chronicle* together with his teenage daughter Sheila. Acting as host was the viticulteur Daniel Querre, a mainspring of the Bordeaux wine trade, described by Whitcomb in his 'Under the Counter' column as 'short, fat, a little bald and covered by one great big smile'. He went on: '[Querre] kisses all of us on both cheeks, nearly shakes the hands off your wrists and invites us back to his home – Château Monbousquet, where he makes the wine.'

Whitcomb also noted that 'John Arlott is just the sort of character to have on this sort of trip. He continues talking amiably in the most remarkable (ribby) French with a Hampshire accent – which he understands perfectly but which is a great puzzle to people of all other nationalities.'

In Whitcomb's autobiography *A Particular Kind of Fool*, published some forty years later, he remembers an idyllic weekend which finished with a picnic on a hillside above the small Gironde wine town of St Emilion. Monsieur Querre's son Alain, much the same age as Stanley Baron's daughter, had joined the party and was devoting considerable attention to her. So much so that he discovered a hitherto unknown ability to converse fluently in English. Whitcomb continues:

> It was a perfect evening. The air was warm and fragrant with the scent of jasmine. As twilight gave way to a starry sky, the lights in the valley below flicked on. On such a night as this it was as clear as the moon to all except one of us that young Alain wished to be talking to the pretty English girl.
>
> The odd man out who did not notice this was John Arlott, and the reason he did not notice it was that he was preoccupied by the extraordinary discovery that young Alain had never heard of the game of cricket: John, speaking uninhibitedly in franglais, was determined, if only out of gratitude to his hosts, to put right this lacuna in the education of Daniel Querre's son.
>
> 'Dans le jeu de cricket il y a deux équipes, you see,' said Arlott, his voice rising alone above the gentle chatter of the cicadas, 'et dans chaque équipe il y a onze hommes. L'équipe qui sont fielding – vous comprenez "fielding", Alain? – sont dirigé par leur capitaine aux leurs places dans le champ – probablement mid-on, mid-off, possiblement silly mid-off, slips, gulley, square leg . . .'
>
> 'Square legs, m'sieu?' inquired Alain, disbelieving.

'Oui, square leg. C'est le nom d'un position dans le champ. Ils sont tous sur le qui vive pour attraper le bal dans les mains après il à été frappé par le batsman.'

'Par le quoi, m'sieu?' asked Alain, bemused and mystified and longing to get away and sit with Stanley Baron's daughter, who was by herself at the end of the terrace, gazing at the moon.

'Par le *batsman*,' repeated John. 'Je ne sais pas le mot en français – peut-être il n'existe pas parce que le jeu de cricket est obviously pas bien connu ici, not yet anyway. Alors, revenons à nos moutons, un des hommes in the fielding side est dirigé par le capitaine à prendre le bal. Il est le bowler. Cet homme marche pour un considerable distance behind le wicket, et puis il commence à courir à grande vitesse en direction des stumps. Vous me suivez, Alain?'

'Oui, m'sieu,' nodded the unhappy but perfectly mannered boy.

'Voilà,' continued John. 'Cet homme, le bowler, jette le bal aussi vite que possible at the batsman.'

Alain sat up, shocked. 'To *hit* heem?' he inquired.

'Non, non, non, non, non, non, non – to get him au dehors. Si le bal frappe les stumps, le batsman is au dehors – he's out.'

At this point the kindly Daniel Querre came over to talk to Arlott, and thereby to rescue his bewildered son, who moved swiftly over to sit beside Stanley Baron's daughter.

When Daniel Querre discovered that John was scheduled to return to the region a month later, he invited him to stay as a guest at the château during the intervening period. After a couple of phone calls to get clearance, John was delighted to accept. Ever after, John used to say that he based his own board on Querre's. From him he assimilated the *rituelles de vin et présentation de table* by which to achieve the maximum enhancement and therefore enjoyment of good food and wine. These maxims were without any affectation; their endurance was founded on simple practicality and passed on rather in the way of a family inheritance. As a natural outgrowth every meal became an occasion, bringing together food, wine, people and conversation: nourishment for the mind as well as the senses.

Château Monbousquet, white and shuttered, is situated beside a lake at St-Sulpice-de-Faleyrens, close to St Emilion, in pastoral countryside. Its origins are thought to go back to 1540, when it was the property of one François de Lesceurs. In 1684 the old house was reconstructed as it stands today by Jacques de Ceres and given as a wedding present to his bride for use as a holiday home. Subsequently a succession of mostly absentee owners led to a deterioration of the building, the grounds and the production of wine. The château was bought by Querre just after the Second World War, in very run-down condition with ivy creeping through the main hall. He quickly set about restoring it to a glory it had not known for at least 150 years. At the same time he was producing and selling wine and travelling hundreds of kilometres to meet potential buyers. Daniel was a man of great energy. When he was not tasting, blending, analysing and vending, he was likely as not to be found chairing discussions at the Conseil Interprofessionel de Vin de Bordeaux. And if he happened not to be there he might be attending to business at his offices and wine cellars in Libourne or seeing clients in the courtyard of the Hôtel de Plaisance, seated with an apéritif at a green wooden café table on top of the ancient monolithic chapel. Gesticulating expansively, pressing a point with volubility, the only accompaniment would be the sudden explosive laughter of his companions at a communal joke. Distant, staccato conversations among visiting church-fanciers and connoisseurs of rood-screens would be audible only to the keenest ear. The periodic clanging from the bell-tower marking the passage of time, though, could penetrate even the dullest. Travelling from one staging-post to another, Daniel would pre-empt his imminent arrival with an imperious blast from his car-horn which was not just noise, it was music. The length and loudness of the sound indicated both the flotsam on the road and the speed of his approach.

Dinner at the château was an experience John never forgot. Daniel would be seated at the head of the table, surrounded by family and friends. Some of the guests might be unanticipated, having received a spontaneous invitation from Daniel that day when he was on his rounds. There was no telephone at the château, so Madame Querre would have prepared in abundance for such an eventuality. She had been busy in the kitchen, helped by girls from the local village, a culinary education for them as well as for the wide-eyed visitor. In later years, whenever John recalled the cooking at Monbousquet, he wrinkled his nose as if trying to recapture the wonderful aromas from the kitchen. 'Fantastic,' he would say. 'The sizzling and the burning of vine prunings and roots on which they roasted and grilled and devilled – "*aux sarments*". One night there would be a dish of lampreys smoking on the table, cooked in red wine, leeks and its own blood – very delicate and not at all fishy. Hard to find, they can only be caught for about a fortnight each year. Henry VIII ate them all (*chuckle*). On another, *Entrecôte à la Bordelaise* with a rare herb sauce, and I remember once we had Agen goose stuffed with plums. Oh, and the oysters from Arcachon.' By this time in the recital, John would have stirred gastric juices that had never really been dormant, and would require details of the forthcoming meal. Having satisfied his curiosity and opened another bottle by way of reassurance, he would continue. 'And the wine was superb. Old Daniel was an immensely kind man. He taught me so much. At the end of the meal, he used to bring out this great shaggy bottle of *eau de vie de marc* covered in cobwebs and say, "Not for boys," and he was dead right, it wasn't.'

Since Daniel's death his son Alain, now married to Sheila Baron, has taken his place with similar charm and efficiency. Those qualities are much needed, for he has to superintend around twenty-five thousand visitors to the château each year, for whom thirteen thousand bottles of wine are opened. The thirty hectares yield some six hundred barrels annually, and the claret is regularly classified 'Grand Cru'. Whereas once there were a hundred grape-pickers, the harvest is now in the hands of five families and modern technology. Although young at the time, Alain remembers John's arrival at the château:

> He was so natural. He had no education in wine at all when he came to Monbousquet but thank God he came, because he really enjoyed wine afterwards. He found the right man to teach him by example for he was sharing our life. My father worked long hours because he had to restore the estate which had been in very bad condition. It was an enormous amount of work, he got up early in the morning and worked till late at night, so he had no time to have a pupil, as I don't have either. They can follow me. I'll take them everywhere. Everything I do they can see. They can put questions, I'll explain why. That's the way to learn.
>
> And that's the way John was with my father. They loved each other. Because my father liked people who were so honest, so open, so direct, so normal. I too, I hate everything which is pretentious and not natural. The first quality of a man is to be natural.

It was during a weekend wine festival in 1991 that I had gone to visit Alain at Monbousquet. Seated on a bench with dusk falling on a balmy June evening, a few metres from where his father now lies buried beside the lake in the grounds, he warmed to his theme. For a moment he could relax. A garden reception for several hundred people was well under way. On a score of tables an astonishing array of provender was to be seen: *anguilles à l'escavèche*; *pluvier à l'ancienne*; *coquilles aux asperges*; *genoise aux fruits*; *Charlotte Malakoff* – the very names watered the mouth. Alongside, beautifully sculpted pastries and delicacies and, standing separately from

the tuck, a choice of château bottles *exclusivité de la Maison Daniel Querre*:
Puy-Razac, Bel-Air Fouroque, Saint-Louis (Saint-Estèphe), Latrezotte
Barsac, Victoria (Landiras), and, of course, Monbousquet (St Emilion).
Forming a perimeter to this ambrosian spectacle were fairy lights which
twinkled ever more brightly on the poplars and the portals as Alain, gently
twirling a nearly empty wine-glass, continued:

> We have the old family system of sharing food. It's practically as
> important as sharing death. I cannot share food with a guy I don't
> like. I avoid doing it. There are people who have never sat at my
> table – will never sit at my table. If you have people around your
> table, it means you want to make a friend with them. And then you
> must be open and say everything that is in your head and your heart
> and wine helps because it is so special. The way you approach wine
> is the way you approach life.

Listening to Alain Querre philosophising, it was easy to see how John
had become a convert to this way of life. The idea of the wine-grower
expressing what the soil has to say, rather in the manner of a good musician
serving and reflecting a composer, would have appealed to him instinctively. The social aspect, too: family and friends gathering for a communal
repast at the end of a day during which they had gone their separate ways
became, with him, a rite almost sanctified. The evening was spent at the
table: to watch television or to disperse to an armchair in another room
would be to lose the sense of ubiety, the condition of being in a particular
place.

Hard on the heels of Monbousquet, the BBC tour of Bordeaux was
like an unserious seminar. Perhaps more than any other person at that
time, André Simon – beguiling, articulate, and above all good-natured –
had preached a fresh standard of gastronomy for Britain, together with
an appreciation of accessible wine. Together with his companions, John
picked up as much as he could, which helped to consolidate his new-found
knowledge and enthusiasm.

Back home again, John adopted the evangelist's role. Much missionary
work needed to be done. The wine revolution in the UK was a long way
off; beer was still very much the macho drink. In his *Evening News* column
'Table Talk' in January 1951, he enlisted the help of a Liberal forefather:

> Mr Gladstone believed that wine was a better drink than beer
> because it was a *family* drink. Wine ought, he said, to be as cheap
> as beer – and as readily accessible to the working man. He reduced

the customs duty to make it so, but while regular wine-drinkers with large cellars took advantage of the lower price, the working man stuck to beer – with no evidence that he had ever even given wine a trial . . .

Now the position that Gladstone contrived has come again. Wine is as cheap as beer – that is to say a bottle of wine can be as cheap as bottled beer for the same number of people. For instance, four pint bottles of beer among four people for supper – and a pint bottle of light ale costs me 1s.6d. – 6s. altogether.

Yet for 5s.6d. I can buy a bottle of wine which is at least equally adequate for four. Certainly it will not knock anyone over, but then neither will a pint bottle of beer apiece and, in any case, wine is not a particularly intoxicating beverage, especially when drunk, as it usually is, with a meal.

That is why there is more liquor drunk – in terms of alcohol – yet less drunkenness in the Latin or wine-drinking countries than there is here.

The article finished with a word of warning:

If a local football team calls itself Basingstoke Arsenal, it will not win the F.A. Cup because of the name 'Arsenal'. By roughly the same token, a wine which calls itself Australian 'Burgundy' is not in fact Burgundy at all. It may be a very pleasant drink but it is not Burgundy because it does not come from Burgundy. Therefore for the first trial, it is wiser to buy the French original.

Once more, John had let his faithful friend, controversy, off the leash. The response was predictable, and it came from C.R. Mackay of the Australian Wine Board in London:

I warmly endorse the greater part of John Arlott's article 'Wine is as Cheap as Beer', but he erred in suggesting that an Australian or South African Burgundy 'is not Burgundy at all because it does not come from Burgundy'. As well say that Ayrshire cattle are not Ayrshires unless they are fed on Ayrshire pastures.

John was not willing to let the matter rest. He felt he had the Australian Wine Board on a tricky wicket, scraping for excuses. Mr Mackay's argument would be a strong one, he wrote, if his Ayrshire cattle comparison was a true parallel:

Cattle are *bred* and, wherever they are bred, exhibit the *constant* qualities of the breed. The wine-grape, however, is in character a product of its environment – the soil – and of climate. The latter has so much effect that a hundred yards' distance between two vine-yards on a Burgundy hillside – with its resultant difference in sun-shine received – produces distinct differences between the two wines.

Thus, the same grape produces burgundy when grown in one district, and champagne in another. In other words, there are, in wines, no such constants as in cattle breeding. Moreover, an Ayrshire cow is unmistakably an Ayrshire, you recognise it at once: how many so-called 'burgundies' are unmistakably recognisable as Burgundy? . . .

There can be only one valid reason for giving the name 'Burgundy' to a wine which does not come from Burgundy. That is, that it is an identical wine – and if Mr Mackay can produce an Australian 'Burgundy' identical with a Corton, a Romanée Conti or a Chambertin, I am his customer for life.

There are good wines in the Empire – wines good enough to sail under their own colours, not those of other countries. South Africa already has such a wine, which has deservedly won itself a reputation – Constantia.

If I buy a bottle labelled 'Australian Burgundy', I shall not be buying what I, and most wine-drinkers, know as Burgundy. On the other hand, I am more than prepared to give a fair trial to a wine from Australia which bears, honestly, the name of its own vineyard or district.

A bottle of 'Yering', or 'Hunter River', or 'Rutherglen' – given the chance – might well establish itself as a good wine, an acceptable alternative to the *vin ordinaire* of Burgundy, in its own right – and under its real name.

History has proved John Arlott right. The 'Crayfish' agreement, whereby South Africa and France have promised not to gazump one another's territory with names, is now established. And an accord is being drafted which will see to it that 'Burgundy' is no longer used as a description of any wine that is not from that unique, scrubby hillside of the Côte d'Or.

12

Football, and a Holiday on Alderney

While he was in France, John went one Sunday morning into the town of Bordeaux, looked in at a church service, took a leisurely lunch, and walked along the Cours Georges Clemenceau. At No. 55 he turned through an archway into a somewhat sparsely furnished sports club. There he found cyclists, runners, players of hockey and pelota and, the purpose of his visit, a clutch of footballers. The Bordeaux side were the reigning champions of France. That afternoon they were playing Strasbourg, unbeaten in their first eleven matches, and topping the table seven points ahead of Bordeaux.

The resultant article which he wrote for *Illustrated* focused on the high watchability of the game, highlighted by the Bordeaux 'ball-laying forward line playing romantic rather than utilitarian' football in their convincing victory. The Continental style of play was then widely unknown in Britain, and John made comparisons with the more physical aspects of the English game.

Football had been a part of his life ever since he had watched the local Basingstoke side as a boy. The only thing Basingstoke had in common with Bordeaux was the ball, which they hacked about on a steeply sloping pitch that was grazed by cattle for the rest of week. In 1954, John recalled the ground's amenities in an article for the *Spectator*: 'It had a corrugated-iron grandstand, two dressing-rooms, and a bath which was filled from the rain-water tank, warmed, a few minutes before the end of the match, with a second boiling of the kettle which was used for tea at half-time. From this ablution – commenced on muddy days with boots on – the players came out shining, if sometimes streaked with mud at the hairline, to walk through the winter evening gloom into the shop-lights of Saturday night and public admiration.'

As a youngster in the 1920s, John had started to support Reading. He would pedal the eighteen miles there, eighteen miles back on an ancient bicycle for an outlay of tenpence: sixpence admission, twopence for a programme and a penny each for two mineral waters for the journeys.

Reading remained his club, although later Southampton received just as much loyalty. After a Reading match at Elm Park he would go to the creosoted wooden hut which was in place before a stand was built, to hunt for autographs and gaze upon stalwarts of the side such as the centre-half Alf Messer; the two internationals, Welsh left-half Dai Evans and Irish left-back Billy McConnell; and the fearless Lancastrian goalkeeper Joe Duckworth.

In the 1930s he got to know the Reading manager Joe Edelston, who, when war came, had assembled a team which was on the brink of promotion back into the Second Division. John also got to know another Reading regular, Joe's son Maurice, and they became close friends. Maurice Edelston played for the England Amateur XI in the Berlin Olympics in 1936 and then, still as an amateur, for the full England side in five wartime internationals. He was an inside-forward who was always in the game and had an exceptional sense of anticipation. His appeal to John, though, lay outside football. He was a classicist who for many years taught French at the Reading Blue Coat School, and he had a fine academic brain.

Hazel Edelston, Maurice's widow, remembers a weekend in the late 1940s or early 1950s when John and Dawn came to stay. At the dinner-table on the Saturday evening, by which time they had been joined by 'the mad Irish scriptwriter' Harry Craig, an argument developed over the scoring of penalties. Apparently, three had been missed in Reading's game that afternoon.

'Anybody can hit a penalty,' declared John. 'Certainly one in three.'

'Oh, can they?' challenged Maurice. 'Well, if you think it's so easy, we'll go out there and try it.'

Next morning after breakfast, Maurice rang Fred May, the secretary of Reading, who agreed to open up the ground for them. 'They were all a bit hungover,' laughed Hazel. 'Harry lined up a ball and Maurice went into goal. It had been raining in the night, absolutely poured, and John ran towards the ball, gave an almighty kick and fell flat on his backside. All his suit was muddy, he hurt his back and didn't have any more attempts after that.'

Having found the hard way to prove that his friend knew more about the difficulties of football than he did, John dedicated his book *Concerning Soccer* (1952) to Maurice Edelston 'in gratitude for much patient and expert instruction in the craft he has mastered with such distinction'. *Concerning Soccer*, claimed the blurb, was 'one of the first attempts to place Association Football on the level of serious critical appreciation'. Although much of the book consists of John's articles which had appeared in such journals as *The F.A. Bulletin, Illustrated, Everybody's Weekly, John Bull, Time and Tide* and the *Evening News*, the writing, as one would expect, is lucid and compelling, with perception beyond the norms of the sports pages.

John had been instrumental in finding a place behind the microphone for Maurice at the 1948 London Olympics. Edelston commentated on hockey, which he did so ably that it led to a career broadcasting on football.

In 1949 John enlisted the help of Maurice Edelston and Wilfred Wooller in the book of recollections of cricket, rugby and soccer, *Wickets, Tries and Goals*. It was well reviewed but, as is often the case with enterprises which try to combine more than one interest, did not empty the public purse.

John had been commentating on football for the BBC for almost as long as he had on cricket, but far less regularly. The measured prose which suited his cricket commentary so perfectly was not so well adapted to football. The game just did not provide enough space for him to amplify and explain, or to draw a character study with pause and pay-off. John had become *the* cricket commentator. For football, it was like putting a close friend, who occupied a treasured and distinct position in a corner of one's life, into another compartment where there was no association of any kind – like finding Raymond Glendenning or Stewart Macpherson announcing the cricket scores. Cricket commentary always remained John's predominant role in the public consciousness, but the dangers of typecasting are well known, and so, particularly in the early years of his broadcasting career, he continued to look for work in other areas.

One of John's football commitments in 1951 was to give a commentary on the final of the Muratti Vase Competition – the inter-insular tourney in the Channel Islands. Although the competition was dominated by Jersey and Guernsey, it had been inaugurated on Alderney. And it was to Alderney that John and his family went on holiday that year. By this time four-part harmony existed in the Arlott household, as son Timothy had been born on 16 November 1950.

Holidays for John had been almost non-existent, nor had he felt any great need of them. He had become something of a workaholic, and so enjoyed every aspect of his busy schedule that not only did he feel he was on a permanent holiday, but to lie idly and inaccessibly on a beach seemed a waste of time. It was Maurice Edelston who urged him to have some consideration for his wife and children. The Edelstons used to rent a place on Hayling Island for their vacation, and in the summer of 1950 Dawn and five-year-old James joined them for a week. 'I remember after they arrived we went straight down to the beach,' said Hazel Edelston. 'The tide was out and Jimmy ran straight into the sea with his clothes on. I don't think he'd seen the sea before, he didn't know what it was. John wasn't a person for taking his wife and family on holiday, you see.'

Having had his arm twisted by Maurice Edelston, and with further persuasion from a neighbour in North London, Bill Tayleur, who told him that a holiday in Alderney would be like nowhere else, John finally took the plunge. Not literally, too often, nor did he spend much time with bucket and spade, for shortly after checking in, and armed with a letter of introduction from John Betjeman, he went to visit the writer T.H. White.

White, who at one time had taught at Stowe and was best-known for his Arthurian sequence *The Once and Future King*, had moved to Alderney in 1946. To strangers he could be disconcerting. He had a sarcastic eye and a sharp, satirical wit, and practised flights of extravagance that were all the more telling because of his normally quiet voice. He also had a flowing white beard, and wore a nightshirt which occasionally became a dayshirt too. Sometimes he didn't wear a shirt at all, but presented a symphony in scarlet – scarlet jersey, scarlet cummerbund, and a cassock of scarlet towelling.

White also tended to have weeks that were devoted to drink. These bouts habitually followed the times when he had been looking after groups of deaf and blind people, and so reflected a release of inner tension. For such periods, White was best left incommunicado. However, there might come a knock on his door, and at last he would stagger down the stairs to answer it. Outside, on one occasion, was a member of a religious sect. 'Have you found God?' was the question. Instead of the usual mild riposte, 'I didn't know he was lost,' White thundered, 'Don't be silly, man! I am God!'

This story, often told in the Marais Hotel at Market Square, never failed to get a laugh. The Marais, owned by Tommy Rose, who had once won the Cape to Cairo air race, was where the Arlotts stayed on that first visit. While John was enjoyably incarcerated at White's house, a team of cricketers from Jersey had congregated at the hotel and were waiting for him to present a cup. In John's enthusiasm to meet the great man, the arrangement had slipped his memory. More likely, perhaps, he was disinclined to tear himself away. At any rate, Dawn, waiting with the cricketers at the bar and keeping them liberally supplied with beer, was looking ever more distractedly at the clock. Eventually, after several hours had passed, and with darkness having fallen, she ventured out along the unlit cobbled streets in search of John. Having at last located the Frenchified three-storey house in Connaught Square, she found two extremely relaxed writers and several bottles that had not been neglected.

'Please come and see to these men,' she implored her husband. John was really in no fit state to see to anybody, but duty having called, and with Dawn's help, he too ventured forth over the cobbles – a slip here and there was par for the course – and back at the hotel he told a joke or two, and all was well.

'Tim' White was to have a profound influence on young Jimmy Arlott's life. He took a great liking to the young lad, now aged six, and over the years adopted the role of a benign schoolmaster with an avid pupil. White taught Jimmy to sail and fly-fish, to draw and paint, to speak verse and act in plays. 'He loved James,' said Dawn, 'and made a little theatre in his garden – a sort of Greek thing, half open-air with a bust of Hadrian. He was so inventive.' Subsequently, White sent what Dawn described as wonderful letters to her son, and there developed such a close relationship between them that for a time she and John actually began to worry. 'John was disapproving of Tim White, because he felt he was more interesting and important to James than he could ever be,' said Dawn candidly. In the end John wrote to White, voicing his anxieties over the attachment. He received a fairly reassuring reply: 'It is not your business to provide Jimmie with a world in which everybody is not his father and mother. The world will do that itself soon enough and at present you *are* his father and mother. The more you try to make him go your way, the more you will drive him the other way, and your only duty to him is to love him. Do relax.'

White, in fact, had complicated sexual alignments; he loved dressing up in his mother's jewellery, but he also recognised Dawn's charms with an offer of marriage (conveniently overlooking the fact that she was wed already – or perhaps that is what was convenient), with the proviso that he could beat her with a hairbrush. Dawn turned him down with a sweet smile. In spite of her earlier misgivings, she is sure there was nothing duplicitous in White's relationship with Jimmy. It would seem he had a genuine interest in and affection for a bright boy, and, like J.M. Barrie before him, there was no one better able to preserve a child's freshness of vision with its constant shifts of moral perspective.

13

Public Figure

During Dawn's pregnancy with Tim, the Arlotts had moved from Crouch End up the hill to Highgate. Barbara Forrester, John's secretary, helped them pack: 'There were so many books it seemed to take all day. But John opened bottles of wine and we sat on the floor and made a party out of it.'

'John said, "We can afford to move now,"' remembers Dawn. 'No. 21 Highgate Avenue was a pleasant Victorian semi. We had an attic converted for the children, which meant about five bedrooms. The dining-room was his library. What was a kitchen had to be the dining-room. I had to work in a place that was originally a scullery, but it was a very happy home.'

Not that John managed to spend any more time in it than he had in Barrington Road. He was a public figure now, and a willing captive of the obligations that came with the position. One Saturday morning, unusually, he was lying in bed reading the papers. The Rostrevor-Hamiltons were coming to dinner that evening, and Dawn was downstairs cleaning and preparing. She too would have liked to be lying in bed reading the papers, but time was pressing. A request in plain terms to John to Hoover the carpet led him to descend from above in his pyjamas. A domestic squabble ensued, during which John threw the vacuum cleaner across the room – which was not the sort of handling the manufacturers had envisaged – in Dawn's direction. The result was one forlorn husband travelling by bus and Underground to Regent Street to have the damaged implement repaired. Dawn now laughs at the absurdity of her fully undomesticated man transporting the very symbol of the house-trained.

Before the advent of holidays in Alderney, she and John used to get away for the occasional short break, with the help of neighbourly baby-sitters. Once they were invited to spend a couple of days at Longchamps by Ronnie Cornwell, the father of the writer John le Carré. Cornwell lived in a mansion in the Chalfonts, Buckinghamshire, and was a company director, property dealer, racehorse-owner and rogue. The Arlotts knew about the first three endowments, but only later became aware of the fourth. 'He was utterly good-looking with sleek grey hair,' said Dawn. 'When we flew over to France I was heavily pregnant with Tim. We had been given a suite at the Ritz and there were lots of parties with jockeys and trainers and film stars and so forth – I remember Michael Wilding was there. We were invited to gamble. John said bluntly, "I have no money to gamble with." So Ronnie Cornwell pulled out a wad of notes and said: "Take this, and when it's gone, stop." He was in the suite next to ours with his girlfriend or mistress or whoever. That night we heard a lot of shouting going on, the door opened, and this pale blue Bond Street lingerie came through it. "I never wear blue! What's the matter with you?" yelled the woman. I said to John, "Does she really mean it? If I wasn't pregnant, I'd pick them up."

'John didn't like horses, but it was an experience – a bit of the high life. He got rather embroiled with Cornwell before he saw the red light. Cornwell thought he was going to make money out of John, so he had to get away from him. He smelled a rat and got out in time.'

At a later date, Dawn and John went to a less extrovert gathering. 'It was a party for debtors and creditors,' said Dawn. 'Cornwell had gone broke for a million and three-quarters. But everything had been put in his wife's name.'

Besides the turf, Cornwell was known in cricket circles. Each year he would entertain the visiting international sides at his impressive home. He also dabbled in politics, standing as Liberal candidate for Yarmouth in the 1950 general election. John was asked to face the hustings as Liberal candidate in that same election by two different constituencies – Basingstoke and St Ives in Cornwall. Of the two, understandably, he favoured the offer from the North-West Hampshire Liberal Association. He was willing to stand, but the BBC 'could not see their way clear to release him during his present contract'. John was not altogether dismayed at being unavailable; apart from what he saw as the improbability of being elected, he had doubts as to whether he could afford to be a Member of Parliament. Nevertheless, the invitations were a recognition of his convincing handling of political issues on such programmes as *Any Questions?*. His Liberal stance, inherited mainly from his mother and grandfather, was endorsed further in the year following the election, when he acted as question-master for a public political Brains Trust to end the party's conference at Cheltenham. Seven prominent members of the Liberal Party were on the platform: the parliamentary leader Clement Davies, Lady Megan Lloyd George, Frank Byers, Jo Grimond, Lady Violet Bonham-Carter, Sir Andrew McFadyean and Dingle Foot. Several of them reminded John that there were future elections and, if he were ever to be free of the BBC, there was no reason why he should not be invited to stand again.

Meanwhile, his bewildering merry-go-round of activity continued. In any week he appeared to be in three places at once, and because he looked like a cross between Denis Compton and Stewart Granger, one correspondent cheekily suggested that they deputised when there was a clash of commitments. His *Evening News* colleague John Carpenter even went so far as to itemise 'One Man's Day' in the paper on 30 April 1951:

> This is my distinguished colleague John Arlott's programme for this evening:
>
> 7.30: Lord's Taverners Ball at Grosvenor House.
>
> 7.50: Leave Ball for Paris Cinema to be quiz-master in *Twenty Questions* at 8.15.
>
> 9.00: Back to Ball to introduce mannequin parade.
>
> 10.20: Broadcast commentary on soft ball 'Test' Taverners v England at the Ball – which is for the Playing Fields Association, of which the President is the Duke of Edinburgh (who will be there with Princess Elizabeth, Princess Margaret, and the Mountbattens).
>
> And today John has a book published (*Maurice Tate*, Cricketing Lives series) and his own weekly 'Table Talk' on page five. Oh, and he did his usual day's work at the BBC, too.

Among the opposing teams in the 'soft ball "Test"' at the Grosvenor House charity ball were Robertson Hare, Trevor Howard, Bill Edrich, Norman Yardley, Doug Insole and George Mann, and Basil Radford and Naunton Wayne, who became famous as Charters and Caldicott, two cricket-loving English gentlemen, in the film *The Lady Vanishes*. The game was played inside a giant net with a trick ball that refused to behave like a normal ball. A bell, signifying dismissal, was rung at inopportune moments, and great fun was had by all. When a *Sunday Chronicle* reporter asked John, who had organised the match, why the Duke of Edinburgh (Twelfth Man in the Lord's Taverners' roll of members) was not picked, he replied that it was due to changing difficulties.

The actual chronology of John's work at this time is unimportant, but the stamina required to sustain it was impressive. At different times his diary reminded him to go to the British Industries Fair to have his hand-writing read by one Delino in aid of a promotion; to compère a hop-picking festival at Paddock Wood; to give after-dinner speeches for cricket clubs at Reading, Salisbury, Stroud, Wantage and Workington. And if 'having to stay in London to sort out a Test match for a national newspaper' was the reason he opted out of a journey to Cumbria – Rex Alston deputised at the last moment – he did venture across the Scottish border to Alloa for the annual dinner of the Clackmannan County Cricket Club.

When he rose to speak he was bombarded with applause for a full minute. 'I realise,' he said, 'that the invitation I had to enter a plain van and go and see the site of Bannockburn was merely a helpful effort by loyal Scots to prevent a Sassenach coming up and speaking about cricket during the football season.' He then went on to recall the imaginary club of which he and so many cricket speakers felt obliged to be members.

The ground had been sold and the money drunk by the committee – finishing about three years before I joined – so it was now a roving club.

One member was deficient in sight and hearing so he was made an umpire; a paralytic was made scorer, and for five years the superstitious secretary refused to remove one man's name from the list. He was dead, but the removal would have brought the number down to thirteen.

I held my place for seven seasons and reached double figures before August Bank Holiday each year – dropped a hundred catches and gave away a thousand runs.

When he was not busy taking the role of a humorist, he was taking the laurels of a reporter from *The Performer* when giving a speech at a Saints and Sinners luncheon at Albany, off London's Piccadilly, which was chaired by the impresario Jack Hylton, with Sir Charles Cochran, George Jessel and the world light-heavyweight boxing champion Joey Maxim in attendance. He retold many of the jokes at a Buccaneers cricket dinner at the Lord's Tavern, where he flippantly named a Test XI, picking Josephine Baker to open the batting 'for having the best possible figure for a number of years' and placing Marlene Dietrich at leg-slip 'for stopping more leg glances than anyone living'. How dated all that seems now. Other commitments included commentating on a game of bat and trap at Ye Olde Beverlie hostelry for a broadcast on *The Roman Road to Canterbury*; chairing a poetry reading by John Betjeman at the Ideal Home Exhibition at Olympia; relaying questions on coffee to a panel at the Carnival Hall, Rugby; acting as a go-between in the provision of Braille diagrams for blind cricket enthusiasts; and interviewing a cow in a pavilion on the South Bank during the Festival of Britain: 'D'ye want to speak, old dear?'

John also found time to share the commentary with Sir Ralph Richardson on *Cricket*, a British documentary for the Christchurch Film Festival in New Zealand. The film was intended, according to the foreword, 'not to teach the game to the unbeliever, but to give pleasure to the converted'.

Actuality broadcast live was in vogue in radio documentaries at this time, in line with improvements in technical equipment and facilities. John took part in documentaries on Plymouth and Bristol where, using a mobile radio transmitter, he described life on the waterfront from a launch going through the floating harbour.

Indoors, he edited volumes of beautifully coloured facsimiles of the maps and text of John Speed's *Theatre of the Empire of Great Britaine* for Phoenix House, and also did the same job in black and white for a number of sporting books for the Sportsman's Book Club. He composed the words to traditional melodies for three hymns for the *BBC Hymnal* – for Plough Sunday, Rogationtide and Harvest Festival. The woman who commissioned this work reacted in total disbelief when told it would be finished the next day. But, after the candles had burnt low that night, it was. 'There's an essential simplicity to lyric writing,' said John, 'which very often a poet doesn't have. Arguably, it's a difference between Thomas More and W.B. Yeats – More wrote better lyrics and Yeats better poetry.' The harvest song of praise, 'God Whose Farm is all Creation', found its way into practically every Christian hymnal around the world and made, as John records in *Basingstoke Boy*, 'several hundred times more per word than anything else he ever wrote'. Britain's Methodists found room for it in their revised hymn-book, but expunged 'God Save the Queen'. In a press report, John Ezard, tongue not entirely in cheek, described John as 'a bucolic part-time songsmith'. He probably would not have disagreed. In later years, when sharing a car with the cricket writers John Woodcock of *The Times* and Michael Melford of the *Daily Telegraph*, John passed by a school on the outskirts of a Lancashire town. 'I've been there,' he said. 'The boys sang my harvest hymn.' 'What was it like?' asked the other two. 'Oh, all right, I suppose,' replied John. 'Only they buggered up the scansion.'

One evening, although he was feeling unwell, John stepped in at late notice to read the *Epilogue* over the air. The *Epilogue* had had a special significance in BBC parlance ever since the night when, it was said, the then Director-General, Sir John Reith, had caught a senior announcer educating, informing, and assuredly entertaining a secretary at the back of a studio. The puritanical Reith wanted to sack the man on the spot, and was only persuaded to adopt a more lenient approach by the pleas of his Director of Personnel. 'All right,' said Reith. 'But he must never, ever read the *Epilogue*.'

On the cricket front, John was a field commentator at Badminton in

Gloucestershire when the Duke of Beaufort's XI played B.O. Allen's County XI in aid of Monty Cranfield's testimonial fund. Wally Hammond, 'Gubby' Allen, Harold Gimblett and Arthur Wellard were among those who paraded their skills for the retiring off-spinner. John also had dinner at Brentwood with the legendary Charles Kortright, of Essex and Gentlemen of England, dubbed 'the fastest bowler who ever lived'. As well as enjoying the occasion, John manufactured a broadcast and an article from their conversation.

These varied activities were, of course, extra-curricular. His main income came from being a full-time employee of the BBC, a commentator on cricket and football, and a writer of books and articles. All of this had to be maintained in order to sustain his life-style. Apart from household expenses, equipping a new property, nourishing a family, school fees, food, an above-average consumption of drink, a car to befit his celebrity status (in the early 1950s John bought a Bentley because he knew that was what was expected of someone in his position – a strange, contradictory act, for he was generally disdainful of public image), there was his susceptibility to expensive short- and long-term obsessions. These were reflected in his diverse collections: books, pottery, paintings, engraved glass, Gladstonian prints, Japanese colour-block, Himalayan herbs – whatever fired his enthusiasm and excited him aesthetically, or was sparked by an association with people. Fortunately the outlay never led beyond the point of fiscal return. 'He inherited a peasant's fear of debt,' remarked Dawn. 'He always paid bills on the dot.'

Much as he tried, however, even John could not do everything that was asked of him. On occasions Dawn helped out by getting into the act. In June 1950, for instance, she opened the Harefield Cricket Club fête, at which the world doubles runners-up at table tennis, Johnny Leach and Johnny Carrington, gave an exhibition.

John's voice – his passport to fame – was a boon for impressionists, amateur and professional. Tony Fayne and David Evans, two young artists touring Britain as part of a variety show, were aping an Arlott commentary on radio shows such as *Music Box* and on the theatrical circuit. Whether at the Empress, Brixton or the New in Northampton, the Arlott impression always brought instantaneous applause. So successful was the routine that the pair were asked to appear as a supporting act for Judy Garland at the London Palladium.

Fayne and Evans were not the only ones to do an Arlott impression. The station announcer at Nottingham Midland obviously felt that train timetables benefited from being delivered in John's unmistakable tones. He became so proficient that during the Trent Bridge Test match in 1954 several passengers, including the Revd. Bert Philip, who played university and Scottish county cricket, and who knew John well, wondered whether the commentator had discovered a new vocation.

Fortunately for the vast majority of his listeners, he had not. Most years 'the Adonis of the ear-bashers' union', as he was dubbed by Eric L. Williams in the *Auckland Weekly News*, came top of the press polls for best cricket commentator. However, in a popularity survey among boys and girls aged between twelve and fifteen in 1950, he was only the seventh favourite male radio star, way behind the winner, Wilfred Pickles. His following amongst youngsters, though, was hardly negligible. In August 1951 the *North Cheshire Herald* repeated a conversation between two schoolboys at a county match at Old Trafford:

'These umpires are wearing white caps. They wore white caps when Glamorgan played the South Africans.'
   'How do you know? You weren't there.'
   'I heard it on the wireless.'
   'The BBC don't tell you things like that.'
   'John Arlott does!'

That particular Glamorgan v. South African encounter at Swansea had given John an opportunity to display his virtuosity. Gron Williams set the scene in the *Herald of Wales*:

Between commentaries, Muncer and McConnon had mopped up the tourists' batting forces. When John, of the apple dumpling tones, had left us in mid-afternoon an opening pair was steadily taking runs in the manner of Test batsmen.

When he returned around six o'clock, zeros dappled the scoreboard in readiness for another match, groundsmen were tending a forlorn discarded square of turf, the captains and the crowds had all departed, a modest county side had won a famous victory . . .

And from his little commentary box, he told us the story, not coldly and statistically in the manner of lesser mortals, but with an excitement which rarely captures the phlegmatic, cynical-sounding Arlott. In the ten existing minutes he recalled each thrill of mounting tension as the stumps toppled. And in his sardonic asides we savoured the full irony of Nourse and company's failure.

There we have the secret of radio's Mr Cricket – his ability to capture the mood of the play he describes. If a Simpson and a Hardstaff are slowly compiling average-boosting centuries on plumb

Trent Bridge, Arlott sounds somnolent, bored, with a tendency to be quietly spiteful. But, if he sees the game in the grand manner, he loses that acquired *ennui* and returns to the tones which, I have no doubt, were always his as a very vocal small boy on West Country village greens. He is radio's Mr Cricket.

A number of cricketers, notably Wilf Wooller, were present when John gave that commentary. Said Wooller, 'They would all vouch for its remarkable impact.'

But not everybody was enamoured of the Arlott commentary style. In the *Spectator* in that same year, 1951, James Overthrow – did he suffer from a predisposition? – begged to differ:

I hope I do not exaggerate if I say that John Arlott has the power to cast a gloom over the whole of my listening life. I believe that Truth hath a quiet breast; but John Arlott doesn't think so. It is the unresting, unceasing, voracious appetite for detail – the umpire's age, achievements in days past, hat, boots and the flap of his white coat, the size of the policeman's boots as he sits by the sightscreen, the habits of pigeons and sparrows, the impressions of natural beauty at The Oval (of all places), the bedrooms at Todmorden, the piece of stray paper that Dai Davies picks up, and an infinity of things like these – that gets my, if I may be forgiven the expression, goat. And interspersed with this bewildering detail come sentences which sound like this: BedserisjustcominginhebowlsRowanmiddlesit ComptonisonitinaflashandflicksittoBrennanwhoreturnsitgracefully toBedser; or dialogue like this: 'Oh dear! That ball gave a distinct pop. Can it be that a spot has developed? I'd better take Arthur Gilligan's opinion about that. Arthur, was I wrong in thinking that that last ball gave a distinct pop?' 'No, John, you were quite right. It was certainly a pop, and I think you may safely say it was a distinct pop.' 'Thanks, Arthur, very much.' 'Not at all, John.'

A.E. Jebbett, in the *Birmingham Evening Dispatch*, had also become disenchanted. Writing about John and Rex Alston, he commented:

Recently I heard them at different matches, and although the old insight into the game was still there, the tang was missing, I felt, in both of them. It had all become too easy, almost too fluent, too much the same mixture as before, with the clichés gathering as thickly as dust on milk.

Nor had there been much human kindness in evidence at the opening of a jointly-arranged MCC and National Book League exhibition in Albemarle Street in London. In answer to a question, one of cricket's diehards, Sir Pelham Warner, said that he deplored the use of cricketers' Christian names. 'Why,' asked Warner, then President of the MCC, 'should Hutton be called "Len" when there is no other Hutton in first-class cricket? I would allow it for cricketers known to millions such as Denis Compton [was Len Hutton not known to millions?], but why Roley Jenkins instead of simply Jenkins? I think it is a little undignified. In these days we should keep cricket on a very high level.'

Sir Francis Meynell, Vice-Chairman of the League, thought differently, and ventured to call Sir Pelham by his nickname, 'Plum'. When it was his turn to speak, John retorted angrily that the same treatment should be given to the most famous cricketer and to the newest county player. 'The day I deplore is that on which the amateur became "Mr J. Smith" and the professional just "Smith". I prefer to refer to Denis Compton as if he were my friend, and not as if he were my groom.'

At a meeting of the Maidstone branch of the Association of Kent Cricket Clubs, John remarked that one of the most unpleasant letters he had ever received was signed by 'Prefects of Sutton Valence School', asking him to tell Douglas Wright that 'he was the worst cricketer playing for England and everyone in England knew it'. This drew a spirited response from the headmaster of the school in the *Kent Messenger*, who admitted the stupidity of the request, but excused his former pupils on the grounds of ultra-partisan support for a 'county other than Kent'.

Controversy was keeping fairly close company with John in this period. As with anyone in the public eye, his mildest comment could attract the most extravagant attention. In his book *Concerning Cricket* he had written that Australian cricketers 'have a single-minded wish to win the game – to win within the laws, but if necessary to the last limit within them'. Nowadays such an observation would probably be taken as a compliment, but at the time it caused a storm. Jack Ryder, a former Australian captain, and the Test players Bill Ponsford and Doug Ring rushed into print to refute what they considered a slur, and pages of print were generated from Dundee to Melbourne.

John also managed to upset the Irish in an article for *Illustrated* in April 1951, under the heading 'The Broth of a Game'. Part of it read:

There is no greater sporting phenomenon in our time than Gaelic football. Mark its extravagant contradictions: it is a deliberately planned sport; its most important achievements were political rather than athletic; and, although predominantly a rural sport, it is the greatest public attraction in urban Ireland. Thus, a Welsh rugby team or an English soccer eleven playing an international match against Ireland in Dublin will draw a maximum attendance of forty-five to fifty thousand. But let Kerry meet Cavan in the final of the All-Ireland Gaelic Football competition, and all Ireland indeed flocks to the capital. Croke Park's eighty thousand capacity will be stretched by those who climb walls and sit on roofs yet there will still be hundreds locked outside. Whole bunches of players rise in the air, bumping and barging, fisting and snatching for the ball. Barbed wire and rails keep back the crowd.

Why does this huge crowd with its brown-robed Franciscans, its bearded Capuchins, its lean black-hatted, dog-collared young priests eager on the terraces, their seniors amply seated in the stands, and with fifty or sixty train-loads of men with heavy boots and the brogue of the country districts – or of Ulster – on their tongues, gather to watch a bishop throw the ball in? Thereafter, why should they cry triumph and indignation to the skies at a game clearly less technically fine and much less far-reaching in its importance than the soccer and rugby which are also at their doors?

The next week, a leader in an Irish newspaper did not mince words:

The article is more than brazen. It is downright impertinent, designed to be insulting, partly inaccurate, and certainly the intended wit is snorted upon by Irish readers, who are not as gullible as Mr Arlott might imagine. The bitter author of this insult is obviously suffering from a jealous disposition. He is apparently ignorant of Irish history, of its games, and probably still enjoys the pig in the parlour joke.

After such a response, John may have felt a certain amount of relief when, a few days later, he found his name plastered all over the newspapers by default. For once, he was not the sinner. His friend Gilbert Harding, 'a verbal sadist of great skills', according to Brian Masters, who also possessed 'the painful courage of honest introspection', had stepped out of line while chairing the radio quiz game *Twenty Questions*. On air, Harding had complained about 'a horrid and upsetting start', and had spoken testily about 'this nonsense'. The BBC decided it was time he took a rest, and as a result John was asked to take over as question-master for a three-week period. The team – Jack Train, Joy Adamson, Anona Winn and Richard

Dimbleby – met John just before his first programme. 'I have played "Twenty Questions" at home as a party game often enough,' said John. 'I shall treat the broadcast tonight in the same way. It's no good rehearsing for programmes like this. All you can do is hope.' Harding telephoned to wish him luck, but his first outing received mixed reviews. Emery Pearce wrote in the *Daily Herald:*

> Deep-voiced John Arlott, thirty-seven-year-old BBC staff instructor and cricket commentator who replaced Gilbert Harding in the *Twenty Questions* programme last night, was a success even if he was bowled out by the 'team'. Frequently puzzled, always amusing, he fenced and tried to foil them but lost by seven questions to four. There was one oblique reference to Gilbert Harding by Arlott when he said at the beginning: 'The first object to kill a question-master is animal.' The team got it in three. It was the *Dragon killed by St George.*

But Robert Cannell wrote in the *Daily Express:*

> Under quiz-master Arlott the programme relapsed into its former dullness. The bite had gone. Arlott was a stonewaller. When he did try to help he overdid it. Often he omitted to give the number of questions. That is a major error in this radio parlour game. It is vital to keep up the excitement. His attempts at humour were heavy-handed. His crosstalk with the team sounded forced rather than fluent. Unless there is a marked improvement in the next fortnight it seems clear the BBC will have to look outside its staff if *Twenty Questions* is to be worth its place.

The next two editions were much sharper. In one of them John teased Jack Train by saying: 'If your eyes were like your mind, you would be able to see round corners.' But the experiment was not considered a great success, and after John's three-week run Kenneth Horne took over the chair. A BBC spokesman, defending stoutly and with the cricket season under way, said: 'This is no reflection on John Arlott who has done a first-class job, but he happens to be our best cricket commentator.'

By now John was no longer a producer. His boss, James Pennethorne Hughes, had moved to offices in Marylebone High Street to become Head of Staff Training. He offered John the job of General Instructor, with the enticement of considerable flexibility in his working hours, giving him the freedom to fit in other activities. It was a difficult choice for John to make. The production of programmes, nursing a concept from embryo to fully-crafted and fledged creation, is a hugely satisfying operation. Nevertheless, and probably in the end because of his genuine affection for Pennethorne Hughes, he had taken up the offer.

'Jim' Pennethorne Hughes was a fascinating man: public-school boxer, poet, writer, traffic apprentice on the Great Western Railway, teacher, broadcaster, talks producer and 'rufous Hanoverian' of distant Royal lineage by George IV and Mrs John Nash. He displayed ambivalent personalities – amiable, amusing and urbane, also sensitive, reticent and shy. He went to school at Oundle where he later taught, and was a close friend of Arthur Marshall, who wrote: 'he had an affectionate if irreverent feeling for his old school and unlike several of his kind and generation, did not grieve about not having been at Eton'. John Betjeman, another friend, observed that 'he was much loved by an intimate few and much liked by very many. He seemed lonely.'

Pennethorne Hughes was also much taken by magic, and was a member of a cult that believed it had repelled a German invasion during the Second World War. Unverified stories were told of a member of the cult who had a terminal illness offering himself as a human sacrifice. In his weekend cottage in Wiltshire, where he greeted visitors with jugs of steaming-hot Turkish coffee and an ornate pipe in case they had need of the weed, Pennethorne Hughes had amassed a possibly unique collection of books on witchcraft, magic and mysticism. This he eventually bequeathed to John. In a preface to Pennethorne Hughes's *Thirty-Eight Poems*, John acknowledged that 'he taught me more than all my schoolmasters; he was kind, convivial and, at times of crisis, clear-minded and helpful'.

The two happy years spent in Staff Training passed quickly, lecturing and teaching broadcasting skills to those pursuing a career, but in the end, John told me, 'it became too difficult for the management to explain to others how I could be doing so much more outside the BBC'. And so, regretfully, came the decision to leave.

John resigned from the BBC on 31 March, 1953. He was still broadcasting as much as ever, and had a firm connection to the editorial office of the *Evening News* at Carmelite House. Once again, the maxims of his security-conscious father came to mind. Had he taken the right course?

14

Exercises in Serendipity

'The world belongs to those who are in love with the new,' wrote the historian Marc Bloch. John was also in love with the old, in all its forms, but in these hustling years of the early 1950s he was constantly seeking fresh accomplishment.

To appear in the pages of Fleet Street newspapers was a natural progression for a now widely-known commentator. On 5 May 1950, some months ahead of John Marshall's invitation to write on wine for the *Evening News*, the editor of the *Daily Mail*, Frank Owen, announced a 'sporting double':

ON MONDAY: John Arlott, radio's no. 1 cricket commentator, writes the first of a new weekly series of cricket profiles . . . intimate, detailed studies by the man who knows them all. The series will be illustrated by Ross.

ON TUESDAY: Gertrude (Gorgeous Gussy) Moran contributes a special article on: Why should Wimbledon be all-white?

Only an editor with a blinkered eye for increasing his newspaper's circulation would publicise such an unlikely pairing.

John's first profile was of the Middlesex captain R.W.V. Robins, a former England player:

They call him 'Cock' – but not to his face. In any case, his bird-like alertness is only a minor facet of Walter Robins, that discriminating enthusiast who, rising forty-four, comes back this season to captain Middlesex . . . The most active cricketer of the thirties, he took batting guard a foot outside his crease, bowled leg-breaks and googlies as prodigal of spin, as erratic of length, and not even the fastest runners dared take a single to him at cover for fear of that deadly throw-in . . .

Still, today, when his burden of years is slightly a brake to his

limbs as it can never be to his brain, you face his bowling at peril
of your peace of mind, his batting at peril of your analysis, his
fielding at peril of being run out. Above all, face his argument at
peril of your opinions, for he disrupts error with a blasting cross-
questioning, and exposes false reasoning with a ruthless analysis.

John went on that summer to give word portraits of Harold Gimblett,
Wilf Wooller, James Langridge (the first professional captain of Sussex,
appointed that year), Godfrey Evans, Len Hutton, Allan Rae (the left-
handed West Indies opening batsman), Jack Walsh and Doug Insole, all
of them highly visible figures in the cricket public's consciousness. He
also turned his attention to the solid workaday professionals who tended
to get overshadowed, and with whom he had particular empathy, such as
John Arnold of Hampshire and Winston Place of Lancashire.

Another profile was of the Bedser twins, who, he noticed had 'synchron-
ously become less alike':

Certainly, two darkly massive men, over six feet tall, identical in
every detail of bone-structure and colouring, and always wearing
identical clothes, can seem indistinguishable to the stranger, but no
one who knows them ever mistakes one Bedser for the other.

Life and experience carve a man's features in a pattern which
nothing can eradicate or counterfeit. Thus Alec Bedser, that mighty
labourer under the sun for Surrey and England, bears the outward
and visible signs of bowling at great batsmen to the limits of physical
effort on pitches doped for run-getting ... The lines of Alec
Bedser's jaw record those overs.

Eric, the senior twin by ten minutes, is still the leader and usually
speaks first, but they do not waste speech, nor, between themselves,
have they much need of it. Perhaps because his cricket is still not
completely fulfilled, Eric's face seems the more sensitive and, simultaneously, less assured. Perhaps, too, because he cannot, like Alec,
immerse himself in such great physical endeavour, his voice is less
strong.

Their visible differences are probably greater than any others, for
between these two men there exists an unquestioning loyalty and
sympathy, a complete lack of need to dissemble or to substitute
politeness for truth.

Here, once again, is reflected the Arlott ability to observe more than
the average onlooker, and to convey his analysis with the exact words.

Describing the Bedsers' Surrey skipper, Stuart Surridge, he wrote, 'fair-haired, explosively rosy with surprising eyebrows and a good sturdy physique, with his long eager run-up – right hand cutting away like a canoeist's paddle'. For any willing captive of Surrey cricket during their record Championship-winning run from 1952 to 1958, there is an instant smile of recognition. John once said to me: 'The books and articles that I've written about cricket are much more lucid about the things I didn't do commentary on than those that I did, because in commentary it just went in through my eyes and out through my mouth, and it was gone and lost and forgotten, for my absorption was complete.'

Again for the *Daily Mail*, and at his own suggestion, John journeyed to Tilbury to say farewell to a short, lean, bespectacled and quietly-spoken man who, together with his wife and five daughters, had decided to emigrate:

> As I stand on the quay, the sun has come out to temper the cold wind of late April, and a figure of cricket history is leaving England for Australia aboard the liner *Orontes*. Bare minutes ago, the ship cast off, and is standing out in the river, the oil smoke running out of her yellow funnels – and the man who has just turned away from the deckrail is 'Lol' Larwood, who, in September 1932, sailed from this same quay, and in this very same *Orontes*, to Australia and an epic Test series.

At that moment John felt that Larwood's place in history had been usurped by the machinations of lesser men. Although the scourge of the Aussies had been made an honorary member of MCC the previous year, John was convinced that the fall-out from the bodyline series still contaminated the minds of an influential few who had found it expedient to neglect Larwood. There was supreme irony in the legendary fast bowler seeking a future in the land in which he had once been so feared, and where his bowling had been instrumental in almost splitting the Empire. John stayed on the quayside long after Larwood had disappeared.

John's writing for the *Evening News* covered all sorts of subjects. His 'Table Talk' column found him tucking in to reindeer meat; he preferred the chunk that was roasted to those that were stewed or grilled. He also found three ways of eating spaghetti without decorating the tablecloth, and yearned to discover secret cheese-presses which produced the seemingly lost Blue Vinny, Cottenham, Smearcase and Yorkshire Cotherstone varieties, 'and made a bread and cheese and beer meal in different regions an exercise for the connoisseur'. Other articles detailed the simple way to make special soups – *Petite Marmite Henri IV* – or tempted readers to try snails; he also discussed railway food and lamented the lack of good pull-ins for drivers.

One day John put forward the notion that the human tongue and tastebuds could not distinguish more than six characteristics: sour, bitter, sweet, salt, alkaline and metallic. 'Any refinement or extension of those flavours which we think we taste are derived from smelling our food or drink while it is in our mouths,' he wrote. Therefore 'a sensitive palate is meaningless against a good nose'.

A friend and mentor who had much more than an informed taste in wine and food was Raymond Postgate. John described him as 'an idealist of unquestionable integrity with a quick, questioning mind, a sense of humour and of justice'. Postgate, dubbed by one newspaper 'Public Stomach No. 1', founded the Good Food Club and its *Guide* and also, in 1951, brought out *The Plain Man's Guide to Wine*. The *Guide* ran to many editions and, a few years after Postgate's death in 1971, his sons asked John to revise it, which he did with pride and affection for its author. Maintaining the *Guide* as Postgate's book brought back memories of an Elizabethan feast they had enjoyed together in the 1950s, at which roast swan was the *pièce de résistance*. On another occasion, John tucked into peacock with TV cook Philip Harben.

John Arlott's 'Sporting Silhouettes' was another feature of his *Evening News* output and ran on alternate days with 'Table Talk' and, subsequently, with 'It Occurs to Me'. The 'Silhouettes' comprised around three hundred words apiece on the footballers of the time – some of them instantly recognisable, such as Walley Barnes, Eddie Baily and Jimmy Logie, and some less so, for instance Gerry Bowler of Millwall and Jack Rawlings of non-league Hayes, who had triumphantly fought his way back to full mobility after suffering a broken leg. In season, the same mix applied to cricketers: Tony Lock, Reg Simpson, Cuan McCarthy (Cambridge University and South Africa), David Fletcher (Surrey) and Alan Rayment (Hants). There were also 'Spotlights' of Test series and analyses of football teams.

'It Occurs to Me' was a column that gave John more scope than practically anything else he had ever written. Much of the material reflected what had recently happened to him and to those with whom he had been in contact, and so for readers and writer it was really an exercise in serendipity. The articles were mostly direct personal statements, couched in a way John came to abhor in later years when he avoided at all costs the use of the pronoun 'I'. They embraced the shared experiences that beset every household, 'beset' being the operative word, for in them can be found the matter and natter of office, pub and home, a good old moan for all to enjoy.

John's approach was to treat trivial things mock-seriously, and those that were not with serious mocking. There is a grin in nearly every line. Resolutions to make an economy drive prompted the thought to put the car away and travel by bus, and to smoke fewer Passing Clouds, the pink, oval-shaped cigarettes to which he was partial at least forty times a day; also a declaration to Dawn to buy fewer books: 'Even the tearing-up of a bookseller's catalogue under her very eyes has not convinced her that I am in deadly earnest – which is hard, because it was very difficult to read it properly afterwards with each page in four pieces.'

Artistic licence with other family members is in evidence in detailing the exploits of Great Uncles Jubilee and Ern, Uncle Hercules and Aunt Magnolia: the elderly lady having to cycle, brakeless, to the next village because only there could she find a stepping-stone which would enable her to dismount; the one-legged fisherman at the end of the pier who refused to accept that the competition was over and that his bait had been eluded. They all had richly comic potential.

Vexations with unforeseen bank charges and Inland Revenue demands gave rise to the story of the man who tried to buy advertising space on income-tax forms. Invasion by builders and the subsequent major spring-cleaning found John not only bemoaning the loss of a favourite cobweb, in which he used to store his matchsticks, but also remembering that the chimney-sweep was due in a day or so. Then there were the precious objects moved in the flurry and never to be found again; the blunders in playing bridge with strangers and the wisdom of giving up squash before it did the same to him. And finding his golf garments were too tight: 'I cannot put on the clothes that I need to wear in order to take the exercise necessary to take off the three inches necessary to wear the clothes,' and so, in despair, undertaking a series of sit-ups with his toes clamped underneath the wardrobe, causing blood vessels to knot and breath to come in husky jerks, before collapsing backwards on top of the baby, who, in sheer wonderment, had crawled up behind him unseen. That same baby, young Timothy, swallowing a tube of what fortunately turned out to be vitamin pills. Visits to Bertram Mills' circus at Olympia and Tom Arnold's at Harringay. Devising a system for doing the Pools. Managing not to mend a tricycle pump. The enjoyment gained from 'lying supinely' in bed with a feverish cold or possibly twinges from an old hopscotch injury – depending on what was thought likely to be the more effective – and trying to drum up sympathy and nursely ministrations in vain. A rummage through weskitry to offset the drabness of men's clothes. Going to a dance

and performing the party trick of lifting a chair with his teeth. And the
stratagems employed to excuse the great domestic sport called 'coming
home late – again'.

But it would be a mistake to think readers were witnessing a life in a
day of the Arlotts, or a divulging of the family chest. They were not. All
they were being given were brief insights enlarged by a journalistic trade
tool. A magnifying-glass does not necessarily reveal all there is to be seen.

Another peep into the glass finds Dawn and the children away for a
change of air. John is left alone with the chores. He remembers – just –
to do the water-softener and see to the refrigerator man. He circumvents
the likelihood of spoiled suppers and the need to wash up by eating out.
He returns to the house late at night and goes into a bedroom to be
greeted with the smell of an electric kettle that has been switched on since
morning. It is, he says, 'a rare experience for the nostrils'. In practice, as
he agreed, the impractical man.

In February 1952 we discover a different mood, in a poignant essay
that brought the chill of fear:

> I suppose most fathers try, when they have the chance, to meet their
> children from school. It is a chance to see one's offspring in the life
> he – or she – is building up as an independent human being. It helps
> one too to appreciate what school-teachers have to endure . . .
>
> Some two years ago the school was closed because of an outbreak
> of infantile paralysis. For weeks afterwards [my son] could do any-
> thing he liked with us. If he said he felt seedy or seemed a little
> languid he might have the top brick off the chimney. Anything, so
> long as he was well. He might be as wicked as he liked so long as
> he was dashing about the place, sound in wind and limb. At last, we
> sighed, he was all right.
>
> Next term the trip to meet him from school revealed one of the
> familiar bunch of boys as now a little withdrawn from the others.
> He had had poliomyelitis. He came to school in a wheelchair and,
> while his eyes still lit up and his shouts were still as piercing as a
> six-year-old's ought to be, he could no longer dash about in that
> fury of pointless activity which is the habit of little boys. Those
> useless legs, a little boy who could not run about – let us be honest,
> the fear that it might happen to my boy – lived with me for days.
>
> I wanted to know what one did about it: what about immunisa-
> tion? Poliomyelitis is not an easy subject to read about, but the first
> thing you find out is that there is no immunisation against it.

For the Infantile Paralysis Fellowship, to which he referred later in that article, John wrote a pamphlet variously entitled 'The Truth About Polio' and 'The Problem of Infantile Paralysis'. He also produced a pamphlet on avoidable fatality, 'Death on the Road'.

'Death on the Road' was an attempt to return to the tradition of the broadsheet which was sold in the streets before newspapers took over. The poem – light verse-narrative for all its serious theme – had first appeared in the *Evening News* on 20 October 1952.

> One more commuter has answered his maker,
> One more cold motor has gone to the breaker:
> One more fatality scored to A3,
> One more dark stain on the road to the sea . . .
>
> In a devilish hurry to get down through Surrey,
> He slashed through the dark in a rain-splashing flurry;
> No checking at crossings; the horn – and ahead -
> And at two sets of lights he nipped through on the red . . .
>
> (BRITISH ROAD SERVICES, gleamingly red,
> Driving to London with ingots of lead;
> A full sixteen tons of it loaded behind
> And supper the thought in the driver's tired mind.)
>
> Jones was laden with sin just as all of us are,
> And it wasn't his soul that was driving the car,
> When the lobes he'd have used if he'd thought about God
> Were smashed in a flash by a hot piston-rod.
>
> We may pity Jones less for his death on the road
> Than the far too brief time that he had to unload
> His burden of mortal and venial sin
> As the bonnet went down, and the engine came in.*

The fact that John had deliberately set out to produce an essay in cliché, couched in a laconic form of verse, and had, incidentally, tried to rediscover an audience which modern poetry had lost, was not immediately clear. Not, at least, to several of his readers, who as well as failing to understand his motive, felt that the composition left a lot to be desired. One wonders if the latent offence to their sensibilities was that of apparent

---

* The full text, with some later amendments, is given in Appendix A, page 353.

levity. Did they see only death-lyrics displayed with cold-blooded cynicism? Or black humour?

Other readers felt inspired to provide verses of their own, and comment on the subject threatened to become a cottage industry before the *Evening News*'s editor, John Marshall, intervened:

> The editor wishes to thank the many readers who have written to him and John Arlott on the subject of Arlott's poem 'Death on the Road'. Some wrote to praise; some to condemn. Whatever their reaction, we feel, apart from its merit as verse, that if its publication saves one life on the road, the purpose of presenting it to our readers will have been more than justified.

Not unexpectedly, John had the last word. Acknowledging the contrary proposals to limit road accidents that were on offer, he rejected the thought that any legislation could be effective, and wrote:

> You may legislate against men driving when they are under the influence of alcohol but not when they are drunk with anger, conceit, speed or impatience ... The second point is the most commonly dangerous one. We are all apt to think that to be correct is sufficient. If our sole concern is to be legally in the right, well and good, but it is possible to have been in the right and yet to be dead.
>
> Last week, on three separate occasions, I approached a blind corner or a blind hill on my proper side of the road at a reasonable speed, to meet an oncoming vehicle on its wrong side of the road, overtaking other vehicles without the speed to get past before reaching the corner or hilltop.
>
> Each of the three was a lorry, though none was a British Road Services vehicle. Is it possible – and I merely muse, I do not venture to state – that some lorry drivers are persuaded into a careless state of mind by the fact that the vehicle they are driving is not their own, and that its weight and strength render them virtually safe against collision with any ordinary car?
>
> My own behaviour, in each case, was in accordance with the Highway Code. I was correct – but I was not safe. To achieve absolute road safety it seems to me that one must approach every bend in the road, every hill and, in fact, every other vehicle prepared for another driver to do something utterly foolish.

In the light of what was to befall his eldest son James just over a dozen years later, there is an eerie and savage irony in all this. But that is to jump ahead of events. Apart from the reaction to the nature of 'Death on the Road', it is conceivable that John was a little bruised by the preoccupation of a few readers with its poetic standard. 1952 was the year in which he was to give up writing verse, and the response could have been an unreasoning factor.

Another effusion of John's in the *Evening News* touched a more concordant theme. A man tried one day to persuade John to buy a piano. Little did the man know that he was talking to someone who had been exiled from music lessons at school. Pianos – those worth having – are not cheap, and John pleaded poverty. But the fact that seven-year-old James showed musical ability – he became adept on the clarinet, even if, at this point, he was standing in muddy Wellington boots on a settee painting the sitting-room wallpaper with indelible ink and a toothbrush – meant that eventually a piano did find its way into the house. Even more eventually it found its way into the attic, in a losing battle with John's books, but the fact is that the master of the house was not wholly unreceptive to music. He may have claimed to be tone-deaf, spavin-fingered and generally musically illiterate, but was this just a defence mechanism?

Donald Barrington, who specialised in legal advice to advertising agencies and who was happily married to Dawn, John's first wife, for thirty-four years until his death in 1994, had definite thoughts on the matter. So did Dawn. In conversation, they disagreed:

Donald: I think John was afraid of music's emotional effect.

Dawn: But he would read emotional poetry. He would cry over that.

Donald: Yes, but music is an even more direct attack on the emotions. He knew how strong his could be when aroused. He didn't want to open a further chink in his armour, so to speak. I think he fought shy. For him, there was an intellectual contact in poetry.

Dawn: I don't think that's it. I would be listening to music on the radio or put on a record and say to John, 'Hey, stay. Listen to this. It's super.' John would say, 'Yes, it is. But the reason I can't start is because it would obsess me.' He was an obsessive person. He wanted to be ever so good at whatever he took on. He knew all about literature and poetry. And the books – we could hardly move in Highgate Avenue for the books.

Quite apart from the volume of books, does a man really decide whether or not he *wants* music? Surely it is either with him – and inextinguishable – or not.

The first time John became a castaway on *Desert Island Discs*, on 21 May 1953, the music was chosen mainly by Dawn. Listeners heard him say to the presenter, Roy Plomley: 'There will be no distress signals flown on my island. The prospect delights me. No telephones, no deadlines, no posts, no bills, no hurry.'

With the exception of Beethoven's Seventh Symphony ('to remind me, if I am on that desert island for life, that eternity is much longer'), all of the eight chosen records were of the human voice. 'I like the human voice,' said the castaway. 'I like it for its connotation, its implications, for the memories it brings – and purely, plainly and simply, as a voice. It is my study, and my business.'

John's choices included the folk songs 'Lord Lovell', 'The Foggy, Foggy, Dew' and 'Little Sir William'; a recording of a Welsh rugby crowd singing 'Land of My Fathers'; the theme tune of his courting days, 'These Foolish Things' (even though a minute or two before he had just denigrated 'the machine-made thirty-two-bar melodies of Tin Pan Alley and Hollywood', a contradiction quickly acknowledged); and the quartet from *Rigoletto*.

'The records I have chosen would bring me the voices of home, the songs of the people of the countryside – my people – songs that originated in the rural nursery or the village pub . . . and the glorious sweeps of trained and rare operatic voices . . . and the world-weary voice of the West End bandstand. But if I were asked to choose just one record to epitomise England, it would be the choir of King's College Chapel, Cambridge, singing 'In Dulce Jubilo'. To attend Evensong in that chapel on a winter's afternoon when the candles are lighted seems to me an almost unbearable glory for the eyes, the ears and the mind.'

Having looked forward to a life of absolute idleness, 'an ambition since boyhood', and reluctantly decided that 'the largest cask of good medium sherry in the world' had to be foregone as his luxury item in favour of 'the biggest second-hand bookshop in the world', John ended his desert island dream by saying: 'Think of the happy years I could spend, browsing and arranging; of the treasures I might find – rare first editions and association copies . . .'

He returned to that desert island twenty-two years later, in 1975. His choice of records then was: Rubinstein's 'Melody in F'; Edric Connor singing 'Mercy Pourin' Dawn'; the traditional Russian tune 'Kalinka'; Dylan Thomas reading 'Fern Hill'; Gerald Finzi's setting 'To Lizbie Browne'; 'Buttercup Joe' from The Yetties (Dorset entertainers who worked several times with John); Burl Ives' rendition of 'Go Down, You Red, Red Roses'; and 'The Boar's Head Carol'.

The accommodation of his luxury this time was much simpler – champagne. The shipwrecked mariner was also allowed one book, and with this he unexpectedly bowled a gentle googly past the guard of his trusting interlocutor, as *The Life and Opinions of Tristram Shandy, Gentleman*, by that early non-linear writer Laurence Sterne, was to be found in the Arlott library in nine volumes. Both Sterne and Arlott would have appreciated the irony.

1953 was also, of course, the year of the Coronation. John was one of the large group of commentators assembled to relay the pageantry on radio, and he was delighted to find that he had been allocated a perch above the Criterion Restaurant, which looked down on Piccadilly Circus. He went up to his vantage point the day before and stayed there overnight, capturing what sleep he could. While the complicated technical preparations were being made, the *commis de rang* at the Criterion kept all the BBC team liberally supplied with refreshment.

At the Coronation rehearsal, John had met the Duke of Beaufort, Master of the Queen's Horse, and told him where he was to be positioned. He heard afterwards that as the Duke rode by on the day itself, he had remarked to his processional companion, Viscount Alanbrooke, the Lord High Constable: 'That lucky young devil Arlott is sitting up there with a bottle of wine while we're doing this, you know!'

The Duke was not wrong, and with a sip from his glass, John began to speak:

> And now the procession makes it stately way out of the curving white-walled gulf of Regent Street, gay with its Coronation decoration theme of roses, and into this warmly peopled Piccadilly Circus – it's been called 'the hub of the universe', but today it's a community of people, and it greets the procession without its usual traffic and with people who've come close together over the last twenty hours. They slept last night side by side and cheek by jowl on the pavements, on newspapers long since trampled underfoot. They were wet last night, dried in the breeze this morning, wet again later today and dried again with sun and wind, and now warm with happiness. A friendly wave for everybody – everybody's a personal friend whether they recognise them or not . . .
>
> Slowly this procession makes its stately way round the great sweep of the Circus with a quality that somehow twists the heart in the chest, and you can feel this coming up down there from the people

who have waited so anxiously and are now, by their faces, more than satisfied.

The RAF drawn up there have become, during the day, their friend. This band down here, the band of the Number 5 Region RAF, have become the people's friends too. They've sung with them, rallied them, applauded them as they marched down, and now they're greeting the procession with a little flutter of torn white paper, somewhere between ticker-tape and confetti falling down like white leaves on the procession and on the black silk wet of the wet road, and the whole procession moving down now through smiling faces, many of them young, with all last night's sleep and cares and cold forgotten, and hands and heads out of even the smallest windows there; and right up into the funnels of Glasshouse Street people packed back against the crush barriers. And over all, Eros, his wings arched and jokingly imprisoned today in a gay golden cage, with flowers white and red and green-leaved at his feet, and the octagonal casing of dark green and white paint, with the gilt fern and the E.R. insignia at his feet, and now the coach comes round and one recalls the words of the 41st Psalm: 'The Queen in a vesture of gold brought about with diverse colours'.

Throughout his vigil at the Criterion John had been fed and watered well enough to chuckle at the note sent to all the BBC crew by the Head of Outside Broadcasts, Charles Max-Muller:

The head of the Procession will reach Piccadilly Circus at 9.00 a.m. Breakfast will be provided in Broadcasting House afterwards at 10.30 a.m.

John had no need of that. Indeed, he stayed at his post to relay the riotous celebrations that went on until the small hours. His commentary after midnight was conspicuously coherent considering the circumstances, though he enjoyed an in-joke with his colleagues when he took his cue: 'The entire Circus is lit up . . .' Those with long memories immediately focused on the elegant, bowler-hatted figure of Commander Tommy Woodruff, returning to his old ship HMS *Nelson* to commentate on the Spithead Review and illumination of the Fleet at Portsmouth on 20 May 1937. Woodruff and his old mates had popped a few corks before the broadcast began (a few, Navy fashion, meant a lot), and the sea air heightened the effect. The listening nation heard a slurred, indistinct voice say: 'The whole Fleet is lit up – Er, by . . . by lights, I mean. The whole Fleet

is lit up by fairy lights.' (This he repeated five times.) 'The whole Fleet
is lit up . . . Now everything has disappeared. The whole Fleet is blotted
out. Disappeared, I mean – can't see it any longer. A few minutes ago
there was a fleet all lit up by fairy lights, and now there's no more fleet.
There is nothing between us and Heaven. There were lots of fairy lights,
and now the whole damn – sorry, the whole thing has gone.'

Announcer at Broadcasting House: 'The broadcast from Spithead is
now at an end. It is eleven minutes to eleven, and we will take you back
to the broadcast from the Carlton Hotel Dance Band.' Poor Woodruff
had been too alcoholically challenged to realise that mischievous comrades
had turned the swivel-chair in which he was sitting to face the opposite
direction. Woodruff's words became part of the rich history of live broadcasting. He was given a severe ticking-off and three months' leave due to
'strain' and a nasty headache.

If the Coronation was one highlight of 1953, winning back the Ashes
was another. The former effectively brought about the capitulation of the
British public to the power of television; the latter re-established their
pride in the power of their cricketers. Naturally, John commentated on
all five Tests, and also took part in a radio discussion on the likely consequences of televising cricket. He warned of the danger of creating a race
of watchers instead of a race of players, and was at odds with the others
around the table, his close friend the Hampshire captain Desmond Eagar,
the writer Denzil Batchelor, and the broadcaster Bill Mallalieu. John had
no need for a camera. He made his own pictures.

Despite having left the BBC staff, John still found himself a prisoner
of its bureaucracy. Since he worked in so many compartments of radio,
and because he had started his broadcasting career in Bristol, the centre
for the West of England Region, and not London where he was now
based, there was endless confusion in the issuing of contracts and their
source. A never-ceasing stream of correspondence passed back and forth
in an attempt to establish a *modus operandi*.

By 1953, John was being paid a hundred guineas for five-day Test
match duty, plus overnight expenses and subsistence. His work now came
under the umbrella of a company shelf-name, Invicta Productions, with
the directors shown on the letterhead to be John, Dawn, and a shipping
lawyer, Brian Dulanty. Son of an Irish ambassador, Dulanty was, for a
time, the oldest show-jumper in the country. He was said to have maintained his stamina by consuming a bottle and a half of whiskey a day.
Initially, Invicta's office was at 32 Bishopsgate in the City of London, but
it moved to 26 Charing Cross Road WC2, where John took a room as a
workplace for his secretary, Valerie France, and himself. The new office

overlooked Cecil Court, that charming precinct between Charing Cross
Road and St Martin's Lane that catered for myriad collecting tastes, so
John had to combat temptation every time he went out of the door.

Valerie had become John's secretary at the BBC when he moved to
Staff Training. She replaced Barbara Forrester, who had looked after him
so well for so long: Barbara left one corporation to join another, BOAC,
as a stewardess, after spending time in Children's Programmes, Television.

Among a range of programmes for which John was now engaged were a
sketch on *Much Binding in the Marsh*; *The Name's the Same*, which involved
meeting another John Arlott and making comparisons (though John failed
to turn up, as he had forgotten the date of the recording); and *Who
Dunnit?*, as a member of a panel trying to guess the solution of a mystery.
Given his knowledge of the criminal mind, John was a quintessential
choice, although he once told me that he had tried to invent a detective
story and failed, because he could only write chronologically.

Perhaps it was writing on cricket, and describing other sports, that
created this 'mind corridor' for him. By the end of 1953, Geoffrey
Whitelock's invaluable bibliography of John's output in the *Journal of the
Cricket Society* reveals that, a decade since his first venture into print, he
had no fewer than twenty-nine titles to his credit. And that figure includes
only the books and booklets of which he was the author, co-author or
editor. It does not include his contributions to the works of others, pam-
phlets, forewords, articles for magazines, annuals and papers, and scripts
for broadcasts. Among the twenty-nine books are accounts of tours, collections of essays, a brief biography of Maurice Tate, an annotated reader's
guide to cricket literature, a sporting anthology, assembled poetry, and
limited edition off-prints. If the standard is not entirely even – 'Some of
them are scissors-and-paste jobs,' said John himself – that is perhaps only
to be expected. Even so, it was quite an achievement.

Besides his writing there was the travelling. The cricketing circus then
did not have the advantage of the motorway system, or powerful modern
horse-power, although there was a railway network that had not yet been
Beechingised. Generally, Sunday was a non-playing day – except for chari-
ties and benefits – devoted to recovery, but John was rarely not going
somewhere.

For the *Evening News* he now made a sort of trial run to Copenhagen
before journeying more extensively into the European hinterland. The
paper's front-page box announced:

> He went there to see for himself the places where history is being
> created day by day. He did not go to collect the official utterances

of politicians, but to see for himself what these places look like, what
the people do and talk about, to create a picture of the background to
the history that is happening about us.

That reads rather like sentences lifted from the persuasive epistle John
must have sent to John Marshall in order to get him to sanction the
project. There was a prologue in Holland – 'a country of canals and
windmills, allotments and goalposts; of care and cleanliness, neatness and
good husbandry' – before John exposed himself to the autobahns of
Germany to reach Detmold and Hanover – where there was little 'idling,
laughter or gossip' – and took a look at Westphalian farms where 'fields
[are] so frugally run that it is not unusual to see a horse and a cow
yoked together in a plough'. Next came the night work and night life of
Hamburg. Having watched the Hanseatic State indulge its pleasures with
grim sobriety, he set off down the Rhine and through the Ruhr valley,
and thence to both sectors of Berlin before crossing the border to visit
the Displaced Persons Camp at Spittal in Austria.

Vienna was 'impracticable, dusty and nostalgic', in contrast to Germany, 'a country where the brain can never rest; curiosity, anxiety about
the future, maintain tension. Think about Vienna for ten minutes and
judgement says that it is an anachronism, a city economically impossible
while the hard realities of modern civilisation rule.' John did, though, find
a new spirit in the Austrian capital. He had last been there in October
1946, when it had been 'a devastated city in which pale, under-nourished
people moved half punch-drunk through a residue of rubble'.

On that previous visit he had been lecturing to the Forces. A beautiful
young woman seconded to the Army Education Corps had been deputed
to escort him for the month. Having assimilated Vienna, they travelled
in what had been one of Reichsmarshall Hermann Goering's Mercedes-
Benzes to Venice. There John underwent what he called total enlightenment; the palaces and paintings, the barcas and gondolas, the splendour
of the setting – all of it overwhelmed him. In essence, he experienced
culture-shock the right way round. And culture – not so shocking – had
come in the shape of the young woman, too: she managed to teach John
a little Italian.

This time, as well as writing for the *Evening News*, he was again lecturing to the Forces. No doubt he wished he could again go to Venice and
learn a little more Italian. And so he did, after finishing his official tour
in Trieste, where he drank *slivovic* with two friendly Yugoslavs in a hillside
tavern on the border – 'the front door went into Italy and the back door
into Yugoslavia'.

The trip had been hard work, and a lot of it had been depressing: Berlin, with Russian look-out posts everywhere, particularly so. His car had been stopped by one of the East German 'Vopos' – the People's Police. The British Military Policeman accompanying John attempted to be jocose: 'What are you? Police, Special Branch, Liberal and the BBC? Huh! Don't fancy your chances. I don't think you'll ever get out.'

A curious incident which took place in Austria a day or so later reveals the state of John's mind after the uneasy cross-currents of Germany. He had been lying on his bed in a sixth-floor hotel room in Graz reading Thomas Hardy's *Jude the Obscure*. Dusk was falling outside, but there was still just sufficient light for him to be able to see the words without turning on the old-fashioned lamp in a corner of the room. 'I had just got to the point where Jude and Sue open the closet door and find the bodies of the three children hanging there – I dropped the book and dashed down six flights of stairs to find anybody who could speak English – I was so frightened.'

Retelling that story ever after, John used to say that nothing had ever moved him so much. For him, *Jude* was the greatest of English novels. But his feelings about Hardy were ambivalent. While recognising him as a supreme novelist, John recoiled at his parsimony and meanness: 'You go to the man who is the greatest in his field and find there is a human being who is tragically disappointing,' he told Mike Brearley years later. 'I think it's one of the greatest disappointments you encounter in life, to find that the man who is great at the thing you admire is third-rate as a human.'

The pervasive air of gloom soon lifted, however. The chills of November began to recede as John prepared to set off in pursuit of Len Hutton's 1954–55 side to Australia.

15

Ashes Retained

The summer of 1954 had been notable for Pakistan becoming the first country to win a Test match on its first visit to England, thereby drawing the four-match rubber. The price had been paid at The Oval for underestimating the opposition. But by the time the MCC side embarked at Tilbury that had been forgotten in the determination to retain the Ashes.

John caught up with the cricketers after the tour was well underway. First, he had business in Singapore and Hong Kong. His old standby of Services lectures meant new places to see and old friends to visit. A chum from schooldays, 'Bunny' Lunn, acted as guide in Singapore – which John found much too humid – and one of his former contributors to *Book of Verse*, Edmund Blunden, filled in the gaps in Hong Kong. In between, there had been fleeting visits to Karachi, Delhi and Calcutta. Blunden, who was Professor of English at the University of Hong Kong, had written to John a few months before:

> Army Welfare is an excellent idea, I find, and I hope it will allow you just a little quiet time in Hong Kong – quietish, for you will be eagerly awaited by several; but the Blundens regard their claim as the best of all, and later on we shall await whatever you feel like doing here. It is especially good news that there should be two occasions – I am glad you will see Japan, though their nonentity in cricket is an old grievance of mine. The victory of Pakistan should encourage them to send a team at once if only XI men who had previously performed only at baseball or cormorant fishing.

Although John found he was much in demand in Hong Kong, nothing was allowed to get in the way of a spectacular Chinese feast of many flavours, which made wok dishes thereafter a muted experience by comparison. His subsequent stopovers in Seoul and Tokyo, where he read Hardy to Blunden's old students at the university, were brief.

John's first impression of Australia was that it was exciting, new, bright and busy. It was also hot. Throughout his life John had bother with the thermometer. Something in his metabolism was prey more than most to high temperatures, and the dehydrating effects of copious quantities of wine did not help that condition, as he was well aware. 'The trouble with cricket outside England is that it's only played in the hot countries – South Africa, India, Australia, the West Indies. And I don't like the heat: not the right climate for drinking claret.'

The comment was made to John Wilkes, who, in an extremely active life, has been a businessman, media commentator on public affairs, Chairman of the Australian Institute of Political Science and a Member of the Security Appeals Tribunal. Wilkes saw much of John while he was in Australia, both on a professional basis and as a host, and remembers the time vividly:

ABC – the Australian Broadcasting Corporation – had copied the BBC's successful *Any Questions?* format, so we jumped at the chance to empanel John when he arrived in 1954. I was a regular panellist and he took part in several of these radio programmes during the tour. Our first performance together was in a community hall in suburban Sydney – we did these as live shows before various types of community organisations at venues in the locality. Our microphones were linked by landline to the ABC's transmitter where intros and sign-offs were added by announcers and the programme went to air about one hour later. On this night there was an extremely violent rainstorm in the middle of our show and only then did we discover that the hall had a 'tin roof' – corrugated iron sheeting. When the rain suddenly turned to hail the din was indescribable and we had to call a halt to proceedings for about half an hour. The panel adjourned to a small office where John opened his briefcase and produced a bottle of Dry Sack. He, Bill O'Reilly, who was also on the panel, and I drank the lot before the programme was able to restart. Our answers thereafter were hilarious, to the glee of most in the audience, though not to our ABC overlords.

On the Christmas edition of *Any Questions?* the panel was made up of John Wilkes and John Arlott again; Betty Archdale, headmistress of a private school for girls, who had played for the England women's cricket team before the war as vice-captain to Charis Fry (daughter of the ubiquitous C.B.); and Lady Cilento (mother of the actress Diane, and herself a prominent medical specialist). One question which led to raised eyebrows was relayed to the audience by the programme's producer, former ABC war correspondent Frank Legge: 'What would members of the panel give a girlfriend for Christmas?' To which John responded: 'Well, Christmas is to celebrate the birth of a child – why not give her a baby?'

Meanwhile, the England side had been asked searching questions on the cricket field. Undefeated up to the First Test at Brisbane, they little expected to be humbled by an innings and 154 runs. There were mitigating factors. The wicket-keeper, Godfrey Evans, had sunstroke and was unable to play, and on the first morning Denis Compton, in trying to save a boundary, ran into the fence palings and fractured a bone in his hand. But England contributed to their own downfall. Hutton misread the pitch and put Australia in, only to see twelve catches go down. 601 was an unassailable total.

John had wrongly predicted the result. Besides his written pieces for the *Evening News* he was giving spoken close-of-play summaries for the BBC. In a letter to the Corporation's cricket correspondent, Rex Alston, he expressed his reservations about the team, and also asked for some advice:

> Strategically, I do not like our side for tomorrow's Test without a spinner, and with such weak catching, but I still think we shall win – or is that the wishful thinking of the exile? . . .
>
> I should be very grateful if you would let me have a line to tell me how my summaries on the Second Test go – both in terms of matter and arrangement and in respect of sound-quality and intelligibility. Do I assume that the score is given by the announcer in the preamble?
>
> Perhaps, too, you could tell me what is anticipated in terms of next season – are you and I to carry through as usual? I shall be taking my holiday early, so I could run on past the final Test to the end of the season. I understand from Charles Fortune that he will be covering the tour for South Africa.

For the Second Test in Sydney it was Australia's turn to wear the shades. Acting captain Arthur Morris – both Ian Johnson and Keith Miller were unfit – emulated Hutton's Brisbane decision and put England in. Most thought it a wise strategy when the tourists were dismissed for 154, in which the top score was 35 from Johnny Wardle. But with fine bowling from Trevor Bailey, Brian Statham and, in particular, Frank Tyson, and a century in the second innings from Peter May, England managed to scramble a victory by 38 runs with a day and a half to spare.

Back in England, Rex Alston responded to John's letter:

I managed to wake up sufficiently early to hear not only all commentary on the Second Test, but also your own pieces, and I thought that the latter were quite admirable. Reception throughout the match was pretty good, the worst day being the last, and thank goodness you came in with the proper headline 'England have won'. Charles Fortune in his attempts to give us the details as soon as possible at 7 a.m. ties himself into knots, and has to get rid of four or five parentheses before he gives us the vital news.

I thought your pieces were very well done. They told me everything I wanted to know, and in the words of Kenneth Adam (at an OB Department party last night) 'John has disciplined himself extremely well in the cause'! I think you were quite right to take us through the day's play without too much statistical detail, and then to finish as you did with an assessment of the position and maybe a prophecy.

The fading in was rather clumsily done nearly every time, and we usually missed your first few words, but that was not your fault.

I have had a look at next year's fixtures, but have not yet definitely been commissioned to fix matches and apportion commentators. I hope to get down to it in the New Year and to let you know as soon as possible. I understand that coverage will be pretty well on the same lines as in previous years, and I expect we shall be asked to do ball-by-ball for South Africa, though at the moment they have not made up their minds.

John spent Christmas with the Wilkes family and friends at Chinaman's Beach, Mosman, on Sydney's north shore. He arrived with the barest essentials of clothing but a two-dozen case of Dry Sack sherry. Bill Bowes, a fellow member of the press contingent who happened to be staying with neighbours of the Wilkeses, had arrived in essentially the wrong clothing – a spectacular Yorkshire blazer. The real essential for the men, though, was that there were enough of them in close proximity and with time on their hands to make sure that the twenty-four bottles of sherry lasted barely five days. With obligations in the kitchen the women had other matters on their hands. John Wilkes has not forgotten that:

At dinner when the last of the sherry was consumed, I pushed back my chair unsteadily and muttered, 'I don't feel very well,' and promptly collapsed on the floor. Shortly afterwards Arlott stood up and said, 'I don't feel well either,' and also collapsed, so the women put him to bed too. By the end of the evening only one of the men was left – an architect friend of mine who, shortly after midnight, marched to his room with apparently all faculties intact. Some time late next day J.A. and I both surfaced little the worse for wear but very contrite. Ted, the architect, was soundly, though not soundlessly, sleeping. He surfaced just over two days later, mumbling, 'Dry Sack indeed – more like a wet sandbag.'

Amidst the jollity there was a moment of poignancy. On Christmas Day, John rang his Highgate home. He had been sending postcards practically every day, but now he heard his wife's and children's voices for the first time in just over a month. To him it seemed like years. They were in another world. The distorted and disjointed conversations, in which everyone tried to speak at once because they did not know what to say, emphasised the distance and separation. 'I think it may have been his first Christmas away from home,' said John Wilkes. 'When he came back to our dinner table he was visibly affected and tearful.'

In replying to Rex Alston's letter, which arrived a few days later, John wrote as much. First, though, he concentrated on the cricket summaries:

Very many thanks for so pleasant and reassuring a letter. I enjoyed doing the summaries immensely – one day you must enjoy the idleness of watching a Test match all day with no commentaries to do and just about enough writing to clarify and order your thoughts on the play – I feel almost ashamed of my laziness and keep looking over my shoulder to see if I am being watched. It makes it an absolute pleasure to do a summary at the end of play for one's first sight of a microphone.

I will remember about the awkward fade-up and make my first two phrases repetitive in substance – thanks.

Although there is a gusty wind it is as hot as a greenhouse here – and in an hour the Third Test starts. The cricket is interesting throughout Australia but otherwise it is a dull country: the people much of a hearty sameness and none of the things that interest me available in more than driblets – virtually no second-hand bookshops, bare bones of worthwhile architecture, no pottery, no glass, no pictures. I had a nine-minute phone call home at Christmas when the baby [Timothy] cried and that so depressed me that I swore I would never make another overseas tour of any length unless the family could come or until they are grown up.

There were other distractions to remind John of the green, green grass of home. A specific one was when John Wilkes practised the ancient Australian art of winding up the Poms: 'When John bought his boxer swimshorts at Spit Junction [a suburb of Sydney] he put them on to show us and I commented that he looked properly dressed for lawn-mowing, as it was very warm indeed. He asked, "Where's the mower then?" and promptly went out to cut our front lawns. It was very hot, he perspired profusely, our neighbours guffawed – one shouted "Better stick to the microphone, John!" – the shirtless and Pommy-white J.A. scorched and later suffered. He never forgave me. Later, whenever we visited him in Alderney, he *commanded* me to reciprocate and I had to spend most of our first day mowing his rather large, walled-in back lawns. His only regret was that both his mowers were powered, unlike the hand model he had used in Sydney.'

While he was in Sydney, Wilkes took John to a Wine and Food Society lunch at the Hermitage Restaurant. The members had a system whereby three of them spoke at each meeting after the meal – one on the food, one on the cheeses and one on the wines. 'Our main course this day was roast pork, and the food commentator happened to be Eric Baume, a senior journalist, ex-war correspondent and later to be a television personality,' remembered John Wilkes. 'He was also very Jewish. When he rose to deliver his expert opinion he said: "This was the finest dish of Gefilte fish I have ever been pleased to enjoy –" and sat down! Arlott roared with laughter. Four years later my wife and I dined with him beneath the large bust of Gladstone at the National Liberal Club in London. We ordered the fish and John remarked, "They cut off the crackling before serving."'

Even though John had complained to Rex Alston about the dearth of second-hand bookshops in Australia, there were enough around to make his luggage heavier at each stage of the tour. In fact, it was in a Sydney second-hand bookshop that he came across a fellow browser, Frank Tyson, taking some hours off from his high-pace exertions. Frank found that he had many interests in common with John, not least the French language and wine. When they went to dine in The Old Australia Hotel in the city, it became apparent that their interest was not widely shared: 'John asked for some Burgundy,' said Frank, 'and I remember the waiter came up and placed this bottle on the table in front of him – there were beads of condensation coming down the sides – and opened it. Literally, he'd had it in the fridge. John looked at this aghast, and the waiter turned to him and said, "There you are, mate – we've got another one like that in the freezer!"'

The Australia of the 1950s was not the Australia of today. Multiculturalism was in its infancy, as were multi-cultural living refinements. 'Then they had the six o'clock swill, when all the pubs closed,' went on Frank Tyson. 'They'd pile into the pubs out of work and drink as many beers as they could in the hour before six o'clock. Since then, the country has become far more civilised – now it's a great country. They've got the mix of nations now, the mix of cultures – you can eat out very well. They have very, very good wines which John would appreciate now. But in those days it was a steak-and-beer country.'

The cricketing convoy moved on to Melbourne for the Third Test. Like any traveller, John had been accumulating impressions, visual images to be resurrected by mere mention of the place-name. Brisbane's homes on stilts, providing cool locations for keg (barbecue) parties; Sydney's welter of white concrete wicket-strips – a breeding ground for aspiring Bradmans and Lindwalls; and now, in Melbourne, the sheer size of the cricket ground, which was being enlarged to accommodate 120,000 spectators for the 1956 Olympic Games. It was hard to comprehend a cricketing venue being able to hold a full house at Lord's four or five times over. There was more general incomprehension at the behaviour of the wicket on the third day, especially as it had been covered. Surface cracks evident on the Saturday had closed completely by Monday morning, and the pitch was far less sporting. After an inquiry, the Victorian Cricket Association and the Melbourne Cricket Club concluded that watering had not taken place. It made little difference. After a century by Cowdrey and a near-century from May, a devastating 7 for 27 in twelve and a half overs from Tyson swept Australia aside.

Following the Test came an excursion to Tasmania for two games. After the intensity of Melbourne, a general sense of *ennui* is apparent in a letter from John to Philip Snow, who had not long before left an attractive posting as Provincial Commissioner, Magistrate and Assistant Colonial Secretary of Fiji and the Western Pacific, to become Bursar of Rugby School:

> I am writing this in the middle of the MCC–Combined XI match at Hobart – a rather boring affair after the excitement of the Tests but relieved by the batting of Rodwell and the bowling of Considine, either of whom could walk into English county cricket and be well worth his place.
>
> Ours is not a good fielding side, and, with the exception of May and Cowdrey, indifferent in batting, but for Statham and Tyson poor in bowling. Fortunately, the Australians are worse.

Years later, when writing his autobiography, John adapted his stance: 'It would be difficult to argue that these were two great teams, but there were some fine players among them, though, at that time, some were past their best and others were still developing. Such names though as Harvey, Archer, Miller, Burge, Benaud, Davidson, Lindwall and Johnston on the Australian side, and Compton, Hutton, Statham, Tyson, Bailey, Bedser, Cowdrey, May and Graveney on the English, have an epic ring about them.' An example of historical perspective changing a view.

At Adelaide for the Fourth Test, Australia were without Lindwall, who had a leg injury. By the end of the first innings only 18 runs separated the two sides. John felt that England would ultimately lose the match to the Australian spinners on a crumbling wicket, but again, after early breakthroughs by Appleyard, Australia was destroyed by the pace of Tyson and Statham. Wanting only 94 to win, England were rocking perilously as Miller rampaged through the top of their batting order; and a score of 18 for 3 became 49 for 4 when Miller held a breathtaking catch at cover-point to dismiss May. John Wilkes recalls how, in his summary, John described four Air Force jets 'galing low and impressively over the ground' as if in tribute to the great all-rounder and ex-RAAF pilot. But Compton and Bailey, with a late strike from Evans, saw the tourists home by five wickets. The Ashes had been retained in convincing style, and the celebrations that followed were distinctly audible, even if, in the city of churches, the bells were silent.

The popping of corks had a stimulating effect on John. In the next four days he visited practically every vineyard in South Australia. The secretary of the Wine and Brandy Producers' Association organised the itinerary, and the two Johns, Arlott and Wilkes, were couriered by the polio-stricken wine grower Bob Seppelt. In spite of his crutches and the searing heat – the temperature peaked at 112°F – Seppelt was indefatigable. His stoicism in the face of such adversity led even John not to complain overmuch about the oppressive weather.

Hardy's, Seppelt's, Berri Co-Op, Stonyfell, Buring and Sobel's, Tolley's, Yalumba, Gramps, Orlando, Reynell's, Woodley's Penfold's Mildara, Waikerie Co-Op and others all underwent copious tasting. At Yalumba, Wyndham 'Windy' Hill-Smith, a former wicket-keeper for Western Australia and nephew of the great batsman Clem Hill, entertained them regally in the magnificent dining-room bedecked with his father's trophies from big-game hunting in India. John remarked that the sight nearly turned him into a vegetarian.

As John had been impressed by the Lutheran-style architecture of the Barossa Valley – a sizeable German community resided in the area –

Bob Seppelt thought that a visit to a winery at Sevenhill run by a Jesuit community might prove an interesting variant. John Wilkes recalls:

> Brother John Hanlon, then thirty-three, had been wine-maker for three years (and was to remain so until his death in 1972), and he showed us around. Arlott, like so many Poms, knew little or nothing about Roman Catholicism, so Brother Hanlon had to explain about Fathers and Brothers and why he devoted his life to producing altar wine for the Mass and the greater glory of God. I think this brought spiritual satisfaction to Arlott. He was delighted to hear that Sevenhill had just started selling commercial table wines, but somewhat taken aback when Brother Hanlon confessed his own addiction to Coca-Cola.
>
> So we went down to the crypt, to find it full of priests, some in cassocks, some in dog-collars and some in casual shirts and slacks. Standing, sitting on barrels, leaning against casks, all were sampling the brew. Nonplussed in this popish gathering, Arlott fumbled for conversational gambits. Finally, 'Tell me,' he said to Father Peter Kelly, 'is there any difference between your various orders, Cistercians, Benedictines, Carthusians and so on?' Peter replied: 'I can only answer by telling you a story. A Jesuit and a Franciscan, pursuing this same topic, couldn't agree so decided to ask God. On a slip of paper they wrote, "Heavenly Father, which order is the more acceptable in Thy sight – the Brotherhood of St Francis or the Society of Jesus?" They set fire to the paper and the ashes drifted skywards. Soon a white paper fluttered down. They fell upon it and read, "My children, in My sight all men are equal. (Signed) God, S.J."'

Once more in Sydney for the Fifth Test – and it rained. The downpours were the worst experienced in New South Wales for fifty years: there was loss of life in the Hunter River Valley, and millions of pounds' worth of damage. Play did not start until two o'clock on the fourth day, which meant that MCC's tour profits were down by nearly £8000, proportionately a feather in the scale. Tom Graveney, with his first Test hundred against Australia, and substantial scores from May, Compton and Bailey, put England into a position from which they could not lose. Indeed Australia, failing by one run to avoid the follow-on, might well have capitulated to the spin of Johnny Wardle for a second time if another hour or so had been available; but a draw it was, with Hutton appropriately getting the last wicket in the final over.

During the England innings, commentator Charles Fortune – often thought to be British in South Africa but recognised as South African in England – had been distracted. Fortune was given to flights of fancy, and this particular one had just taken off from Kingsford-Smith airport. Was the plane going here, or going there? Around the world? Really? What make was it? How much turbulence would it encounter? Were the passengers able to see the cricket? What kind of meal were they having . . . Meanwhile, Lindwall bowled Bailey. A sudden interjection: 'Oh my God, he's out!'

John and Alf Gover, who, having finished his splendid bowling days for Surrey and England was also in Australia for the press, were standing at the back of the commentary box. John, of course, had not been participating in the ball-by-ball commentaries. Gover recalled: 'John stepped in and took up the commentary. He kept it going and waved Charles to keep quiet as if it was normal for him to come in, and continued for five or six overs. Then he referred to Charles and handed back, at the same time pointing towards me. Charles took the hint and after a few balls asked me a technical question. And so it went on, and appeared natural for people listening in and not as if Charles had gone off-beam. "Doesn't know enough about the game," said John afterwards. "Couldn't even knot a club tie!"' – referring to Fortune's foible of wearing the length of his tie *over* the knot, rather than through it.

Alf Gover and John spent much time together on the tour. Once, after doing a studio recording, they went to a fish party at Rockhampton in Queensland: 'It was thrown by a woman who ran a hotel who was a Charles Fortune fan,' recalled Alf. 'He had this wonderful educated voice and women in Australia loved it. They thought he was marvellous, which he was – he was a lovely chap, Charles. Anyway, between us we demolished forty-nine oysters and we had no ill-effects. I kept saying, we can't eat any more, and John would reply, "Come on, they're wonderful." And we had beer with them, not wine. John said, "Don't drink wine with these oysters, otherwise you'll have tummy trouble." It's the only time I ever saw John drink anything other than a glass of wine.'

The socialising never seemed to end. The rain which had delayed the start of the last Test allowed many of the English squad and most of the Sydneysiders in the Australian team to attend a riotous forty-first birthday party held for John by the Wilkeses. His fellow-commentators were also there in force – notably Alan McGilvray, Charles Fortune and Michael Charlton, who was eventually to find his way to BBC TV's *Panorama* desk. (In the 1960s, Charlton was to turn the tables on earlier patronising remarks by English commentators when, during a Test in Sydney in which Alan Davidson captured early wickets, he said: 'There goes Davo, with his hands fairly dripping with the blood of Englishmen!') At the party too

were Bill Bowes, with whom John shared a flat in the King's Cross district
of Sydney for a time, and Alf Gover. Denis Compton could not make it,
nor could Len Hutton, the stresses of captaincy even now bearing down
on his shoulders.

This presumably left John free to produce his Hutton story. Not that
the subject needed to be out of the way for him to do so. John was a great
lover of funny – some might say bawdy – stories, and always had an ear
ready to catch the latest on the circuit, giving the lie to the theory that
the principal sources of jokes are those with little sense of humour themselves. As with his commentaries, though, the words are better heard than
read.

The Final Test – not the one happening in Australia but the 1953
Terence Rattigan film – starred Jack Warner, Robert Morley and George
Relph. According to Halliwell's *Film Guide*, it was 'cluttered up with real
cricketers and stymied for lack of action'. A number of the current England
side played themselves, including Hutton as the captain. The crucial
moment arrives when the veteran batsman, played by Jack Warner, leaves
the pavilion to play his last innings for his country. Everyone hopes for a
century. An encouraging pat on the back from his captain: 'You've done
it before – do it again.' John Wilkes relives Arlott telling the story:

> *Lights, Camera, Action.* Hutton placed his hand on Warner's shoul-
> der. In a hesitant, artificially-modulated voice, pausing between
> every word, Hutton produced an alarmingly stilted 'You have done
> it be-fore – do it a-gain.' The director [Anthony Asquith] decided
> on another take – begging Len to do it naturally and in his own
> accent. No better, so another take and another and another until
> the light curtailed all shooting until the following Monday. He took
> Len aside, urged him to get a corner seat on the train home to
> Pudsey, hide behind that day's copy of *The Times* and repeat to
> himself over and over on the journey 'You've done it before – do it
> again!' in strict time with the rhythm of the wheels, which Len duly
> did. Over and over, also all through supper. In the early hours of
> Sunday morning he was rudely awakened by a nudge in the ribs
> and his wife exclaiming: 'That's all very well, Len, but you have to
> co-operate!'

Apocryphal or not, Wilkes continued with a tale about the teller:

> John had met a young woman friend of ours who shared his interest
> in poetry and writing generally, and their friendship developed

BBC Staff Training Unit, General Course, May/June 1951. J.A. sitting next to his boss James Pennethorne Hughes *(3rd from right, front row)*.

Left to right: Omar Kureishi, Pakistani cricket writer and broadcaster, Hanif Mohammed and his wife with an expansive J.A.

Prepared for the hustings: 'I shall remain a Liberal all my life.'

A Liberal gathering at Lady Noel-Buxton's home, High Beach, Upshire. *Left to right:* J. Vincent Chapman, Chairman Epping Liberal Association; Lady Noel-Buxton; J.A.; Vicky Hoddell, wife of John's agent; Howard Davies, President of Epping Liberal Association; Norman Hoddell (*largely obscured*); and Marjorie Chapman.

Following his benefit in 1957, Leo Harrison commissioned this engraved glass by Laurence Whistler as a present for John. Whistler describes the picture on the glass as 'a bedside table with a lit candle and a glass of water, matches, book of poems, apple and watch ... A moth has whirled about the candle and landed by the candlestick. All its circles are engraved as though they existed simultaneously; for such is the illusion in real life, where by the speed of its movement the moth is a scribble more than a defined object in motion.'

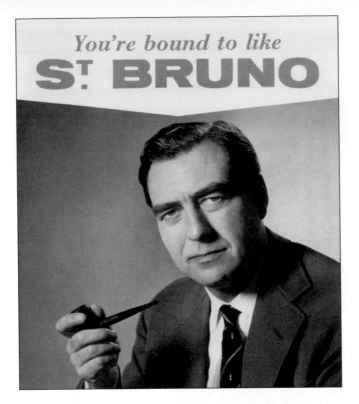

Before anyone thought of
Government health warnings
and cholesterol intake.

Poured correctly, label uppermost.

Surely it's not corked?

Below-stairs at Alresford, where John disregarded Tovey's dictum that 'Your stomach is your wine cellar; keep the stock small and cool.'

With thirty-two-year-old David Frith at the back of The Old Sun in 1969. Kitchen to the right, snug and library immediately behind.

Golf during Alresford Week, October 1974. J.A. putting for a birdie with *(left to right)* Dr Sam Saunders, John Samuel and Maurice Edelston looking on.

Christopher Fielden with John at Beaune, 1976, at the time when they were collaborating on their book *Burgundy Vines and Wines*.

Awarded the OBE. With Valerie, Robert and Tim in 1970.

Pat and John married at Winchester Register Office, 6 April 1977.

With Fred Trueman for the BBC Television series, 1977. 'I'd bowl 'im a yorker right through 'is legs!'

to the satisfaction of both. The paperback edition of the Ernest Hemingway novel *For Whom the Bell Tolls* had been published in Australia some months earlier, and our friend had delighted in it – especially the romantic interlude between the American, Roberto, and the Spanish girl, Maria. You will recall how this climaxed in Roberto's sleeping robe, described then by Maria as 'when the earth moved'. Rashly, a little later, I asked our friend, 'And did the earth move?' to receive her immediate reply, 'Yes – but you should just see his earth-moving equipment!'

John's return home from this cricketing crusade was, as after the South African tour of 1948–49, not direct. In letters to Philip Snow, John had sought advice about accommodation and presents for the family which could be found in Fiji. Snow put him in touch with Mosese Bogisa, a member of the talented Fijian side that had played in New Zealand in 1948. On that tour Mosese had leaped over the boundary fence at Canterbury to fetch a six-hit, only to land on the far side at a much lower level. He hurled the ball back, but could not climb the fence, so he started to run around the circumference in the direction of the entrance. Play resumed on the upper level, with the fielders puzzled as to Mosese's whereabouts, as he was totally obscured from view. Eventually, having reached the gate, Mosese found himself stopped by an official who refused to believe he was taking part in the game, with the result that Fiji fielded for some time with only ten men.

On meeting John at Nadi, Mosese took him out of the town to the village where he was born. There they met Taite Nalukuya, whose reputation as a ferocious fielder had not been harmed when he fractured the skull of an unwary batsman with a spearlike return. Together with a convivial cricketing all-rounder, the New Zealand chemist Clarence Angleson Adams, commonly known as Gerry, they made John's stay memorable. The local ceremonies and dancing, and much kava, the potent brew whose roots are allied to the pepper family, meant that somebody was bound to end up with a headache. In the event it was Adams, who had easiest access to a quick remedy. John's opinion of kava, a cement-like concoction tasting of toothpaste, which has to be swallowed in one go, is not recorded.

Further stops in Hawaii, San Francisco, Chicago and finally a week in New York – writing paid for the extended diversion – revealed new sights and fresh faces. A friendly *old* face was the most significant encounter. While John had been on the far side of the world, John Marshall had ceased to be editor of the *Evening News*, and had become a representative of Associated Newspapers Ltd in America. His place in the editor's chair had been taken by his former deputy, Reg Willis. John had heard of the change, but was anxious to have details at first hand.

Back home, he steeled himself for a professional confrontation. A discreet and unofficial message from a friend in the editorial office at the *News* had warned him that the new incumbent would no longer be requiring his services. On hearing this, John had quickly to lined up a job with the *News Chronicle* in Bouverie Street, just across the road from Carmelite House.

When John entered Reg Willis's office, the new editor had no idea that he already knew of his impending dismissal, or that he had secured a new post. And, crucially, John knew that he did not know that he knew. Hesitantly, Willis outlined the changes he proposed to make, in which there would be no place for Arlott:

'I see,' growled John. 'And I suppose that means you won't even be signing my expenses.'

'Of course we will,' replied the uncomfortable Willis, wanting to be as placatory as possible. 'There's no question of us not doing that.'

'Very well,' said John tautly. 'Perhaps you'd be kind enough to sign them now, please.'

Whereupon he produced several sheets itemising extensive financial outlay over the four months he had been away. In different conversations I had with John in later years, the total figure varied from £18,000 to 'Can't remember,' but we can be sure that it was a lot of money, for on seeing the amount, Willis blanched. He opened his mouth as if to speak, then thought better of it. He signed with a flourish.

John's close friendship with John Marshall had not helped. Inevitably, there had been some in-house jealousy about their rapport, as John had been writing regularly for the paper without having come through the ranks of journalism or having professional playing credentials. But this was small irk compared to the envy, dislike and probable insecurity of E.M. 'Lyn' Wellings, the *News*'s number one cricket reporter. John got on well with people. Wellings did not. The two never did see eye to eye. And it is likely that Wellings felt his position usurped when John was engaged to write summaries for the 1950–51 MCC tour of Australia. On John's death nearly four decades later, a reporter rang Wellings at the instigation of Matthew Engel of the *Guardian* to ask what he thought of Arlott. He received an emphatic reply: 'Yes, I'll tell you what I thought of him. He was the most evil man I ever met. He was hated throughout the building. And what's more, he knew nothing about cricket.' Which undoubtedly reveals more about the speaker than the subject. Wellings successfully pursued a thin line of acrimony in most of his dealings throughout an entire lifetime.

The *News Chronicle* was a reporters' paper, which meant that the sub-editors interfered as little as possible with their copy. It was also a paper of principle and purpose, which meant that it retained a loyal and devoted staff. Moreover, with its predecessors, it had been John's family newspaper for three generations, which meant the Liberal tradition was strong. Above all, it was a friendly newspaper.

John covered cricket and football – although Crawford White and John Camkin respectively were in pole positions for those sports – as well as wine and general interest items. Under the last heading was his defence of the so-called cranky behaviour of Lieutenant-Commander Bill Boaks, who had been held in custody for seven days after obstructing traffic in the Strand in the course of his campaign for road courtesy. Was the fact that Boaks's car had painted stripes, and his use of a loudspeaker to pro-nounce safety slogans, unacceptable eccentricity, John wondered. If so, what were publicity agents wishing to sell chewing gum, or election cam-paigners touting for votes, going to do in the future?

In that year, 1955, John first stood as Liberal candidate for Epping in the General Election. The long run-up to polling day demanded much of his attention and energy. At the same time, working for the *News Chronicle* meant that his attention and energy were divided.

Roy Nash, education and labour correspondent for the paper, who wrote a long series of articles exposing Communist troublemakers in the electricians' union, remembers John's approach when it came to making proposals: 'As a freelance he was able to go to different departments. He was always welcome because he was known to be helpful. At that period he was a journeyman journalist, and he would come in and say, "I've got the makings of a good idea." It wasn't for self-glorification – he was genuinely interested in the paper.' Unusually, John would sit in on edi-torial meetings, always called 'The Conference'. At those meetings would be Michael Curtis, the editor until Norman Cursley took over; Tom Hopkinson, the features editor; his deputy Ian Law, cartoonist; Bill Pattin-son, news; James Cameron, foreign affairs; John Camkin, football; Craw-ford White, cricket; Bill Hicks, the sports editor; David Walker, chief leader writer; and Geoffrey Goodman before he went to the *Mirror*. People would come and go. 'There would be discussion not just on the day's paper but long-term planning,' commented Nash. 'The paper was in difficulties. Some wild ideas were bandied about. But John brought wisdom and sane thought.'

Whether in the offices in Bouverie Street, the staff local The Feathers, or The Mucky Duck, around the corner in Tudor Street, John enjoyed the camaraderie and felt part of the paper's heritage. He had made many friends among the *Chronicle*'s staff. One he had known, but who had died before John became part of the paper, was the master feature writer Ian Mackay. When offered a job at the *Chronicle*, the Highlander Mackay, with his craggy face, hispid hair, and beaky nose, is reported to have said he would take it if his politics were thought acceptable. 'What are they?' he was asked. Mackay replied: 'I regard Stalin and Trotsky as a couple of old crusted Tories.' His stall had been set out, and he got the job.

Mackay had spent many drinking hours with John. He was a dozen characters in one, with a tremendous store of general knowledge, always having the time to explore the fantasies with which his life abounded. The *Chronicle*'s crime reporter, George Glenton, relates that 'his story-telling won him more friends than any man in Fleet Street. He often boasted that he had been political, industrial, dramatic, architectural, cricket, soccer, naval, military, agricultural, musical, art and fashion correspondent at one time or another in his career.'

'Did you know Ranji had a glass eye?' he once asked John in the middle of a discussion on Bowdler. John did not. On another night, at a dinner shared with Teddy Knox, Clarice Mayne, Ronnie Waldman, Gerard Fay, Dawn and John, he started to sing neglected music-hall ballads – and remembered all the words. It transpired that the day before he had taken a train to Wigan in order not to break up an interesting conversation he was having with a man who had to go there on business.

As well as being a fine essayist, Mackay was a fearless opportunist. Enjoying a tipple in a reporters' drinking hole during the war, there had been four full glasses of whisky on the bar counter when a flying bomb cut out overhead. His three companions ducked to the floor, the bomb came to ground elsewhere. When the three stood up again all four glasses were empty, and Mackay was trying very hard to simulate surprise.

John had a great affection for 'The Great Bohunkus', as Mackay was called:

> He created a mythology so imaginatively true that no technical expert could have discredited it – out of the cricket that he had watched. Although he was, so far as we know, not a practising cricketer beyond waste-land standard, we relished it far more deeply than the wisdom of many self-declared *aficionados* of the game. Ian perceived, always, not only the man under the flannels but also that man in relation to his cricket. He understood that theirs is a world which becomes dull if it is real; that it is, in essence, a fairy-tale

kingdom – and he knew how rare and valuable the true fairy tale is. Indeed, he himself often told fairy tales, true fairy tales, because they were concerned with the finest truth, which is the truth of imagination.

John could almost have been writing of himself. His own efforts for the *News Chronicle* reveal something of his philosophy. Reporting on the 1956 Australian tourists at Grace Road, he wrote:

> The Australians are in a strong position against Leicestershire: figures make that clear. Cricket, however, has feeling as well as figures. Feeling says that this side has not the giant air of the other post-war Australian sides.

In his 'Sporting Column', there was evidence of John's feeling about a home-grown player:

> I have heard Tony Lock accused of playing up to the gallery; in fact, he is one of the last cricketers in the world to be aware of the 'gallery' at all, for a cricket match absorbs him completely. Here, indeed, is a single-minded cricketer, twisting himself into agonised knots as if to *will* the ball to hit the stumps or come to him as a catch. With each ball he bowls, in his heart, he means – even expects – to take a wicket.

In the close season, John found himself at Highbury observing true histrionics:

> Arsenal are something of a test case of rough play. Derek Tapscott is the most impassioned tumbler in the business: his falling is so dramatic that if he were not such a successful goal-poacher he could make a fortune on the stage as the victim in murder plays.

The *News Chronicle* began to lose money in 1956. Circulation had dropped by nearly a quarter of a million, a sixth of its readership, and the paper's much-predicted demise took place in 1960. It was swallowed by the *Daily Mail*, and the *Chronicle*'s night-sister, the *Star*, which had problems in attracting advertising revenue, was merged with the *Evening News*.

By then, John had been contributing to other papers as well for several years. His awareness of the *Chronicle*'s financial position had made it advisable for him to find space elsewhere. In the late fifties and the sixties the

Guardian, the *Observer* and *The Times* all benefited from Arlott typescripts. In fact, his football debut for the *Observer* coincided with an extraordinary match at White Hart Lane when defences were breached more often than the Möhne Dam: Tottenham Hotspur triumphing over Everton 10–4 on 11 October 1958.

Some of John's writing was published under the *nom-de-plume* 'Silchester' – chosen because of his grandfather's connection with the North Hampshire village, and used because rival dailies did not necessarily want to make it obvious they were employing the same columnist. Not that that concerned him too much. His priority was to service the many and frequent self-imposed demands on his pocket with a steady cash flow. To keep solvent he either had to pare down the collecting indulgences which brought him so much pleasure, or carry on seeking and committing himself to a fearsome work outlay. The first he found difficult to contemplate, the second easier to accept.

Life in the freelance fold, however – enjoyable though he found it – has its own disciplines, and a price. Part of that price was the amount of time he had to spend away from home. The premium was the break-up of his marriage.

16

Break-up

No single incident led to the eventual termination of the Arlotts' marriage, rather a series of absences that loosened the bond. As Dawn said frankly: 'We were in love, quite passionately, but the endless trips away and tours abroad .. All right, he had to go to South Africa and Australia, after all he was a cricket correspondent, and that was his job. But the needless trips to art galleries around the world where he would send back copy – it was no funno. The chain each time was a wee bit weakened.'

On these excursions, John invariably received much hospitality. With his innate generosity he would repay it by offering accommodation at Highgate Avenue to any who were planning to come to London. If he happened to be out of town when they arrived, the imposition on Dawn was considerable.

'He would say, "Oh, go and stay with Dawn," you know. I think I was grieved about that. The cricketers came to stay, didn't they – tried to rape me in my bedroom (*laugh*). Far worse than intellectuals, I have to tell you. Anthony Asquith the film director, Robert Frost, Walter de La Mare – I liked them more than the cricketers. Being brought up in Ireland, I knew nothing about cricket. Mind you, there were some nice cricketers. Bill Bowes I liked enormously. The West Indian lot were very pleasant – well-behaved, quite charming, Jack Cheetham and some South African players, the New Zealanders who were quieter than the Aussies, and Leo Harrison from Hampshire, he's a lovely man, and Joan, his wife, is lovely too . . .

'It was all lovey-dovey when John came back. I said, "Well, X was staying here." He said, "Don't go on, I've had girlfriends." I said, "Well, a man of your inclinations would have done." He said, "Speak not." And we didn't. And nothing of that was very important. We were very honest with one another. But he spent long times away. Even though we had French and German au pairs it was slightly selfish of him.'

There were still times they spent together, of course. Perhaps in tacit response to his absences, John would take Dawn away for the weekend, but even then his own interests remained paramount, with antiquarian bookshops en route warned to stay open in the knowledge that this particular customer could never leave empty-handed. Trying to persuade Dawn to collect cookbooks after she had been kicking her heels for an hour or so was a vain hope. All she was interested in at those moments was being able to consume portions of what appeared on the pages . . . and that nice hotel at Midhurst was only a few miles down the road.

On the whole they remained faithful, Dawn says. At one time she wondered if there was something between John and Margot Fonteyn. Returning from Venice he said he had met her on the Bridge of Sighs – they had known one another, of course, since those days with the Ayrtons in All Souls Place. Any kind of liaison, however, seems unlikely. Other people have speculated about a relationship with the striking-looking cookery writer Elizabeth David, whose books and articles on Mediterranean cooking in the early 1950s reminded insular Britons of culinary delights beyond food-rationing. The sketched head and shoulders of her which adorned the Arlotts' dining-room often triggered this thought. Again, it is conjecture. Innocent friendships can sometimes seem less so than less-innocent ones.

At dinner parties John was not averse to launching into men-only reminiscences which would culminate in pay-offs like 'and the Aussie woman said, "If only my husband could see me now."' 'Male chauvinism' was an expression which was not marketed until later, but in those roving days John did develop a habit of taking a bottle and visiting lady friends, which put one of his confidantes in mind of the Flanders and Swann song 'Have Some Madeira, M'Dear'.

The realisation for John that he had fallen in love with his secretary, Valerie France, was far from immediate. She was the second daughter of a general practitioner in Bromley, Kent, who had been shot in the chest in the First World War and had only survived as a result of excellent Canadian surgery. In fact his death in harness in 1957, nearly forty years later, was an indirect result of those wounds. Both Valerie's elder sister Gillian and younger brother Richard were to become doctors. She was educated at Bromley High School, was interested in sport (being good enough to play netball for Kent), and had a healthy intolerance of pretension. Having taken 'A' levels and a course at secretarial college, she got a job at an institute of engineering before starting work at the BBC with the drama producer Royston Morley.

The spell in Staff Training with John followed, and then the subsequent move to Cecil Court in 1953. The Salisbury public house with its glorious Victorian glass at the St Martin's Lane end of Cecil Court became a kind of unofficial office for them both, a place for a whistle-wetter with visitors before adjourning to Sheekey's Restaurant nearby. As always with John, the divisions between his business and social life were comfortingly (to him) indistinct, and it was natural for Valerie to became part of his family circle. She would sometimes drive her employer to and from his various activities, and she also joined the Arlotts and others of their friends on holidays on Alderney.

John's description of Valerie in his autobiography barely conceals his feelings: 'She was short, with gentle, direct eyes, a humorous, easy-smiling mouth, and a good sense of fun, as well as sound common sense, and she was utterly reliable and efficient at her job.' Her passion was sailing and, having inherited a love of literature from her father, she collected books on the subject. She also, later on, had a select collection of scarce books on Native American Indians, 'Partly,' surmises her brother Richard, 'as a defensive rebound to John, with all the dealers' catalogues coming through the door in great numbers.'

Valerie was not just a reader, she was also a doer. In 1956 she was a member of the crew of the seventy-eight-ton Brixham trawler *Provident* in the first Tall Ships Race from Torbay to Lisbon, as one of fourteen 'amateur cadets' – seven women, seven men – under the expert guidance of ex-Royal Navy skipper Peter Godwin. Among the motley mariners, recruited from the Island Cruising Club of Salcombe in Devon, were a medical student, a nurse and a doctor, and two civil servants; they were therefore amply provided for in the event of accidents – some to tend to the wounded, others to fill in the forms.

As it happened, the weather during the five-week voyage was stormy, and one of the cadet ships was reported as having sunk. John spent anxious days much concerned for Valerie's welfare. Happily, *Provident* emerged unscathed.

In his autobiography, John juxtaposes the Tall Ships Race with his realisation of his love for Valerie during the Glamorgan v. West Indies game at Swansea at the beginning of August 1957. Although the two events were a year apart, they somehow became conjoined in his mind. On the back cover of John Corin's book *Provident and the Story of the Brixham Smacks* (1980), there is a photograph of the ketch bound for Lisbon in 1956, with Valerie standing in the bow. John wrote about the race in his *News Chronicle* column on 26 August 1956, quoting the captain's report, 'If we were not the fastest, we were the best-fed,' and noting that on their return the crew wore the 'vague look of those who gaze out, for days, over sea miles and sea miles of wide open space'.

There was potential for further squalls when the Arlotts and their friends, including Valerie, gathered for a holiday on Alderney in 1957. Valerie felt that John had allowed things to meander on long enough, and was hoping for a resolution to the situation, in the shape of a declaration from John to Dawn of his intentions.

Due to work commitments, John would usually arrive on Alderney after the rest of the family. At the most he would take two weeks' holiday, while Dawn and the children would have much longer, spending some of the time in a hotel and the rest in rented accommodation or with friends.

'Alderney was a bit like a club in those days,' said Dawn. 'Everyone would entertain like mad and spend a lot of time sailing and swimming. John was always exhausted when he arrived. I never got the impression that he liked it much. He never went for walks or spent much time on the beach. He would bring his work with him. Valerie would be sitting there typing his letters. I said, "For God's sake, Valerie, throw all these letters into the sea."'

Dawn had long been aware of the mutual interest between John and his secretary. 'He did say, "I think I'm falling in love with this girl." I thought, you old bugger, you. No subterfuge up front. When he broke his ankle and worked from home she'd come over and take letters and she'd say, "Can I peel a mushroom?"

'Then one time he was doing this cheese film in Yorkshire and he said, "I'm taking Valerie, but you know it will be bedroom 1 and bedroom 80." I said, "Oh, yes, like you used to take me to London – bedroom 1 and bedroom 80!" That was long before we were married. And when they went to Yorkshire, I lost an expensive earring that he had given me because I was so upset that I rolled on the floor like a dog, and I never found it.

'Anyway, when he told me about Valerie he couldn't have been more tactless. "Pippin, I want to speak to you." Having come back from a boat party – four naval corvettes had recently been built and were anchored in Braye harbour; the officers had been doing their utmost to uphold the tradition of stiff measures – I said perkily, full of eighty-nine gins, "Oh, yes." He said, "I'm going to marry Valerie. And she's very afraid that you'll be cross. Will you go upstairs and say you don't mind?" (*laugh*) We had a houseful at the time – thirteen in all. And I went up to the bedroom and her face swelled up with nerves. One side was out like a balloon. And I was so pissed that I did speak to her. I said, "All right, Val, it's happened – OK then." I staggered down a flight of stairs and then went to bed. Did I have a hangover.'

The next morning, realisation sank in. Added to which Dawn was faced with the task of frying twenty-six eggs for breakfast – doubles all round. It was too much. 'I was hysterical what with the news and the eggs. In the middle of a family holiday was the wrong time. Typical of a man brought up by doting women. Fortunately, Leo Harrison was on hand to lend a comforting ear and a cooling light ale. "Don't mind. pet," he said soothingly. "You'll find somebody else." And I did.'

Towards the end of John and Dawn's marriage, there were many recriminatory rows. They had been growing apart for some time, and had developed different interests. Dawn went to stay with 'the robust Harlequin' T.H. White for six weeks, and John moved out to take up residence at the National Liberal Club in London. He described his sojourn there as a 'peculiar night-monastic life', which defines the aura of so many gentlemen's clubs which, apart from their smell of cabbage, combine the feel of a cloistered retreat with a sense of unutterable loneliness – particularly in the dormitory hours. Certainly John had moments of isolation. During one, he rang his former secretary Barbara Forrester, who had left her job with BOAC to marry and have a family. She was now living in Essex.

'He rang up and asked me to have dinner with him. Unfortunately, I was unable to get a baby-sitter and couldn't go. He'd only rung in the afternoon for that evening. He was obviously lonely. I much regret that I did not go. I wonder what would have happened. I feel I let him down.'

However tactless and unfair his conduct towards Dawn had been, and however much he was in love with Valerie, John himself was much affected by the break-up of his marriage. The past had a great hold on him, and he had not realised the extent to which he would miss his two sons, Jimmy and Timothy. Often he was racked by guilt. Among his friends was Leslie Gutteridge, at that time presiding at the Epworth Press in the City Road as the premier cricket bookseller in the world. Leslie and John would often drive together to cricket club meetings and dinners at which John was speaking. 'Once, when John came back to our tiny house in the early hours of the morning,' remembered Leslie's partner Norma, 'he was musing about life in general in a rather gloomy way and said something like, "I enjoy my sons very much, but Dawn had to have them, and it couldn't have been a very pleasant experience for her," which I thought at the time was one of the most enlightened things I had ever heard any man say.'

John was too much a social animal to stand for long a place which had been organised for just that purpose. The National Liberal Club contained a little too much chipped Victoriana and a little too many aloof portraits, and bar bores quickly palled. So he moved with Valerie into a two-floor flat at 69 George Street, just off Baker Street. Initially, Dawn was understandably bitter, and made scenes outside the flat: 'I was jealous as hell of

Valerie in the beginning, but then one learned to admire her and like her. She was good for John . . . Val was a great woman.'

John and Dawn filed for divorce on the grounds of his adultery and were granted a decree nisi on 6 April 1960. By now Dawn was eager to get the whole process resolved, as she wanted to marry Donald Barrington, an American whom she had met on Alderney. Donald had been to school at Malvern and went on to Magdalen College, Oxford, and was then working for a subsidiary of a public relations firm. Dawn laughed, 'I had to be very careful what I said before the decree absolute, because of the Queen's Proctor. I couldn't be too keen to get free.' After the divorce had been announced in the papers, an unexpected missive arrived on Dawn's doormat. It was from Father Caesar, the Southampton priest who had married them nineteen years before. It simply said: 'I expected better of you.'

Three weeks after the decree absolute came through, Dawn and Donald were married at Kensington Register Office, on 27 July 1960. Nine days earlier, on 18 July, John and Valerie had been married at St Marylebone Register Office – appropriately, since they had first met just down the road. Afterwards, at the reception in the Pier Hotel, Chelsea, John had a mild scare: 'There was no champagne available for guests till 11.30 a.m. because of the licensing laws. Fortunately, we didn't have to wait long.'

The couple went for a few days' honeymoon at The Compleat Angler by the River Thames at Marlow in Buckinghamshire. 'We were overjoyed and were engrossed with one another,' said John, 'and I suppose we were making rather a lot of noise in our bedroom late at night. All of a sudden there was a loud knocking on the wall on one side of the room. "Why can't you two keep quiet and let decent people get to sleep," came the complaint. Immediately, there was another knocking on the other wall. "You miserable sod, how can you say that to young people who are so gloriously happy? Leave them alone."' A long silence ensued, with much suppressed laughter from the newlyweds. Although there was a captive audience, ears agog, John felt that, for once, comment, let alone commentary, was entirely unnecessary.

17

Survivor

Although many people were aware of John's domestic upheaval, it scarcely seemed to impinge on his work. Valerie had been the secretary *par excellence* for a number of years, and simply continued to be so. She had, of course, done far more for John than is implied by the term 'personal assistant'. When business contacts or friends called at the office she had often cooked meals for them. Hazel Edelston was one of several who had been surprised that secretarial duties went so far: 'Maurice and I went to visit John in his office at Cecil Court, and I realised there was more to the relationship when Valerie prepared a very good lunch for us all to eat.'

Michael Hastings, later to be known as Tuke-Hastings, from BBC Outside Broadcasts, wrote to thank John for the hospitality after a visit to George Street: 'Do congratulate your secretary on her cooking. The artichokes were superb.' John responded, 'We'll try the artichokes hot next time.'

The *decrescendo* of John's marriage to Dawn was matched, to a certain extent, in his public exposure. This was perhaps inevitable, after the heady years of setting forth in so many directions. The public now felt they knew their man, where to place him and what to expect from him. Accordingly, he had been given an established place in their affections.

The second half of the 1950s was a period of change and reassessment in John's life. The personal traumas had a chastening effect and heightened his insecurities in some of his professional encounters. That much is obvious in his correspondence.

During the summer of 1958, for example, at a function in Southampton, John had met the Director-General of the BBC, Sir Ian Jacob. Sir Ian had informed him amusedly that, after a recent church service, a man had berated him about Arlott's broadcasting style. For Jacob, this was no more than inconsequential conversation. For John, mulling over his words afterwards, it was a cause for wondering uneasily whether there was a hidden agenda. He wrote on 19 August:

Dear Sir Ian,

Ever since we met at Southampton, I have felt a little sad that your sabbath should have been disturbed by the man who disliked my broadcasting so much. In fact, I think the balance of commentators is such that few people like all three [Rex Alston and E.W. Swanton were the others] – which ought to mean that most people like one of them. I cannot resist, however, sending you this letter which perhaps you may feel cancels out your importunate church-goer.

The letter enclosed was from a resident of an old people's home in Canterbury, a Mr J.W. Filde, who had written on 7 August:

Dear Mr Arlott,

I do wish to thank you for your commentary on the Kent and Hampshire match. Owing to ill health I was for the first time in many years unable to attend the [Canterbury] Festival, so I was and still am grateful, not only for your observations on the play but for your vivid description of the setting in the marquees, the pavilion and stands, and the famous tree on the boundary – that brought the scene to life, so that I could imagine myself at the match. I could almost say that I know and love every blade of grass on the St Lawrence Ground, and if, as is quite likely, I never attend another Cricket Week, your broadcast commentary will remain a happy memory while life is vouchsafed to me.

From my heart I thank you.

There were unsettling moments, too, in John's somewhat taut relationship with Charles Max-Muller, who had taken over from de Lotbinière as Head of Outside Broadcasts (Sound) in April 1952. Whereas 'Lobby' had been approachable and avuncular, John found Max-Muller quite the reverse. As far back as 1954 he had written that he was 'ever grateful for granting [an interview] so promptly as to relieve my anxiety' (John had been worried about the lack of definite outside broadcast dates in his diary). He went on: 'I shall look forward to such O.B. engagements as you think me right for, and trust you will appreciate that – perhaps in the way that George Robey yearned to play Shakespeare (note he did well as the ghost of Hamlet's father) – I yearn from cricket towards a scrap of football.'

Max-Muller had reservations about John as a football commentator. He felt he did not really know enough about the game, and had placed him fourth on the list of commentators. This meant that he only covered a handful of matches every season, and few of these were from the First Division; mostly they were Second and Third Division rough and tumbles: Luton v. Sheffield Wednesday, Rotherham v. Stoke, Southampton v. Southend. This last match, in March 1956, had been a dull encounter and attracted internecine sniping within the Corporation. A number of Midland Region people, who were pushing the case for local commentator Harry Walker to be used nationwide, were of the opinion that John Arlott was 'like a duck out of water' where football was concerned. 'His delivery was flat and monotonous. He seemed to concentrate very much on the players rather than the teams for which they were playing, so that if one joined the programme late, it would be difficult to distinguish which way the ball was going,' were among their criticisms.

Five years later, in another game at Southampton, at which Liverpool were the visitors, John was again criticised. Listeners wrote in complaining that he was 'blatantly biased in favour of the local team' – which, if undesirable, was hardly surprising. On this occasion John had given his enthusiasm ample scope. With his fellow commentator Maurice Edelston working next to him, a friendly competitive element had developed, in which there was much overtalking about the 'reds' and the 'blues'.

Max-Muller did, however, give praise when it was due. In April 1958 he was the first to thank John after the Outside Broadcast team arrived at Highbury to find an Arsenal game postponed. John helped transport equipment and crew in his car across North and East London to Upton Park, and managed to give a commentary on most of the second half of the West Ham match. 'And all this in spite of the fact that you could not have been feeling too well with your eye trouble,' wrote Max-Muller, referring to treatment that John was then undergoing at Moorfields.

At the end of the 1957 cricket season Max-Muller had written to John: 'I think one can say that the new experiment of broadcasting ball-by-ball commentaries in this country has been a resounding success. No one contributed more to this success than you did.' Unfortunately, the fact that each commentator was told, identically, that no one had contributed to the success more than they had somewhat reduced the individual glow.

Conveyor-belt compliments had not been dispatched from Max-Muller's office two years earlier when, during a cricket commentary, John had done a spot of inadvertent advertising. 'I am sure that as soon as you said it you realised the stupid mistake you made at Old Trafford on Tuesday evening, when drinks were being given to those in the field,' wrote Max-Muller. 'You referred to the fact that on most days in this country "a hot cup of Bovril" would be more suitable. A very nice plug for the firm concerned!' Unintentional as the remark had been, humble pie was eaten: 'I now go about in a perpetual state of jitter that I shall mention something else *verboten*, but I will do my best not to – apologies.'

These incidents are no more than a typical part of any assault course over a long period on the broadcasting front line. The human factor can always be discerned over a live microphone – preference, fault, vulnerability, insecurity. There is nowhere to hide, and no immunity.

John's programme miscellany remained rich – even if his bank manager did not think so: *The Week's Good Cause* (refugees); *Topic for Tonight*; tributes to Len Hutton and Denis Compton; a royal visit to Romney; youth programmes from the Lake District; *My Word* with Frank Muir and Denis Norden; a review of London's policemen for *Town and Country*; and *Any Questions?* (by now he had long been restored to favour) in towns around the country. During a Bournemouth edition of the programme, he shared a platform with MP Tom Driberg, who remembered John as a policeman at Southampton during the war, giving him a permit to go to the Isle of Wight to give some Army lectures. 'When are you going to write some more poems for *Horizon*?' John had asked. As Driberg remarked, 'Not the kind of thing that policemen usually say to one.'

A regular commitment was *Sports Special* summaries for the famously idiosyncratic editor Angus Mackay. An inquiry for Schools Programmes, *Is the Provincial Theatre Doomed?* required John for just one session in the studio. He also received an invitation from the Light Entertainment producer Dennis Main Wilson to appear on *Hancock's Half Hour*. It had not been so many years since John, in the course of compiling a piece on theatrical terms, had sought the advice of that great stage raconteur Dennis Castle. They met at the Lord Belgrave pub in Whitcomb Street off Pall Mall. Dennis expounded on such matters as 'skip baskets', 'putting on slap', 'on the green', 'flies', 'pros arches', and when the 'ghost' walked. John and his companion listened earnestly. When Dennis had finished there was silence, and then a confession. 'This is all news to me as well, John,' said Tony Hancock.

A whiff of theatrical surrealism is evident in another excursion that also started in a pub. One evening in 1956, John was sharing an early-evening glass with a West End theatre manager, who happened to remark casually that the visiting Soviet leaders Bulganin and Khrushchev were dining with Prime Minister, Sir Anthony Eden, at Claridge's. The Cold War isolationism of the time made anybody from behind the Iron Curtain seem like a being from another planet, and so, emboldened by a few more drinks, the two comrades set forth to see B. and K. for themselves. Confidence enabled them to walk through the security cordon, and having reached the hotel lounge, John attempted to strike up conversation with a large man in a paper-thin suit with bell-bottomed trousers whom he mentally christened 'Tovarich'. Dumb-show about the Moscow Dynamo football team was quickly being exhausted, when all of a sudden the door of the private dining-room opened. It was a cue for previously invisible security men to surge towards one another, shoulder to shoulder. In the mêlée John's large 'friend' toppled him backwards into an armchair, while the theatre manager looked on open-mouthed. Recovering from the shock, John managed, through the legs of the burly phalanx, to register the emerging Bulganin twitching irritably and Khrushchev looking rosily moist. He also registered the fact that he now had a bruise on his hip from the jolt of an extremely large firearm in his large friend's pocket.

Normality returned with the cyclical cricket fixtures. Anxiety always surrounded the allocation. When would the list of days and venues arrive? What else could be fitted in? Were there job clashes? Travelling time? Hotels? Article and book deadlines? What about that USA trip under NATO auspices? Politics always intruded, and John was never quite convinced that he would be asked back for the next season. Of course, he always was. Eventually, in late January or early February, an envelope would arrive on the doormat. It was time to assemble the jigsaw. 1958 was a typical season, although initially there were a number of matches left open in case a close-run County Championship proved more attractive than the New Zealand tourists, who were not a strong side

Saturday 3 May:	Leicester v. the New Zealanders at Leicester
Saturday 10 May:	Warwickshire v. Sussex at Birmingham
Saturday 17 May:	Derbyshire v. Leicestershire at Chesterfield
Saturday 24 May–Tuesday 27 May:	Glamorgan v. the New Zealanders at Cardiff
Saturday 31 May:	Hampshire v. the New Zealanders at Southampton
Thursday 5 June–Tuesday 10 June:	FIRST TEST AT EDGBASTON
Saturday 14 June:	Sussex v. the New Zealanders at Hove
Thursday 19 June–Tuesday 24 June:	SECOND TEST AT LORD'S
Thursday 3 July–Tuesday 8 July:	THIRD TEST AT HEADINGLEY

Saturday 12 July:	Gloucestershire v. Nottinghamshire at Gloucester
Saturday 19 July:	Match to be decided
Thursday 24 July–Tuesday 29 July:	FOURTH TEST AT OLD TRAFFORD
Saturday 2 August–Monday 4 August:	Match to be decided
Tuesday 5 August–Saturday 9 August:	Match to be decided
Wednesday 13 August–Friday 14 August:	Northamptonshire v. the New Zealanders at Northampton
Saturday 16 August:	Match to be decided
Thursday 21 August–Tuesday 26 August:	FIFTH TEST AT THE OVAL
Saturday 30 August:	Match to be decided

In 1959, the encroachment of football into the start of the cricket season caused John to miss the first few matches. He had been covering soccer for the *Observer* for six months. The job had come his way after his agent, Bagenal Harvey, who headed an organisation which represented many sportsmen and sports writers, had a quiet word with Chris Brasher, the Sports Editor of the paper. With an impending divorce, maintenance, school fees, his own lifestyle and a second home to support, John needed every penny he could accrue.

Previously, as second correspondent, he had been writing the Friday football lead in the *Guardian*, which was simultaneously one of the most stimulating and unrewarding jobs on the sporting pages. By Friday any worthwhile matter from the weekend before had been thoroughly masticated in the press, until it was unpalatable to both writer and reader. In January 1958, seeking fresh topics, John asked the *Guardian*'s Sports Editor, Larry Montague, 'a charming and literate idealist', if he might take in a European club game. At the end of the month Montague rang to tell him he could report Manchester United's third round European Cup tie against Red Star in Belgrade the following week. John was delighted. Normally H.D. 'Donny' Davies, who held the number one slot as football correspondent, would have been expected to go to such an important match on foreign soil. For some reason, he was otherwise committed.

John went to Highbury on the Saturday to watch 'the Reds' go through their paces against Arsenal, a useful reconnoitre for form and background information. The biggest crowd of the season at Highbury, sixty-three thousand spectators, saw Manchester pip Arsenal 5–4 in a thrilling attacking game. John duly rang in his report, and later rang again to get copy clearance. Then came the bombshell: 'Oh, by the way,' said Montague casually, 'Donny now finds it is possible to travel to Belgrade after all.' John swore volubly. 'No use cursing,' said Montague. 'Donny is the soccer correspondent, and it is his choice.'

The details of the 'Busby Babes" 3–3 draw with Red Star, their aggregate 5–4 win and progress through to the semi-finals, forms the first paragraph of many epicedia of the Munich air disaster. The refuelling at Riem Airport, the icy conditions, the second take-off attempt, the overrun and crash into a house on the perimeter of the airfield, the death of eight gifted young footballers, three club staff, eight journalists, the co-pilot, a steward, a travel agent and a United supporter is a well documented tragic episode in soccer history, although the profound impact of the catastrophe was incommunicable. Rarely recorded has been the incongruity of the pre-Lenten carnival of Fashing and its low-life bacchanalia, leading a young lady in fishnet stockings to vamp BEA's funeral director as he arrived to inspect the mayhem. Or the great skills of Professor Georg Maurer, the surgeon who saved lives that seemed lost, and who could conceivably have resurrected the mighty England centre forward Duncan Edwards had dialysis equipment been as advanced as it was to become not many years later.

John was unaware of the grim news. Ever since being told he was not going to Belgrade, he had been doleful and restless. On the fateful day – Thursday 6 February – he decided to submerge his irritation with newpapers by seeking distraction in print. He visited a succession of bookshops, all of them usual haunts, and eventually arrived at Bertram Rota's in the Savile Row area of London's West End, which specialised in modern first editions, private press books, English literature and literary autographs.

As he was delving among the shelves, an assistant tapped him on the shoulder: 'There is a phone call for you, Mr Arlott.' Considerably surprised, John picked up the phone. 'Ah, I was tracking you south through the shops,' began Valerie. 'You're to ring Larry Montague before the *Guardian* switchboard chokes. The Manchester United plane has crashed. Be ready to write a lot of obituaries – starting with Donny's.'

John sat in the Press Club with the *News Chronicle*'s John Camkin, sifting through the cables with their chilling bulletins. He turned at last to his typewriter. A mixture of disbelief, shock, nausea and guilty relief flooded through him. People he had known were on that plane – friends, acquaintances, colleagues. He could – perhaps should – have been with them. Writing was not easy. Wine, for once, did not help. Piecing the narrative together beyond midnight, as the *Guardian* asked for more and more copy, was a morbid experience. There were so many stories. This one ended:

> No club in the history of football had ever shouldered such a burden of strain as the Manchester United team of the past two seasons, which strove so mightily for the triple honour no British team has ever attained.
>
> Yet, even under that weight, they invested the playing of a game with something near, indeed, to glory in the imaginations of hundreds of thousands who had never come within miles of Manchester. This was to have been another triumphant homecoming to Old Trafford. If their triumph has become a wreath, it is one which, in many memories, will not fade.

Try as he might, John could not forget Donny Davies. For a short time in the 1920s, Davies had been a middle-order batsman with Lancashire. At other times he had played football for Bolton Wanderers, and won an amateur international cap. He had written under the *nom de plume* 'An Old International', and was fond of interposing literary quotations, especially from Dickens, in his match reports.

Fairly soon after Munich, Donny's widow suggested to Larry Montague that an anthology should be made of her late husband's writings on football. Montague mentioned John's name as a possible compiler. Mrs Davies, however, did not want John involved in any way. Hearing of her reaction, John wondered what he had done to offend. Was it possible that Davies had contrived an explanation for going on the trip at the last moment that put his number two in a bad light? Sadly, Donny's wife and John were never in touch again.

It is feasible that John either misconstrued the meaning of the widow's wishes, or read more into them than was intended. There could be a simple, straightforward reason why she preferred that he not participate in the proposed anthology. Or maybe, in some complicated and cathartic way, John had to believe that her feelings towards him were inimical because he himself had been reprieved.

Whatever the reason, this postlude to the horrific Munich episode was something he agonised over privately forever after. It was not the only calamity that caused him to wonder why he was a survivor.

18

'I Shall Remain a Liberal All my Life'

If it is true that, as the saying goes, a Liberal is a person who lacks true commitment, John was in the wrong party. His Liberal roots ran deep – at least as far back as his maternal grandfather, and probably further. But then, as he once said, his family's mythology was centred on prime ministers, 'whose reality is always carefully hidden'. Not altogether true today, where reality is often carelessly exposed.

John's maternal grandfather, ploughman Thomas Clarke, worshipped William Ewart Gladstone. He even looked like Gladstone – tall, wide, bony shoulders, bushy eyebrows, white hair, whiskers, jutting browline, hard jaw and intense eyes. Grandfather Clarke died when John was a small child, too young to glean anything at first hand. But what he learned at second and third hand was that the old man had once come face-to-face with his hero.

In his middle twenties, and still single, Thomas Clarke had worked in Brockenhurst in the New Forest. He would habitually go at lunchtime, with his bread and cheese or bacon, to the more lowly of the village's two pubs, The Rising Sun. Tucked away behind the long wooden seat in the bar would be the latest issue of the *Daily News*, which two generations later, in 1930, was to merge with the *Daily Chronicle* and become the *News Chronicle*. But in 1868 it was considered impolitic for a working man to be seen reading a radical paper in High Tory rural Hampshire. Feudal characteristics died hard. Let John himself take up the tale, as he did in a 1950s edition of *Liberal News*:

> One ploughing day, my grandfather ended a furrow close by the churchyard wall, tethered the horse, filled its nose-bag and, throwing a long leg over the wall, walked quickly through the grassy graves, out through the lych-gate, turned to his left and went unhesitatingly in through the door of the four-ale bar. He called for his pint of beer, took a long pull to wash away the dryness of the morning's work, set the pot down on the scrubbed plank bench and, alone in

the bar, drew the forbidden paper out from its hiding-place between
seat and wall.

As he settled to eat, cutting the thick bread with a jack-knife
against the press of his thumb, he began slowly to read it, starting
at the top of the left-hand column of the front page and working
steadily on. Sometimes, at a long word, I fancy, he needed to follow
it letter by letter with his finger, for his reading, like the rest of his
education, was self-taught.

Now, he read that Mr Gladstone was to come to the new town
of Bournemouth – he frowned, calculated – on this very night, to
talk about his proposed education bill which would bring into being
such and so many schools that every child in the country, however
poor its parents, would be taught to read and write and count.
He looked unseeingly across at the whitewashed wall. William
Gladstone: in person: think of that now.

John's grandfather knew he had to see Gladstone. If he did not go now,
he might never have another opportunity. He knew he would be sacked
if it became known in Brockenhurst that he had left work early to go to
the meeting, so he could not go to the railway station. He had no recourse
but to walk.* Having persuaded one of the other hands to groom and
stable his horses, he set off. John's powers of visualisation enabled him to
see clearly the gaffer on his pilgrimage:

He wore a billycock hat; his grey jacket buttoned almost to the
throat; his heavy corduroy trousers were tied an inch or two below
the knees with rough string, and his boots were of leather, harsh as
iron, with soles too thick to bend. Making a circuit to avoid being
seen from the farmhouse, he walked those hot July roads, the yellow-
white dust rising in puffs at each step . . .

When he arrived at the hall, hungry and dry, for there had been
no time for refreshment, the place was crowded and the main speech
was well along its course. The place was full, they told him, looking
with some suspicion at the layer of dust that had settled on his sweaty
face, the beads of perspiration that glistened on his moustaches and
at the roots of his strong, dark beard.

Away down at the end of the hall, under the gaslight, he saw

* The distance from Brockenhurst to Bournemouth is ten miles. In an account in *Punch*
in 1967, John gave the venue of Gladstone's speech as Romsey, fourteen miles from Brockenhurst. In his first year as Prime Minister, 1868, Gladstone spoke on 'England's duty to
Ireland' at Romsey, and also outlined plans for an Elementary Education Bill.

the white head, the sadly-strong, lined face he recognised from the pictures he had seen so often.

He said nothing, but, moving to the right of the door, he set his shoulder against the wall. Gradually he drove along close to the pitch-pine panelling, pushing behind those who leant against it. Most of his victims were irritated; many voiced their irritation, only to be shushed into silence by the remainder of the audience.

He answered none of them. Before they could justify their outcry or stop him, he was past, edging the next listener away from the wall.

The chairman frowned urgently at the disturbance moving down the side of the hall, but he took no notice. Soon he stood, tall, silent and curious, at the side of the platform, staring intently at the speaker.

It was true then. It was true for this was Gladstone – Gladstone himself, and so close he could have touched him with a rake – and he was saying so. Country children were going to be educated. The men should hear of this in The Rising Sun tonight – or tomorrow if it went on as long as he hoped.

He moved along the front a yard or two, was hissed at to sit down and sat on the edge of the platform and looked up at Gladstone.

The speech ended. Mr Gladstone sat down and, as the applause rose, pulled a great table-cloth of a white handkerchief from his pocket; and wiped his mouth and forehead. The chairman rose to propose the vote of thanks but my grandfather ignored him, staring firmly at the Old Man.

He seemed tired yet, at the same time, full of a strange energy which reminded my grandfather of a revivalist preacher who had once come to Brockenhurst. He looked keenly at my grandfather; returning the earnest, half-incredulous stare, with no embarrassment on either side. Then he looked away again.

The chairman was reaching the climax of his speech. How wonderful it would be, he said, when, with the passage of Mr Gladstone's new bill, the working classes would all be educated – how wonderful!

My grandfather was now, literally, sitting at the feet of the leader of the Liberal Party, when the great man interjected – so quietly that only my grandfather and perhaps the chairman, heard him say it – 'Yes, indeed – until they learn too much.'

In that story, surely, lies the germ of a novel that was never written. On Gladstone's death, John's grandfather transferred his allegiance to David Lloyd George, although direct contact was to be reserved for his daughter and grandson.

As a bustler for the Basingstoke Women's Liberal Association, John's mother has been described as forceful, upright, dignified and bosomy. She was largely self-educated and, whenever there was an opportunity, always reading. Undoubtedly John inherited much of her strength of personality. After becoming secretary to the Basingstoke Constituency Women's Liberal Association, Nellie went as a delegate to the national conference before acting as agent for the first Liberal MP for the town, Lieutenant-Commander 'Reggie' Fletcher in 1923–24. That is how she came to be serving tea, bread and butter and home-made damson jam to Lloyd George in the Cemetery Lodge.

The former prime minister had come to Basingstoke to speak at a meeting in support of Fletcher, and Nellie and young John had met him at the station. They waited at the barrier as the train came in – silly to waste pennies on platform tickets. 'A little man stepped out and came along the platform springy as a dancing master, his bobbed hair bouncing, as if each strand had an extra, vibrant life of its own,' remembered John. 'My mother gave him a nod that was almost a curtsey, but when he put out his hand to me, it was agony to overcome the feeling that, if I touched him, I should receive a terrifying electric shock.'

The tea, the amiable chat, and the speech in the committee rooms all went well. And that, for a very long time, was that, as far as encounters with prime ministers were concerned. For the young boy, however, the Liberal pedigree had been established.

In later years Donald Barrington used to tease John gently about his Liberalism. John might be expounding to friends on part of the Liberal Party manifesto, such as workers' share in the control of industry. Donald would quietly drop in inflammatory comments about their Whiggish fathers being totally against anything that interfered with ruling-class profits, and indeed humanitarian reform itself, like Wilberforce's attempts at anti-slavery legislation. Having rattled sabres at a serious level, Donald would remark, apropos of nothing in particular, that W.G. Grace and William Gladstone were one and the same person (this theory had also been suggested in an essay by Monsignor Ronald Knox), which was why Gladstone never attended a Test match in which Grace was playing. For just a moment the unexpected change of pitch gave John pause; there would be a worried frown and then, as the joke sank in, a face creased in smiles.

With his background, it was not surprising that John acquired forty-two volumes about Gladstone. He was, after all, a natural Liberal. Or was he? I put the question to the one-time Labour MP and Minister of Sport, and long-time friend of John, Lord (Denis) Howell.

'I talked with John on many occasions about his political views. He was an old-fashioned libertarian of the *Guardian* school – that was his life and his purpose. There was no way you'd have got him into the Labour Party, although he was, as I was at the time, of the very strong view that the Labour Party and the Liberal Party were going to come much closer together – if it were possible to get some sort of working relationship. We were faced with the prospect, which later turned to a reality, of years and years of Conservative rule, and that was anathema to both of us.'

Denis Howell's last comment brings to mind a caveat given by John to Robert, his youngest son, on the threshold of manhood: 'You could commit rape, you could commit murder – I would still be on your side. You could always come to me, I would do my best to help you. But, my son, don't even *think* of voting Conservative.'

On one West Region broadcast of *Any Questions?* John was in more serious vein when answering the question 'Has the Liberal Party more in common with Tories or Socialists?'

The Liberal Party is a separate and independent party. Mr Gladstone, who was at one time a Conservative and who joined the Liberal Party, put it quite clearly – and I think it's the best exposition of the difference I know. Gladstone cherished conservatism, there's no doubt – particularly with a small 'c' – he wanted to save many of the things that were good, and rich, and traditional. Yet he said: 'My sympathies are with the Conservatives, but my opinions are with the Liberals.'

What he meant was that there were some things he was *not* prepared to fight to conserve, because he believed a number of welfare reforms were more important. Now, there is the fundamental difference. And I would remind you that the basis of the British Liberal Party is the radical movement, which is fundamentally, and always, an anti-Conservative movement. Because it existed long before there was a Labour Party it was the original opposition to the Conservative Party. The Liberal Party must always be radical, and a true Liberal will always be opposed to Conservatism. He will obviously have some sympathies with the socialists, because he will have sympathy with the welfare methods introduced by the socialist party, but he will also deplore any loss of individuality, of individual freedom.

On *either* side he will abhor the loss of freedom and liberty; he must at all costs be a *liberal* person – that is, have a belief in the individual, be prepared to be generous on both sides; he must be prepared to grant liberty and freedom, which is his creed. He isn't a Conservative and he isn't a socialist – he's a Liberal.

Having become President of the National League of Young Liberals, John took the decision to stand as the Liberal candidate for Epping in the general election of 1955. The decision was not taken without misgivings. Apart from the remote possibility of actually being elected, there were the unceasing demands on his time to consider. John wondered whether, in the turmoil of an election campaign, there would ever be chances to see his family. His pride was also at stake, as he had to capture enough votes to make sure the deposit was not lost.

Howard Davies, the president of the Epping constituency party, successfully allayed his doubts. Howard, the brother of Rupert Davies of *Maigret* fame and a former Liberal candidate himself, having opposed Winston Churchill at Woodford, had a persuasive tongue. He also had a considerable supply of whisky – until the day a Liberal team descended on the district to hold an *Any Questions?*-type forum. John had arranged for Jeremy Thorpe, Frank Owen, Frank Byers and Gilbert Harding to join him on a platform at Waltham Abbey. Harding had agreed to participate, he said, not because he was a Liberal, but because he was most definitely *not* a Conservative.

John picked him up at his flat near Broadcasting House. Harding was still in his socks and suspenders, and nowhere near dressed. By then he was a very sick man, and he sank a couple of large gin and tonics to wash down his pills as a prelude to the tiresome journey across London. Once into John's car, he lit a cigarette, then promptly fell asleep. Fortunately John, who was concentrating on manoeuvring his vehicle through the rush-hour traffic, noticed in time, took the cigarette from Harding's lips and stubbed it out. A little later the sleeper awoke with a startled shout when his 'chauffeur' had to brake sharply in order to avoid colliding with a car that had cut in. John described the incident in his *News Chronicle* column shortly afterwards:

> I cocked my ears for a characteristic judgement on the driver, but Gilbert wearily closed his eyes. Five minutes later came the remark: 'The nation has two things to thank me for – I do not drive a car and I have no children.'

Before going to the forum, the celebrated team gathered at Howard Davies's house. The Epping constituency party chairman, Vincent

Chapman, was there as well. 'John had warned Howard Davies that Gilbert enjoyed whisky. As they left for the hall, Howard looked ruefully at the empty bottles. The evening was a huge success.' Given a packed house, the repartee of Thorpe and the whip-like retorts of Harding, that was hardly in doubt.

There were other similar sessions during the campaign at which Liberal colleagues appeared, and John reciprocated in kind in support of their candidacies. One visit was to North Devon to champion Jeremy Thorpe, and the two later shared a farm wagon in the main square at Hereford to back Frank Owen in a by-election there.

Thorpe recalls John 'immaculately dressed, rasping out, "I am an ordinary man. I only want 'paice'." I told him afterwards that although he was to be commended for his quest for peace, his role as an ordinary man was not flattering to himself, nor were the facts borne out by the evidence.'

Jeremy Thorpe found John a refreshing and sincere speaker. And that aspect of campaigning gave John no qualms whatever. He was a natural performer. Less so when it came to knocking on front doors. Marjorie Chapman, the wife of the local party chairman, remembers his reticence. 'I felt with him that he regarded it as an invasion of privacy. He was no door-to-door salesman – he was very shy and retiring about himself. I knew a lot of people who worked in Epping, and on market day I went with him and introduced people in the street. That was all right – he was fine then.'

Canvassing caused John to shudder: 'I was the world's worst canvasser. I went to two houses only. The first one, I asked the lady who came to the door if she felt she could support the Liberals in the election. "What election?" she said; and the second one I asked the same question, and she slammed the door in my face.'

In spite of John's inability to doorstep he did well, capturing over 7500 votes and easily saving his deposit. But the Tories had topped the poll with 26,065 votes, 3500 ahead of Labour. Liberal supporters felt that, in the circumstances, their candidate had achieved a minor triumph.

'Election campaigns are a dizzy, almost giddy life of absolute high pressure with your mind set on only one thing: and it did, I found, as nothing else has ever done, obliterate everything else,' remarked John retrospectively. 'You found that you were going past bookshops, antique shops, good restaurants, and not giving them a thought. You were just ploughing on with this. You really feel, or I felt, that you owe so much to the people supporting you that every hour you take off seems like letting them down.'

John's second campaign, in 1959, also in Epping, was regarded as another triumph. During the intervening four years, his continuing interest in the constituency had enabled many money-raising activities to prosper – jumble sales, coffee mornings, barbecues, supper parties, dances, fashion shows, and even a cricket match at Harlow, the rapidly expanding new town where the would-be yuppies of the day had been transplanted from decaying London streets into a glass-fronted design for twentieth-century living. John brought a smattering of first-class cricketers to take on the enthusiastic local Liberals, who adopted a few airs and graces in pursuit of an inevitable defeat. 'A nicer bunch of vice-presidents I haven't seen anywhere,' remarked John.

The 1959 campaign began badly. John was in hospital nursing a broken ankle, so he sent tape-recorded messages to be played at the first functions. The organisation surrounding this second attempt, however, had improved beyond recognition since 1955. Local Liberal membership had multiplied by twenty, committee rooms by three, and the canvassing average by seven. The expanded constituency of 100,000 was one of the biggest in the country and covered Chingford, Epping, Harlow, Nazeing, North Weald, Roydon, Theydon Bois and Waltham Abbey. Speaking at three meetings a night, there would be helpers planning every inch of the candidate's trail. John would arrive, from London, perhaps only half an hour before the starting time of the first meeting, not at the hall itself but at Divisional Liberal Headquarters. A furnished bungalow at 73 Forest Drive, Theydon Bois, had been made available to the party, and it became both a temporary home and an election office. On arrival, John would go into a room for ten or fifteen minutes on his own, having been given his brief for the night by either his agent, Norman Hoddell, or the chairman, Vincent Chapman. 'His ability to digest a complicated brief in such a short time was extraordinary,' said Chapman. 'He had a wonderfully retentive memory and fielded every awkward question like an expert.'

The issues ranged widely and contained the warhorses of every election – pensions, education, trades unions and the H-bomb (only in recent times has that issue receded somewhat). The debates and speeches were many and long. In village halls and school assembly rooms applicant Arlott was on his feet – often for ninety minutes at a time. The *West Essex Gazette* followed his progress:

> Answering a question about the H-bomb and rocket bases, Mr Arlott said that Britain should take the lead and stop the manufacture and testing of atomic weapons. 'I believe the more weapons, and the more people that have them, the greater the threat of war.'

To another question, on nationalisation, Mr Arlott said he was not in favour of nationalisation, re-nationalisation or de-nationalisation. 'It would be fatal to de-nationalise coal; the railways would be none the better now for denationalisation; and the steel industry should be left as it is. But if the steel industry needs it to run efficiently – then nationalise it.'

On pensions. 'Every human being is entitled to a pension that keeps him above subsistence level.' But this should be pinned to the cost of living, with the right to increase the pension by subscription.

On another night, in another hall and in front of another audience, juvenile delinquency, Teddy Boys and flick-knives were in the spotlight:

Tell me, do you like the ugly knots of narrow-trousered, horribly-barbered louts who gang up on the street corners?

When they jostle you and show, or hint, at their coshes or bicycle chains or flick-knives – are you ashamed that they are your people? . . . But they have not happened by accident – they are the product of the society in which they live, the society we have made.

If you want that sort of civilisation, then vote for either of the two major parties. If you think it unavoidable, then refrain – don't vote – but if you want to protest, then vote Liberal.

At the adoption meeting, John had told a crowded Mornington Hall at Chingford that he had entered politics because he was indignant – 'because what I've believed in was being violated by the government of this country. I still feel as angry now as I did then, now I suspect that the anger is shared . . . I have no personal political ambitions whatever, materially I can make a much better living out of politics than in them. If I were returned I would drop the ordinary living that has made me an income because I would have a duty to you in the House which I could discharge in no other way than by a full attendance in the House.'

He went on to say that he did not like professional politicians, and had no wish to be one: 'I should hate politics to be my career, I should hate my income to depend on politics. I am in politics because I believe in Liberalism and that reason only. I am a completely unrepentant Liberal.'

He continued with a tirade against the British manufacture and testing of the atom bomb and against capital punishment: 'I am not prepared to modify one of these opinions one iota for a vote, a hundred votes or a political seat.'

He wound up by extending an invitation to meet the Labour and

Conservative candidates on any platform at any time during the coming weeks: 'They can have any conditions of debate they like, they can look at the questions before and I don't want to.'

The offer was not taken up directly. Graeme Finlay, the sitting Conservative MP, instead issued his own challenge in a telegram to the Liberal Party HQ: 'Please persuade Liberal candidate in this division to share his privileged monopoly of radio and television and let Labour and Conservative candidates have the opportunities to reach electorate.'

Finlay, described in the *News Chronicle* as 'a forty-two-year-old rather self-effacing barrister', then complained: 'Mr Arlott doesn't have to trudge around meeting people in their homes. He can go in on the air.' John's riposte was quick: 'I don't control TV – where I would certainly love to meet Mr Finlay before the electorate. I would have thought he had two chances of televising. One was for his own party to ask him and the other is for the BBC and ITV to ask him.'

The Labour candidate, Donald Ford, was a novelist and a London County Council committee chairman. He commented on the matter of media advantage whilst fondling his lucky black cat buttonhole, once owned by the late Sir Stafford Cripps.

In fact, John featured twice in BBC and ITV television transmissions two weeks before the election, and several times on radio. He had other concerns: 'Let's make it a clean fight,' was his appeal. 'At the last election one or two things happened that left a bad taste. Last time they thought we didn't count. This time they know we do. Let's not muckrake, let's not break up other people's meetings. Let's use our loudspeakers and vans decently. If the other candidate is in the area canvassing, leave him alone, give him a fair break. If he calls at your house be courteous to him, and be firm.'

Given that last behest, there was more than a degree of gamesmanship in John's treatment of a Conservative candidate who had called at his home in Highgate Avenue during the previous campaign. John was ensconced in his study, chatting to Leslie Gutteridge. Fifty minutes later, Leslie gently reminded him that the candidate was still there, waiting in the hall. 'I'm well aware of that,' replied John. 'The longer he's kept sitting there, the less damage he can do.'

During the 1959 election trail John came across Alan Gibson, a fellow BBC commentator and prospective Liberal MP for Falmouth, in a loud-speaker van, talking to an audience of three cows looking over a hedge. John assumed he was rehearsing a speech, and Gibson was obviously making an impression, as 'the beasts looked interested'. A light-hearted conversation ensued between the two friends. 'The canvassing returns are really rather ominous,' said John. 'I'm going to do rather well. How soon can a Member of Parliament apply for the Chiltern Hundreds?'

By present-day standards, the contest in Epping was comparatively civilised. There were the usual thrusts and counter-thrusts in the press; in one John found fault with the Labour candidate's association with a nuclear disarmament demonstration, given the system of block vote and 'my friend Mr Aneurin Bevan's recently expressed attitude about the dangers of going "naked into the conference chamber" without H-bomb protection'. But no lethal missiles were thrown.

Away from the hustings, John brought his well-rehearsed aptitude for making work fun. He was amazed at the organisational skills being shown in ferrying him from meeting to meeting with the minimum of fuss and time. 'It's incredible,' he remarked on more than one occasion to the party workers. 'And none of you are getting paid.'

'John had bought a Rolls,' recalled Marjorie Chapman, who had assumed the secretarial mantle for the local association, 'but he sold it because it wouldn't get up to a hundred quickly enough for him, so to get to meetings he went in Norman Hoddell's little Ford.

'When it came to hecklers he just wiped the floor with them, because he turned it into a joke. And then they would all get back to the bungalow at midnight for a meal. I never knew how many people were coming. He would often have invited people along the way. During the run-up I might be cooking at any time of the day or night – he would bring all these marvellous bottles of wine – but he was such a lovely person that nobody minded at all.

'You see, Norman and he slept at the bungalow a lot of the time, and during the last week of the campaign he would say, "Come for breakfast tomorrow morning at six o'clock." And we would have kidneys, bacon, strawberries, red wine and champagne, all before a day's work!'

Valerie, soon to be John's wife, helped as much as she could, but discretion had to be used with a political candidate in transition between announced marital states. On one occasion Valerie had been driving the election car around all day, with John sitting beside her speaking through the loudspeaker. Absolutely exhausted, she finally returned to the Forest Drive bungalow and drove straight into the open garage beside it – forgetting that the loudspeaker was still on top.

Marjorie Chapman remembers other human touches. 'At the time of the election, he had become well-known for his St Bruno pipe tobacco advertisement. I said to him, "You'll have to get some, John, people will expect it of you." So he'd go down to the village to the little shop that stocked it, buy a packet, come back, put it in the drawer and then smoke a cigarette that he really liked. He'd put the pipe in his mouth unlit.'

The Arlott supply of unlimited energy was fully stretched. Working while eating, he would ask for quiet to listen to a football commentary and make notes for a report he had to make. Even during an election, his concentration could not afford to be totally undivided. One day a letter of encouragement arrived from the party leader, Jo Grimond, for whom John had great respect and admiration:

> I send you my very best wishes for your success on October 8th.
>
> We want more Liberal voices in the House of Commons and there is none I would wish to have more than your own. With your deep Liberal convictions, your sincerity of approach to all the everyday problems and your great kindliness you would be a tremendous help to us all on the Liberal benches.
>
> I have every confidence that your supporters in Epping will do their utmost to bring this about.

Eventually the hour arrived, and so did the three candidates. Unfortunately, there was only room for one, and it was not John. His local supporters, however, were delighted that he had increased the Liberal vote to nearly twelve thousand. His agent, the tireless Norman Hoddell, slapped him on the back: 'The same percentage increase in two more polls and you'll be there.'

Knowing that he had had no realistic chance of winning did not prevent feelings of utter deflation and overwhelming tiredness. Immediately after the count John told a reporter: 'I shall remain a Liberal all my life, but I am undecided whether to stand again.'

Two months later, in December 1959, he was no longer undecided. The Epping Liberal Association had invited him to become their prospective candidate for the third time. He replied, thanking them for the offer:

> As you may have guessed, this matter has been much on my mind for some time. I have had to decide, sadly but, I think, rightly, that I cannot undertake it. Let me say at once, however, that if I were ever in a position to stand again for Parliament, I should want first to offer myself again to Epping.
>
> As it is, I find myself, through my working commitments, unable to 'nurse' a constituency as I feel yours deserves. Our two election advances argue that there is a hard core of Liberal support in the

constituency which could prove to be the basis of a winning Liberal candidate.

I am sure, however, that that potential can only be realised by a candidate free to be in the constituency far more frequently than I can contrive.

We must, too, contemplate a situation, arising from redistribution, which splits unrecognisably the constituency as we have known it in the last two elections.

Whatever may happen, however, I should be grateful to be allowed to continue to help, to support my successor and to work for the constituency in general . . .

At a post-election and farewell party at the Blacksmith's Arms, Thornwood, John was presented with an engraved glass goblet and a framed map, 'Morgan's Essex, 1720'. Howard Davies said: 'He has done invaluable work for the Liberals in Epping. Any doubts that he did not do his job brilliantly are in his own mind and not with us.'

Many have wondered what impact John Arlott, MP, might have had in the Commons. 'Oh, there would have been some brilliant and impassioned speeches. But he would have hated the dog-fighting,' is the view of Denis Howell. 'Mind you, I'm quite sure that if John had been elected, he would never have allowed the wretched Robert Maxwell to sell off our wine. Maxwell was approached by the Treasury because the refreshment department was losing money and I believe he was then asked to take over the chairmanship of the Catering Committee and get it in balance. What nobody expected, including the Treasury, was that he would get it in balance by selling off all the best wines. Maxwell was never forgiven in this place for selling all the great wines accumulated over many years and replacing them with bloody plonk.

'I said to John, "Had you been a Member of Parliament, you'd have died at the Bar of the House rather than allow the dissipation of a marvellous cellar of wine."'

John continued to support Liberalism all his life, and on a practical basis as President of the Winchester Constituency after he returned to live in Hampshire. There was a suggestion that he might be ennobled into the House of Lords, but nothing came of it. At one time, too, overtures were made to him to stand for North Dorset, which the Liberals always had a good chance of capturing. If he had accepted and been elected, the post of Chief Whip beckoned, a job that was eventually given to Jeremy Thorpe; and Thorpe, of course, took over the leadership from Grimond. Unreasonable speculation?

'I sometimes wake in the night with my hair almost standing on end . . . I couldn't have done it. I wouldn't have made a party leader, any more than I could hire or fire. I would never have made a party leader.'

19

One Team, One Individual

The idea for a Fijian cricket tour of England originated with Philip Snow. He had been a Provincial Commissioner in Fiji and the Western Pacific for many years, and was a brother of C.P. Snow, the novelist and Labour peer. Philip Snow had led the Fijians on their remarkably successful tour of New Zealand in 1948, when they had played seventeen matches in two months, being undefeated in eleven two-day games against the minor provinces and beating Wellington and Auckland in their five three-day games with first-class provinces.

With their natural quickness of eye and movement and high spirits, reflected in their unorthodox yet spectacular fielding and hitting, the Fijians captivated the crowds. Added to which, their dignified bearing with bushy, hedge-shaped fuzzy hair, shimmering split sulus, and bare feet seemingly immune to the hardest knocks, created a visual impression that stayed in people's minds long after the game. As if all that were not enough, they entertained the public during intervals in play with spontaneous singing in harmony. Near-record attendances in New Zealand proved they were a very marketable proposition.

Snow arranged to meet John in 1952, at a pub close to his home in Highgate. John had T.H. White in tow, together with the latter's large labrador dog. White was in one of his prickly moods, ready for an argument on any subject, and questioned Snow with some asperity on his reasons for leaving what he regarded as a South Sea paradise to take a job at Rugby, 'amidst the pernicious atmosphere of a public school'. Apparently he was dissatisfied with Snow's answers, because he left fairly soon afterwards in a huff.

John quickly became supportive of the idea of a Fijian tour, but he was conscious of the difficulty of securing funding. The bandleader-turned-entrepreneur Jack Hylton was approached, and the two would-be promoters waited in an ante-room in his Savile Row offices for an hour and a half before being ushered in to see the great man – which did nothing for John's humour. Hylton did not feel he was the right person to undertake the operation, and suggested various people – including even Billy Butlin.

Philip Snow recalls: 'After the talk with Hylton broke up, we all piled out into Savile Row – Hylton into a waiting open Rolls-Royce. As he was driven off into town, he started to munch an apple in full public view. We walked off humbly to our separate assignations.'

Some time after this, the Manchester Sports Guild showed an interest in the idea, but that interest was never transformed into action. With time passing, John at last suggested that Lord's be asked officially to sanction and organise a Fijian visit. He felt that 1959 would be viable, as the Indians were scheduled for that year and might not prove very exciting box-office. A counter-attraction might catch on.

'The MCC Secretary, Ronny Aird, agreed that John and I should address a meeting of county secretaries at Lord's,' continued Philip Snow. 'It must have been around late '56 or early '57. John spoke first with his usual eloquence and I followed up with the necessary detail. I had to leave early, but John told me afterwards they were impressed with the idea, except that Trevor Bailey had a few reservations. Nevertheless, after that meeting all the counties were going to offer matches, with half the gate going to Fiji plus £100. That doesn't sound much now, but then it was quite a figure. I had thought that only the county sides in the lower half of the table would come in, but Surrey and the top teams agreed to matches, as well as MCC at Lord's and the two universities, which in those days were quite strong.'

All seemed set fair. But then an internal coup within the Fiji Cricket Association, in which the secretary, Harry King, was deposed, effectively scuppered the plans. King, who had been party to the protracted course of events thus far, could only watch helplessly as his successor undid all his good work. K.C. Gajadhar, the new secretary, was part Indian, part European, and both parts anglophobe. Once in office, he declared publicly that any Fijian touring side would consist of only thirty per cent Fijians, the rest being Indians.

'This seemed to me absolute nonsense,' said Snow, 'because in my time, eight years before, only one Indian was anywhere near the representative side. It was a mischievous remark to have made. Much publicity was given to it, and John and I developed cold feet over it. Also the thought of a Fijian side coming over three-quarters Indian had little attraction, especially as the representative side from India would be touring at the same time. So with much regret and embarrassment, we wrote to the county secretaries and said we're afraid we shall have to call it off for the time being. And, in fact, for the time being meant in reality for ever, because there was never another opportunity.'

Years later, in 1979 and in the 1980s, the Fijians did come to Britain to take part in International Cricket Council tourneys, sponsored successively by Adnan Khashoggi, who had property developments in Fiji; Earl Jellicoe, the Chairman of Tate & Lyle; and that tremendous supporter of cricket in all sorts of areas, J. Paul Getty. But these were one-day ventures. From the late 1940s to the early 1950s, after a bow to the seven Test-playing nations, the Fijian side could make a serious claim to be the best of the rest. A tour of England then, against testing opposition, could have provided an impetus for their cricket which might now see them as a member of the major international scene.

For Philip Snow, the dream remains to be realised. For John, a different dream was about to unfold, not with the Fijian cricketers, but with Basil D'Oliveira.

The letters, written immaculately in green ink, started to arrive in 1957 or 1958; John could never be quite sure of the year.

> 14 Upper Bloem St
> Cape Town
> South Africa

Dear Mr Arlott,
    I daresay that this is only a minor detail compared, I presume, to your other escapades, but I am sure that you would try your best and use your powerful influence to assist me . . .

Basil D'Oliveira, born in 1931 and designated 'Cape Coloured' under South Africa's race laws, went on to explain his mission. What he did not say – it was left to his close friend Damoo N. Bamsda, in a note forwarded by the BBC, and later to S.J. Reddy, the joint editors of the *South African Non-European Cricket Almanack*, to provide the information – was that he had scored over fifty centuries, one a stupendous 225 in seventy minutes, thumped 46 off an eight-ball over, and had a career batting average of 100.47. Three times he had taken over 100 wickets in a season, including one return of 9 wickets for 2 runs. All these figures were achieved on matting or earth pitches in games against Kenyan Asians, Malays, Bantus and Indians.

Initially, however, none of this was wholly relevant. 'The idea was,' said D'Oliveira, 'not so much to come and play in England, but to take the coaching course and then go back and coach in South Africa, because we had no coaches . . . I saw the development of our game in South Africa along these lines – that we needed somebody to teach our lads what they ought to know about the game. But then it drifted to the playing side of it.'

John Arlott was asked to be an intermediary because 'as far as we were concerned he was "the voice of cricket", there was just something magical about it'. It quickly became apparent to John, however, that finding a job for an unknown cricketer in England was not going to be easy. Lord's was approached, as were some of the counties, but to no avail. Suggestions were made and rebuffed, correspondence winged forth and back, time passed, and progress could more accurately be described as the elimination of possibilities. 'Coaching, possibly at the Alf Gover School?'; 'How good a player is he?'; 'Northants?' 'Too big a staff'; 'The Leagues?' 'They're not losing a single player in 1960, as they do when the Indians, Pakistanis or West Indians come.'

So it went on. John persevered. The cricket correspondent of the *Manchester Evening News*, John Kay, became involved, working the League circuit with which he was familiar. The trouble both he and John had was to give a yardstick of D'Oliveira's achievements in terms of first-class opposition. As John wrote in his autobiography: 'Cite his batting achievements and a county secretary would retort, "Of course, on plumb wickets." Point to his bowling figures and they would say, "On rough pitches, of course." '

John Kay, writing to John, reflected the response of the Leagues: 'No crowd appeal; cuttings might help.' John's reply to Kay emphasised a wider horizon: 'I would not give a tuppeny damn if he were just an ordinary cricketer in one of the Test-playing countries, but this could be such a fine thing to do. The last thing I want out of it is credit, but I would love to see it happen.'

At long last, a breakthrough occurred. Middleton in the Central Lancashire League had dismissed the volcanic West Indian bowler Roy Gilchrist, and had been awaiting a decision from his chosen replacement, Wesley Hall. Hall, trying to juggle commitments to the West Indies authorities, delayed his negative reply for so long that it was too late for Middleton to engage any prominent professionals.

Enter the Kay brothers, John and Edwin, closely connected with the club and needing a solution to their problem. Re-enter John, in a letter to D'Oliveira in Cape Town dated 26 January 1960:

Dear Basil D'Oliveira,
    Now I have an offer for you to play as a professional in England this summer, but it is imperative that you cable me your decision

about it at once . . . the offer is £450 for 20 weeks. In addition, every time you scored 50 or took 5 wickets in an innings you would receive talent money (21 shillings or 25 shillings) and a collection around the ground, which usually averages between £10 and £12 . . .

John went on to point out the difficulties of transferring to and playing on English wickets, and to warn D'Oliveira that he should be aware that it was no easy task.

'I had just got married when the letter came through the post,' Basil D'Oliveira told me. 'We were staying in a room at my Mum and Dad's place. My wife was on the small balcony attached to this flat, and she was cleaning up and my mother brought this letter to me and I opened it. It told me about the job, how I would have to pay my own fare and digs, and that it was my last chance and he advised me to take it.'

D'Oliveira had reached a stage in his life where he was seriously considering giving up cricket and football. He had achieved all his aims locally and was losing interest. He was working in a printing office, having been thwarted in his ambition to be a doctor by leaving school early to help the family finances. 'I showed the letter to my wife and she said, "Well, it's up to you. Whatever you want to do."'

Basil immediately went to seek his great friend Damoo 'Benny' Bamsda. 'He always showed interest and wrote articles about me. He was a barman at the Grand Hotel. I tried to go upstairs, as I couldn't get through the front door because of the laws and regulations, but the guy said, "No, you can't go upstairs," so one of his other mates smuggled me through the back door – the service lift – and I got upstairs that way. Benny was behind the bar, and got the shock of his life when I walked in. I said, "Look, I've just got to see you. I've got this letter from John Arlott and he says it's the last chance." And Benny said, "You've got to go." There was no question of discussing the matter, he said. "You've got to go. We must contact John straight away. Leave it to me. I'll do all the necessary work from here on in" – which he did. And it's that letter that day, which dropped through the post, which is the reason I'm here today.'

Back with his family, Basil once more opened his bottle of green ink. His mind was racing, the words a blur:

many many thanks . . . noted contents . . . do appreciate it will be uphill battle to do well, especially coming from matting to turf . . . however, I will be practising four times a week on a turf wicket . . . will try to bowl tight . . . I think the whole non-white community will go wild when the news hits the local press this week.

As Basil flew in to Heathrow, he thought of the sacrifices and efforts that had been made back home by his family and friends on Signal Hill in Cape Town to get him this far. In this new world, he had to succeed for *them*. A stewardess handed him a note; it was from John Kay: 'Don't say anything to anybody until I meet you in the lounge.'

'I saw all those photographers there,' laughed D'Oliveira, 'not thinking for one moment they were there for me. And they all wanted to talk to me. I was gone – I was too emotional – I was scared.'

Having stumbled through a television interview, Basil allowed John Kay to drag him away from the throng, who were more interested in his views on apartheid than in his cricketing ambitions. As Kay was to write later: 'Make a note of the date. It was 1 April 1960. Was it merely coincidence that it was All Fools' Day?'

A visit to see John in his flat in George Street, some reassuring words, a drive past Lord's and then the train to Manchester. 'When we got on the train,' Basil said, 'the seats were all plush and soft, whereas in South Africa I was used to wooden benches whenever we travelled. And I was surprised that you could actually have a meal on the train.'

Another flash-bulb reception in Manchester. 'It was cold, damp and snowy. It was all too much. I didn't see the significance of what was going on until much later when I worked it out.'

Quickly on to a dinner at a golf club, some much-needed sleep and into the safe hands of a redoubtable Lancastrian landlady, who was totally unimpressed by the media hordes waiting on her doorstep.

Every Saturday night for the first six or seven weeks, John religiously rang John Kay to find out how their charge had fared on the field.

'I had a disastrous time at the beginning,' said Basil. 'I was way, way out of my depth. And John got nightmares about the whole thing, thinking he'd done me a lot of harm by snatching me from the so-called back streets of Cape Town and sticking me into the League over here. He started to question his own judgement.'

The D'Oliveira début at Middleton on 23 April 1960 was a local derby against Heywood, and was not really as bad as it has since been made to sound. He scored 27 and took 3 for 45 off 19 overs, but was overshadowed by a flamboyant century from the West Indian Clairmont Depeiza, his professional counterpart with Heywood. Understandably, Basil took time to adapt to the wet, slow pitches. Eric Price, the former Lancashire and Essex slow left-armer, helped him as much as he could, and then, one Saturday, the sun came out. 'We were playing Werneth at Middleton and the pitch was dry, and I got 78 and it took off from that innings, and it just went from there.' By the end of that first season he had scored 930 runs, at an average of 48, and taken 71 wickets at 11 runs each.

As he climbed each step of the cricket stairway, D'Oliveira was only too conscious of his fellow players in the nets saying, 'He'll never make it, the way he plays.' But make it he did, and history has more than adequately recorded much of the rest of his story: the move to Worcestershire, with four other counties showing interest and John still anxious, 'Are you sure it's a wise move? You're doing well. Why don't you stick where you are?'; playing for England; being the catalyst in the schism with South African cricket; and a glorious career crowned with the OBE and much meeting of the good and the great, and even prime ministers: 'Sir Alec Douglas-Home said a lovely thing to me. He said, "Don't ever get off the cricket field, Basil." And what he meant was, you get in there and play your game and let it speak for itself. I told John about that and he said, "Yes, that's absolutely one hundred per cent right."'

On the occasion of D'Oliveira's retirement dinner, on 1 November 1979, John turned down an invitation to attend a Downing Street reception for the England tour party to Australia, journeyed to Worcester and, astoundingly, eschewed the grape. 'I met John in the bar beforehand,' said Basil. 'He asked for an orange juice. At the dinner he gave the most brilliant speech for twenty minutes. In reply, all I could say was, "I can't follow that."

'We've spent hours talking about what happened. I wasn't that good a player. When I see other people playing these days, I wonder how I got this far. I really do.'

The happy conclusion to the D'Oliveira story gave John the greatest feelings of joy and fulfilment of any episode in his life. Although the issue was of the utmost importance to him, ultimately, as always, it was the individual who mattered.

Basil summed up: 'I often asked John why he picked on me to help. He said, "Because you sounded so nice in your letters." He took a hell of a gamble . . . I don't know, I haven't got the words to describe it . . . but it's . . . it's just that . . . there was a thing between him and me that was just defeating the whole object of apartheid in South Africa. Without shouting the odds, you know. We never shouted the odds.'

20

Return to Hampshire

However much John's activities, since he left Southampton in 1945, had revolved around cities and towns, he was still essentially a countryman, even if a countryman with a cosmopolitan view. But living in the centre of London was starting to become irksome. He and Valerie were cramped for space in the George Street flat; every spare inch was taken by books, and parking was getting to be difficult. It was, he felt, time to move out.

There were other contributory factors. John's father had died in 1959, after being ill for some time with Parkinson's disease, and his mother was now living in a small house which John had bought in Beaconsfield Road, Basingstoke. Since moving to London, he had seen less than he would have liked of his parents, and with his mother now widowed, he hoped to find somewhere to live in Hampshire, close at hand. Also, Valerie and he needed larger accommodation in order to put up friends, and a place in the country would not preclude John from seeing his sons, Jimmy and Tim, at weekends.

John had first seen the Hampshire village of Alresford in 1921 as a seven-year-old boy: 'I cycled wheel-rim-deep through the dry grit of the Basingstoke Road into the summertime village that moved at walking pace.' Forty years later, early in 1961, he came by car.

Close to Alton and not far from Winchester, Alresford's main thoroughfares are in a T-shape, with the imposing Broad Street forming a perpendicular to the town's east and west wings. The one-time Saxon free borough has a rich history. Some of that history has been relatively uneventful – corn, woollens, poultry, farming and sheep-marketing – and some of it full of jeopardy – conflagrations over six centuries destroyed much property. All of it has left a mark.

In the eighteenth century, Alresford had five grounds that had been used for cricket; in the nineteenth a railway – the Mid-Hants or 'Water-cress' line is still puffing nostalgically for enthusiasts of steam. In the twentieth century, the buckling of deep-sprung pure water, gravel seeding and chalk bedding in the streams of Bighton, Sutton and Alre produced plentiful watercress. And throughout, behind brick and timber or wattle and daub, the insidious woodworm works its timeless invasion.

It was Valerie who spotted that the first building on the eastern edge of the village was for sale. The Arlotts pulled into the yard, inspected it, bought it, and moved in on 28 February 1961.

The Sun Inn had served its last customer about three years earlier, and had then been taken over by an antiques dealer. It was thought to date from the 1640s or 1650s, during the English Civil War, and probably replaced a previous one which had been burned down by retreating Royalist cavalry as revenge for a rout by Ironsides at Cheriton, two miles away. Alresford was known for its strong Parliamentarian affiliations.

For centuries 'The Sun' was known as the last drovers' inn before Winchester, and when there were markets and fairs in the vicinity cattle and sheep were housed in the sheds around the courtyard. The shepherds, when not watching their flocks, slept in the lofts above, along with the drovers and dealers. In the eighteenth century the victuallers were known to act as fences for illicit spirits brought by smugglers to a cottage in nearby Brandy Mount from the tidal inlets along the Solent and Portsmouth shores. The section which was to become John's sanctum, built out at the back of what had been the interconnecting bar, tap-room and smoking-room, had a secret cellar. Under part of the solid wooden floor was an opening which gave access to a cavity in the chalk some six feet by nine feet and about eight feet high. The contents of that little snuggery were definitely not available for inspection by officers of the Excise.

The main cellar, with lime-washed brick walls, extended under most of the main block. This was shortly to house what the wine connoisseur Michael Broadbent described as 'one of the most interesting and imaginative collections in private hands in the country'. In time it would contain over five thousand bottles lying in state.

Without sacrificing the character of the building, and by restructuring rather than reconstructing, John and Valerie made what they now called 'The Old Sun' their home. The place became indistinguishably part of them, an extension of their personalities. The original bar made a restful yet distinctive hall; the landlord's retreat became the dining-room – the focal point of wondrous conviviality and refreshment for many a gathering; and the spacious lounge-library (added to the inn in 1912 as a billiard-room, with the occasional conversion to a dance floor for Saturday-night hops) translated into John's 'Long Room', a stall for a goodly number of the valuable books which had taken 136 packing cases to transport from London. The potential of that particular room was a governing factor in their decision to buy.

John was in his element at 'The Old Sun'. Sitting at the head of the long dining-room table, surrounded by invited friends and unexpected visitors, expounding on national affairs and listening to village gossip, encouraging everyone to refill glasses still three-quarters full, foraging in the cellar for even more bottles, and eating delicious food prepared by an exceptional cook – those memorable evenings were relished by all who were there. 'Have some more Stilton. Quails' eggs? We'll have a goose this Christmas.'

A glance around the table, and John would quieten the happy hubbub and prove the indestructibility of his thick-stemmed, wide-brimmed wine glasses, thought to have been made in Czechoslovakia, by holding one in his fist and crashing it down on the old oak table. He might then call for a toast, not so much as a formal offering, but as an excuse for recharging the glasses with full measures.

Newcomers were led comfortably into the conversation, old sweats were soon animated. Spare broadcasters, jobbing journalists, itinerant cricketers, truant pub landlords, estate agents, accountants, shopkeepers – what they did, where they came from, was of interest but did not matter. Who they were, counted – good people bonding together. John Bevan could arrive with punnets of fresh watercress from his stocks in the village; Laurence Oxley might look in with a new catalogue from his eclectic bookshop in Broad Street; Dr Sam Saunders, a Southampton GP, and his wife Doris, known to everybody as 'Mingo', who had first met John when he called at their house with tickets for a police ball, would dispense Jewish humour; Desmond Eagar, the architect of Hampshire's post-war cricket as the club's captain and secretary, would sit, urbane and exact, in the corner; Leo Harrison, John's oldest club friend with the youngest complexion, in the centre chair regaling the assembly with a story . . .

Leo Harrison's elfish grin frames Mudeford vowels. His stories have flavour – and also the quality of compassion which every good wicket-keeper should possess. An injured batsman receives instant first-aid; a batsman out, an immediate dry quip: 'Hard luck, mate; it ain't half a bloody game, is it?' That catchphrase of Leo's was adapted by John for the title of a short story about the lot of a professional cricketer which appeared in the magazine *Lilliput*.

'Arlott,' Leo would call out, affecting the French pronunciation. 'Arlo! Pay attention. Listen to this . . .'

'He thought he'd get into fishing, didn't he.' Leo slowly twirled his glass of wine, remembering the good years, which seemed like yesterday. ' "We'll have a holiday in Ireland," he said. "Good fishing out there." So

Joan and I left it to him and Valerie and they booked up. Posh hotel. County Mayo.'

At that time, in the early 1960s, neither John nor Leo had attempted much fly-fishing, though having spoken for five minutes on angling for a radio programme called *Time Out of Doors*, John felt confident. No doubt he was working on the premise that anything in the water could be got out – somehow.

'We had to decide what gear to take,' went on Leo, 'and J.R. Hartley hadn't written his book, so we took spinners – which is very infra-dig – for trout and things.'

Having flown from Heathrow to Dublin and spent a night at the Gresham Hotel on O'Connell Street, where John was charged 3s 6d extra for a pear in lieu of breakfast, the four set off westwards in a hired Chrysler.

'When we entered the foyer of the hotel where we'd booked, we couldn't believe our eyes ... Three sides slabbed with marble, and on this marble were these trout ... What a size! From then on we were on a hiding to nothing.

'Anyway, we booked in, went to our rooms and came down for a drink before dinner and everybody was in dinner suits. We were in lounge suits. Immediately Arlott was put off this hotel, plus the fact we had been put in two bad rooms – over the kitchens and above the ventilators.

'At the end of that evening, he said, "We ain't stopping here any longer." So I said, "But we're booked in for a fortnight." "I don't care about that," he said. So next morning he goes to the reception and says, "We're booking out!" The receptionist looked at him and said, "But you've booked for a fortnight." "I don't care about that," he said, "we're booking out." She says, "It's going to cost you a lot of money." "Not on your life," he said. "If you don't give us a full refund, I'll make sure this is published, and you won't have a very good reputation at the end of it."'

Having managed to extricate his party from financial penalties and saved them from the embarrassment of watching experienced fishermen use the right fly, John found more modest accommodation at a little market town three miles down the road.

It was no better – in fact, it was much worse. The beds were on a dais, the blankets did not fit and the bathroom was full of rust. 'It was a tatty ol' place, but the food was magnificent. We had a good time,' recalled Leo. Boats and ghillies were hired at five pounds a day and the whiskey they consumed came to about twice as much again. 'Ghillies cost us a fortune, and in two weeks we never caught a bloody fish. They invited us to take part in the Westport Angling Competition. I remember Joan and

I had just got back to shore where they were weighing all the fish, and we stood and watched John rowing a boat through the mist – rowing so slowly (*laugh*). Mind you, Val had rowed most of it. John had taken over the oars just as they were in sight.'

John never seemed to have much luck with his fishing. On another occasion, again with Leo Harrison, at a sea-trout pool in Christchurch, they were securely anchored and hoping for trout. 'How John ever did it, I do not know. But he cast downstream and he must have pulled the rod 'cos the spinner went right through the window of this very nice bungalow a few yards from the edge. And we had to pull up anchor and go in and ask, "Can we have our spinner back?" Bloody embarrassing that was.'

Leo laughed again. He was warming to his subject. 'Just shows you how bad he was at fishing. We got an invite to go salmon fishing along the Avon. First I'd ever done it. First time he'd ever done it, obviously.' At this point Leo digressed to mention that a certain Hubert Wheeler, who ran a sports shop in Bournemouth, and his mate John Pitts, who had played piano for Paul Whiteman's band in the 1930s, were fishing-mad. 'These two told us what to do: "If you get a fish on – gaff 'im. Don't just lift 'im on the bank, 'cos he'll flip back in the water, if you're not very careful. Throw 'im back a bit – you know, from the bank." So off we go. He'd got his Bentley by then. We'd got stacks of vino, of course. Cheese – he was into double Gloucester at the time. Nice day, it was. Soon as we got there, he got his chair and he got his vino out and he got his cheese out.'

John soon convinced himself that his day's work could best be done fast asleep, so Leo wandered off down to the river's edge. 'I must have been a hundred yards from him when I'm into a fish. So I yell, "Aaaarlot." You know how long it would take John to do a hundred yards. By the time he eventually gets there, I've got this fish on to the bank. So I said to him "Gaff it – don't forget, gaff it."

'If he had one try at gaffing it, he must have had fifteen,' chortled Leo. 'He eventually gaffed it. And it must have gone through his mind, throw it back a bit. So he grabbed the fish, threw it, and it finished up in some rhododendron bushes about twenty yards away.' A long laugh and a pause to replenish his glass.

'So we had to go into the rhododendron bushes to get the fish back, or rather I did. Unhooked, brought it out, put it on the bank, hit it on the head. And he looked at it and he said, "It's a bit bloody thin, isn't it?" I said, "What d'you mean?" He said, "What I'm saying, it's a bit bloody thin." He said, "It's a kelt." I said, "You're only bloody jealous of it just 'cos I caught it."

Kelt it was, though, and the spent-out salmon was buried unceremoniously in Leo's garden. John must have pondered the words of Izaak Walton, 'As no man is born an artist, so no man is born an angler.' In a way, his old friend T.H. White could be held responsible for the infatuation, though he had warned John once in a letter:

Of course you can have the wrecked fishing rods, but I advise you not to. If you are going to take up trout fishing, which is the most terrific sport in the world, far more difficult in timing than the most perfect on-drive at every cast, and far more breathtaking than breaking the sound barrier, and far more subtle than middle-eastern politics, you will not be content with less than the best tools brand new . . .

I have given it up for moral reasons, one of the great sacrifices of my life, and ought not in theory to encourage you . . . Whales are nothing, coelocanths are nothing, salmon are fools and governed by the laws of chance, coarse fish are mostly worms and bent pins, but the trout, the trout, the chalk-stream trout is emperor of all. You fish for him all day with the cunning of a maniac – and the skill of a Hobbs or Woolley – glorious, graceful, classical strokes – and the suffocating excitement of dicing with your own death, and at the end of the day you don't know that five minutes have passed . . . I warn you, that if you really take this up you will ruin yourself, as you will have to give up cricket and soccer.

That humorous warning was too late as far as playing football was concerned, as John had not kicked a ball for many a year, after succumbing to a leg injury in a scratch game at Basingstoke. And cricket had finally given him up, rather than the other way round. Although John thought he had played his last game during the war, in 1950 Jim Swanton managed to entice him to take part in a charity match at Didsbury between a Didsbury and District XI that was laced with some distinguished old players, and a team of cricket writers.

Having managed to stave off a few balls from medium-pacers, John found himself facing the former Lancashire opening batsman and slow left-arm bowler Charlie Hallows. On wicket-keeper George Duckworth's suggestion, Hallows was bowling wide of off-stump in order to get John off the mark. John lunged at the first five deliveries without getting anywhere near them – it did not help that the public address announcer kept saying, 'Now, here is the man who tells us all about cricket' and so on. Hallows saved John further embarrassment by bowling him with the sixth ball. John compounded his lack of success by remarking as he returned to the pavilion, 'Ah, old Charlie can still bowl a chinaman.' He sought reassurance from 'Billy' Griffith of Sussex, who had also been playing: 'Hope I didn't make a fool of myself.'

After that inept display, did memories return to John of his younger days in a different class of cricket? Of playing for Old St Michaels and Sherborne St John? Of a match at Tylney Hall, and his best-ever analysis of 6 for 10 bowling bumpers at his aunt's boyfriend? Or the charity game at Much Marcle in Herefordshire in 1939, when he hit the solitary six of his career, and in doing so split the bat that Reg Perks had been keeping for the Test match?

Leo Harrison remembered an occasion much later, when John went in to bat at number eleven in a game on Alderney. 'Frank Tyson was playing. John didn't have a jock-strap, so he thought he better put a box in. So he puts a box in without a jock-strap. It finished up guarding his knee-cap.'

Having returned to his native Hampshire, John set about re-establishing close contacts with the county team. He had never really been out of touch, but now, living on the doorstep, he could get to know better the younger players as well as renewing friendships with the more senior professionals – and this in their Championship-winning season. Colin Ingleby-Mackenzie was the admirably starch-free captain, having succeeded Desmond Eagar in 1958. 'John hung his hat on Hampshire cricket. We had a close relationship, which may be thought surprising – John with somebody of my background: public school, Old Etonian. He had definite views on who should be playing. We normally discourage people from coming into the dressing-room, but John was always welcome. For him the door was open any time.'

Long gone were the days when John first picked up a microphone and the Hampshire players of the time had nicknamed him 'Housewives' Choice' because they pretended that nobody with any cricket knowledge would be listening – only women. Or when he was commentating on a game at Worthing and describing the flint church by the ground and the Sussex Downs beyond, and the players had sent him a telegram: 'Never mind the scenery, what's the score?'

John's attachment to the Hampshire side throughout the years is reflected in a number of limited-edition monographs that reveal yet again his remarkable ability to assess character. The pen portraits were first printed in the annual *Hampshire Handbook*, sometimes accompanying a benefit year. But it was not just well-known or current players who were brought to life so vividly. A youngster like David Rock in the 1970s, or an ancient oak like C.B. Llewellyn, the South African all-rounder from the turn of the century, who was tracked down to a trim bungalow on the edge of Chertsey, would receive equal care and attention. And John still tried to cover away matches with the team whenever he could manage it. In the past he had enjoyed going for meals with Leo Harrison and another long-standing friend, the opening batsman Neville Rogers: 'We just automatically went out with John, because we were the ones who'd known him before the war. I remember a wonderful meal we had at a place called The Squirrel just outside Taunton. He started, as he often did, by pouring sherry into his soup. It was a fad of his. We always had what he had, because he was the expert. We knew we couldn't go wrong.'

There was no question of the expense of eating out at the better establishments stretching the limitations of the average professional cricketer's purse. Neville Rogers said: 'He would never put you in a situation where he thought it might embarrass you. He'd often put his hand in his pocket. He was incredibly kind and generous like that.'

At home, John's hospitality would extend to entertaining complete teams – often the overseas tourists during their game with Hampshire – and this could be worth at least a couple of wickets to the home side next day. When in Somerset, he would arrange a skittle evening for the competing sides, and with scrumpy, beer and wine on offer nobody would admit to drinking lemonade.

During the annual Alresford Fair in October, John and Valerie would have a houseful of guests who were well aware of the rituals to be observed. A set of golf clubs was essential baggage for the men. Denis Howell reminisced:

'John always had a golf tournament to coincide with the fair. The course there had nine holes and we used to have a practice round the day before with some very good entertainment in The Old Sun. I'd introduced him to the Wine Society and he took me down to his cellar, and I remember him saying, "This is my fortune maturing and appreciating at one and the same time."

'On the day of the fair some more people would join those who had stayed the night before – an assorted bunch, John Samuel [one-time sports editor at the *Observer* and later the *Guardian*], Hampshire cricketers and other odd bods, and we'd play nine holes in the morning. Then we'd stop for a sumptuous lunch in one of the pubs in Alresford, and at about three o'clock went back for another nine holes.

'John always acted as handicapper. He stood on the first green and decided what each player's handicap was going to be as a result of the first hole. And then in the afternoon he did the same thing, and of course the handicaps were totally different to what they'd been in the morning.'

Hazel and Maurice Edelston were frequent guests. Hazel was in no doubt about the score: 'John was a very bad player and so was my husband. Maurice could play most ball games, but not golf. The ladies would meet them in the pub for lunch and I remember the thing to do was nobble the other golfers before the afternoon round, get them so tight they couldn't even see the ball.'

'In the evening,' says Denis Howell, 'we had this great party at The Old Sun, which Val had got together for us all – marvellous lady. Other people came in and joined us – extraordinary occasion.'

'Traditionally, Val would always cook the same meal,' said Hazel. 'It was a lovely old place, but the tiniest kitchen you'd ever seen – minute and old-fashioned. And I can picture Val sitting on the floor making watercress soup, because there wasn't room anywhere else. And we always had venison as a main course. They would set up these trestle tables and certainly twenty people would sit down for this lovely meal, and the wine always flowed, of course.'

'John made an announcement after the main course and said that we now had to visit all the pubs in the village as was the custom, and pay our respects,' chuckled Denis Howell. 'Apparently the pubs at Alresford were kept open virtually all night for the fair, which was right down the main road. And so we all got up from the table and went round pub after pub after pub, meeting the landlords, talking to the locals, having a couple of drinks before moving on to the next one,' remembered Howell, reliving every minute. 'Then we went back to The Old Sun at about one o'clock in the morning and John would say, "We shall now resume with the sweet course," and we carried on with the meal.

'My contribution to all this was to introduce a few songs. I think I started by singing, "Hey ho, come to the fair", which everybody joined in, and John said, "This is a new development. We haven't had this at my party."'

'After coffee some would leave, but the remainder would settle down to play poker,' said Hazel Edelston.

'It was a wonderful occasion, typical of John, of course – a very generous host, very generous hospitality . . .' Denis Howell paused, and then reluctantly let go of the memory.

One of the strongest links John maintained with his home county was to write for the monthly *Hampshire: The County Magazine*. The editor, Dennis Stevens, had first met John in Southampton during the war. He would remind John of those days and the appalling scenes at a slaughterhouse near the Spa Tavern at the back of the *Southern Daily Echo* office, where he was working as a messenger. 'Sheep and cattle were driven from the station about half a mile away down a crowded main shopping thoroughfare to meet their end. They even terrified bullocks when they broke away and ploughed into shops and stores like Woolworth's. John used to chuckle and say, "Yes, but you should have seen what was going on at that time in the bloody parks."'

John's move to Hampshire meant that engagements in London counted as an away day as far as work was concerned. Writing for the *Observer* on cricket and football was still a weekly commitment, as it had been since 1958, but no longer could he entertain the sports editor, Chris Brasher, to a lavish lunch at his George Street flat, catch the 2.41 from Marylebone Station to Wembley for a weekday international match, leave two minutes before the end and be home with a glass of sherry half an hour later.

Socialising was now confined to winter Saturdays and lunch in a Fleet Street pub called Auntie's. The football and golf writer Peter Dobereiner recalled these lunches: 'The purpose was to discuss the sports department's policy, since it was the one occasion when the free-ranging correspondents could meet the battery staff of the sports desk, but John diverted it into broader topics. He started the convention of bringing guests, and introduced people such as the West Indian writer C.L.R. James to widen the scope of his debating club: John became so involved in these political, musical and literary debates that he brushed aside reminders that they would be kicking off at Highbury in five minutes. His reports tended to dismiss the first half and concentrate on the latter stages.'

John was meticulous, however, about looking in to check copy before the third and final edition of the paper went to bed at 10 p.m. He was one of a catholic band of writers on soccer for the paper at various times around the 1960s: Tony Pawson, Bob Ferrier, Professor A.J. 'Freddie' Ayer, John Sparrow, Warden of All Souls, and the proprietor of a night-club in Sloane Square attached to the Royal Court Theatre – Clement Freud.

The inspiration behind some of these unconventional choices was Chris Brasher. He remembers a night in January 1960 when he was sitting with John in 'the god-awful *Times* canteen in Printing House Square', which was being shared by the *Observer*, when a sports-room messenger arrived at around eleven o'clock with a Reuters cable about a riot at the Second Test between West Indies and England in Trinidad. 'It was only chance that we were there at that hour. We had to re-do the whole of the back page. And John just sat down and wrote it all from the tape.'

All this time, John's broadcasting carried on apace: a programme on the poet John Clare; reading Masefield's poem '85 to Win'; recalling

Albert Craig, the cricket rhymester; *Round Britain Quiz* with Alan Gibson and question-master Roy Plomley; a portrait of Lord Birkett; an interview with Georges Simenon; *Any Questions?* with Michael Foot and Nancy Spain; a debate at the Oxford Union during the Lord's Test of 1963; a feature on the West Indian tourists of that year; an appreciation of S.F. Barnes; and, memorably, a trip to the Kent coast to meet the creator of Billy Bunter, Frank Richards – or, to give him his real name, Charles Hamilton. John described him in the programme:

> He was a little, neat, rather bird-like man, with bright, busy eyes, and a slightly fussy attitude. He wore a skull-cap, and a dressing-gown, and carpet slippers, and he sat in a rather straight wing-backed armchair . . . He talked about his work, seriously, enthusiastically, and very illuminatingly. You see, every one of his major characters was to him real, and had been made of an amalgam of real people. Some of them he'd met as boys, some as adults. In some cases, he took the physical attributes from one person, the Christian name from another, the surname from a third, and the character from a fourth. But they were all for him real, and he felt that he'd really taken those people as they'd been when he found them, and lifted them up and made them bigger and better. He had the pride of a creator in this respect, and he referred to them familiarly, friendlily; he said how for fifty years he'd written about them sometimes to the tune of over twenty thousand words a week, and every bit of every story typed on the same typewriter.

Naturally, John was entertained to tea in the study. '*Floreat* Greyfriars. It was the usual lavish spread from the tuckshop around the corner, cucumber sandwiches with paste, bread and butter, a choice of strawberry or greengage jam, meringues, eclairs, plum cake, Darjeeling tea and . . . and sugar.'

Did he, John asked Richards, ever go to a public school? 'He was very, very evasive on this point. He wouldn't say that he did, but he more or less dared me ever to say that he didn't. I came away, I must say, with the impression that, like so many of his boyish admirers, he'd never been to a public school. He wished he had, and perhaps indeed, after all those years of writing, in his heart, and in his mind, he really believed that he had.'

Retrospectively, John felt that Hamilton had been extraordinarily adept at concealing all the things he had wanted to conceal. He sent the old man a script of the programme he had prepared, and received an immediate and unequivocal response: 'Unless you excise the sentence saying that you don't think I ever went to public school, I will sue for libel.'

In January 1962, Neil Crichton-Miller, a talks producer at the BBC, had asked John to take part in a programme in the series *What's the Idea?* The aim of the series was to give a minority idea an airing in testing circumstances, with two cross-examiners trying to expose its logical deficiencies. In this particular programme, Mary Stocks, one of the trenchant regulars on *Any Questions?*, a feminist and Fabian socialist, and John agreed to take the inquisitorial role, with Dr Donald Soper, the Methodist preacher, defending his views on total abstinence.

> *Arlott:* Dr Soper, is it merely that you yourself do not care to drink alcoholic beverages or drinks, or that you think no one should?

> *Soper:* I have an aesthetic objection to alcohol as a beverage, but that's not the important one. I have, first of all, a moral objection to drinking alcohol as a beverage for myself, and inasmuch as I believe that it is right for me – and I am a member of the society and not in any way a peculiar member of that society – I believe that it's also right for other people. Therefore, I should advocate the same total abstinence for others as I believe proper for myself.

Soper then stated his view that, as a professing Christian, he was under an obligation to bear other people's burdens and to share in community life.

> *Stocks:* I had an aunt who was deeply religious, but like St Teresa of Avila sometimes expressed religious truths in unconventional language, and I remember her arguing with somebody who advocated vegetarianism on moral and religious principles, and she ended the argument by saying, 'Well, what I say is, if Our Lord went to his crucifixion on roast lamb, that's good enough for me.' Now, could you not say the same about wine?

Soper responded by saying that the Christian faith did not depend on a slavish adherence to the things Jesus did or did not do. Local circumstances at the time prevailed. Water was unsuitable for drinking, therefore he drank wine. If Christ were alive today, he would take an attitude consistent with the circumstances in which alcohol has become a public menace.

The argument continued: there was nothing in the scriptures to forbid alcohol; abstinence would be a sacrifice for the common good; alcoholism as a disease; the seductiveness of advertisements; the Highway Code; traffic accidents, and legislation controlling temptation; taking away the pleasure of life.

> *Arlott:* To say that drinking, that the taking of a glass of wine by a man who hasn't got a motorcar, in his own house with his supper, or the taking of a glass of whisky by somebody whose nerves are jangled before he goes to bed, be forbidden on the grounds of drunken driving seems . . . what you are doing is saying, "Because I don't like bull-fighting, nobody should be allowed to eat beef." This doesn't follow. To take a glass of beverage which happens to be alcoholic with a meal does no harm at all . . . If you say, to drink before you drive is dangerous, then I agree with you. But what you're arguing is total abstinence, not temperance. If you argue temperance, I will agree with you.

The polemic went on: life-enhancing qualities; total abstinence a predisposition that could be psychosomatic or physical; medicinal advantages; insurance for drinkers; delinquency problems; betting a luxury; smoking; sexual licence.

Mary Stocks shifted ground slightly, coming down in favour of restraint of advertisers and drivers, but not prevention and encouragement 'to give up entirely something that may conduce to the comfort of their lives'.

> *Arlott:* I will tell you something. Drinking is pleasurable, betting is pleasurable, smoking is pleasurable, and, if I dare say it on the air of the British Broadcasting Corporation, sex is pleasurable and exciting. And if you two are going to attack the pleasures of life –

> *Soper:* Oh, no.

> *Stocks:* We're not.

> *Arlott:* Oh, yes you are . . .

It was, after all, the pantomime season. A draw would seem to be a just result. John celebrated the end of the programme with half a bottle of wine.

Rum punch was the order of the day at the beginning of 1964. John had accepted an invitation to go on a short trip to Jamaica with an International Cavaliers team organised by Bagenal Harvey, his agent. The five-match tour was sponsored by the tobacco firm Carreras, and the side had an England eleven flavour about it, with players like Peter Richardson, Ted

Dexter, Tom Graveney, Denis Compton, Trevor Bailey, Fred Trueman and Jim Laker. The first match against Combined Parishes at Montego Bay, a one-day affair, was won comfortably by the tourists. Then came a journey along the north coast to the sugar centre of Monymusk for a two-day drawn game with a Colts and Country XI. The commentary box at the Gray's Inn ground was basic, a squared arch supported by walls of still-green bamboo stakes with a roof of emerald-coloured palm fronds. The elderly rum-punchers and excitable youngsters leaping to their feet successfully obscured John's view whenever anything worth describing was happening.

The ground had reminded him of Swansea's St Helens, with the railway and station as a front-drop to the distant sweep of, in this case, the Caribbean. The island's post office had not been able to offer lines nearer than ten miles away, so very high frequency, or VHF, was having to battle local short-wave din. However, John felt he was better off than he would have been at Ellis Park, Johannesburg, where the commentator was obliged to stand between the boundary line and the fence, wearing shoulder-straps to support 'a board like a muffin-man's tray with a microphone standing in the middle'.

In Kingston, the Cavaliers won two of their three matches against Jamaica to complete an enjoyable and relatively undemanding tour. The home side was still somewhat in the doldrums after the death in a car accident of the talented all-rounder Collie Smith, despite such figures as Frank Worrell, Easton McMorris, Reg Scarlett and Alf Valentine playing in these games.

Steering his sweep through every conceivable angle in the first game, Compton scored a nostalgic hundred, to be upstaged in the second by Ted Dexter making 103 out of 128 (although Roy Marshall was the batsman at the other end) before being bowled by Worrell for 176. Tom Graveney was also among the runs, with 108 not out. In the last game there was another century from Dexter. Of one off-drive in this innings John wrote in *The Cricketer* that it 'never rose more than ten feet above the ground as it went for six into the stand at long-off with such force that it was providential that it passed between the spectators: had it struck anyone on the head, its force must surely have killed'.

Without realising it, John had made an impression in the West Indies. Not just from that one short trip – his only visit to the Caribbean – but from his cricket broadcasts generally. A favourite pastime, especially with the younger generation, was to try to imitate 'the voice'. The ITN newscaster Trevor McDonald used to listen in Trinidad. 'Arlott's influence in the West Indies was very interesting. He was non-Oxbridge, you see.

People from Hampshire could also broadcast cricket. We embraced him for that. He wasn't nakedly partisan. He enjoyed the game and he was aware of his international audience. We thought this was great.'

John was barely back from Jamaica before he was attending the memorial service for his idol Sir Jack Hobbs at Southwark Cathedral. Just over a year before, for Hobbs's eightieth birthday on 16 December 1962, John had gone down to Brighton to record the great man's reminiscences:

> The best and best-loved cricketer of modern times and still simply, Jack Hobbs, in the memory of cricketers all over the world. And it's a privilege to speak for them, and for myself as one of them, to wish Sir Jack many happy returns of the day. Sir Jack Hobbs, the man who made batting seem easy. Who developed that craft more nearly than anyone else to the point of perfection. Invested it with such ease, subtlety, and invention, that in his hands it could seem an art.

It was nearly a decade since the foundation of a club dedicated to, and named in honour of, 'The Master'. One day in 1953 John had received a telephone summons from Jack to 'come over to Emil's and pull a cork'. He did not need a subpoena. The proprietor of the Wellington Restaurant next to Hobbs's sports goods shop in Fleet Street was Emil Haon. Haon would often open a bottle of champagne in his cellar for an eleven o'clock refresher for Jack and his friends, though Hobbs never allowed himself more than a couple of glasses before a little claret at lunchtime.

A little later, John went again. This time he was joined by Kenneth Adam, a *Guardian* journalist who later became a senior BBC executive, and Frank Lee, the Somerset left-hander and Test match umpire. On this occasion two bottles were opened, followed by lunch upstairs.

'That was the first of several such parties,' related John in an article on the club for a Surrey CCC handbook. 'Alf Gover was one of the earliest to join in. At one lunch, it was suggested quite spontaneously that we should form a club, with Sir Jack as its perpetual guest of honour. He modestly, but clearly happily, acquiesced. What more fitting title for it than that bestowed on him by his fellow players? So "The Master's Club" came into existence. Then came Greville Stevens, Hugh Metcalfe – prewar film star, actor and stage manager – Jack Ingham who ghosted for Sir Jack in his newspaper days, Alec – now Sir Alec – Durie, Stuart Surridge, Tom Pearce, Doug Insole, Morley Richards, John Bridges of the BBC.'

John Bridges recalled: 'John asked me, "Would you like to come to the Master's Luncheon Club?" "Would I? Yes, of course, I'd love to."

I'd never been to anything like it, and it attracted me because I thought it was a marvellous Regency idea – eight to ten people getting together to lunch with one great cricket player. Jack tapped the table very gently and said, "I would like to welcome a new member. John, you are very welcome, and here are two little decanters, one for oil and one for vinegar, because I know you like collecting old pieces of glass." Nobody knew better than John how *Alice in Wonderland* it felt for me, because everybody there was famous.'

Over the years a historic phalanx turned up to greet Sir Jack at the lunch on his birthday – George Gunn, Maurice Tate, George Geary, Bob Wyatt, Herbert Sutcliffe, Frank Woolley, Wilfred Rhodes, Herbert Strudwick, 'Tich' Freeman, George Duckworth, Bill Hitch, Andrew Sandham, Learie Constantine, Robert Menzies, Donald Bradman, and many more.

The club had only two rules – no speeches, and only one toast: that of 'The Master'. 'For years,' continued John, 'with the port it was customary to demand – and not to count it as a speech – Alf Gover's story of the day he went in first with the Master. Yes, it did happen, with only a few minutes left for play at the end of a first day at Northampton in the early 1930s. With doughty defence, Alf not only managed to stay there that evening, but for quite a long while on the next day. In the end Jack said to him, "D'you mind getting out, Alf? There's a lot of good players waiting to get in." Sadly, Alf tired of telling it at the point where the other members knew it so well that they used to recite it in unison with him.'

After Emil Haon's death in 1957, Master's Club luncheons were held at The Mitre in Fleet Street, The Bedford Head (Henri's), St Stephen's Tavern in Parliament Square, and in recent years at The Oval. It exists now to commemorate Sir Jack and all that he stood for, and to help further those ideals with young cricketers. John, the founder of the club, was eventually elected its Perpetual President.

Hobbs died at the end of 1963. At the beginning of that year, he had become godfather to the latest addition to the Arlott household, a role he shared with Leo Harrison and Ted Mason, scriptwriter of *The Archers*, who had journeyed with John to many a match around the country. A bonny son, Robert, was born on 4 February 1963. Valerie had spent many weeks in hospital in Hammersmith during her pregnancy. Her doctor brother, Richard France, explains: 'She had a strange kidney condition which resulted in her having high blood pressure. She had an unhappy time in childbirth. A baby daughter, Lynne, was born prematurely in October 1961 and died after a few days. Val was fortunate this time in having one of the outstanding gynaecologists and obstetricians of his era looking after her – J.C. McClure-Brown. He worked pretty hard monitoring her condition.'

It was a growing awareness of health risks, and also of his own lack of breath, which led John to give up smoking around this time. Instrumental in the decision had been the alarming statistics he heard quoted when he took part in a Home Service feature on the subject. 'He smoked heavily until he gave up, and he always inhaled deeply. Officially, he smoked a pipe – good for the image,' commented Richard France. 'He was given large quantities of tobacco and a tobacco jar as Pipe-Smoker of the Year sometime around 1960, which he passed on to me. But it was really all cigarettes and the odd cigar. He gave it up with the single-mindedness with which he did everything he wanted to do.'

Sometimes Valerie had smoked a clay pipe to keep John company. This too was put away, as her husband took to a cigarette-holder with a fake cigarette to help break the habit.

John and Valerie's delight in their new son was infectious; but that happiness was to be shattered on the last day of 1964. A tragedy that affected the rest of John's life ushered in a dreadful New Year.

21

Jimmy

The policeman had been gentle, but professionally neutral. His words still echoed in John's brain. He was unutterably stunned by what he had been told.

His mind was a vacuum, yet saturated with memories. Jimmy, his eldest son, a reporter on the *Southern Evening Echo*, his life stretching before him, was dead. The word in itself did not mean anything. How could that be? He was alive. He always had been. He was so good-looking, so full of intrinsic charm and so much loved . . . a boy who had a mind of his own. At Highgate School in his early teens he had possessed a beautiful treble voice . . . a chorister under Martindale Sidwell . . . 'Oh for the Wings of a Dove', the solo James sang on television . . . And his clarinet – how he had enjoyed his jazz sessions with black musicians in London clubs.

The policeman's knock on the bedroom door had been discreet – at first John thought it was one of his sons – and the beam of the torch was obscured as he switched on the light and apologised for disturbing them at this time – past five in the morning. Did he know the man?, John wondered. Had he seen him at the Police Club? John was always dropping in when he was commentating on a game at Southampton, helping with the raffles and charity boxes – he had never forgotten where he started out.

He had to be stopped from seeing the body; he knew the procedures at times like this, and eventually gave way.

The memories continued to come – that horrifying time when Jimmy fell out of the passenger seat of the car on Alderney, fortunately only cuts and bruises. And Jimmy's love of mischief and mimicry. 'He used to ring up the pianist Howard Shelley's mum next door,' recalled Dawn. 'She was an amateur cellist, and he used to pretend he was a strange East German with whom she occasionally played – "Well now, Ann" – and then dissolve with laughter. And he used to trick Kingsley Amis as well . . .'

'I remember James in Swansea in 1958,' Amis smiled. 'He had a very good Indian pronunciation. "Lal Gupta here," he said. I was taken in completely. He pretended to be a professor from India, and could he come and talk to me? He was most persistent, very anxious to meet. "Well, not really," I said – it was a Sunday morning, I remember – "I'm sorry, I'm just going out." "Well, in that case," he said, "if I could come down to where your house is and just stand and look at it." So I said, "All right, I can't really prevent you doing that." And that was it. And then John and his sons turned up and I started telling them this, and when they all started crowing with laughter, I couldn't understand why. And then James broke into Mr Lall's voice.'

Amis laughed at the memory, and then became pensive. 'John was devoted to James. They were close – they were very good pals.'

Jimmy had left Highgate School in 1961. He had done well there, and the expectation was that he would get into Cambridge. Unfortunately his 'A' level results were not quite good enough, so he had taken a shorthand course with the intention of becoming a newspaper reporter. The job with the *Southern Evening Echo* had come after John – with the help of the paper's sports editor Denis Treseder – managed to arrange an interview. And so in 1962, with Tim remaining with his mother and stepfather in London, James moved in with John and Valerie at The Old Sun.

The jury at the Alresford inquest returned a verdict of accidental death. A staff reporter from the *Echo* had attended the hearing:

> Driving home from a New Year's party in Southampton, James Andrew John Arlott, twenty-year-old *Echo* reporter, probably fell asleep at the wheel of his sports car which ran into the rear of a lorry.
>
> Jim Arlott, son of broadcaster and author Mr John Arlott, of The Old Sun, Alresford, died from severe head injuries in the crash.
>
> A little earlier the Winchester Deputy County Coroner, Mr A.K. Freeman, reminded the jury of the evidence given by Mr John Arlott when the inquiry was originally opened.
>
> 'You may think that the evidence from Mr Arlott that his son had a tendency to fall asleep may well be the explanation of this accident,' the Coroner said. 'You may think that in fact the driver did fall asleep. Clearly he does not appear to have taken any avoiding action.
>
> 'You probably all know this road. It is absolutely dead straight, and it is clear from the evidence that the lorry had its lights on.'

James and a girl he had met that evening had left the party at 3.45 a.m., and he had driven her to her digs. In her evidence, she said that James had been with her at the party from 11.15 p.m., and that during the evening they had each drunk four gins and a little wine.

The Coroner: 'Did you notice anything about the manner in which he drove?'
'He was driving perfectly all right.'
'Did he seem all right in himself?'
'Yes, he did.'
After dropping her home, he had driven away to his home.

The inquiry then heard police testimony. Visibility was clear for at least three hundred yards in both directions at the scene of the crash on the A31 about a quarter of a mile east of Temple Valley filling station. The road surface was damp, but there were no skid or tyre marks to indicate avoiding action. Scientific analysis showed an alcohol content of 92 milligrams per 100 millilitres.

The Coroner: 'I think I am right in saying that 150 milligrams per 100 millilitres is the unsafe limit?'*
'Yes. 92 milligrams are equivalent to about 2½ pints of beer or five single measures of spirits.'

The unfortunate lorry driver then took the stand. He had been driving an unladen Austin articulated lorry and, just before the accident, had stopped at the filling station.

I pulled out of the filling station and was going downhill at about 20 to 25 mph when I felt a crash at the rear of the lorry,' he said. 'I was on the near side of the carriageway.'
He stopped at once and found the sports car had gone under the rear of his lorry. He had neither heard nor seen the car before the accident. So far as he could remember no traffic was approaching at the time on the 'down' lane of the dual carriageway.
In reply to his solicitor, the driver said he had checked the lights on the lorry before leaving Bishopstoke that morning.
In addressing the jury, the Coroner said it was tragic indeed that a young and talented man had lost his life. The jury were not directly concerned with the reason for his death.
It had been clearly stated in evidence that James Arlott had had

* The legal limit of 80 milligrams per 100 millilitres was set in 1967.

a little to drink, not a very great deal, and from the report of the
pathologist the amount of alcohol in his blood was certainly very
well below the level recognised as necessary if a person were unfit
to drive.

The Coroner expressed his deep sympathy with Mr John Arlott
and his family in their tragic loss – a sentiment in which the jury
and Sergeant W. Bishop, on behalf of the police, joined.

John never really recovered from his son's death. His emotional state,
so easily touched, had been plumbed to a depth that could not be reached
by others. The cross-currents of grief and guilt swirled dangerously out
of control. Utterly distraught and for a time irrational, his outlet was
anger. The MG sports car, which he had bought for James as an interest-
free loan, became to him a symbol of culpability, and the lorry that of a
destroyer. In the weeks following James's death, John would keep his foot
firmly on the throttle in the face of heavy transport while overtaking.
Several lorries found the only escape route was by way of a ditch. Had
his verse-narrative of a decade before come back to haunt him? Should
he have been the victim?

At times of death, people often attach significance to previous – often
unexceptional – incidents. To rationalise the inexplicable, to search for
logic in the fall of the cards, is to keep at bay the deadly hand of fate. At
home a few days before he met his death, James had been asked by his
father to decant some port. Richard France was there: 'Jimmy was having
terrible difficulty with this bottle of pre-war Quinta do Noval. I remember
saying to him, "Well, the cork must come out," and I seized the bottle
with a cloth, and gave it an almighty tug. The bottle gave way at the
shoulder and my hand went down into the broken crown. I sustained a
severed tendon. Finished up in Winchester Hospital and, what with one
thing and another, it took about six weeks to get better. Jimmy died a
week after it happened, and I've always reflected in a rather macabre way
that if it had been his hand and not mine that had gone into the bottle,
he would never have been killed, at least not on that day. He wouldn't
have been driving.'

The funeral in Southampton was a private affair. Only family were
present at the cremation. John had been insistent. No friends, no flowers.
'John drank brandy after James died – he cried up and down the streets,'
Dawn recalled sorrowfully. 'It was a pathetic funeral – Valerie and me,
John and Donald – no funeral meats – nothing to eat.'

While Valerie tried to bring calmness and stability to John, the pain for
Dawn remained indelible. She needed the comfort of being able to share

her grief with those who cared. 'A number of people were very annoyed at not being invited,' she said. 'Some of James's friends were outside our house all night – *all night* – no word – a silent protest that they hadn't been asked to the boy's funeral. I don't know why John didn't want it.'

Perhaps the intensity of John's emotions was such that he could not bear to share them with more people than was absolutely necessary: the private man reacting to his public image.

John sought solace the only way he knew how – in work, companionship and drink. Shortly after Jimmy's death, he covered Aston Villa's match at home to Coventry, and then Fulham's local derby with Chelsea at Craven Cottage. The veteran journalist and agency man Reg Hayter, also covering the match, was sitting in the next seat. 'I was amazed to see him. I'd heard about his son on the radio. I just put my hand on his shoulder and said, "John." He said, "Thanks, Reg," that's all. Nothing much else you can say, is there? I read his account in the *Observer* next morning – magnificent, accurate reporting. I know the show must go on and all that, but what professionalism. I don't think I could have done that in those circumstances.'

Soon after, an old mentor and friend found a way to let him know of his commiseration. John Betjeman adapted a recent poem, 'Autumn 1964', copied it out in his own hand, and sent it 'in memory of James Arlott':

> Red apples hang like globes of light
> Against this pale November haze,
> And now, although the mist is white,
> In half-an-hour a day of days
> Will climb into its golden height
> And Sunday bells will ring its praise.
>
> The sparkling flint, the darkling yew,
> The red brick, less intensely red
> Than hawthorn berries bright with dew
> Or leaves of creeper still unshed,
> The watery sky washed clean and new,
> Are all rejoicing with the dead.
>
> The yellowing elms have still some green,
> The mellowing bells so hopeful sound:
> Never have light and colour been
> More prodigally thrown around;
> And in the bells the promise tells
> Of greater light when God is found.

Three months later the future Laureate was in contact again. 'Keep heart,' he wrote. 'Don't exercise the will too much and share your sadness with others. It helps.'

But John could not be placated. His inner outrage at the overturning of the natural order was unabated. At Alresford Fair he saw some youths behaving badly, and reacted furiously by kicking some cars. He almost got into a fight, and had to be restrained. A well-intentioned friend introduced him to a Roman Catholic priest with the idea of helpful counselling, but as soon as the term 'divine providence' was used, John stormed off in fury. His fellow commentator Alan Gibson felt that John's faith wavered after Jimmy's death. These incidents took place over a period of time, giving the effect of a quiescent volcano unexpectedly erupting. Even three years later, having failed to turn up for dinner with Michael Parkinson, John was found on the floor of his room in the Midland Hotel in Manchester, prostrate with grief. Said Parkinson: 'I had eventually got the porter to open the door. John was in a terrible state. The death of his son had affected him deeply. Something had brought it all rushing back to him.'

It is impossible to over-emphasise the effect his son's death had on John. Jimmy's youthful shadow tailed behind him for the remainder of his life. Whenever he needed to wear a tie, he wore a black tie. It was an emblem of mourning, yes, but also an act of defiance. As the years rolled on, some people wondered whether there was an element of wanting or needing to play a role, the reason for which had vanished long ago – vanished in others' minds, that is. Had the tie become a public prop for bouts of depression? For looking lugubrious? Or was it an excuse for wallowing in self-pity, and an acceptance of tacit sympathy? Probably bits of both, and lots of neither. If only John could have allowed his grief to become a friend . . .

Nearly twenty years later, in 1984, the former England captain Tony Lewis, who by then was well into his broadcasting career, suggested a programme on John's seventieth birthday for BBC Radio 4. Which is how, soon afterwards, Tony and I found ourselves in Alderney with recording equipment and microphones at the ready. After the broadcast, I received a telephone call from an American woman who had never heard of John Arlott, and who had been listening by chance. She was in tears. 'It was the most moving thing I've ever heard in my life,' she said, weeping.

Tony had very sympathetically drawn John back to a Saturday night at the Angel Hotel in Northampton early in the cricket season of 1965, the one following Jimmy's death. The Glamorgan team were there, there was no play the next day, and the communion continued all night. John had poured out his feelings:

I should say it floated me back into cricket. Oh – it's . . . things like that – they leave a mark on you that never comes off. You're a different person. You are, I think, a lesser and a reduced person, because you know a piece has come out of your heart, and that boy, I – I just don't miss, but you see, you never . . . People say, 'He gets over it.' You don't get over things like that, they're – they're part of you, they're absorbed into your consciousness, and it's no good going around bleating about it, but it does change you. Poor boy, he . . . he wasn't even drunk – the Coroner made that very plain. I remember saying it at the inquest when they asked me, they said was he drunk? I said, no, I'm sure he wasn't. A, because he didn't get drunk, and B because most important of all, he was a happy person who didn't need drink to be happy. And then the coroner came out with the fact that the post-mortem had shown only a very small amount of drink in him – he'd just gone to sleep at the wheel. Because, like me, he falls asleep unless he's sitting up with the Glamorgan team.

22

The Cricketers' Association and the South African Debate

After Jimmy's death, John's life continued in much the same manner as before. Outwardly, there were few signs of the void in his soul. A tendency to become morose, an increasingly low boredom threshold and, on a banal level, no more games of poker – memories of his dead son trying to look impassive before declaring his hand were too painful for that particular pastime. John's practice of cramming a dozen lives into one carried on with the same inexhaustible stamina and seeming lack of hurry he had always shown. One day he would be broadcasting an appreciation of S.F. Barnes, on another giving a commentary on a Gillette Cup match between Suffolk and Kent at Ipswich or interviewing that man of the sea Uffa Fox for *The World at One.*

In 1965 he appeared on an *Any Questions?* programme from Cardiff, in which the Conservative MP for Finchley, Margaret Thatcher, gave early evidence of her ability to unsheathe her claws. The absent victim was the Foreign Secretary, George Brown, and the question concerned his suitability for the job. Mrs Thatcher – 'a Margaret yet to be fully blessed', to adapt Norman St John Stevas's phrase – was of the opinion that he should not hold office, whereas Michael Foot and John were predictably supportive of the beleaguered Brown, whose penchant for appearing 'tired and emotional' was beginning to make the life of press cartoonists very easy.

Instinctively John always backed the underdog, the person down on his luck who needed not only sympathy, but practical assistance. He had strongly identified, for example, with the old Hampshire stalwarts Philip Mead and George Brown (no relation) in their years of declining health, and had played for the police in a charity game near Ringwood in 1941 in what was to prove Mead's last public appearance at the crease. Already half blind and playing from memory, Mead scored nearly half the total runs for Lady Normanton's Estate XI. John loved the dry asides and eccentric rituals that made Mead such a character. As a batsman he was a master of deflection, exact in his placing. 'There's no need to belt the cover off the ball,' he would say. 'Hard enough for four is hard enough.'

As for Brown, John regularly visited him in hospital when he was dying. The one-time brilliant if inconsistent England all-rounder with 'the features of a Red Indian chief' had finished his working life as a car-park attendant in Winchester. In 1961 John took some of the Australian tourists to meet him. Their evident indifference to the old player wounded John's sensibilities. To him, Brown was a hero. Mutual embarrassment and a lack of common ground between the generations no doubt did not help the situation. John had meant well, but perhaps Brown felt patronised and the Australians awkward. However, John was a man of the players, and had an empathy with professionals who had achieved their position through their talent and not because of who they knew.

In the winter of 1967–68 the newly formed Cricketers' Association was a shapeless body, looking for a leader. A meeting held at Edgbaston was attended by forty-five players. Jack Bannister, then bowling fast-medium for Warwickshire, who has since held every office in the Association, explains what happened. 'Various names were tossed around to be a senior officer – Len Hutton, Peter May, Alec Bedser, even the Duke of Edinburgh. Suddenly, Don Shepherd of Glamorgan said, "What we want is somebody with an active feel for the game – presumably what we're after is a president?" Yes, of course – general agreement. Silence for ten seconds. Then Shepherd said, "Well, what about John Arlott?" Within a very short time it was settled – it was unanimous. We wrote to him and asked if he would do the job. Now, John had been keen to get on the Hampshire Committee, and it was my understanding that he'd only been on it for a matter of months or a year or so when we gave him this offer. He said it was the most gratifying thing he'd been offered in cricket, and immediately resigned his committee membership in case there was a clash of interests.'

Whether or not it was convenient for that to be thought, John actually resigned from the Hampshire Committee over what he felt was its lack of support for Basil D'Oliveira's cause after he had been omitted from the 1967–68 MCC touring party to South Africa, having just scored a century in the final Test against the Australians at The Oval. He was incensed – but not surprised – by the duplicitous actions and political manoeuvring of MCC and their cohorts both at home and abroad.

In the press he gave a long-term view: 'MCC have never made a sadder, more dramatic or potentially more damaging decision ... If politics, in their fullest sense, now transcend cricket in importance, it might have been wiser to take D'Oliveira to Soth Africa though he were not good enough, than to leave him at home when he is not merely good enough but eminently suited for the tactical situation the side will face ... No one of open mind will believe that he was left out for valid cricket reasons ... This may prove, perhaps to the surprise of MCC, far more than a sporting matter. It could have such repercussions on British relations with the coloured races of the world that the cancellation of a cricket tour would seem a trifling matter compared with an apparent British acceptance of apartheid. This was a case where justice had to be seen to be done.'

John was equally sure in his reaction to the players' offer. He was delighted, and it remained for him the cricket honour of which he was most proud. Over the years he was to become, as the former Lancashire captain David Lloyd pointed out, 'like a Dad to all the players'.

John was not merely a name on a letterhead, but an active president. In the first years of its existence the Cricketers' Association was entirely dependent on a few hundred pounds annually from Lord's, accompanied by suggestions on how it might be spent. 'Together with Harold Goldblatt [the Association's financial adviser],' says Jack Bannister, 'John negotiated for four years a sum of money which in 1970 seemed a lot – starting at around £2000 up to £5000 a year over the period – from the John Player Organisation, which made us independent of Lord's and really set us up. It gave us the time and elbow room to start conferring for things that were, at that stage, unheard of in cricket, such as a minimum wage, a group pension scheme to replace in part the importance of a benefit. Not entirely – it never could. A benefit was so crucial to everybody. But if a player was three-quarters of the way down the road towards a benefit and had fallen out with his employers, he daren't move, because that was him gone. Those things were set up thanks to John Arlott.'

From 1969 to 1983, when increasing frailty made journeys from Alderney hard to sustain, John chaired an average of six Cricketers' Association meetings a year. Some of them were attended by only a handful of people, others by over two hundred, such as in 1977 when the Kerry Packer 'intervention' was a contentious issue. 'We had two or three Extraordinary Meetings and the arguments got very heated,' said Bannister. 'I could well have seen those meetings degenerating into shouting matches and even the Association being split down the middle – polarised views, swingeing suggestions about refusing to play with or against Packer players in county cricket. John's chairmanship of the whole lot was terrific, simply because he'd got the respect of all the players. He held it together, kept the lid on and, at the same time, steered it into quite a reasonable debate. And then, eventually, he led the way into unlocking the entire stalemate.'

Jack Bannister laughed unexpectedly as another recollection came to his mind. 'We had a meeting with Packer in the Harlequin Suite in the Dorchester Hotel, Park Lane. My car broke down at Hendon at the end of the M1, and I was late getting there.' A sweaty and grimy Bannister found his way to the suite and spied David Brown, the England quick bowler and Chairman of the Cricketers' Association at the time, John, and the huge figure of Packer, at the far end of the room. 'The anti-Christ', so called by Jim Swanton, came rushing up to shake hands. 'Ah, you're the bloke who is trying to get all my players away from me. Be careful you don't end up in court. Come and sit down and have a drink.' Bannister laughed again. 'All this, and I hadn't said a word yet. And we're sitting and talking and there was an onyx table and a cigarette lighter and Packer's on about litigation and it's second nature and it doesn't bother him and he doesn't get emotionally involved with these cases anyway. And John suddenly said, "Well, forgive me for saying so, but I think you are emotionally involved in this particular cause, and that's the problem." There was a slight gear-shift and Packer replied, "I'm not emotionally involved – I don't get involved in my causes – I don't . . ." "Well, I think you do." "Well, I assure you I don't." The decibels were rising, and John continued, "I really think that's the problem between us." Next thing, it was like Packer had got a little moustache and it was Adolf Hitler. His hand came down on the table really hard, the cigarette lighter jumped up in the air. "I am not emotionally involved," he hissed. "I never have been and I never will be." He absolutely blew his top.'

John's own emotional involvement was not in doubt. His passionate concern for the players' welfare was constantly manifest. 'Sometimes he found it difficult to take two steps backwards from the centre of the action,' observed Harold Goldblatt, always at a close vantage point throughout John's presidency. 'But he was very able at handling meetings.'

In fact, John's feelings about Packer were not unambiguous. Part of him was entirely in favour of a tilt at what he saw as the feudal relationship between the masters of cricket and their servants, particularly if, after the dust had settled, there would be lasting benefits for the cricketers. But he was also aware that Packer's interests were elsewhere. For him the players were merely marketing pawns in a bigger game about the ownership of television rights. In late April 1978 there was a meeting at Lord's in connection with the Packer crisis. The Cricketers' Association wanted the International Cricket Council (at that time the International Cricket Conference) to send a letter to member countries suggesting they begin talks with Packer's World Series Cricket to try and resolve the stalemate. David Brown, the Chairman of the Association, could not attend, as he had to play in Warwickshire's match against Oxford University at the Parks (as it turned out, practically the whole match was washed out by rain). This left Jack and John with the task of persuading David Clark,

Chairman of the ICC, and Jack Bailey, MCC and ICC Secretary, that the letter was in everyone's interests. As soon as he passed through the Grace Gates, John began to feel uneasy. Lord's was a place where he never felt he belonged, and his anti-establishment instincts started to play up. As he made his way to the Committee Room with Jack Bannister he said, 'I don't trust them. I don't trust them. Never have.'

The battered, faded brown briefcase, beloved by those who knew it always contained several bottles of the palatable medicine so necessary for his well-being, was placed on the table. It was a symbolic gesture, really – rather like marking out territory or setting up a first line of defence. Jack Bannister continued: 'After about an hour's discussion they said they didn't want to do this, they saw it as player-power of the wrong sort. But Arlott kept on at them, and eventually they said, "Well, can we have an adjournment? You stay here, we will just take ten minutes."

'As they left the room, John said, "I told you we couldn't trust 'em." "What do you mean?" I said. "They've listened for all this time. They're going to discuss it." "No", he said, "A: they haven't offered us a drink, and B: if they had, they probably haven't got a bloody corkscrew." With that he opened the briefcase, took out a corkscrew and a bottle of Beaujolais.'

Shortly afterwards the letter was sent, with the text, as far as Bannister knows, unaltered. The aftermath for the Packer players in England was tricky negotiations with their counties. John adopted the role of mediator in several of these disputes, notably when Dennis Amiss was isolated by Warwickshire.

The controversy over the rebel tour to South Africa in February and March 1982 proved to be another test of John's chairmanship. Although his views on South Africa were well-known, he remained objective and was able to ensure that the view that players should have a right to coach there was communicated to the authorities.

Years earlier, in 1970, as the culmination of what had started out as the D'Oliveira affair came into sight, John was faced with a dilemma. Not morally – there was no doubt about his thoughts on the matter – but pragmatically. To commentate on the forthcoming tour of England by South Africa would be repugnant to him, and he wished to opt out of it, but for someone who broadcast as much as he did, there were other considerations. Put simply, he was worried that if he made another public statement on apartheid he might be dropped from future commentary, and also other broadcasts. He had not forgotten his suspension from *Any Questions?* Never far beneath the surface was an insecurity that few discerned. Discreet enquiries as to his position within the battleship berthed at Portland Place took a little time. Some broadcasting and journalistic colleagues who were looking to John to take a stand on the matter began to be impatient. Was he, they wondered, abnegating responsibility? But on 17 April 1970, in a *Guardian* article entitled 'Why I'm Off the Air', John left no room for doubt:

For personal reasons, I shall not broadcast on the matches of the South African cricket tour of England arranged for 1970. The BBC has accepted my decision with understanding and an undertaking that my standing with them will not be affected by it.

This course of action has not been dictated by mass influences. Apartheid is detestable to me, and I would always oppose it. On the other hand, I am not satisfied that the cricket tour is the aspect of apartheid which should have been selected as the major target for attack. It would have seemed to me more justifiable, more tactically simple, and more effective, to mount a trade embargo or to picket South Africa House. Surely the Nationalist South African Ambassador is a thousand times more guilty of the inhuman crime of apartheid than Graeme Pollock who, throughout the English summer of 1969, played cricket for the International Cavaliers XI with eight or nine West Indians and, before he went home, said, 'What great chaps – there couldn't have been a better bunch to play with.'

Jack Plimsoll, the manager of this touring team, was an intimate friend of mine on the South African tour of England in 1947, before the election of the first – Malan – Nationalist government and the introduction of apartheid. Every one of the South African players of my acquaintance has already played with, and against, non-white cricketers. Indeed, only a multi-racial match, played in South Africa before the Nationalist government banned such fixtures for ever, provided the expert assessment of Basil D'Oliveira's ability which enabled me to persuade Middleton to give him a contract to play in England. Not all South Africans are pro-apartheid.

Crucially, though, a successful tour would offer comfort and confirmation to a completely evil regime. To my mind, the Cricket Council, acting on behalf of British cricket, has failed fairly to represent those British people – especially cricketers – who genuinely abominate apartheid. The Council might have demanded – and been granted – terms which would have demonstrated its declared disapproval of apartheid. It did not do so; nor give the slightest indication of a will to do so. To persist with the tour seems to me a social, political, and cricketing error. If I were a supporter of apartheid I would feel the same. It seems to me destined to failure on all levels, with the game of cricket the ultimate and inevitable sufferer. If it should 'succeed' to the extent of being completed, what is the outcome to be – a similarly contentious tour four years hence?

It is my limitation, or advantage, that I can only broadcast as I feel. Commentary on any game demands, in my professional belief, the ingredient of pleasure; it can only be satisfactorily broadcast in terms of shared enjoyment. This series cannot, to my mind, be enjoyable. There are three justifiable reasons for playing cricket – performance, pleasure, and profit – and I do not believe that this tour will produce any of them.

The terms of the BBC's charter do not permit expression of editorial opinion. It would not be professional or polite to disagree with my fellow commentators on the significance of the tour within the hearing of listeners. It therefore seems to me unfair, on both sides, for me to broadcast about the tour in a manner uncritical of its major issues, while retaining the right to be critical of them in this newspaper.

It is my hope to write and talk about cricket in which the minor issue of a game is not overshadowed by the major issue of principle.

Principle was not the underlying reason for the eventual cancellation of the South African tour. Meeting an imposing MCC delegation led by former president G.O. 'Gubby' Allen, who wielded enormous influence within the club, at the House of Commons, the Labour Home Secretary, James Callaghan, told them that he had insufficient resources to police London if there was a crisis resulting from the proposed protest march. The potential size of the march, the blocking of fire engine routes and the threat of public mayhem at venues around the country meant that the tour had to be stopped. Faced with that ultimatum from Callaghan, the delegates returned to Lord's where, John heard, Allen remarked, 'This is the decision that has won us the next general election – it's worth a quarter of a million votes.'

The Minister for Sport, Denis Howell, came to the support of his colleague. 'I took the strong view that I didn't want these people here on ethical grounds, given the make-up of cricket and sport in South Africa at that time. Jim Callaghan was taking a much more practical line that, as Home Secretary, he couldn't allow widespread public disruption and disorder.' The South African issue was a hot potato that had refused to cool down. It had occupied the editorial columns and sports pages of newspapers for months. Denis Howell and John had been invited to take part in a televised debate from the Cambridge Union on 10 November

1969, opposing the motion 'that political commitment should not intrude upon sporting contacts'. Ted Dexter and Wilfred Wooller, both old Cambridge men, were the proposers.

Before the debate, John rang Howell and asked to see him. Over drinks in the minister's office, John related a story about Wooller's experience in a Japanese PoW camp. When the camp was relieved by the Americans, Wooller had asked for a full muster, together with the Japanese guards. After everyone had assembled, he had marched the Commandant over to a deep grave, and thrown him in head first.

'It was a very interesting insight into John, I think,' remarked Howell. 'Because he clearly had a degree of affection for Wilf Wooller, and because he knew we were going to have a passionate debate about South Africa and apartheid, he was very anxious that we kept personalities in proper proportion. "I don't know how you're going to get on with Wilf Wooller," he said. "You may find him a bit difficult to deal with." In fact I liked Wilf Wooller very much, and we've met many times since, not least on the occasion I was up on a great big digger which was digging the first soil at the Welsh National Sports Council behind the Glamorgan Cricket Ground. Just as I was about to perform this ceremony, high up in the air, surrounded by microphones and buttons, the back door of the pavilion opened and out came Wilf Wooller. I was able to say, "I'm delighted to see my old friend Mr Wilf Wooller appearing. I'm looking for an old sod to turn over." '

During the debate, Wooller paraded the double-standard argument: 'Why should MPs suggest we should not play against South Africa when they're busy trading with South Africa?' He also appealed to idealists: 'If you bring politics into our sport, you're going to destroy the last bastion of sanity we have.'

Batting last, eschewing notes and with his hands thrust deep into his pockets, John spoke for fifteen minutes:

> I should perhaps at an early stage state that I have known the honourable third speaker [Wilf Wooller] with great admiration for some thirty-seven years, in close personal contact for twenty-three years, during which we have dined, wined and argued together, and in that entire period I have been completely amazed at the political naivety of one so shrewd in other matters, and I must admit, Mr President, with due humility, that if the honourable third speaker had continued for the time that has been allotted to me he might have done the cause of the opposition more good than I could. [*Applause*]
>
> There is a time in the growth of some political beliefs when they so offend against common morals that they are recognisable as evil

and obnoxious to right-thinking people. I cannot believe that any gentleman on the other side of the house would happily have played a round of golf with Hitler or Goering, nor I trust do any of them want to make up a football match with the people who directed or carried out the suppression of the Hungarian Revolution or who battered down the rise of thought in Dubcek's Czechoslovakia. This, sir, is not a question of nationality nor of race, but of political commitment, which is a personal matter. The ultimate clash of political commitment, Mr President, is war, which breaks down all contacts between nations, except those between the bankers gathered in Switzerland. [*Applause*]

Mr President, I would go so far, I think, as to argue that political commitment is the only valid reason for breaking the sporting contacts. To see what other reasons we can find: national differences won't do, the World Cup proves that. Nothing in football is more exciting than to see, for instance, West Germany playing against Brazil and a clash of method, of character, of approach and of physique. And so, in the Glamorgan cricket team which won the Championship this year, race was unimportant. It had West Indians and a Pakistani – whom it's most happy to see here tonight, Majid Jahangir – who played distinguished parts in the winning of the Championship and were very happy members of the team in the dressing-room and in its hotels. Not nationality, not race, I would say not, Mr President, difference of sex, for as you may have heard, men play many games with women. [*Laughter*]

It is political commitment and political belief that can make a man think that his opponent's views are so obnoxious that he will abstain from playing any game against him, as a protest against what the other man believes and also, lest it should be assumed that by taking part in any activity with the supporters of that view, he gives it his tacit approval.

Any man's political commitment, if it's deep enough, is his personal philosophy, and it governs his way of life, it governs his belief and it governs the people with whom he is prepared to mix. Mr President, sir, anyone who cares to support this motion will not exclude politics from sport, but will in fact be attempting to exclude sport from life. [*Prolonged applause*]

John's deep conviction swayed the voting to his side – the motion was defeated by over 2 to 1. Ian Wooldridge felt the same in the *Daily Mail*: 'He won the day not only with sane persuasion, but a faultless flow of

English so beautiful in its construction that you could almost hear the commas and semi-colons fall into place. He sat down to a standing ovation.'

'John made a brilliant speech – easily the best,' said Denis Howell. 'Majid Khan, who obviously worshipped Wooller, sat at his feet throughout the whole debate. We watched with great interest as with great reluctance he went and voted for us. It was a moving moment. Afterwards, John and I sat up most of the night in the hotel – we outdrank the students, which we regarded as a bit of a feat – passionately arguing the case. When, in the early hours of the morning, Dexter and Wooller said, "Well, we concede you *might* be right – you *might* bring apartheid to an end by having this boycott rather than going to play – changing it that way," we decided to call it a day.'

The Cambridge debate attracted widespread attention. Some time later an envelope bearing the House of Commons insignia arrived at Alresford:

My dear John,

    This letter is long overdue. However it has this advantage that instead of writing on my own behalf I write additionally on behalf of the whole Parliamentary Party to express our heartfelt congratulations on your firm, courageous and honourable stand on the S. African Cricket Tour. Frank Byers who saw the recent TV discussion said: 'John played a straight bat, and made one feel proud to be a Liberal'! And he's not easily given to praise!

    Bravo. We are all delighted. I hope those bloody fools call it off.

    Yours, Jeremy

Jeremy Thorpe's hopes were not in vain, and it was to take two decades for the division in cricket to be mended.

Ten years later, in 1980, John was offered the chance to debate the subject once more, and I acted as go-between. The invitation came from Hugh Purcell, the Assistant Head of Current Affairs and Magazine Programmes at the BBC: would John be prepared to go to South Africa and take part in a debate at Stellenbosch University which would be broadcast? John thought for a long time. 'No, I don't think so,' he said finally. 'It's very tempting, but it would be misconstrued.'

So, the lion's den waited in vain for its Daniel, although for John that element did appeal. It took courage to refuse. He felt that any changes that had been made in South Africa were merely cosmetic. Capital would be made out of his visit to the country by both sides. Did he want to be kicked around in a political arena again? Of course not . . . but a pause to ponder. The indecision was final. He did not go. But he wanted to.

23

The Voice of Cricket

In 1968, John was appointed full-time cricket correspondent of the *Guardian*. In recent years he had been mainly serving the *Observer*, with occasional contributions to *The Times* under his 'Silchester' pseudonym. But now at the *Guardian* he was conscious of inheriting a gown of office that had rested on distinguished shoulders.

His predecessor Denys Rowbotham, just deceased, had, apart from a year's interregnum, done the job for over twenty years. Before that, for a brief period after the war, Terence Prittie was in position before moving on to become the paper's Berlin correspondent. And before that, illuminating the years between the First and Second World Wars, was the incomparable Neville Cardus. A touch of impishness is evident in Cardus's appreciation of John's appointment – 'It was as though a cricketer went in to bat after Hobbs and Sutcliffe.' More seriously, he went on: 'I have always admired Arlott's economy of words, his ability to depict a scene or character as though by flashlight ... Arlott can imprint on imagination by means of swift, accurately-seen etching; he has a gift for the word photographic. He is never the literary mandarin, yet he is one of our most civilised writers.'

The move from the *Observer* had been engineered by the *Guardian*'s deputy editor, soon to be sports editor, John Samuel, who had himself taken the same route some time previously. Samuel was chary of the influence John's agent, Bagenal Harvey, wielded at the time, so the deal was done directly. Harvey had many leading media and cricketing personalities on his books, and he organised the International Cavaliers tours as well as the limited-overs matches played for television on Sunday afternoons. A director of the Bagenal Harvey Organisation, Geoffrey Irvine, who sensitively supervised many of John's affairs from 1969 onwards, says: 'I recall Bagenal telling me that during the fifties and sixties John was generally disorganised and usually in financial difficulties. Bagenal's friendship with Clifford Makins and Chris Brasher at the *Observer* enabled him to get John the job which was, at least, a source of reasonable regular income for John, who very much needed it. Subsequently John accepted an offer from the *Guardian* without involving Bagenal, for which Bagenal never fully forgave him – particularly because he felt compromised with his *Observer* contacts.'

John, no doubt, had his reasons for negotiating alone. He probably felt that the *Guardian* offer had come his way because of his own contacts – he had known and liked John Samuel for some time, whereas Samuel and Harvey had crossed swords before. To have involved Harvey would have unnecessarily risked the venture. Also, John knew that the Bagenal Harvey Organisation would have wanted to set a fee far in excess of the *Guardian*'s expectations. Said Samuel: 'John would never screw something like the *Guardian*. He had an awareness of your budget and what you had to spend and what was fair and what wasn't fair, and he knew the price had to be paid and that there was only a limited intelligentsia to pay for the things he wanted to do or write about.' Certainly in the past John had limited Harvey's control where his broadcasting work was concerned. A letter to BBC Contracts in February 1964 confirms as much: 'Bagenal Harvey is authorised to negotiate *Sportsview* and *Grandstand* contracts only on my behalf.'

With Geoffrey Irvine, John had an amicable relationship. They first met at a business dinner with representatives of an advertising agency who were keen for John to front the St Bruno pipe tobacco campaign. It was an occasion, Irvine remembers, at which John obviously felt he had to impress, so he fell into his monologue routine. 'The dinner was highly successful from a business point of view, as the campaign was agreed, but there were times when our host's eyes seemed to glaze over at the prospect of yet another Dylan Thomas story. Eventually, our host enquired with an air of finality which certainly did not invite a positive response, whether we required anything more. As he turned to summon the bill, John said, "Thank you. Another bottle of claret would go down very well." Forty-five minutes and several Dylan Thomas stories later, I was afraid we might lose the deal. Happily, we didn't.'

Over the years, John was engaged for a number of commercials besides St Bruno: Brylcreem, Double Diamond, Fragrant Cloud, Cracker Barrel biscuits, and Qualcast lawnmowers – 'A lot less bovver than a hover'. The onlookers who had laughed as he perspiringly mowed the Wilkeses' lawn in Australia back in 1954 would have been amazed. Reward at last. 'To get paid £10,000 for standing in a field in Cambridgeshire, I'd say virtually anything,' John chuckled to me at the time. He also put his credibility on the line extolling the virtues of the Spanish wines of Rioja and enthusing about the 'Goldseal Priory' biscuits of Huntley & Palmer: 'When summers were just a bit longer and hotter, when we still had pounds, shillings and pence – and guineas – and you listened to wirelesses not transistors and you travelled to Devon on the Great Western Railway. If you can remember any of these things, these Huntley & Palmer biscuits will take you back a bit' – he crunched into one – 'I'd almost forgotten a biscuit could taste as good as this.'

According to John Samuel: 'A lot of people said, "A pity John appears hawking his personality." But he marketed himself because he had pretty tall needs in terms of wine and other interests. I think anyone in the public eye learns to market themselves. He used Bagenal Harvey because he had to. There was no one else at the time.' Samuel thought for a moment, and then went on. 'John had a good scale of values. He hated meanness, puritanism, that's where the cavalier came in. But he was a person of such sanctity, almost, of moral purpose, that you always felt you could go to him, and he had enough distinction of personality to say what one should or should not do and what would be the wiser course in the circumstances.'

John's wisdom and business acumen were in evidence in 1981 when he helped twenty-five-year-old Marcus Robertson, son of the tennis commentator Max Robertson and Elizabeth Beresford, the creator of the Wombles, set up his sponsorship and PR agency Craigie Robertson. 'John was enormously supportive,' commented Marcus, 'and agreed to be chairman. His name, of course, gave us credibility, but he wasn't just a figurehead. He attended all the board meetings and was very knowledgeable about contracts and articles of association – changing clauses that weren't right and noticing what was missing. He gave a lot in the way of ideas and suggestions. When we asked him what fee he wanted as chairman/director he replied, "I don't want anything." We pressed him and eventually he said, "Oh, all right, I'll take a share of the profits," which meant that he was out of pocket.'

At the first meeting of the agency, Marcus's partner, Judy Brierley, made him promise not to reveal the identity of her father – John Stanning, who had won a cricket blue at Oxford and played a few games for Worcestershire just before and after the war. She was certain John would never have heard of him. But Marcus could not resist teasing her by doing so. As she kicked him under the table, John looked up. 'Oh, yes, fair-haired, good-looking young man – caught Maurice Leyland at Stourbridge in 1939.' Judy remains amazed.

John's association with the *Guardian* was a happy one. He would sometimes go back to the paper's offices in Farringdon Road after a match for a drink with colleagues, or go and pass the time of night with those working into the small hours – he always respected the honest toiler. He was aware that, increasingly, sports writing was tending to concentrate on the sensational and superficial side of a story. He came from a different school.

'He was always worried about his inability or refusal to acknowledge a news story,' said John Samuel. 'There was the time at Lord's in 1971 when John Snow ran into and knocked over Sunil Gavaskar in a Test match. Here was the son of a Bognor vicar who had apparently flouted cricketing conventions in going for the ball first and knocking the batsman over, and this was shown on BBC Television News in report after report on the Saturday night.'

John was in the habit of ringing Samuel to let him know that he had finished his piece for Monday's paper, and this time he phoned from a motorway service station on his way home. Samuel: 'I knew his potential weakness here, so I said, "You've mentioned that incident, have you, with Gavaskar and Snow?" There was a long silence, and he said, "What do you mean? You don't want that." So I said, "Yes, as it's been on BBC Television News showing the actual incident." He said, "What do you want me to be, an Alex Bannister then?" So I said, "Come on, did you see it? If you didn't see it, tell me."

'I was a bit shocked, because I'd taken into account that he might have been doing BBC work or was off for a liquid lunch, but he said, "Of course I saw it." I said, "Don't you have any views on it?"' Samuel then reminded John of a discussion they had had after a Wembley Cup Final, when booing had occurred for the first time. In those long-forgotten days when soccer was still seemly, John had agonised over whether to mention the event, for fear of encouraging its recurrence.

'You can't pretend it's not happened,' said Samuel. 'John was defensive initially, and we had some pretty hot words because I think he'd had a drink or two, and after I put the phone down I can remember my three-year-old daughter saying, "I thought you and John Arlott were friends." I said, "We are, but you've got to get through to the old bugger."'

Two hours later the telephone rang again. John was still on the motorway. It was 11 p.m. and he was at a different service station. 'All right, all right, I'll do it.'

John Samuel laughed. 'He'd spent two hours mulling it over ... It was still a very moderate comment, though. John was often much more vehement in private than he ever was in print. He believed that once you appeared in print even the mildest observation could be a real lash.'

Until around Easter 1974, John's *Guardian* output included football. He had become progressively disillusioned with the cynicism that pervaded the game, and after then his closest contact with it was to listen to matches on the radio or watch them on television. John hated the professional foul, the financial chicanery and the unrealistic demands on managers and coaches that had become the norm, the creed that demanded success at all costs and that players be thrown back into the fray too soon, the pain of unhealed injuries numbed by needle and drug, resulting in long-term damage and shortened careers. Most of all he hated what someone once called the 'cigardianship' of chairmen and directors in their sharply-cut suits and mohair overcoats, and the size of whose brains was in inverse proportion to that of their bank balances.

But it was not all that alone that stopped him going through the turnstiles. On two separate occasions when returning from matches by train he had become involved in affrays with football hooligans. Both times they were wearing the colours of Manchester United. John defended himself bravely in each incident – a wine bottle can be a lethal weapon in practised hands – but to see the youth who had just hit him with a knuckleduster sprawled across the platform as the result of a retaliatory blow was small consolation. The prospect of spending more Saturdays being spat upon, kicked, punched, jeered and abused did not bear contemplation. After the second incident, John walked down the train in search of a drink at the buffet-bar. He asked the steward, 'How on earth d'you handle these hooligans? I've just had a crowd of them.' The steward leant under the counter and produced a big iron bar. 'I keep this by me, Mr Arlott. It's very necessary after a football match.'

Some time later, John was talking about his experiences with Denis Howell who, as Minister for Sport, was searching for ways to grapple with what had become a national problem. Said John, 'There'll be no more iron bar with me on the train. I'm packing it in – it's not worth the candle.'

Before then, he had received a letter from J.B. Priestley, who had seen his article in the *Guardian* on 3 November 1972, in which he diagnosed the public disenchantment with football.

> Along with my old friend Neville Cardus, you are one of the few bright spots in the *Guardian* as it is now, so feverishly determined to attract the young.
>
> I have particularly enjoyed the football piece today, a very perceptive article indeed. As in cricket, we compel our players to play far too much, so that they so often find themselves at a disadvantage against players who are not so hard-pressed or so stale.
>
> I never see a soccer match now, except on television. In my boyhood and youth, I played a great deal of soccer, always at full-back. Up to the First War, which undermined me in various ways, I was

a very healthy and strongly-built youth, and could play hard against some very tough opponents. But sixty years ago, the game was very different from what it is now. As full-backs we hadn't to run ourselves ragged and rarely left our own half. On the other hand, we were expected to turn quickly and do some huge clearances. These were often absurd – I can well remember booting the ball clean over grandstands – something the crowds loved. But at least we were not eternally passing the ball back to the goalkeeper, a tactic that slows up the present game and often can be quite dangerous when all is slippery. And of course these vast throw-ins from touch were never allowed and it would be better if we didn't have them now. You are right in thinking that many of the bad fouls we see now come from tiredness and too much tension, itself partly the product of too much money and publicity – and, as you rightly say, lack of enjoyment of the game. I never enjoyed our international side that rather luckily collected the World Cup. Somehow Ramsay took the panache and sparkle out of the game. The earlier Manchester United and then that wonderful Blanchflower Tottenham team were better in my eyes than England itself. But I mustn't run on. Again, many thanks for your today's piece – and scores of others too. Keep going!

PS. Life was rough when I was young in the North. But it never had the shocking viciousness it displays now, when we seem to be stranded in a dying civilisation.

Despite Priestley's exhortation, John had no intention of keeping going. An invitation to cover a match at Luton on Boxing Day 1973 brought the matter to a head. The mental association of 'Boxing' and an injury sustained by weapons more lethal than fists gave rise to the morbid thought of an obituary with the final sentence 'He was clubbed to death outside the Luton ground.' Facetiousness aside, John had had enough of football. The decision led to an argument with John Samuel, who eventually persuaded him to see out the season.

Samuel much regretted that there would be no more Arlott on football. 'He was a fine football writer – some of his very best prose. He wrote about soccer in the old-fashioned sense – from what he saw. He was so perceptive as an observer, and he saw many things in a soccer match that the players themselves hadn't seen. He was able to absorb what players had to say, but you would never get John to make a statement in quotes. That was not part of his aim. He absorbed what players said and then through the filter of his own eyes and vivid imagination retold it.'

The same was true of his writing on cricket. His 1971 biography of

Fred Trueman, *Fred: Portrait of a Fast Bowler*, dedicated to his son Timothy 'who deserves far better than my faults' (the lingering guilt of domestic upheaval?) contains few quotation marks. Without doubt it is one of John's best books, with many revealing psychological insights into a complex character. Because of the lack of direct quotation, one is only casually aware of the considerable research and journeying undertaken. As well as lengthy conversations with Trueman – 'duo monologues', somebody called them during a 1977 collaboration for a BBC-TV Further Education series – John made several visits to Leeds, Bradford, Doncaster, Stainton, Scotch Springs and Maltby – Tyke territory. On those trips he ferreted information about 'Fiery Fred' from luminaries including Arthur Mitchell, Phil Sharpe, Brian Close, Doug Padgett, Ronnie Burnet, Billy Sutcliffe, Don Brennan and Bill Bowes. The writing was vivid and exciting, giving the lie to those who thought John's literary style better suited the things he had not seen than those he had:

He was a cocked trigger, left arm pointed high, head steady, eyes glaring at the batsman as that great stride widened, the arm slashed down and as the ball was fired down the pitch, the body was thrown hungrily after it, the right toe raking the ground closely beside the wicket as he swept on.

Coming in almost from behind the umpire threw his left shoulder up and helped him to deliver from so near the stumps that sometimes he brushed the umpire. Indeed once, when Sam Pothecary was standing at Taunton, Trueman felled him, as he passed, with a blow of his steel right toe-cap on the ankle so savage as to leave that mildest of umpires limping for a fortnight.

John's writing continued to operate in different directions – one unlikely example being his book on snuff (*The Snuff Shop*, about the house of Fribourg & Treyer in The Haymarket, published in 1974). But it was, of course, the cricket commentaries which had made him a national treasure. Occupying pole position in the box, dispensing wisdom and imagery through his words, he attracted the 'voice of cricket' cliché so often it became almost meaningless. Graeme Wright, the former editor of *Wisden*, reflects on his technique: 'John created a picture simply by putting in all the positions, saying exactly what happened but not hurrying it. So that he may have been half a minute behind the play but by the time the bowler got back to his mark, he'd always caught up with it again. A lot of commentators don't have the confidence to do that – they rush it, so they don't get behind play too much. John described it as a poet does – using the right number of words.'

What did his colleagues think of the star in their midst? Robert Hudson first met John when auditioning as a cricket commentator at a county match at Lord's in 1946. He sat in whilst John commentated. 'I thought to myself, "My God, no one with an accent like that will ever get anywhere." ' Twenty-three years later, he thought very differently. 'He was an irreplaceable genius as far as cricket commentary was concerned – I always saw him as the Denis Compton of the microphone. Nobody could copy someone like Compton, and you couldn't copy Arlott, although one or two people have tried.

'When I became Head of Outside Broadcasts in 1969 he gave me lunch at the National Liberal Club, and almost with a shaking voice and trembling hand asked me if he was going to be used on the Test matches, quite apparently thinking that he wasn't. My predecessor, Charles Max-Muller, didn't like John and didn't think much of his broadcasting. This was Max-Muller's fault and not John's, because he didn't have the ability to appreciate a genius when he heard one. The result was that John was very insecure. Even at the height of his powers, he never seemed to think that anyone would ever ask him to do another commentary. When I took over, he was terrified that I might follow the same line as Charles Max-Muller, which, of course, I had no intention of doing whatsoever. In fact the first thing I did was to sign him up for all five Test matches. We had a very good lunch.'

Hudson, perhaps the most unsung and unassuming of all commentators, eventually became known as 'Bob of all trades' because of his coverage of all types of occasion. As an administrator, he was responsible for appointing most of the *Test Match Special* team, including the producer Peter Baxter, whose job is to organise all the facilities for cricket on radio and to direct broadcasts from the commentary box. Baxter was aware that John's bronchial condition, brought on by his earlier excessive smoking, made the negotiation of three or four flights of stairs at Lord's and other grounds something of an ordeal. 'He would arrive,' Baxter told me, 'in a terrible state in the morning having fought his way up the stairs, and then he would sit there panting for a bit. You knew that before he recovered his powers of speech you had to have a cup of black coffee at his elbow. The silly thing was that he would never drink it until it had gone cold, but it was there – that was the important thing.'

Having regained his equilibrium, John would scrutinise the commentary rota which Baxter had pinned to the wall. 'He regarded it as an opening of negotiations, really. It was soon covered in black ink as he altered this and that, and other commentators would arrive and see the black ink and say, "Ah, I see Arlott's been up."'

It was a performance repeated many times. 'Oh, no, no, no, no, no,' John would rumble, his pained tone stepping down sepulchrally to a diminished fifth. Peter would know immediately that John had a lunch date or some other pressing engagement.

By the mid–1970s John was doing only two twenty-minute spots before lunch and one after, as his contract stipulated that he had to be free by ten past three so as to give him time to write his piece for the *Guardian* in the press box. Peter Baxter: 'He would decamp and move his operation, and he would get pretty cross if he'd forgotten something, like his glasses from time to time, because then he had to come back *down* the steps of the press box and *up* the steps to the commentary box and there are quite a few grounds where that is the case.'

John's mobility decreased as he grew older, but he still liked to wander around the ground or go off and talk to people when he was not actually broadcasting. 'The result was he rarely heard what the other commentators were saying, so when he came back into the box a fraction before he was due on air he often launched forth into something that had just been said,' remarked Robert Hudson. 'He never seemed to listen to any other broadcasts of cricket. In my experience he had very little to say about other commentators.'

Other commentators, however, have a great deal to say about him. Trevor Bailey: 'John is the best painter of word pictures as far as sport is concerned that I have come across – easily. He was an artist in this particular field. I would put as one of his highlights the twenty minutes he did at Lord's in the Second Test against India in 1979, when the covers were being put on and taken off – a brilliant piece, absolutely superb:

This mammoth uncovering is going on – you might almost call it an unveiling. The old 'taking off the covers' – which was only running a couple of trolleys of corrugated iron off the pitch – was nothing compared with this. This is a real Cecil B. de Mille job, with – four, five, six, seven, eight wheeled covers, huge tarpaulins – eight of them – and a whole team of removers. They seem to be in two shifts. Those in the red jerkins removing the covers and those in the white jerkins admiring them – which is not quite a fair division of toil, but it does give an impression of labour to spare out there.

Anyway, two furled covers are now off, and out comes this wonderful Emmett-type tractor to take them away. You can probably hear it, the roar of its engine. It's rather like a First World War aeroplane in its engine note, and it scoots about the place. I should think it's the ambition of every boy on the ground staff to be the tractor driver. They drive it as if for fun.

Now the wheeled covers are coming off. Any moment now the umpires will appear. The object of immense attention. Meanwhile the England players are out loosening up, just bowling to Bob Taylor. Six of them – Lever, Hendrick, Randall, Edmonds, Gooch, Miller. I can also reveal that – one, two, three, four – four bars have been opened, but for some reason the people have all clustered round one. I can guess why, but I'm not certain. A few of the early-morning drinkers there at the Taverners Bar.

A man in a red curtaining coat – a very odd job indeed – is over there by the bookstall, and now another wheeled cover is off. Now we're getting down to the real nitty-gritty, and the bolsters, and the blankets and the wadding, they're under these things. It's really a sort of cover removal spectacular. The real fact is that if you have to uncover it, there's time for another storm to come up while you're getting the pitch opened. No sign yet of the umpires. In fact, there may be quite a bit of wheeling to be done yet. There's a strange clamp that joins the two tall covers. The tall ones actually are quite splendid for the ground staff because they're a comfortable height for leaning on – and five of them are having a little lean at the moment. Add two – and the chief groundsman. No, he's sprung into action now, and he's handing over to his redcoat, and another cover's being moved. It looks as if it's being moved back into position, Fred.

Trueman: I think they're just taking it down the hill, John, getting it ready for the tractor to hitch on to pleasure riding. That could go on for hours. We'd better leave that for a moment . . .

Arlott: Well, now the umpires are out looking at the pitch, chatting together. Groundsman Jim Fairbrother standing beside it as if he didn't want to intrude on their private conversation, and Dickie Bird there looking very worried, stroking his chin, hands on hips, one in the pocket. Poor old Dickie. All the troubles in the world, always, hasn't he?

As has been said before, words on paper scarcely convey the vocal impact. Trevor Bailey continued: 'John appreciated that *Test Match Special* was not a sports programme – he said it was "folk". Just how folksy it is you realise when people write in and say they prefer it when it rains.

'One thing. John hated to be corrected. I think he always thought he was right and couldn't accept that somebody else's view might be right. He might say "And that was another google [*sic*]" and it was a leg-break, or "That has happened for this reason" and he got the reason wrong. As the summariser, if your commentator makes a mistake it can be difficult not to make it obvious, particularly nowadays, when it is on television at the same time. But you tried to do it gently, as he was very sensitive to any criticism.

'He was essentially a critic – rather in the same way as Milton Shulman was in the theatre – he was brilliant on that, but he wouldn't be able to act. John was a great critic, but he couldn't play cricket. Steeped in the history, but the techniques of the game were all very much second-hand.'

To those for whom cricketing techniques had been a first-hand experience, John could appear vulnerable. He had not seen eye to eye at various times with the Australians Jack Fingleton, a former Test batsman, and Alan McGilvray, who had opened the bowling for New South Wales. The tact of Bailey and others was not over-used by Australians. 'McGilvray had no time for Arlott, and vice-versa,' said Bailey. 'McGilvray was a very good commentator *and* a very good cricketer, and it jolted. There was a clash of personalities.'

'He was a good commentator in his own way,' commented McGilvray, 'but he didn't give the score or the card. I mentioned this to him and he said, "Who wants the score? I'm not interested in the score." You should give the score three times in a six-ball over. He had a different technique to mine, more intimate, but he didn't care about the Aussies not listening – a lot of what he said was way above their heads.'

Australian-style commentary tends to be more straightforward, concentrated, informational and terse than the English version. Poetic licence, pauses for effect and colour are mostly absent. John was not about to adapt. His alterations to the commentators' roster sometimes made the timing of McGilvray's pre-arranged commitments to the ABC in Sydney difficult to manage. 'We had a niggle over this, but he would not accommodate me. All he would say was, "Yes, that's the way it is."'

McGilvray, known as 'the whispering commentator' because of his habit of speaking so close to the microphone – even those adjacent to him in the commentary box could hardly hear his words – did, however, overcome another problem. On this occasion John had enjoyed a lunch with plenty of shallots – pared, no doubt, with his own penknife as was his wont – washed down with wine. As McGilvray came to take over from him at the shared microphone, the lingering aroma was more buzzard than balm. With his nostrils twitching in protest, he requested another microphone, which was forthcoming. He also asked John, in so many words, to forgo pungent flavourings before similar hand-overs. John apologised and said he would do so.

With Jack Fingleton, John had a guarded relationship. As David Foot has pointed out in his perceptive essay in *Beyond Bat and Ball*, the Australian was a member of the proletariat who also liked toffs. A paradoxical man: warm, hard, humorous, pungent, a bearer of grievances, overtly generous, and surprisingly reactionary. His nature made him uncomfortable in an atmosphere of easy complacency; he would often puncture it with a challenging remark. He was a man aware of his own mind. In that, he resembled John. They both liked to get their own way.

Robert Hudson: 'John didn't like being on with Jack Fingleton, because Jack tended to be rather blunt, and very often would query what people were saying. He wasn't beyond telling commentators they were talking rubbish. We had to go to quite extraordinary lengths to keep them apart. This was done without either of them being told the reason.'

Nonetheless, both of them were obviously undeceived. Fingleton claimed publicly that Arlott refused to work with him, and said as much to John. 'But you do take the piss out of me,' is the reported reply.

There had been times when they had worked together amicably enough, though a certain forced politeness can be sensed in this exchange during the Third Test between England and Australia at Leeds in 1964. Peter Burge was playing the decisive innings of the match for Australia:

Arlott: The field again is spread wide for Burge; one, two, three, four, five, six, seven men guarding the boundary. Trueman bowls, he shapes to cut, and it goes through to Parks.

Fingleton: Have you ever seen a field set like this before? To a new ball?

Arlott: Certainly not to a new ball.

Fingleton: It's an odd one, isn't it?

Arlott: Quite shattering, isn't it? This is the measure, of course, of the mental dominance that Australia have gradually built up over the last five hours of play. Now then, it's Trueman again, comes in, bowls to Burge, and Burge gets a thick inside edge to a ball that moved just a little, and it trickles out on the on side.

Fingleton: Well, John, these aren't the correct tactics by Dexter to my mind. He's got to try and confine Burge and keep down the runs to a minimum and concentrate on calling up the other end. Burge must be a very tired man by now.

Arlott: Ah, but I think with 160 to your name, it takes away a lot of fatigue, Jack. Trueman comes in, bowls to Burge. He hooks him. He's caught it, Burge caught sub, bowled Trueman, 160. Australia all out 389. They now have a lead of 121. Listen to the applause for Burge.

On the other hand, John was very much at ease with the home-grown commentators and summarisers. Considering the disparate personalities that were herded together in such a close and closed environment, the general working relationship was remarkably good. However, the irrepressible and frothy banter of Brian Johnston was as far removed from the measured *gravitas* of J.A. as it was possible to be. How did they relate to each other?

'We were not close friends, really,' Brian Johnston told me. 'He had a lot of different ideas to me. I used to give him lifts sometimes to a Test match and run him back. We had shouting arguments about South Africa – he felt very deeply about that, and I felt the other way. But as a broadcaster, he did more to spread the gospel of cricket than anybody. All that time when radio was supreme, the Hampshire burr was just cricket, wasn't it?'

Yes, it was, although the voice was strictly speaking not so much Hampshire burr, or even Basingstoke bronchial. It was just John, an individual instrument, God-given.

Brian Johnston continued: 'Give him a scene where they were changing the covers [besides the one at Lord's quoted above, there was another epic covers commentary at Headingley in the 1970s], or the streaker running on, and he would do a perfect piece. Lucky he was on for the streaker – I'd have made a balls of it!'

The streaker incident has been replayed on air *ad nauseam*. It took place during the Second Test against Australia at Lord's in 1975. In stifling heat on the fourth afternoon, an exhibitionist later identified as one Michael Angelow ran across the playing area carrying little noticeable excess baggage. A buzz in the crowd alerted the commentary box, where Trevor Bailey shouted excitedly, 'It's a freaker!' John picked up the term and assumed control of the commentary, dealing magisterially with the brief happening – it seems impossible to refer to it without a leery *double entendre*.

Not very shapely . . . and it's masculine. He's now being marched in a final exhibition past at least eight thousand people in the Mound

Stand, some of whom, perhaps, have never seen anything quite like this before . . .

And so on. In retrospect, John was not best pleased with the effort. Too late, he thought of the perfect tailpiece: 'Perhaps his greatest disappointment is not to be deprived of further cricket, but that he managed to straddle the stumps without even dislodging a bail.'

'Johnners' went on: 'He probably wondered about the public school element in broadcasting – Howard Marshall, Swanton, Alston – me, no doubt. He was suspicious of Michael Tuke-Hastings, who he felt threw away the tapes of his best commentaries. He felt bitter about that.'

Michael Hastings, later Tuke-Hastings, had been the producer of the cricket commentary team before Peter Baxter took over in 1973. Potential archive material did not then receive quite the attention that it does today, under the supervision of manager Mark Jones, and there was constant pressure on space for tape storage from the daily conveyor-belt of the radio networks. In the 1960s there was an annual cull of commentary tapes, with an emphasis on keeping only 'the crucial moment'. Reflective passages often received short shrift as a result. The canvassing of producers to prune holdings is still unremitting, and it is to Peter Baxter's great credit that he built a local archive in order to retain as much material as possible. John believed that Michael Tuke-Hastings concentrated on short-term expediency at the expense of long-term considerations. Ironically, both men ended their days living on Alderney, where there were unavoidable reminders of their disunion.

'John was a most hospitable man,' remarked Brian Johnston. 'If you went to his house – which I didn't do often – always waiting for me was a bottle of Pouilly Fumé – most generous with his entertainment. He introduced drink into the box. At one time Alan Gibson got into a row for having a pint of beer in the box, and it wasn't until John, with his case and bottles of Beaujolais, that it became an acceptable thing – and then, of course, a glass of wine with the sponsors altered that pattern. He often arrived with a good story – told slowly, but well.'

John loved to pick up the latest yarn on the circuit, embellish it, polish it, and perhaps even re-originate it.

Which England batsman had sex in the middle of an over? Even those who had heard the story before pricked up their ears. How was more intriguing than who. An easy explanation – onset of heavy rain, gloomy weather forecast, quick return to hotel room, compliant chambermaid. Or which England captain was too mean to buy a bidet? What? Well, his wife said to him, 'Why can't we have one of these new bidets?' and he replied, 'What's wrong with doing a handstand in the shower?'

A wheezy chuckle accompanied these non-malicious yarns. General laughter, a glass to hand, and the day took on a rosy hue.

Another from the annals concerned Wally Hammond. Apparently John and others had been playing bridge with Hammond during a rain break. On the resumption of play Hammond had gone out, scored a double-century, and when dismissed he returned to the dressing-room, chucked his batting gloves into his bag and said, 'Three no trumps.' John always emphasised *double-* century, as if defying sceptics to scuttle to their record books. (It may have been during the 1930s, when John was a fixture in the Hampshire dressing-room, or in 1946 at Bristol.)

Brian Johnston resumed: 'I don't think he ever quite approved of my schoolboyish humour – and he was a real wit. I think he thought me a bit childish, and he used to pull my leg. "Send as many cakes as you like," he would say. Which was a bit annoying, because people then did it. "Do go on writing to him because he does love it."'

An instance to hand, courtesy of cricket chronicler Bill Frindall's lode of lore: 'John sighs, "He was a little upset on Friday, because he didn't get anything, which means that a lot of you are actually eating your own food ... In case any of you have missed those three wickets that have fallen during the catalogue of groceries ... Mrs Matthews of Penge, I'm afraid he doesn't think much of your nut brittle, because that's been discarded by the microphone ... He's just gone off with a wheelbarrow full of produce, and all I can say is that if you've got any old, musty, dirty bottles of red or white liquid, just put a label on them and send them to me."'

In 1973, during the Third Test at Headingley between England and New Zealand, a parcel did arrive for John. It felt squelchy and suspicious: definitely not bottles. The local constabulary took an interest and, after some demurring, an officer gingerly carried it to the centre of the adjoining rugby ground. Carefully opening the parcel, he found not gelignite, but – jelly babies.

During one spell of shared commentary duty between Brian and John, news came through that Emrys Walters, a regional reporter used occasionally on the national network, had died. Reputed to have been defrocked from the priesthood, Walters was not a good commentator. His great asset, as far as producers were concerned, was his ability to bring out a live report to the specified second. Neither Arlott nor Johnston knew him well, and on hearing the news, they reacted in unison: 'Good Lord, he must have been listening to one of his own commentaries!' They both laughed guiltily. Then Brian said, 'Who are we going to attribute that remark to?' 'Oh, put it down to me,' replied John. 'You're supposed to be the nice one.'

'John was in charge of the commentary box,' said Brian. 'I came back into radio from television. There was no rivalry, because we were so dissimilar. I did find it rather strange, though, at a most dramatic moment in his life, when he had just retired in 1980, that he came out of the box and said to Don Mosey, "That's stuffed Johnston. He won't be able to retire for at least three years now." I was never jealous of him, because I couldn't ever have achieved what he did.'

Was there a touch of grammar-school solidarity raising two fingers at public-school privilege? When it came to helping or comforting colleagues of a different generation, however, John was above reproach. Christopher Martin-Jenkins remembers:

'I was a family man with a young family and perhaps he felt that that part of his life hadn't gone as smoothly as he would have liked it to have gone. During a Test match, I used to go dashing back on a Saturday night to have Sunday at home and then back on a Monday morning. One terrible morning, I drove up to Old Trafford and hit a cyclist – in fact, the cyclist rode in front of me, he thought he was in the middle of a dual carriageway – and, thank God, he was OK. I was therefore late, because I had to report it all to the police, and John could not have been more sympathetic. He was extremely supportive.'

A sentiment echoed by numerous reporters, writers and commentators including Richie Benaud, Alan Gibson, Tony Lewis, Tom Graveney, David Foot and Frank Keating: 'If there is a collective of his apostles and advocates,' said Keating, 'count me in.'

Bill Frindall would also be among their number: 'The thing he did for me was to inspire me with confidence. When I took over from Arthur Wrigley in 1966, J.A. arrives wearing something akin to a MASH jacket and carrying a battered briefcase causing him to walk with a bit of a tilt. I thought, "My goodness, he's brought his entire library."

'We were introduced. "Morning, welcome. What d'you give to a woman who has got everything?" And I'd brought all these books. I got everything out. I thumbed nervously through the file of Worcestershire players and it opened at the page of one of the greatest womanisers. All I could say rather weakly was, "I don't know, Mr Arlott. Encouragement?" "No, penicillin," he replied.

'It was an easy baptism. Aware of the professionalism of the man, I told him I was rather scared of him. "Don't know why, my children aren't afraid of me." After just a few overs J.A. turned to me and said, "You'll be all right. You've got a scorer's mind. You concentrate on that and shut us out." It rained for most of the three days. Without very much happening, and with the aid of one tool, a stopwatch, he could give a two-and-a-half minute summary, a six-minute summary and a half-minute summary and come out on the button every time. He didn't seem to be doing anything except chatting, it was all effortless, and if you analysed what he said, it was all there.

'He was the easiest man in the world to work with. Now we have people – I have to carry books on Bristol wildlife, helicopter charts and bus timetables and all sorts of things – who don't actually keep to the cricket. But with J.A. all you needed to pass to him was another glass or the bowling figures and you could go on to automatic pilot, record the dotto and chat to Brian Johnston about rather important things like that night's dinner arrangements.'

Bill Frindall is one of several who perform Arlott impressions on the after-dinner speaking circuit. There is no one who is closer to the original; the inflections, nuances, and phrases are uncannily accurate. And the sound he reproduces is particularly true to John's later working period when he had almost become part of folklore, an icon to be cherished. With an ear for the public response, John matched their perception by representing himself as he thought they would have wanted. It could have slipped into self-caricature but it was never that; more an enlarged photograph. He more than once laughingly said to me, 'If they want an impression of my voice, I can do a fairly good one.'

Bill Frindall was also one of several who took turns to ferry John to and from the cricket after he had decided that driving long distances was becoming too tiring and dangerous. Having fallen asleep a couple of times at the wheel and mounted a grass verge, he had alarmed not only himself but also Valerie.

'He was a terrible navigator,' said Bill. '"Turn left back there," he would say. I remember coming to the outskirts of Manchester with him on one occasion and he suddenly woke up, realised where he was and then sank back into the passenger seat before remarking, "Manchester is the only city in the world where they teach lifeboat drill on the buses."'

At the Racecourse Ground, Derby, there was a time when there was no commentary position. For county matches Frindall would sit in the driver's seat of an Outside Broadcasts van with a lectern-top over the steering wheel, on which he would place all his paraphernalia. The commentator would work from the passenger seat. At one match between Derbyshire and Hampshire in 1968, John's lunch arrangements were different from normal. His cheese, Ryvita, tomatoes, engraved glasses, vine-root corkscrew and bottles of claret all remained in his case on top of the lone *Playfair Annual*. As the players left the field, from the old grandstand appeared a white-hatted chef bearing a silver salver, on which there was heavy duty by way of bottles and food, with all the trimmings. The Arlott lunch was conveyed with aplomb all the way round the back of the meagre crowd who were sitting on benches, and was handed in at the van door. Having let the wine breathe with the diesel fumes for a few seconds, consumption began. Some time later, replete and content, John fell fast asleep.

'I had to wake him up because a transmission was due,' said Bill. 'He came to with a start, grabbed a glass, and started commentating into that, suddenly realised – "Oh, sorry" – and picked up a lip-microphone.'

During the afternoon Bill inadvertently put on the fog-lights of the vehicle, without realising how he had done it. The driver and the rest of the crew were nowhere to be seen, and John was dozing again. But not for long. The van was parked just by the sightscreen, and the fog-light beam was shining directly into the batsman's face.

'Turn those bloody lights off!' Umpire Cec Pepper's voice was raucous rather than Bashan roar, but still loud enough to waken the dead. John duly surfaced. 'What have you done now, Frindalius?' 'Well, I think I've put the fog-lights on, John.' 'Oh, Christ.'

'John starts moving things and I'm putting on switches all over the place. The crowd were laughing, so were the players by this time. It went on for several minutes – "No, that's not it, try another one", so I put another one on – "No, not that one." We were lit up like Blackpool Tower. "Where's the driver? . . ."'

'Luckily, someone in the crowd who had driven one of these vehicles in the war when they'd been field ambulances put us out of our misery. It turned out my knee had knocked a little switch on the steering column, and I hadn't thought of looking down there. The only thing we didn't do was take off and drive straight down the pitch.'

After laughing long at the memory, Bill became reflective. 'You know, he had a caring mentality. He was very caring about a young man coming into the profession for the first time – how he would be thinking. The core of his whole broadcasting was the brain behind the man batting and bowling and how it would relate to the others. So many commentators now don't think about that. They just describe the bare picture without the workings of what's going on behind.'

An example of this is to be found in John's commentary during the First Test between England and Pakistan at Edgbaston in 1978:

There's no doubt to my mind that this patch is becoming increasingly difficult, and the batsmen increasingly aware of it. Liaquat to Brearley, then – he mistimes an attempted square cut, and this is a state of mental conditioning where a batsman must watch this particular spot if the ball lands near it. He's got to assume it's going to lift and keep away from it, otherwise he can play a stroke, and it's a schizophrenic state of existence which was apparent in that stroke of Brearley's then.

The editor of *The Journal of the Cricket Society*, Clive Porter, who acted as scorer/statistician for BBC 2's coverage of the Sunday League in 1980, was another receiver of John's beneficence. 'From the outset, John was supportive and encouraging. I remember the first match was at Ilford, Essex against Somerset in early May – the cherry blossom was out. At lunchtime John offered me a glass of claret. A bundle of nerves, I said, "No, thank you. It might affect my concentration." With a twinkle in his eye, he nodded understandingly. "Perhaps later in the season?" ' With the match underway, John continued to cast a protective eye. 'How are you feeling? Are you enjoying it?' And at the end of the day, a warm 'Well done. Thank you for your help.'

'He alone took the trouble to say it,' remembered Clive. 'He was always most thoughtful. He never sprang a demand for information while we were live. You always knew where you were with him. Typically, he often acknowledged on air my contribution when he used background material I'd prepared.'

For John, the Sunday League was a chore he could well have done without. Generally he disliked the bastardised limited-overs form of the game, but the financial inducement to commentate was too attractive to resist. Sharing the microphone with Jim Laker, he would take the first twenty overs of each innings of the 'forty-over bash', so as to be on the road homewards soon after five o'clock. In most games the predictable pattern of play quickly lost his interest, and sometimes he would fall asleep while on air. As I joined him in the box at Headingley one Sunday afternoon, he asked me to give him a nudge if I noticed that he was nodding off. He started to do so, but I hesitated to wake him, in case he was startled into an unguarded remark. After a long period in which not a word had been said, John opened his eyes and observed, 'The last four overs were entirely nondescript, and did not deserve comment.'

Jack Bannister remembers a match in the 1970s when, squeezed into confined spaces at either end of a long table, neither he nor Irving Rosenwater was able to reach John to alert him to the increasingly urgent tones of the director over the headphones to 'Say something – anything. For, Christ's sake, just give the score!' Eventually, after several overs of non-commentary, and with the production team in the Outside Broadcasts van on the verge of apoplexy, John resurfaced during the nineteenth over, glanced at the scoreboard and gave the details. 'I fully expected him to press the off-air switch and apologise profusely,' laughed Jack. 'Instead, he calmly said, "Oh, just remind Jim he's on at the end of the next over, will you?"'

There was one occasion during a match in the West Country when John uncharacteristically but gently chided a fellow commentator. Conscious that he was occupying a seat next to the master of apt imagery, the commentator searched for some descriptive colour. Unfortunately, he did not possess John's bottomless vocabulary. Again and again, as the bowler came in to bowl the listeners were told he was doing so with 'the sun sinking slowly in the west'. At last John could stand it no longer. Taking the microphone, he said, 'Bertie Buse is coming in to bowl, and by the way, the sun is still sinking slowly in the west, and if by chance it should decide to sink anywhere else, we shall be the first to let you know.'

The word-pictures and *bon mots* could fill a book themselves:

Umpire Bill Alley, the solitary dissident.

Butcher drops his head, both hands behind the back, and looks sheepishly down the wicket like a small boy stealing jam.

I do not think cricket is under Bradman's skin, but I believe that it is under his skull.

Ernie Toshack's batting: like an old lady poking with her umbrella at a wasps' nest.

Gilmour comes in, bowls – and Lloyd hits him away over mid-wicket for four, a stroke of a man knocking a thistle-top off with a walking-stick.

David Gower: You can sense the warmth of the applause for this young man. He's captured the enthusiasm of English crowds – looking almost frail with a half-sleeve shirt clinging closely to a not very substantial physique. He passes Boycott, who's got his helmet underneath his arm, like a knight at arms alone and palely loitering.

Dennis Lillee: Beginning to show a bit of a bald patch – lightly tonsured, you might say.

Keith Miller: like a cross between a Viking and an irresponsible schoolboy.

Botham runs in like a shire horse, cresting the breeze.

One recalls the immortal words of one of my partners in a house second team match many years ago: 'Don't worry, we can get these off the edge. I think there's no danger of them coming off the middle.'

His bat has as many holes in it as a Henry Moore sculpture.

Kardar seems at the moment to have about four fieldsmen and seven missionaries, you know, as they used to say in Victorian days, sent into distant fields. They're still in Trent Bridge, but only just.

What I really want to know, Bill, is if England bowl their overs at the same rate as Australia did, and Brearley and Boycott survive the opening spell, and that the number of no-balls is limited to ten in the innings, and assuming my car does 33.8 miles per gallon and my home is 67.3 miles from the ground, what time does my wife have to put the casserole in?

In response to Brian Johnston's quip about a turbanned left-arm slow bowler, 'I suppose that if this chap's next delivery eludes both batsman and wicket-keeper and makes its way to the boundary, the resultant runs could be termed Bedi-byes': And I suppose that if the same thing happened at the other end, they would be known as Abid Ali-byes.

On Dicky Bird scrutinising the pitch after rain: Not so much examining the pitch as pecking at it.

After Trevor Bailey's comment, 'Here come the umpires, wearing their new short coats, looking rather like dentists': It occurs to me, Trevor, that it is rather suitable for the umpires to look like dentists, since one of their duties is to draw stumps.

John's commentaries have also become linked with great cricketing events – Compton's highest Test score at Trent Bridge in 1954; Laker's 19 wickets at Old Trafford in 1956; Loader's hat-trick at Headingley the following year; Dexter's imperious treatment of Hall and Griffith at Lord's in 1963; Lloyd's stupendous knock in the World Cup Final in 1975; the George Davis incident at Headingley, when the pitch was damaged by protesters – the list is endless.

Although John never gave commentaries of MCC tours to India,

At The Oval in July 1980, on the fourth day of the Fourth Test against West Indies. The match was drawn.

Four musketeers at Dean Park, Bournemouth on a freezing day in summer 1980. *Left to right:* Basil D'Oliveira, Ian Botham, J.A., Leo Harrison.

A tumult of mixed emotions: farewell to commentary.

A none-too-subtle hint from Shadow Chancellor Denis Healey
to Leader of the Opposition Jim Callaghan. Callaghan retired a
couple of months later in November 1980.

The battered brown briefcase which accompanied John wherever he went, containing the restoratives so essential to his well-being.

The Old Sun, Alresford. At the last moment, he had to be persuaded to leave.

With Chris Gittings (*The Archers'* Walter Gabriel) and June Spencer (Peggy Archer)
after being named Radio Sports Personality of the Year at the Pye Awards gala luncheon,
Savoy Hotel, October 1980.

The Vines, Alderney.

The new Long Room.

D'Aquino figures on Grace table which was bought at a pub in Cardiff.

Sharing a joke with the author.

Basement studio, Broadcasting House, 1983.

Penelope Lee, Valentine Dyall, J.A., Robin Holmes at the recording of *Pitch a Wicket*, a seasonal glance at the words and music of cricket for BBC Radio 3, July 1983. John is trying to look contrite, having accidentally tipped a bottle of Rioja over the mixing desk.

With Jack Donovan, a friend for sixty-six years.

A sugar-lift aquatint by Norman Ackroyd, regarded as the leading etcher in Britain. John had a life-long fascination for aquatint engraving and enjoyed discussions with Ackroyd on its history and technique. Basically, the process is to brush marks on to a copper plate with gouache or Indian ink, sugar and washing-up liquid (a speciality of Ackroyd's), which is covered with varnish. The unpainted area is then dressed with a resist. On immersion in water the black solution rises, exposing the marks which are etched by the acid.

On John's left is Bryan Timms, former Hampshire and Warwickshire
wicket-keeper, then Mike Brearley and, just discernible, Neil Jenkinson,
Hampshire solicitor and the author of a book on Philip Mead. Opposite,
Timms's partner Maureen Serle and Graeme Wright, former editor of
Wisden.

St Ann's churchyard, Alderney. The quotation is from John's poem to
Andrew Young.

Pakistan or the West Indies – apart from the temperature, he disliked being away from home for any length of time – he was near-deified on the sub-continent and in the Caribbean. Peter Baxter was always being asked why John Arlott was not there, and it was sometimes difficult for him to explain that for 'a man who would leave the windows open at the North Pole', to use Arlott's friend John Woodcock's phrase, a hot climate was an unbearable burden. 'He hated heat,' said Peter. 'There was a constant battle to have door and window open – awkward in some places if it was noisy. Also, for a lot of the time he was commentating we had Robert Hudson in the team. Bob himself says that he's got this terrible two-star blood and feels the cold all the time, so you'd be opening and shutting doors and windows throughout the day. Arlott would be perspiring hugely and Hudson would be freezing. Travelling would have got him down. Nowadays, you seem to be forever going through airport lounges.'

Expatriates or those working abroad would tune in to John's broadcasts, relayed on the World Service. The writer Geoffrey Moorhouse bemoans the fact that he always seemed to be out of England when the best cricket was to be seen. He relishes memories of sitting up night after night, in distant Auckland, listening to John's voice fading in and out as it fought a continual contest with the atmospherics. 'Little vivid things John would say used to make you weep with nostalgia: "There's a young chap in front of the broadcasting box who's using today's cold breeze as an excuse to keep an arm around his girlfriend," or "Roley Jenkins, who takes his cap and walks off with a constabulary roll" – quite incomparable.'

Robert Hudson remembers another quirk: 'John was very much at his best when there was an audience in the commentary box, for example the director-general or a controller or somebody important. Even if the cricket was dull he perked up and would give a virtuoso performance.' Christopher Martin-Jenkins agrees: 'He could turn it on. I remember when Ian Trethowan was Managing Director, Radio. He came into the box – I think it was earlier on the 'streaker' day – and John really was in sparkling form. One felt he was putting on a performance. He could play in two gears, and his first gear was still better than most people's second. He never lost the insecurity of the freelance.'

'On the other hand,' said Hudson, 'if there was not someone important in the box and the cricket was dull and didn't engage his interest, he very often gave a sub-standard performance. Although a genius, he didn't always employ his talent to the full – he was up and down; brilliant many times, he could also be rather poor. Nearly poor.' He qualified further: 'Nearly everybody, when they're writing about people, usually because they can't think of anything else to say, uses the word "professional". I wouldn't employ that word with John, strangely enough. He was a genius with words and a marvellous commentator when on form and in the right conditions, but I wouldn't regard him as a great professional. Because a professional always maintains a good, level standard whatever is happening. John didn't always do that, he could fluctuate. Having said that, I do remember one occasion when the match was so exciting, and his commentary so scintillating, that it produced a round of applause in the box on the air from his fellow commentators. Whoever was on next said it was the most brilliant commentary he'd ever heard. John took a mock bow and then went off wandering around the ground as usual.'

Some commentators like to indulge in repartee and badinage with their summarisers. Not J.A. Peter Baxter again: 'The likes of Fred Trueman and Trevor Bailey knew well enough that when John was really flowing there was nothing for them to say and no reason for them to say it. That sort of commentator doesn't need the interruption of a summariser or anyone else.'

'If a summariser started a conversation in the middle of an over, John would have found that irritating,' confirmed Christopher Martin-Jenkins. 'Because he liked to take it at his own pace, the sound of the crowd coming through every now and then. The modern thing is that some of them feel they have to speak all the time. I'm not sure it's a good thing.'

Such was John Arlott in his pomp, unmatched. And when out of sorts, unpredictable. Where to next? What other mountains were there to climb? John was not a compartmentalised being. For him, there were other things in life besides cricket. His attention needed to be engaged. His temperament demanded challenge. For those who take more than their fill of life or achieve much, fate demands a price. Part of that price was to be another devastating blow.

24

Relationships and Friendships

A lasting memory for many visitors to the Arlott home at Alresford is of Valerie performing a concerto on the typewriter to John's dictation. The keys responded to her virtuoso playing at thrice the speed of John's two-finger honky-tonk approach. When John attacked a typewriter, it was with an individual hefty, chopping motion that came from the shoulder – almost as if he was attempting to brutalise it into submission.

While doing the typing, Valerie would also be preparing wonderful meals and entertaining guests. The six-in-one job – secretary, public relations assistant, housekeeper, cook, chief glass-rinser and wife – called for dawn-to-dusk dedication. The demands of John's lifestyle were enjoyable, but exhausting. Only someone deeply loved and in love could have continued to keep up with them. The only help came from a trio of domestics, Myrtle Andrews, Margaret Betteridge and, after the move to Alderney, Helen Critchley: the redoubtable Misses A, B and C – though Mrs Critchley was never called Mrs C.

The Old Sun always seemed to be full of people: those calling in for a brief chat and a drink, and those who had been invited for lunch and who did not leave the table until after dinner. It was not a question of outstaying their welcome. John liked to conduct his affairs from the festal board, and when he was not away from home he wanted, in fact needed, people there. The inn was not a place of gossip but of genuine conversation and controlled activity. The hive kept John's adrenaline running, engaged his interests, gave him comfort. It was a sort of community within a community: a cottage industry.

Sometimes the factory produced around five thousand words a day, a phenomenal work rate. An early start, responding immediately to a stack of post, followed by an article here, a foreword there, and yet another book chapter underway. The phone would ring frequently with callers requesting this, asking that and wanting more. The ABC on the line from Sydney: could Mr Arlott please do a spoken piece on so-and-so, the cricketer, who has just died? When? Oh, right now. We only want a minute and a half. A little later, it might be a promotions person from the Bristol Wine Fair wondering if he could say something at the opening ceremony. And just as the evening meal was about to be served, a call from the *Guardian* news desk: a ruling on a knotty issue has been announced by the Test and County Cricket Board, and the paper needs an analysis for tomorrow's edition.

In such cases John would ask for a copy typist to ring back in twenty minutes. His son Robert would be dispatched upstairs to fetch a particular volume that was to be found in the second bookcase on the left, third shelf from the top, just right of centre. On Robert's return John would check a fact and the meal would begin: normal conversation, everybody chattering. The telephone rings on schedule. And without notes or any kind of written material as an aid, John dictates a column for the *Guardian*, giving punctuation points as they occur. Guests around the table look on in silent admiration; many of them have seen it before.

Dennis Stevens, editor of the monthly *Hampshire*, remembers one visit, ostensibly for the purpose of discussing the articles John would provide for the magazine. 'It was during the time Valerie was in hospital having Robert, in early 1963. John's mother, Nellie, who was living in Basingstoke, had come to look after him and served us lamb chops for lunch. She was in cracking form, berating him for his way of life, which she thought rather shiftless. She preferred people who had regular and steady places of employment. Her eyes twinkled all the while, though – she was obviously pretty proud of him. She toddled off after lunch and we continued. It must have been the Alresford record lunch as we did not rise from table until after midnight, having consumed among much else four bottles of vintage port.'

Dennis's admiration for John's output – as well as his intake – remains undimmed. 'His association with the magazine lasted twenty-five years. Never once through bereavement, ill-health, enormous pressure of work – never once did he miss an issue. The articles he supplied were never "pot-boilers" or easy pieces which he could dream up – they all took a lot of research and thought. What is more, they were written, re-written and polished. He usually did a rough draft, a revision, and a final polished draft which he went through with a fine-tooth comb. I was always astounded, because we didn't have a great deal of money to pay him. He became a director of the company and remained so for twenty years. He said in many ways, of all his work, he was most proud of his writings for *Hampshire* – he loved the county.'

John had his own way of eliciting information. He would invite to dinner people in key positions who were able to mould events – or, at least, react to them – county councillors, community figures, occasionally Members of Parliament. Without indulging in any kind of manipulation, he would engage them in frank exchanges. At the end of the evening he would often have the basic material for a fresh, exclusive article, better-informed than many of the local newspapers.

John's range of subjects appeared to have no limits: rare handkerchiefs, great parties, Christmas customs, the churches of Bournemouth – the reader would not know what to expect. 'John loved to work stories into his text,' said Dennis Stevens. 'One I liked was in an article about Bournemouth, in which he wrote: "Bournemouth, even before it was removed to Dorset, was never really part of Hampshire, but a town of pensioners many of whom came from far-off parts. Its presence in Hampshire was purely coincidental." He told of a man visiting a village pub not far from Basingstoke one summer's day. The pub was almost empty and in the lounge bar the man regaled the landlord with his life in Hampshire and how marvellous a place it was to live in. He said he came from Bournemouth. There was a silence, and then from the bowels of the public bar came a deep Hampshire voice: "Be I Hampshire? Be I buggery!"'

Other pieces were of a more prosaic nature: technical surveys, roads, housing development, local government reorganisation. Dennis Stevens: 'Often tremendously detailed. His piece on the Chandler's Ford by-pass even had the number of trees used for screening and included drainage and re-siting of cricket and football pitches. There have been a lot of changes of mind since, but his article still stands up. It was accurate, long-view and sensible: the work of a master craftsman who knew his subject inside out and rather better than many of the experts involved. But this for John was a side issue, which makes it all the more remarkable.'

When the Alresford by-pass was a subject of controversy, a public meeting was called. John had invited his old friend John Betjeman to stay for a night or two to attend a public gathering and put his view. The meeting was chaired by one of Hampshire County Council's few Labour members at the time, Charlie Watts. Watts was a rare phenomenon in Hampshire, a successful socialist from a rural area – in his case, Hedge End. He had become chief of the planning committee, and was a man of definite opinions. That much soon became obvious, as Dennis Stevens recounts: 'After the meeting had been going for a while John stood up and told the chairman that they were fortunate to have in their midst a man of tremendous foresight who cared passionately for the English landscape, for small towns and architecture, and he was sure they would be enlightened by John Betjeman.

'"Does he live in Alresford?" responded Charlie Watts. "Of course he doesn't live in Alresford. He's not a local man," replies John.

'Whereupon Watts adopted a procedural stance. "Well, 'e can't talk 'ere. We don't want people talking 'ere who don't live 'ere. Anybody could turn up. We could be 'ere for days," he said. An indignant sniff. "People turning up and talking ..."

'John again pointed out John Betjeman's reasons for wanting to speak at the meeting. He enlarged on his background and experience and his concern for proper civic planning. "No, no," said Charlie, "'e can't talk 'ere. We start this, we open the floodgates."

'In the end, John at his most persuasive managed to wring from the chairman the concession that John Betjeman could speak for four or five minutes. Thereafter, as far as John was concerned, Charlie Watts was something of a marked man. I said to John, "Oh, well, he's possibly got good intentions." "Yes," responded John, "but he's bloody daft and he's bloody stubborn." No rapprochement was achieved. Eventually, the by-pass went through.'

Another literary confederate to visit Alresford was Laurie Lee. He, though, did not have to face the obdurate Charlie. John always maintained that he first met Lee when he was a policeman in Southampton during the war, and had ordered him to move on because his busking was causing an obstruction on the pavement. Lee's companions at the table on one occasion were Dennis Stevens, the then Women's Editor of the *Guardian*, a poet from the Isle of Wight who wrote thrillers, and a bookseller who had parked his Rolls outside and who advocated Salcombe in Devon as the finest holiday spot in the world. 'I can't remember their names,' said Dennis, 'but it doesn't matter. It was as people they were important.'

Other days, different crowds. Fellow commentators; a female athlete; well-known journalists; an outstanding foreign correspondent, Trevor Fishlock of *The Times* and later the *Daily Telegraph*; an Antarctic explorer; a bank manager; a furniture restorer called George Watson; family and friends such as Welshman Dan Dando, a teacher, and Alan Charlton, an arts lecturer in Eastleigh. Spirited argument often ensued, encouraged by John. He enjoyed the meeting of minds. It might be a fierce head-to-head between John and his son Tim that would cause others around the table to fall silent. But it was always a disagreement, never a quarrel. The shocked face of a newcomer to such a clash would lead John to quick reassurance: 'Don't worry, the Arlotts enjoy arguing.'

His younger son Robert knew John's tactics only too well: 'He would speak an exaggeration of his thoughts in such an extreme way as to provoke a reaction from people to stimulate a conversation. It was fun, but worrying when people started taking it too seriously, because you then had to start apologising.'

Another time, fired by alcohol, guests might be loudly contesting sporting points. John, having been up since early morning writing to meet his many deadlines, would appear to have nodded off. It was, after all, the end of a long day and some memorable bottles. At the height of the ruction he would lift his head, open one spanielly eye, growl, 'It's only a bloody game,' and then sink into slumber again. Self-conscious giggles from the assembly, then uproarious laughter. Perspective had been put.

Valerie often took a pertinent part in the debates. She would argue with quiet passion against social injustice and for a united Ireland. She would take John on, and often interrupt him – sometimes it was the only way of being heard. The contradictions came coolly and without a qualm. 'She was a great debunker,' says Richard France of his sister. 'She had the ability to tell John he was a silly old sod and to shut up, he was making an idiot of himself. She would needle him with comments like "All policemen are fascists" – that sort of thing. This kind of debunking was quite important, especially when he was surrounded by people who lionised him. It introduced a rather more human dimension in him at times.'

Maybe Valerie was also demonstrating sexual mastery, a way of gaining equal footing in public. Neither of them ever parroted the conventional wisdom. There were no received thoughts. It was fascinating fodder for the listener. As Valerie went off to the kitchen to collect the next course, John would say with a wry shrug, 'She's very good for me.' As she came back within earshot, he would pick up the thought. 'I don't know what I'd do without you.' 'I know what you'd do without me,' she would reply. 'You'd soon get somebody else.' They were devoted to one another.

For Dennis Stevens, John was the hardest-working man he had met. A lot of that work could not have been done without Valerie. The strain of entertaining day after day, typing innumerable books and articles, and simply being Mrs John Arlott, with all that that entailed, would have taken its toll of the healthiest body. Valerie did not have the healthiest body. She had a rare kidney condition, which resulted in high blood pressure. She put a remarkably brave face on her hypertension and never discussed it. Although her sister, brother and brother-in-law were all doctors, nobody could help. In effect, she was living every single hour under Damocles' sword. One day it was bound to fall. In early 1976, it did.

Dr Peter Sleight, a distinguished heart specialist and the husband of Valerie's elder sister Gillian, describes what happened. 'If you have high blood pressure, you have a risk of developing blow-outs on the arteries of the brain – sometimes they rupture and cause subarachnoid haemorrhage, which is what she had. The tragic thing was that she seemed to recover pretty well for a day or two, and then what happens is you get a sort of secondary spasm of the arteries. That now is more treatable – it wasn't then.'

It is trite to say that Valerie's death devastated John. Never could anyone have been more overcome by anguish and desolation. First the loss of his son, now his soulmate. Valerie had been taken from him in such a short space of time. The visits to the hospital in Southampton had been despairing. There lay Valerie, receding before his eyes, shorn of her hair in a shell-like state. The cerebral bleed wreaking its devastation. Brain-dead . . . and then . . . declared dead. Where would it all end?

His sons Tim and Robert did all they could – cooking meals, just being there. Friends and relatives rallied round. Some were almost apprehensive about entering the house because of John's emotional condition. The former Hampshire opening batsman Barry Reed and his wife Shirley kept close. 'You can treat grief. You've just got to work harder,' said John to Barry, with total lack of conviction. Bill Shepheard of the large bald dome, who manned the public address at Hampshire's home matches, and his wife Jean were endlessly supportive. But nothing could comfort John.

Valerie's death had been announced in the *Guardian*, but I had missed it, indeed had not even known she was ill. Since seeing them both in fine form at dinner in Alresford three weeks previously, I had been out of the country. On my return I rang in cheery mood to catch up on what John had been doing and to arrange a get-together. That unmistakable voice answered in the same way it always did.

'Alresford 2197.'

'John,' I said.

'David . . .' The emphasis on the first syllable. How many have experienced the warmth of his greeting?

The beginnings of a conversation, then, still unaware of disaster, a casual enquiry, 'How's Valerie?'

There was no pause. Just two words, dully. 'She's dead.'

Shock has many reactions. Mental paralysis is but one. Stunned to silence and then, because of the physical distance, a need to impart my feelings. Mere babble. 'I'm sorry. I didn't know. I . . . I . . . just don't know what to say.'

John's gentle understanding over the phone. *He* was comforting me.

'I'm coming down,' I said. 'I'm taking you out.' At least it was doing something. Useless, maybe, but positive.

As I drove down from London my mind was elsewhere . . . The programmes we had worked on together, for the BBC and for record companies. I had driven him to Sherborne once, to meet those engaging entertainers from Dorset, The Yetties. He had complimented me on my driving, how relaxed I was at the wheel. I realised it was really a way to encourage me to go faster. Better take care now . . . When we had reached Sherborne, John had said something about the geographical layout of country towns. It made it easier to pinpoint our destination . . . what was it now? I couldn't remember. How he had liked the lads from Yetminster. It was the start of a fruitful association. The meals we had enjoyed together, at Alresford, with Valerie and at Wheeler's in town. Oysters – what was it, two dozen? . . . Well, I certainly hoped he would have a good meal tonight. Dear John, he had been so generous so many times . . . a chance at last to repay a little.

The restaurant, O'Rourke's, was just down the road from The Old Sun. Fairly small, but with an enviable reputation. There was one other couple sitting at the far side of the room. Good. Peaceful vibrations. After such a harrowing event, it was a time for quiet companionship and maybe gentle distraction. The menu was select and the dishes all the better for it. John had anticipated our choice and we had decided to start with a very acceptable white Burgundy – Macon Prissé – to accompany the hors d'oeuvre. The main course was to be honoured with a magnificent '61 Château Pétrus from his own cellar that would forever be indelibly etched on the palate.

John started to talk, and soon began to cry. Emotion was always with him, just below or on the surface, but this was not just part of his normal make-up. Here was a close friend, riven deep to his roots, whom one desperately wanted to console, to help. But how could anyone help? What was he to do? Who would look after thirteen-year-old Robert? Still at school, and without a mother. The cricket season was about to start. Who would look after him? 'I don't have the dignity to live alone,' he confided tearfully. Should he pack it all in? Should he . . . ? The questions continued to come across the table, hopelessly seeking a solution. The answers barely formed, never made it back beyond the flowers in the middle.

The bottle of thirst-quenching Burgundy had been mostly consumed, the Pomerol, *cru exceptionel*, was uncorked, awaiting our assured appreciation. Two waitresses busied themselves with our plates and cutlery, fussing unnecessarily. Napkins fluttered – an unguarded gesture – a bottle tipped – an involuntary cry – the contents spilled over John's lap. A look of sheer horror passed over his face. I buried my head in my hands. Surely not? A quick glance. The joy of relief. Chateau Pétrus remained standing, steady as a rock.

John's old friend Kingsley Amis had a subsequent conversation with him in which one sliver of sunlight shone through the clouds. 'I always liked Valerie very much. I thought she was a splendid woman. And John told me about having some friends round shortly before she died and, as Valerie was just about to serve the meal, John produced a special Burgundy, the best he had, and made a speech, saying, "I'd like to drink a toast to my wife with this, if I may say so, exceptional wine, because she is not only the best secretary I ever had and the best friend I ever had, but in bed beyond compare." And he said to me, "I was glad I said that because soon after she was dead."'

In the vacuum following Valerie's death, her only surviving child, Robert, grew close to his father for the first time. 'He was a man who had a lot of affection for children, but was never a man to get involved with them,' says Robert today. 'As a youngster, I recognised he was a very bright and inspiring man and I was in awe of him. Not terrified, but respectfully and fondly. And unsurely. I'd see him mostly in evenings during the winter, or at holiday time, early ones in Lyme Regis and later on the Scillies, but I had communicated with him mostly through my mother.

'When she died we were thrown together. He was very good at that time. He was a very emotional person, but not particularly subtle. I was not sure then that I wanted the great love and physical affection he offered me. Probably he was doing it for himself as much as me, because he felt very lonely. It was a replacement for Valerie, I suppose. But it was a bit sudden and I think I was probably too young at the time to feel comfortable with it. Mind you, he was terribly good in many ways. At that age, I'm sure I wasn't sensitive enough to his feelings. If your mother dies, you do tend to be a bit selfish in the way you respond to it.'

In the late 1940s, at Lord's, John had met Patricia Hoare. She was then working for the Assistant Secretary, Ronny Aird, which meant that she was in the room next to the commentators. 'I thought he was a good-looking young man, a bit different to most of them. We went out for a couple of meals and a few drinks. He used to get me tickets for shows. Then, some years later, I left Lord's to work abroad.' There followed stints in Paris, Rome, Geneva 'and all over the place', working for amongst other organisations, the United Nations (narcotics division and conference work). Over the years Pat and John were in touch intermittently on her brief returns to England. She was in Switzerland in 1976 when a letter from John arrived.

'In it, he asked if I'd like to come and work for him, keep house and look after Robert. I suppose he'd remembered I was keen on cricket, and anyway I was thinking of coming back to live in England. Mind you, I had mixed feelings. I was a secretary more than a housekeeper. I had a well-paid job at the UN, a good salary, tax-free, lots of holidays. As I was freelance, I came and went fairly freely. Anyhow, I eventually came back, tried it, liked it, seemed to get on with Robert, enjoyed the life, and the next year, 1977, John and I got married.'

Which is jumping ahead a little. Pat forbore to mention that John, trying to entice her back from Geneva, had offered to pay her double her UN salary if she accepted. 'No you will not,' replied Pat immediately, and named the figure she was getting a week – John must have blanched – 'But I'll come over anyway.'

And so she did, and brought stability once again to John's life. It cannot have been easy fulfilling the various roles she had to perform, but she soon won the affection and admiration of those who cared for John. Previously, Pat had only had to worry about cooking for herself. Now she was faced with a man used to the culinary arts practised at a very high level. It is to her immense credit that she began to measure up to her predecessors in such a short time. As she settled in as housekeeper, cook, secretary, surrogate mother and friend, did John ever recall his own words from a decade ago on an *Any Questions?* programme, when asked what qualities he would look for in a wife. He had replied, 'Speaking purely as a husband, I'd like a wife who was a non-smoker, a teetotaller, an early riser, good cook, very industrious, reluctant to have paid help in the house, and the possessor of a large private income. If you want me to be virtuous I'd give you a completely different answer, but it wouldn't be quite as truthful.' Everyone laughed at the time. The thought of John looking for a teetotaller was amusing in itself. It was just a jokey end to the programme. But Pat met most of the other criteria.

John's relationship with his sons Tim and Robert gave him cause for pride. The intensity of argument in their family disagreements only reflected the strength of feeling they had for one another. John was fond of telling how, when they met again after an absence, they would greet each other with a kiss full on the lips. He also enjoyed the company and close friendship of several young men who would have been around Jimmy's age. His elder son's untimely death had robbed John of the joys of observing and helping him to make his way in the world. Consciously or unconsciously, that gap was filled to a partial extent by a paternal interest in the lives and careers of England and Middlesex captain Mike Brearley, *Wisden Cricket Monthly* editor and author David Frith, the cricket photographer Patrick Eagar, son of Desmond, the much-travelled wine

expert Christopher Fielden, the present writer, and, of a younger generation, Ian Botham. There were others as well.

'He was a great figure when I first knew him,' Mike Brearley told me.
'I was a very ordinary county cricketer who was in his thirties and didn't
look as if I'd play for England or have any expectation or much ambition
of doing so. His paternal and avuncular attitude towards me was very nice,
very personal and very real. I felt there was a great pride if I did well, a
great pleasure and a great encouragement, and that was helpful to me. It
was the generosity of a father to a loved son.'

David Frith's friendship with John had begun and blossomed in 1966.
In 1971, following the death of his mother, David and his wife Debbie
had left England, the land of his birth, to return to Australia, the land of
his upbringing, to look after his father. 'Good luck on the long trek' was
John's inscription on a farewell present, his new book *Fred*. Six months
later the Friths were on their way back, without anywhere to live or jobs
to go to. Thirty-seven boxes of belongings went to the barn at The Old
Sun until a house could be rented, and while Debbie helped Valerie mend
some curtains, David discussed his career prospects or lack of them with
John. Several glasses of claret later, life looked much more rosy.

It was not long before John was acting as David's advocate for the
editorship of *The Cricketer* – a job he was to do for six years. 'I don't think
it would have happened without John, and I've been grateful to him ever
since. You don't forget these things. In all truth John was my English
father since the mid to late 1960s; my own father was living in Sydney all
that time until 1989. John filled that role for me. He was a man to whom
I could talk and upon whom I could lean in times of crisis – and there
were one or two. And I just loved him as a man loves his father. I think
it made my own dad a little jealous when I used to go on and on in letters
about John. He never actually said to me that he regarded me as a son,
and I never said to him – yes, I did actually, I did say, "John, you know
you're my English father," and I think he thought I was joking and I let
it pass at that.'

Christopher Fielden was working in the heart of the Burgundy wine
trade when he first met John. Living in France was a pleasurable and
peaceful experience after having, in the course of his travels seeking sup-
pliers and customers, been expelled from Gabon, refused admission to
Guatemala, left Surinam by dug-out canoe and entered Albania by mail-
van. The date of their initial meeting was November 1972, and John's
visit was in the course of his job as wine correspondent of the *Guardian*,
a role he had undertaken a short while before.

A year later John and Valerie returned, this time staying with

Christopher and his wife Ann in their house in the hills outside Beaune. 'I remember when he arrived, he thought he was suffering from food poisoning, and he asked what he should take and Ann suggested herb tea, so he went to the local village shop and bought them out of every imaginable herb tea they had. John was someone who felt that if a single measure would do you good, a double measure would do you twice as much good,' laughed Christopher. 'And any remedy that involved a glass was probably the best you could find.

'We got to know John and Valerie very well, and I don't know, but I wonder whether, to a certain extent, he saw something slightly in me of his eldest son who died in the car crash. Tim was away a lot at that time, abroad. Whether it was as a replacement I'm not sure, but I felt he needed certain people of a certain age to fill the gap for him in his life. I know he made me feel loved.'

During that second visit Christopher remarked idly that there was a need for a good book on Burgundy in English. 'All right, we'll write it together,' was John's response. In 1976 *Burgundy Vines and Wines* by Arlott and Fielden was published. 'John enjoyed wine but didn't know a great deal about it,' was his literary partner's assessment. 'He liked to talk to the real professionals about the subject. He was not a serious wine-taster or cork-sniffer. He would not write in depth about the flavour of a wine. John's strength was to get his pleasure in drinking across to the readers. He was a genuine enthusiast and as a wine writer he was great. Not in his knowledge, but in the same way as he was a great cricket commentator, in his description of wine. I think his book on Krug is one of the most readable wine books there is.'

Fielden went on to say that John's technical limitations did not lessen his importance as a wine writer. His long series of 'Honest Bottles' in the *Guardian* was evidence enough of that. Undoubtedly many a one-time non-wine-bibber was persuaded by his down-to-earth approach to venture into areas of the supermarket or off-licence that they would not have contemplated before. As with cricket, much of John's wine writing centres on the characters in the trade, both great and humble: Harry Waugh 'of the million-dollar palate'; Fritz Hallgarten, 'the best nose in the business', in his Spanish-style house at Winkel in the Rheingau wine country; Libero Raspa, who owned a small vineyard in Brufa di Torgiano in central Umbria and was still working on it at one hundred years of age; and Ernest Aujas in Beaujolais.

John's piece on Aujas was specifically mentioned when he was named Glenfiddich Wine Writer of the Year in 1978:

You are on the north road out of Juliénas when you pass the Coq d'Or and Chez la Rose, next door to each other on your left. Tiny as they are, they are two of the dozen best restaurants in the entire Beaujolais. The road, like any other in Beaujolais, never continues straight for more than a few metres; but soon it runs like a shelf let into the hillside of south-east facing vineyards. After perhaps a kilometre, a stream, less than a yard wide, comes sparkling down the hillside on your right. It crosses the road through a shallow conduit and then leaps into the wall of a grey stone house, of which only a single windowless storey shows at road level.

This is the home, presshouse, cellar, and bottling shed of the vigneron Ernest Aujas. There is no footpath; the wide wooden doors at the end of the building give directly on to the narrow road and, when they are opened, the ancient hand wine-press can be filled directly from trucks standing in the roadway.

At the other end, the path, just wide enough for the family truck, turns, hairpin, quickly down to bottom-floor level of the house, while the hill tumbles on steeply away; so steeply indeed that the plough is drawn up the vineyard slope by a winch. The cellar yard is cut deeply into the hill and on the bank rest the carcasses of a couple of cars, a dozen or so worn-out tractor tyres, a heap of gnarled, grubbed-up vine roots, and an orderly mountain of empty, green burgundy bottles waiting to be filled.

The ground floor of the house, its windows looking out across its own hill to others, and the cellar, are one solid, stone-built unit, running far back into the earth. The stream bursts from its under-floor tunnel, across the yard and gushes on, between the rabbit hutches and the dog kennels, through the garden patch and the olive trees, and down the hill.

Ernest Aujas is strongly built, six feet tall, sixty years old; his face weather-beaten to a brick red; a sun-bleached beret partly covers his white hair; the frilly stub of a hand-rolled cigarette clings to his lower lip. No spendthrift of words, he answers questions with the quiet certainty of a man who has worked out his problems.

He shares the labour of a six hectare (14.4 acres) vineyard with his son. They split the proceeds 3½/2½: the son will inherit. Roughly speaking, the son cultivates the vineyard, the father maintains the cellar, vinifies, bottles and packs. This, though, is a harsh workload possible only with family help from wives, cousins, even grand-parents, at busy times; and a team of as many as two dozen Portu-guese – mainly students – in the ten- to fifteen-day *vendage*.

The cellar is gravity-fed from the press at road level; five vast and four smaller, but still mighty, barrels hold the wine. In March 1978, the 1976, big and tannic, was still unbottled. M. Aujas, content that he had a fine vintage, did not propose to hurry it. It was safe in his cellar, where the temperature is safely static, and he takes regular samples of all his wines – and allows them to his visitors – in the traditional tastevin which hangs, worn and gleaming, from a tape about his neck. He never fines nor filters; his is a natural wine that throws a natural deposit.

He bottles it himself – as many as twenty thousand bottles in a good year – in his primitive one-man bottling machine. His 1976 was still a big tannic wine last spring. As always, he refused to bottle except when the wind was in the north and the moon on the wane.

Here again we see John taking a romantic view of the honest toiler in the field. If only cricket could have been played in the Latin countries – John's idea of bliss. At various times, he went far afield on wine trips – France, of course, many, many times, Spain, Portugal, Italy, Hungary, Germany, Austria – invitations arrived on a fairly regular basis at his *Guardian* office. According to Christopher Fielden, the job as wine correspondent was appropriated in a charmingly undemocratic way. 'He claimed there was this editorial meeting during which it was thought there ought to be a wine correspondent and John said, "Oh, I have the job as of right." "Why's that?" he was asked. "Well," replied John, "I'm the only person here who could genuinely claim to open two thousand bottles of wine a year."'

Nobody queried the claim. John and Valerie habitually opened five or six bottles a day throughout their marriage; one must remember that visitors were arriving on a regular basis, and I have been present when a dozen or so empty bottles comprised the debris of two conjoined sittings. If this seems excessive – and it probably was – balance the conviviality and pleasure to receivers and givers.

There was a memorable evening at a motel in Mere, Cheshire where, on the Saturday evening of an Old Trafford Test, Christopher and John engaged in an undeclared drinking contest. It was not planned, or even admitted. But it was obvious to the rest of the group who, recognising that we were striplings in comparison, filtered away to our various bedrooms as saturation point was reached, leaving Messrs Fielden and Arlott still amiably opening bottles well past midnight. The next morning the two finalists were bright-eyed and sparkling; more than could be said for the rest of us.

Christopher himself says: 'I think the heaviest single day I had with John was on Alderney, when in the course of twenty-four hours we drank twenty-three bottles of wine, and there were never more than four people there.'

One of the trips John took for the *Guardian* was to Château Mouton-Rothschild for an interview with the unconventional Baron Philippe. The baron, as well as a preference for designing his own jackets, had a mischievous reputation. He liked to decide on a daily basis where his meals should be served, and the dining-table would be moved to suit his whim. On this occasion, before tasting some memorable *premiers crus* over lunch, John toured the legendary cellars, where a treasure-repository of over a hundred thousand bottles of the finest and rarest clarets in the world was to be seen. He also inspected the priceless wine-related artefacts and artistic works in the private museum. That evening dinner was taken in one of the best restaurants in Bordeaux. The baron was otherwise occupied, so his public relations officer acted as host. Patrick Eagar, assigned to take photographs of John with Rothschild, was also present: 'We started with a champagne in which the baron had an interest, then a 1971 Mouton with the main course, and when we came to the cheese, this huge gilt-bound wine list with wonderfully smart prices was produced.

'The PR man said, "Now, Monsieur Arlott, would you like to choose cheese and wine?" "Thank you," replied John, with a slight twinkle in his eye. "I think I'd like a bottle of Beaujolais."

'A stunned silence. In Bordeaux, anything outside Bordeaux doesn't exist. I frantically looked up and down this large wine list and there, at the bottom, was one solitary bottle of Beaujolais – which we all enjoyed.'

John had a great appreciation of Beaujolais, especially for its thirst-quenching properties, but he obviously enjoyed the opportunity to puncture a little of the preciousness and mystique that can surround wine. Never afraid to give an opinion, he once said of a popular Spanish wine, 'Corrida going down is like vomit coming up.'

On another trip, this time in Alsace, John was determined to find a bottle of Rouge d'Alsace. The region is famous for its Riesling and Gewürztraminer: white wines. Some said a red did not exist; others would not admit to not having drunk it. Every enquiry in café, bar or restaurant led to the appearance of a rosé. The not-too-serious quest ended with the realisation that it was necessary to read the label to know which was rosé and which was red. The colour extraction from the Pinot Noir grape resulted in a fairly uniform light wine.

Driving the car around the Vosges and Haut-Rhin was Barry Reed. John was in the front passenger seat, Christopher Fielden and Patrick

Eagar in the back. Patrick was navigating, or trying to: 'We got hopelessly lost in our efforts to get from one part of the valley to another. We'd go into thick fog and then, as we were crawling uphill, break through cloud into brilliant sunshine. The sun was really hot. John suddenly said, "Stop the car. We shouldn't be here, Patrick." I looked at the map and then at the sign on the side of the road. "This is the wrong place we're trying to get to," I replied. "Nieder Morsahewhir ... plus ... Look, John, it's a four-kilometre word." He was reduced to fits of giggles. He often talked about that.'

Michael Parkinson tells a story about he and John meeting as they passed through the Grace Gates into Lord's. There was a drizzle in the air, and John was wearing a bulky raincoat with a poacher's pocket; room enough for a vintage red. 'I've got the best job in the world,' said Parkinson, who at the time was writing a column for the *Sunday Times* and doing a regular programme for Granada Television. 'I'm paid to go to the cinema and watch sport.' 'Oh, no, no,' said John. 'I'm paid to watch cricket and drink wine.' Pause for reflection. 'Mind you,' John chuckled at the thought, 'Cardus said, "Mine's better. I'm paid to watch opera, and I'd rather sleep with a soprano than a wine merchant."' Which was a branch line of John's oft-repeated joke about the lady who knew nothing about music but was very fond of musicians.

In the last few years before his retirement in 1980, John started to feel the strain of his many commitments. He was approaching pensionable age, and his way of living, which had become part of the legend, made demands that in his youth he had shrugged off.

The constant travel and pace of work, along with his gradual disillusionment at the way market forces were dictating the future of cricket, made him long for a less pressured existence. Pressure was not a word he ever used or a thing he admitted to feeling, even to himself, but it was there. Incredibly, he still managed to fit in everything he wanted to do without the appearance of hurry, but the price was rising. The tax was on his body, the toll was on his health. His heavy social schedule, some of it unavoidable, brought uncomfortable bulk. How could he be expected to change the habits of a lifetime? Never one to compromise, he imbibed just as liberally and shared just as much. He would often return to the press box after an elastic lunch break with the game having restarted some time before: what Cardus had called 'constructive watching'. He did not need to see every ball to know how a player had performed. If a particular batsman did not get out that way, it was the way he jolly well ought to have got out.

Not that John practised any kind of deceit. A few questions to colleagues, and in a short time his typewriter was submitting to another dose
of heavy finger-chop. The resulting copy conveyed the situation as if he
had been glued to every moment of the game: a masterly exposition envied
by those in the vicinity who could not understand how he did it. The
readers would get their full measure of Arlott and had no reason to doubt,
while only a cricketer actually involved in a certain dismissal might perhaps
occasionally wonder.

By the late 1970s sponsors' hospitality tents had become an everyday
feature of big cricket. Lunch breaks fizzed by at important matches, and
words only dried up when glasses were empty. During a Cornhill Test
match at Edgbaston in 1979 against India, a loose press assortment called
the Black Fish Club was enjoying its second serving. (The name was the
brainwave of someone who had spotted the resemblance to fish of the
soaked-off black labels swimming around in the unfrozen pool of water
at the bottom of an ice-bucket). It had become the club's practice to have
a five o'clock refill, chilled rosé to stimulate tired minds with impending
deadlines. John had noticed some bottles of claret stored below the press
point, and made his preference known to his former *News Chronicle* colleague Crawford White, who was acting as PR liaison. Patrick Eagar
describes what happened: 'John's bottle of red soon disappeared. Being
the generous soul he was, he would share out with anybody who preferred
red. Crawford was wise to this – he had a couple more up his sleeve –
but after the third bottle of red, the fourth was not exactly forthcoming.
To which John riposted, "Look here, Chalky, you wouldn't want us to
write about the *Prudential* Test match, would you?" "Oh, all right John,"
sighed Crawford, and he goes down and gets two more.

'Anyway, there's been a bit of a running battle where John is seeking
his ration of red and Crawford is fed up going down to the caterers seeking
something which is not on his normal list. He's quite happy to supply
rosé, but red is rather more difficult. By now, John has got imprinted on
his mind that the match is something to do with the Prudential. He starts
his copy – "First Prudential Test match here today . . .". Now, in John's
defence, he first of all handed it to Irving Rosenwater, who was doing his
dictation. And Irving, who knows his cricket, dictated "First Prudential
Test match" down the line. It gets to the *Guardian* sports desk, sub-editor,
editor – nobody spots it. And they run a photograph on the front page:
"The First Prudential Test Match". I think John was rather contrite. Next
morning, a lot of red faces.'

David Frith, who has shared many moments of cricketing and human
drama with John, outlines the subtext: 'After the test of will with Crawford,

a Freudian process took over. He did actually type "*Prudential* Test match", so he was culpable. So were the others who should have picked it up. You can imagine Cornhill were furious and John was absolutely horrified. It looked as if he'd carried out his threat, but he hadn't meant to. He would never have wanted to do that.'

Given John's method for putting his thoughts on to paper, it was perhaps surprising that mistakes of a crucial nature had not occurred before. 'I've got some of his early newspaper copy,' commented David, 'and it is like an abstract sheet of graffiti. It used to fascinate me that he would type a sentence and, having got halfway, he'd realise the construction or the words were wrong, and he'd go on typing the right ones. I used to panic, looking over his shoulder, and think, why doesn't he cross out what he doesn't want? Because he might forget to cross it out and some idiot is going to put the whole lot through. But he'd go back with that thick black nib and he'd scratch it all out eventually. I've never known anyone do it the way he did it. It was all in his head. He had to get it all on the paper and then he subbed it. Apart from that time when "Prudential" should have read "Cornhill", I think it was all OK.'

During that Edgbaston Test in 1979, David Frith hosted the first editorial board dinner of his new cricket magazine, *Wisden Cricket Monthly*, at Walsall Golf Club. The members of the board made an impressive group: 'I wanted to build up a matchless team of writers with Patrick Eagar's photography. John was the most important element in that. He agreed very readily and that was a great comfort, and it meant a lot to know that he was there together with Ted Dexter, who always liked a new challenge, and Jim Laker, who actually said "This is exciting." Can you imagine Jim saying that? Bob Willis was with us and so was young David Gower, who'd scored 200 not out that day, but still came, which I valued. I told them all how thrilled I was they were supporting me.' *Wisden Cricket Monthly* went on to become an integral and respected part of cricket's new testament, and John continued to contribute to virtually every issue for the remainder of his life.

The press box is an unholy sanctum, or should be. Invited visitors and friends tend to regard it as a privilege to be there, and speak, if at all, in reverentially hushed tones, so as not to disturb the scribes at work. At Lord's, it being Lord's, particularly so.

Over the years, however, there have been some unlikely invaders, including the actress Linda Lovelace of *Deep Throat* fame. One of the oddest was the youngest son of a peer of the realm. David Frith recollects: 'He had come straight from Ascot wearing a carnation and a pink shirt and was done up quite grandly. He must have sunk several bottles and sat in the back row talking in this plummy, penetrating voice to no one in particular, just rambling on about his views on cricket and sport generally.

'John was trying to write his story three rows in front and he turned round and gave this fellow a glare. He didn't stop, so John glared once again. In the end, he simply turned round and said very loudly, "Out!" The chap bridled, but being drunk it took a while to register, so John shouted "Out! Out!" three or four times. He then had to elaborate. "I'm trying to work! Can't you see that? You have no right to be in here!" And so the Honourable finally left. John knew who he was because he told me later. I don't think any of us could have got rid of the man, but John, by the sheer volume of his voice – and it was a quite frightening turn of anger – managed to do it. He had every right to be tetchy, I think.'

When it came to John's final farewell to the commentary box – a sort of epilogue after the benediction – the last Gillette Cup Final at Lord's in 1980 between Middlesex and Surrey, following the Centenary Test, was he baiting an old adversary, or just poking fun at his father? As the lanky Vintcent van der Bijl, Middlesex's South African seamer, bald pate glinting in the sun, turned at the Nursery End and rolled in to bowl, John described him as 'looking like a younger, healthier, more athletic version of Lord Longford – but not nearly so tolerant'.

John's own tolerance had not been too noticeable on the plane to Australia for the first Centenary Test in Melbourne in 1977. A cocktail party at Heathrow for the cricketing convoy had made a lot of people very happy, and free champagne on the plane had only enhanced the mood. The veteran journalist Reg Hayter, sitting next to Bill Edrich, was aware that his companion was tippling merrily, having had three bottles put in front of him. Reg remembers Bill saying, 'I must go and speak to Arlott.': 'I think John had taken a sleeping tablet and was lying flat. Bill, unsteady on his feet, tripped and poked him. John shot up involuntarily and punched Bill in the eye. He had a stunning black eye next morning, a real shiner. At the hotel in Melbourne, all the Australians were coming in and teasing him about it, pretending not to know, although they'd heard how it had happened.' John's old sparring partner Jack Fingleton immediately christened him 'the Alresford Mauler'.

For John, the trip was fairly miserable. He was still missing Valerie dreadfully, and found it hard to come to terms with all the jollity surrounding the Centenary celebrations. Frank Tyson, now living in Australia, had met him at the airport. 'I took him to the Hilton Hotel. He was exhausted from the flight and fell fast asleep with his head on the bar. The waiter said, "Take that man out – he's drunk". I said, "He's not drunk, he's absolutely knackered." That's the sort of thing John didn't like – he hated that sort of thing. It was a long time since I'd seen him and he had deteriorated physically, but his intellect was still as sharp. He had encouraged me to write. Very supportive when I did *A Typhoon Called Tyson*. He told me he thought it expressed the feelings of a fast bowler very well. "Always remember when you're writing, Frank," he said, "that the English language is a marvellous instrument. For every feeling, every sentiment, there is an exact word that describes it. Look for it." With spoken language, he was always looking for it – the exact word.' Tyson paused for a moment. 'I don't know whether John liked my marrying an Australian. He never really liked Australians, did he, honestly?'

The witnessing of an unpleasant incident had confirmed John's personal prejudice. 'He saw a big, fat feller on the bridge at Jolimont near the Melbourne Cricket Ground thumping his kids (including a fostered Asian girl), and on the strength of that – this is a clue to how perturbed he was at the time – he took a down on Australia generally.' David Frith, with dual loyalties, spoke with warmth. 'I had some pretty heated arguments with him around that time. He was irrational. He'd written off all Australians because of this nasty Oz and I said, "Is there no such thing as child abuse in England then?"' Here were echoes of that scene in South Africa nearly thirty years earlier when he had seen an Afrikaner kicking a black man into the gutter.

For John, the physical punishment of children – indeed, of anyone – was unforgivable. His own experiences at the hands of Percivall, his abhorrence, in days gone by, of police flogging convicts, and his tender treatment of his own sons, were the cause and result of deeply ingrained views. Once, after some misdemeanour at his preparatory school in London, Norfolk House, James had been left over a weekend, anxiously awaiting probable chastisement on the Monday morning. John spoke to the master concerned, pointing out that although it was his right to punish a transgression, it should be done at the time. It was cruel to leave a boy wondering what fate had in store over such a long period. Apparently the logic was accepted and the punishment rescinded.

As for John's attitude towards Australians, individually he liked many of them very much indeed – Keith Miller being a prime example. The manifestation of the 'Ocker' image was what offended him; the cluster crowing at an opponent's discomfiture; jokes, unfunny because they laughed at and not with; and an inability to smile when on the receiving end of humour. 'They are not the world's greatest losers,' John remarked to Mike Brearley during their television conversation in 1986. 'Nobody gets so bitter as Australians.'

The few days spent in Australia did, however, have a brighter side.

John acknowledged the quality of Australian wines, and looked to the future. 'I suddenly realised one morning that he'd brightened up a little,' said David Frith. 'He announced that he'd phoned Pat over in England the night before and they had decided to get married, so there was a sort of recovery from Valerie's death.' In fact John had proposed and been accepted before he left on the trip, so he had obviously chosen his moment to make the public declaration. 'I admire Pat enormously,' said David. 'She'd got the third innings, really. A cricket match is two innings each, isn't it? John was telling all his mates in Melbourne that he was going to make an honest woman of her and suddenly he was surrounded at the bar. They all wanted to be with him, because he was always able to lift an event into an occasion.'

In due course there was to be another occasion; one that could truly be described as unforgettable. But before that could happen, he had one more decision to make.

25

Farewell to Commentary

Soon after Peter Baxter had been given the job of guardian of the cricket commentators in 1973, he was taken out to lunch by John: 'It was part congratulatory, part welcoming on board, a nice sort of signalling of my arrival. We had a free-ranging discussion, not just about the business of cricket commentary, though that did come into it, but about all kinds of other things. During the course of the meal he did say to me on two or three occasions, "You will tell me when I'm past it as a commentator, won't you?" Now here's this young man of twenty-five just been appointed to produce the great Arlott – I'm really likely to say to him "You've had enough, go." '

But, years later, had the situation altered? 'No, it never got to that stage, because for every session that he wasn't perhaps quite at his best, there were sessions where he was quite brilliant. He would still turn in three or four in a Test match which were absolute gems.'

By his own standards, however, John knew that his best broadcasting was done. His breathing was an increasing problem. Bronchitis, or 'my old wheezy chest, which does sometimes sound like a pair of bagpipes full of dust', as he put it, brought on by the heavy smoking of his younger days, made it a real effort to string together a long sentence without gasping for air. Also, after so long on the circuit he was simply tired, and needed an escape from the tyranny of broadcasting and reporting deadlines. He wanted to seek fresh pastures and, moreover, he knew where to find them. Importantly, he wanted to go while 'people are still asking "Why?" rather than "When?" '

Early in 1979, John asked Peter Baxter whether he was intending to employ him for the following season, 1980. Somewhat surprised, Peter answered in the affirmative. 'In that case, it shall be my last,' said John.

The decision taken, John made plans. He had seen a house on Alderney which was shortly coming on the market. He wanted to move there. It would be a wrench to leave Hampshire, and particularly Alresford, but he knew that if he stayed he would be 'too weak-minded not to work', and as his mother had died in 1974, there was no reason to be close to Basingstoke. Alderney had sentimental attachments – family holidays when Jimmy was alive. There were no juggernauts, no vandals, unlocked front doors, fresh air – he needed that – and considerable tax advantages.

Financing the move and the purchase of the new property was the next consideration. Over dinner at The Old Sun, we discussed possible ways of disposing of his cricket collection. Auction? 'Too much of a lottery'; specialist dealers? 'I doubt', he said, 'if any of them could afford six figures or more.' A long pause. 'D'you know any private collectors?' The enquiry was made more in hope than expectation. 'Hang on', I said. 'There is a chap. Tony Winder asked if he could meet you next time we're in a studio together. Comes from Yorkshire. Inherited his father's electrical firm. Pretty wealthy. Always seems to be left clutching the booty at the end of cricketing sales.' John smiled. 'Bring him down to dinner.' It was one of those offers that could not be refused.

I took Tony Winder to Alresford the next week. He was excited at the prospect of seeing the famed cricket book collection, let alone buying it. He had only been collecting for a few years, but already he had some prized items, bought with a view to their scarcity value and fine condition. Before and over dinner, John expounded on this and that bibliographical rarity, how difficult it was to get hold of a complete set of Lillywhite's *Guides*, where else would there be such an extensive cricket photograph collection . . . Boxall, Lambert, the many editions of Nyren, Pycroft, an obscure cricketing register of 1833, *Felix on the Bat*, *Bat's Manuals*, scarce eighteenth-century overseas annuals . . . ? All right, one could perhaps pick up an individual item without too much difficulty, but to acquire the fruits of a life's search and purchase *en bloc*. . . John excelled himself. It was a masterly piece of salesmanship. Tony was hooked, I could see that. But John was not so sure.

'I'll have to think about it,' said Tony at the end of the evening, 'but I'm *very* interested.' Afterwards, over the phone, John thanked me and said, 'I suppose that's the most you can expect any Yorkshireman to say straight away, that he *is* interested.'

Within a short time the deal was struck. The doyen of cricket booksellers, E.K. Brown, came in to take items that duplicated those in the existing Winder collection. The floor of the Long Room was strewn with pieces from John's past, each of which told a story. John retained the standard grammar for future cricket writing – his sets of *Wisden* and the fifteen volumes of Haygarth's *Scores and Biographies of Celebrated Cricketers*. And he decided, at the last, to keep a copy of the almost unprocurable 'Epps scores' ('A collection of all the grand matches of cricket played in

England, within twenty years, viz. from 1771–1791') – an inscribed present from his father shortly before he died in 1959. The book had probably been obtained from Leslie Gutteridge's lair at the Epworth Press in the City Road – the old man wanted to give John something by which he would be remembered.

Cavalier thoughts of smuggling around five thousand bottles of John's wine by boat at dead of night through tricky currents on to Alderney's rocky shore lasted as long as it took four of us – all non-sailors – to drain a magnum. The tax situation made transfer impracticable, so the auctioneers Christie's sold the bulk of the cellar, which fetched a little short of £30,000. During the sale, John was in a press box covering cricket and, having made a phone call, suddenly intoned, 'Gentlemen, you may be interested to know that the lunch score here is 217 for 5, and at Christie's it's seventy cases of Bordeaux for £7,000.' Laughter and delighted applause. Maybe some remembered the time one of their number had offered John a glass of what looked like red wine. He took several sips before realising he was drinking Ribena.

That final year with the cricketing circus was like an extended coronation: lunches, dinners, receptions, parties in his honour wherever he went. Counties, clubs, promotions, private functions, public acknowledgements, award ceremonies. Friends he knew intimately and those he never knew he had, all began to realise they were going to experience a real sense of loss. He was *part* of people, *part* of the household. 'Part of summer, just like the lawnmower,' someone said irreverently.

As always, John hated disappointing anybody, and in the last week or so before his retirement he was sometimes attending two lunches a day, with cocktail and drink sessions thrown in. Television, commercial and BBC, national and regional; radio similarly, plus local; press, it seemed like every newspaper in the land – they all wanted interviews, and John obliged. After his farewell to the John Player League at Edgbaston, Russell Davies in the *Sunday Times* noted: 'John Arlott, excused from commentary, and almost militantly glass-in-hand, said a last goodbye during the tea interval, thus bringing to an end the most exhausting cycle of interviews any man has undergone since Rudolf Hess landed in Scotland.'

The last two acts were played out at Lord's. First there was the Centenary Test against Australia from 28 August to 2 September, and then an encore a few days later on Saturday 6 September with the Gillette Cup Final, Middlesex v. Surrey. The night before, the *Daily Mail*'s star sports columnist Ian Wooldridge and his wife Sarah had gone down to Alresford and taken John and Pat out to dinner. 'He was very quiet, introspective, and then, after two large brandies, emotional – understandable.'

But the Centenary Test was the real moment of departure. The match itself turned into something of an anti-climax, with over ten hours lost to rain. When John started his last twenty-minute period on the final after-noon, some wondered how it would all end. The play was uneventful and, somehow, timeless. That, perhaps, was appropriate.

Arlott: The sun bright, the wind still, and just fluttering the flag – the MCC flag on the works office . . . and Lillee turns, six feet tall and wide shoulders, he comes up, a little stammer in the middle of his run, but then he gets it straight again, bowls short and – Boycott hooks that. That looks like being four, it is four, and I imagine we're going to hear somebody on the public address at any moment asking the spectators over there to get back inside the boards, because several of them are lying on the grass inside the playing area – any moment now I think the voice of Alan Curtis will be heard in the land. And Lillee turns then, 60 for 2 now, 8 to Gower, 26 Boycott . . .

Two more to Boycott then – 28, 69 for 2, and the batsmen out in the England innings remembering they were set 370 to win in a minimum of 350 minutes – now it's Bright to Boycott – pushes this away on the on side – little trouble in reading the flight there – Gooch bowled Lillee 16; that was 19 for – 43 for 2, and Bright again going round the wicket to the right-handed Boycott, and Boycott pushes this away between silly point and slip, picked up by Mallett at short third man, that's the end of the over, it's 69 for 2, nine runs off the over, 28 Boycott, 15 Gower – 69 for 2, and after Trevor Bailey it'll be Christopher Martin-Jenkins.

[Suddenly the unexpected sound of spirited clapping within the commentary box.]

Trevor Bailey (over applause): Well, the applause is . . . I'm very lucky really to have been on while John completed his last commentary, and on behalf of the *Test Match Special* team and listeners . . . we thank him very much indeed, and would he open that bottle of champagne a bit quickish . . .

Christopher Martin-Jenkins: . . . and let's hope it's launching a happy retirement rather than finishing a great career. Here comes Lillee bowling on the off stump to Gower, who plays that up to mid-off, and there is no run, Gower now 15 – 28 to Boycott, 69 for 2 – the cricket full of tension. But . . . the box, in a way, tense too, because that was the final twenty-minute session of John Arlott's career as a Test broadcaster, although he'll be back on Saturday here for the Gillette Cup Final, and I sincerely hope will be broadcasting and writing at least occasionally during his what we hope will be a long and happy retirement.

Alan Curtis, in control as usual of the Lord's public address, had earlier spoken to BBC producer Peter Baxter. 'I asked Peter roughly the time of John's last stint, and he said about 3.15. I was certainly aware that the crowd were very politely watching the last rites of what mainly, due to Boycott's selfishness, had become a dull Test match. If the game had been as exciting as it might have been I most likely wouldn't have said anything, because it would have been an intrusion.

'I'd heard the applause in the commentary box and everybody had been taken aback by how matter-of-factly John had signed off. About ten to fifteen per cent of the spectators, who listen to radio, would also have been aware that he had just finished. By then Lillee had just started an over, so I had to wait for four or five minutes until it was completed before speaking. I just said, "Spectators might like to know that John Arlott has just finished his last Test match commentary."'

Trevor Bailey: And the applause was for John Arlott, his last commentary.

Christopher Martin-Jenkins: And Trevor, the entire Australian field is clapping – Geoff Boycott having a clap there, and I'm sure the entire ground is clapping at that announcement by Alan Curtis that John has just done his final Test match session – a moment indeed of nostalgia in a very nostalgic match.

Alan Curtis again: 'I certainly didn't think it would get the reaction it did. There were about five to six thousand spectators in the ground. I remember Lillee was just adjusting his headband and took it off rather like a Roman gladiator, walked up to where he knew John would be and waved it in the air. And Boycott actually put his bat down, took his gloves off and applauded.

'The sad thing was John didn't twig any of this, because he'd gone from the main box immediately to the next-door box to do a commentary down the line for BBC South or something like that. I knew he was talking and wasn't really aware of what was going on.'

Eventually, John came out of the box and started to descend the steps to a lower level of the pavilion, where he was to present the Man of the Match award to the Australian captain Kim Hughes. Members were patting him on the back and calling out. The presentation did not happen immediately, because as John came onto the balcony to be introduced by Alan Curtis, the whole crowd, and all the players and officials, gave him a rapturous ovation that went on for several minutes. If they had not been on their feet already, they would have stood. 'He was visibly overcome,' said Alan. 'At last he said, "You'll have to stop applauding, otherwise I won't be able to speak."' In fact the applause had gone on for so long that it appeared that John's public, for once, did not want him to speak. It was a most moving and heartwarming gesture of admiration and affection that nobody wanted to end. Because when it did, they knew they would have to let him go.

During that journey from one side of the pavilion to the other, John had met Tony Lewis. As he leant against the rail, mopping his brow with his piratical red-and-white spotted handkerchief, Tony reminded him of those last words of commentary. 'I thought you'd say something more romantic than that,' he said.

'There's nothing more romantic than a clean break', replied John.

26

Emeritus Years

That occasion should have been the end of the story. John could then have sailed away towards his island home and his own special sunset. Of course it was not, and he did not. As the exhausting round of farewells was drawing to a close, John told everyone he was looking forward to sleeping for six months. But within a very short time he was working again, in fact he never really stopped. No more commentary, daily journalistic deadlines or rushing round the country, but still the occasional broadcast, writing of reviews and articles, and working journeys. And his annual survey of the year's new cricket books for *Wisden*. If, after a lifetime's conditioning to produce material on demand, John expected to be totally idle, he was hardly displeased to find that he was as busy as he wanted to be.

At the last moment before moving to Alderney, John had had an attack of cold feet. The pull of his beloved Alresford and Hampshire made him reluctant to sign the deeds of the new house. But having done so, he convinced himself he had made the right decision. He managed to withstand a temptation to return to commentary in the early 1980s; the offer was made, but a family consensus persuaded him to take the right decision. There was to be no continuing series of farewell appearances. A three-way conversation with Jim Swanton and Rex Alston by phone link from Alderney was organised by Peter Baxter on one occasion, but that was it. Nor did John return to watch others at work.

'What I found very sad was that he never came back to Test matches, except to open the Neville Cardus Stand at Old Trafford,' remarked Brian Johnston shortly before he died. 'He stayed for one day. I find that very difficult to understand. I took a day off yesterday, the first time I've gone to a first-class match where I haven't commentated since 1946. I sat and watched and I loved it. It's given me great hope that when I give up I shall enjoy watching cricket.' Unhappily, that was not to be.

Alderney is the most northerly of the Channel Islands, shaped irregularly like a slice of cheese. Three and a half miles long by one and a quarter wide, its gorse-covered hem encloses a population of about two thousand souls. With the island's encirclement by fourteen forts, much reinforced concrete betrays the German occupation during the Second World War when four camps – Borkum, Helgoland, Norderney and Sylt – housed prisoners from North Africa, eastern and western Europe and Russia. References to a possible induction camp, Citadella, have also been found. Ill-treatment and atrocities resulted in many deaths from starvation, dysentery and exposure, and slave-labourers were thrown over the cliffs after collapsing during the digging out of gun emplacements. Only about a third of the population returned to the island after the war, which partly explains why, alone among the three larger Channel Islands, Alderney's *patois* is extinct.

'Balmoral', or 'The Vines' as John quickly renamed it, is an impressive residence on the Longis Road, the nexus between St Anne, the tiny capital, and the lighthouse at Mannez in the north-east corner, near to where Ian and Kathy Botham have a holiday home. With a granny flat on one side and a newly designated Long Room on the other, a paddock, and an extensive back garden ending with a granite wall beside which vines were planted with the avowed intention of suckling Château d'Arlott (nothing came of the idea), John and Pat settled in. The hilly incline behind the house overlooks Braye Bay, and beyond that the next landfall is North America. 'No need to draw the curtains when you get undressed,' John always used to say when he showed me to the bedroom.

The house had been one of the last strongholds of the occupying German forces before they were rounded up in 1945 and the cellar, soon to be restocked with an Arlott wine collection mark two, had been amateurishly booby-trapped. The shaven wires on the wall at the top of the steps are still visible.

A year or so before he moved, John had been tempted to put in an offer for Raz Island, a fort in Longy Bay, once a German machine-gun nest, subsequently a restaurant, that had a causeway which made it inaccessible at high tide. It was a romantic notion that appealed to the part of John's nature that enjoyed reclusiveness, but the idea was never practical. Apart from the inconvenience of being marooned on one side or the other for hours on end, the damp and salt would have very quickly ruined many of John's treasures. A distant Hardyesque fantasy, mentioned by Dawn, may have surfaced momentarily, in which John responded to being jokingly called 'Master' by imagining a huge house or castle and lots of servants kneeling as he walked past to lead morning prayers. Mike Brearley had a not dissimilar notion: 'I felt he could have been a sort of left-wing country squire in Henry VIII's time, surrounded by minstrels with lots of hunting, food and drinking.'

The quiet and the relaxed pace of life on Alderney had a dual effect on John. In one way, it was just what he had been seeking; in another, it caused restlessness. The adjustment from his hectic existence to something approaching monastic calm did not come easily. To combat the change, he sought things to do.

In 1983 he undertook a nine-day lecture tour of theatres and halls around England: starting just upstream at Newport on the Isle of Wight, thence to Shropshire, Yorkshire, Surrey, Wiltshire, Somerset, Essex and Kent, finishing at the Surrey Hall, Stockwell. Full houses, rapt audiences everywhere he went. By the end of the tour, the boot of the car taking John and his minders from place to place was full of books. At every opportunity he had raided bookshops along the route, enjoying the chance to indulge in his old pastime. I journeyed with him some of the way. The performance at the Towngate Theatre, Basildon, was typical. The house lights dimmed and a single spot centred on a bare stage. The applause was of an emotional intensity that surprised the audience themselves, as was obvious in the ensuing release of their laughter after John had seated himself on the solitary chair alongside a small table which supported an empty glass and a full bottle. 'Thank you – bless you,' he said, as he stretched forward with a smile to pour from one to the other. 'You couldn't possibly expect me to begin a talk without first taking a glass of wine . . .'

The audience had missed him, and they settled back to enjoy once more the sound of his voice and the stories they had probably heard before. Hobbs, Tate, Percy Chapman, Alex Skelding, the Hampshire legends, Nyren and the Hambledonians all came to life again. John, without a note in sight, regaled his audience with a story he had once put down on paper, of how he had visited Hambledon in the company of Harry Altham, chronicler of the pioneering *A History of Cricket*, a President of MCC, and a man absorbed in every aspect of the game:

We left the Bat and Ball and walked out across the pitch at Broad-Halfpenny Down. We were at about the centre of the wicket, when his eyes lit with that eager, inner fire so characteristic of Harry. In a voice trembling with emotion, he said, 'Look – look at that slope down the hill. When one of the great players, John Small or "Silver" Billy Beldham, really got it in the middle and it went down there, how many runs do you think they made? All the hits were run out. How good a thrower must have been Noah Mann to get it back up that slope after chasing it down to the bottom?' Harry, by now, had transported himself to their time. He was not expecting answers. Having drawn a deep breath he said, 'What air – what air to breathe.'

John never quite finished the story on a public platform. In private, for instance in conversation with David Frith, he could just about get to the end before dissolving in laughter. 'John told me he'd had a very big night out and was full of wind, and as Harry was saying "You can smell the history here, John," he was wholly unable to prevent himself punctuating the remark in an appropriate way. Harry Altham's nostrils were raised to the air as he tried to pick up the scent of Nyren and Beldham, and slowly his face turned into a strange grimace as he recoiled.'

John visited Hambledon twice in the 1980s, once to record a presentation for Frith's video *Benson and Hedges Golden Great Batsmen* in 1983, and again in 1985 as the special guest at a celebration match for the bicentenary of *The Times*. Although there was some cricket, the match between Collins publishers' team and the boys from the broadsheet was bedevilled by the weather. John Woodcock, highly respected writer for the paper, was one of the umpires:

'John had flown over for it. Filthy weather. He had been sinking Beaujolais and during lunch at the Bat and Ball his head was dropping, he was tired and sounded maudlin. When it was time to make a speech, he got up and he was absolutely brilliant. It was almost as if he'd shed a skin and pulled himself out of himself. He quoted large chunks of Nyren in his inimitable style. People from outside came to the door. Initially the voice was weak. Everyone listened in wonder, spellbound, there was total silence. After twenty minutes he finished and a great cheer went up. He sat down again and slumped into a chair.'

Other occasions during his emeritus years included manning the public address at The Oval for a match in 1983 between Old England and Old West Indies. David Frith, headlights blazing, had raced up the hard shoulder for miles on the A3 to avoid a traffic jam and get him there on time. The game was full of poignant reminders as everyone recalled their salad days. A year later, returning to the site of his *alma mater* in Basingstoke, John was unable to finish a story about visiting the old Hampshire and England stalwart George Brown in hospital. It somehow seemed as if he was identifying with the dying Brown, and his voice revealed the extent to which he was moved. As John sank into his seat, the chairman jumped up and started speaking to cover the general embarrassment. John covered his own confusion by being heard to mutter, 'This chairman's a boring old bugger!'

Increasing decrepitude was making John vulnerable. His health was a

constant problem. Chronic bronchitis, a form of emphysema, a couple of
brain bleeds, a heart attack which led to him being fitted with a pacemaker,
cancer of the bowel and a splintered spine could have sent six normal men
to the mortuary. 'He was fast becoming a bionic man,' affectionately
remarked David Roper, a friend from Alresford. 'When he was told he'd
got to have a pacemaker, he immediately went out and had two bottles
of Beaujolais at the Clump in Chilcomb.'

Yet John survived. He had the constitution of an ox. But over the years,
the effect of his illnesses was unremittingly debilitating. Bronchitis was
always with him. The nebuliser, which gave temporary relief and much-
needed oxygen, was a continuous aid. Its nose and mouth mask simultaneously resembled an old lip microphone and a fighter pilot's headgear.
I used to tease him about Biggles giving a cricket commentary in, rather
than on, the air. He smiled with his eyes.

During the first years in Alderney John would take an early-morning
saunter fifty yards up the road and on to a bank which overlooked the
Beaumont Hague and Flamanville atomic power stations on the French
coast, there to do his 'coughing practice and to check that France was still
there'. His bouts of coughing were accurately described by David Frith
as 'operatic'. Later on, with a walking frame, that stroll was beyond him.

Hypochondria, to which John had always been prone, was a relative
thrice removed from all this. Early fears of going blind, when he possessed
extraordinarily good eyesight; putting special preparations on his hair
when he thought he was going bald; dabbing his gums with iodine because
he thought they were receding. Those were manifestations of an achiever's
hidden anxiety, a young man searching hard for an ulcer. But this, now,
was an old man who, despite himself, was struggling desperately to survive.

Periodic visits to the Forest Mere health hydro, near Liphook in Hampshire, lasted for a week or more. Friends living within a hundred-mile
radius would get a phone call from John, sounding terribly depressed.
Usually he was trying hard not to adjust to a relatively spartan existence
in pleasant enough surroundings. 'Bring a couple of bottles of Beaujolais,'
he would say as he signed off. 'How much are you paying a week for
staying there?' I asked him once when he rang from his room. 'Oh, about
£400,' he replied. 'So, what's the point in forking out all that, if you're
going to carry on as usual?' I was not really being unsympathetic, because
at the same time I could not help laughing.

Passing reception at Forest Mere was like going through the green
channel at customs with undeclared goods. One tried not to look guilty.
John's face lit up when he saw my hard-backed attaché case bulging at
the sides. Once safely in his room, I took out two or three bottles and

suggested putting them in the wardrobe. Only then did I become aware that there were half a dozen or so empties unsuccessfully hidden by his shoes waiting to be taken away. 'You couldn't just dispose of these for me, could you?' John nearly managed to look like the small boy stealing jam of whom Tony Lewis was so fond.

On the night of one visit, England were playing Denmark in a soccer international at Wembley, and John had the television on. We opened the newly-brought wine and settled down to enjoy the match. Suddenly there was a knock, and the door opened. A medical orderly entered, carrying a tray on which were a bottle of barley water, two slices of lemon and a glass. The barley water had been expertly wrapped in a napkin as if it were choice Château Médicine Liphook. The man looked startled when he saw the bottles on the table, and mildly disapproving. Neither John nor I said anything while he found room for the contents of his tray, but we were careful not to catch one another's gaze.

In these breaks for rehabilitation, John was looking for others to provide the will-power and restraint that he lacked. In his home environment, which he loved, that would have proved impossible. Once, padding down a corridor at Forest Mere to escape for a short while to a nearby hostelry, we passed the open door of a room in which a gathering of earnest-looking inmates were receiving a lecture on the benefits of healthy living. A large wink and then a murmured 'Silly buggers.'

After one visit to the health hydro in the early 1980s, a letter arrived accompanying a presentation copy of *Rites of Passage* from that maned lion of literature, William Golding, who used to read pieces for John in his poetry producer days. 'I hope Forest Mere was successful and that the vile body is dried-out but not desiccated! I am a bit dried-out and underfed and moving towards the desired haven of being not wicked but slim!'

At Forest Mere, John made new acquaintances. One day when he was out for a walk in the grounds, a track-suited woman approached, jogging. She stopped and informed him that he knew her father. He later realised that he had been speaking to the Duchess of Kent, whose father was Sir William Worsley, President of Yorkshire CCC. This led to an amusing sequel some time later when she visited Alderney. Michael Aireton, a resident of the island who quietly and efficiently helped with all those jobs around the house that John, even before he was ill, was congenitally incapable of doing, tells the tale: 'John said to the President of Alderney, Jon Kay-Mouat, "I know the duchess quite well. D'you think there's any chance of saying hello to her while she's on the island?" And the president replied, "Well, we've already set up the programme. She's only here for an hour, you know, just to meet officials and shake hands. If you want to meet her, so will everyone else. I don't think we can manage it this time. We'll see what we can do next time."

'Anyway, John's wife, Pat, discovered the duchess was to go on an island tour and that the route would take her straight past their house. It was a lovely summer's day, so John put a card table and chair just outside his front gate, and on it a brandy and water to keep him company. He then sat down there to watch the duchess go by. As she came past in the car, John waved. There was a tremendous screech of brakes. The car stopped and reversed. The duchess leapt out of the car. "Hello, John, how are you? How lovely to see you!" And then she stopped and had a conversation, admiring the house and saying that she would like to come back to Alderney for a holiday and see John again, while all this time the President was standing alongside looking embarrassed. Eventually she got back into the car and off they went.'

Nothing seemed to go quite straightforwardly when John met members of the royal family. On his way to being presented with a Sports Presenter of the Year Award by Princess Margaret in London in 1981, the car driven by his trusty chauffeur from Alresford days, Dick Corbett, broke down. A water-pipe sheared near the Fleet service station on the M3. 'We were stuck by the side of the road,' said Pat, who was with him. 'There was a great panic. Dick's wife Joyce, who is also a driver, was due to be coming back from Heathrow on the opposite carriageway. Dick rang the police, explained the situation, and they flagged her down and escorted her round to our side. She picked us up and we got there just in time.'

Pat laughed at another recollection. 'We'd been invited to a cocktail party at Number 10. Beforehand, we'd had some sandwiches in the National Liberal Club because John said, "Oh, we won't get any food in there." In fact there was a very nice buffet. Mrs Thatcher was showing everybody these paintings of prime ministers on the walls and explaining who they were – every single one was a Conservative. And John said, "What happens if you get a Liberal?" She ignored the question.'

On another occasion, a member of the Thatcher clan had shown a more unreserved response. Among a party, including John, which was visiting the Torres vineyards in Catalonia was Mrs Thatcher's daughter Carol. She became alarmed on John's behalf when he was arrested at the airport in Barcelona for carrying a Stanley knife: 'Stop, everybody. We must wait for John. We can't go without him.' John's explanation, that he used the knife 'for cutting my toenails', failed to impress the Polizia, but in the end they let him go.

Another Conservative, a one-time party agent, hotelier, and a Yorkshireman, though not necessarily in that order, became a loyal friend on

Alderney. Geoffrey Rennard was to give great assistance to Pat in the last years as John gradually became more immobile. In the early 1980s he accompanied John to St Emilion for the annual judging of the vintage by the Jurade. The presentation ceremony, at which the twelve successful vignerons receive their trophies and their twelve wines are served with the preceding banquet, was attended by a posse of Lincolnshire farmers. The previous evening John had given a sparkling speech at Château Mon-bousquet, but on the day of the award-giving he was feeling rather poorly. 'He was not at all at his best,' remarked Geoffrey, 'and perched right down the far end of the hall. Knowing that he was due to receive an award, we wondered who was going to collect it on his behalf. But this group of Lincolnshire farmers on hearing the name Arlott started exuber-antly whistling and shouting, to the amazement of the French – the sort of thing you'd hear in a sports arena – and borne along by this tide of applause, John rose from his seat, floated down past our table with a broad grin, never noticed us at all, collected his parchment from the president and wafted back. His feet hardly touched the floor.'

There was a clutch of friends on Alderney whom John saw regularly: Jim Morgan and his wife Stephie, who made a market garden from an overgrown hillside; Elizabeth Beresford, author of *The Wombles*, who with Ronnie Cairnduff plotted three '1920 classic silent movies' – all filmed on the island – of the adventures of 'Rosebud', in which J.A. featured in several unlikely roles as 'Sir Arlott Johns'; Barbara Benton, whose colourful career had encompassed being a continuity girl at Radio Luxembourg, secretary to the conductor Stanford Robinson at the BBC, working in Burma and Palestine and more recently as a Channel TV representative; and Count André D'Aquino, a Polish artist and sculptor with one of the oldest Italian titles – he is the 48th count.

D'Aquino had been specialising in portraits of animals in porcelain and John actively supported his idea of producing a series of cricketers, 'the immortals of the game', with advice on poses and mentions in articles. From the D'Aquino ceramics studio finely sculpted figures were soon being marketed in the cricketing world.

André was one of several people who used to drive John on his daily tour round the island. John's own driving days had come to a spectacular end after a multi-vehicle pile-up in a car park. That is an exaggerated way of saying that he was driving in slippers, one of which caught on the accelerator pedal. Although no one was hurt, damage was caused.

John's friend John Gatrell explains what happened: 'It was about 10.30 in the morning and John had just come out of the Seaview Hotel, where he had been making some arrangements for Christmas. He had been having foot trouble and rammed a whole row of cars. The police had to charge him with careless driving and he was arraigned before the local bench. The Jurats were fairly sympathetic, because he said he would not ever be driving again, and gave him a small fine.'

There were times in John's driving career that would have been quite mirthful, if the possible outcome had not been so serious. The former editor of *Wisden*, Graeme Wright, remembers the occasion when he and Bill Frindall were helping John take empty cardboard boxes from his cellar to the local tip. 'It's halfway down the side of a cliff, and the single track winds round and round. It was the last journey and we were coming back up in John's automatic Maxi. A van was coming down the hill and somehow, I don't quite know how, John put his foot down on the accelerator and not the brake and rammed the van at 5 mph.

'Instead of saying, "Oh, my God," or anything like that, he looked round and asked, "Did he toot?" as if, you're my witness, if he didn't toot we're OK.

'The radiator was damaged on the van, and when we got back to the house he said to Pat, "Terrible, terrible. We had an accident – need a drink. Must have a brandy. First accident I've had in my life." So Pat said, "John, what about the time you drove into the post office wall?" "It's the first time I've had an accident with anything that was moving," he replied indignantly.

'The builder who owned the van arrived half an hour later, and John said urgently, "Find a very good bottle. We'll have to sort this out."'

While John was still driving, he used to meet visitors at the airport and give them a guided tour of Alderney. I remember waiting with him to greet Tony Lewis, whose plane had been delayed by fog. When Tony eventually arrived, a celebratory bottle was opened on the check-in counter, under the appraising eye of customs, and in no time at all the two were reminiscing about their antique-seeking days. As we wended the well-rehearsed route we passed Clarence Wright, the *ITMA* veteran ('Good morning! Nice day!'), whose walking stick waved an acknowledgement, and then further on stopped at The Moorings, a hotel run by Geoff Shaw, ex-Triton of television lighting. The next day John's car gave up the ghost at Crabby Stores. It is pointless to have a posh car on Alderney, because the salt from the sea erodes body and parts in a matter of months, and neither John's Maxi nor later his Maestro was immune.

Tony Lewis had come to the island to interview John for the seventieth-birthday broadcast for Radio 4 which, when transmitted, was heard by the then producer of *Any Questions?*, Carole Stone. She rang and said she was intending to do an edition of the programme on Alderney – would

John still be up to performing in front of an audience? 'His breathing gives him trouble, but I'm sure he would,' was my reply. 'But don't go to Alderney if you decide not to ask him. Having been a founder member he is an obvious choice, and it would be deeply upsetting not to invite him.' In the event John was on form in a vigorous programme. Describing himself as a 'former broadcaster' he was joined round the table by Katharine Whitehorn of the *Observer*, the Conservative MP Edward Du Cann, chairman of the 1922 Committee, and Ian Mikardo, the veteran Labour MP. David Jacobs, who had chaired the programme with charm and poise since Freddie Grisewood retired, spoke first:

> Now, just before we go to the first question, may I say personally what a joy it is for me to have John Arlott in the team, because he was on the very first *Any Questions?* programme all those years ago in the late forties, and was also the man who took the trouble to teach me how to be a broadcaster.

The first question centred on issues raised by a dock strike at Dover. John was exercised by wider implications:

> I've been a trade unionist all my life – my father and grandfather under threat of the sack founded the NALGO branch in Basingstoke – I'm no anti-trade unionist. But the fact is, you see, the trades union movement has become sloppy. People like Ernest Bevin and Aneurin Bevan would have been picked up by the modern educational system, they'd have gone to university, they would have become university dons, they'd never have been in the trades union movement at all. Now the modern educational system scoops up all those with good brains and takes them away and it leaves those who can't pass their 'O' levels to be trades union leaders *[laughter and applause]*. If your intellect is thus limited and for this reason you have a chip on your shoulder, you're not an ideal leader of working people.

In November that same year, 1984, I was visiting Alderney with John's son Robert, who was then working in the wine business and later became a pilot. I had arranged to pick him up in my car in London; 'Anywhere just past Harrods' had been his supremely optimistic suggestion. The traffic was thick, and it looked as if we would miss our flight. Searching anxiously through a steamed-up windscreen, I could see no tall and handsome young man at any kerbside, and there was nowhere to stop. All of a sudden, in the mirror, I was aware of a frantic figure carrying a large case hurling himself down the centre of the road and shouting at the top of his voice. Robert still had enough breath left to phone John from the first available kiosk. There was no way we could make the plane. The last flight of the day was scheduled to leave Eastleigh Airport at 4.30, and here we were at 3.30 still stuck in Knightsbridge. 'Not to worry,' said Robert, returning after the call. 'Dad will ask the plane to wait.' 'What?' I said incredulously.'They're not going to do that!' 'Oh, I think they will,' countered Robert. 'He's one of their biggest customers.'

Having moved to Alderney, John reasoned that those he really wanted to see and who wanted to see him would make the effort to fly over. As it turned out, that was not always the case. The expense, the distance and the time involved were often determining factors, and put some people off, as did worries about the flight. Even so, Geoffrey Moorhouse was one who strapped himself in on four occasions:

'Although I'm not bothered by flying, I've been nearly bothered by flying in that bloody little flying cigar box – that Trislander. Sitting at the back, realising there was no way out except by the side of the pilot. If that damn thing went down in the drink, there was no way you were going to get out, with one pilot and maybe eight people in front of you. I can't hold my breath that long. But I did feel guilty about not going more often.'

Letters from John to friends, former colleagues and acquaintances usually ended with 'When are you coming over?' David Foot had first met John when he was a junior reporter at Yeovil. Years later, John wrote an introduction to Foot's acutely observed book on the Somerset cricketer Harold Gimblett. He invited him to Alderney:

'There he was waiting at the minuscule airport. The conducted tour straightaway of the postage-stamp island. Bad driver. Top gear at 10 m.p.h. Much jerking, about which he seemed oblivious. Nominal discussions about landmarks and historic battlements: but frankly I didn't form the impression he LOVED the place. Nothing that he said, but I sensed there were still regrets about leaving Hants.

'We sat down to the table (of cold meats, left by Pat) at about 3 p.m. and, apart from minor diversions – like the brief arrivals of neighbours for a nominal drink – didn't really leave the table till just before midnight. Once, maybe twice, we descended to the cellar for new bottles. That experience was rather like going into a public library. "Let's try that one – second shelf on your left. And that's a nice little feller, waist-high in front of you." Touch of cricketing language, "waist-high", I suppose. We went up with bottles under both arms and in our hands. Both got discreetly mellow. John did most of the talking. Catholic as ever. Cricketers who never put their hand into their pocket to buy a round, village life (he was interested that I came from a line of gamekeepers), on to philosophical matters, son's death – on which he recurrently pondered aloud – and declining faith.

'Next morning he was late for breakfast. His chest was full of vocal rebellion. Pat, the gentle companion, mentioned in passing that she'd found him asleep on the loo. "Just contemplation," was his riposte. He encouraged me to browse in the splendid library, got me very flatteringly to sign several of my books.

'Excellent correspondent. Whenever I wrote, perhaps with a minor query, his reply came within forty-eight or seventy-two hours. He liked to make little alterations to the original in that thick-nibbed fountain pen. The strong signature never really changed.

'He could be quite scornful about those he didn't like. I'm not sure he always approved of his more waspish private comments. To me, and many others, he was kind and encouraging.'

Geoffrey Moorhouse was another who found him kind and encouraging. 'In my hearing, whenever John said something outrageous about someone, I thought it was always richly deserved. I don't remember him saying anything unpleasant about a decent person.'

In 1981, John's son Tim and his wife Tricia were working in Tokyo. Tim, apart from holding a senior position with Visnews, was opening the bowling for Yokohama. John flew out to visit them, and on his return, with a number of Japanese masks which were soon to decorate the wall of the dining-room, he vowed never again to take a long flight. The journey and the dehydration at altitude had exhausted him. Yet four years later he had apparently forgotten his resolution. This time he set off for Jamaica, having been invited to make the major speech at a banquet in honour of Clive Lloyd during a cricket festival. He got no further than Heathrow, where a doctor had to be called. The spirit was willing, but did not always win.

After that, there were few journeys. The Old Boys' dinner at Basingstoke and the annual Winchester breakfast, a happening which had started when friends had met doing Christmas shopping and decided quite spontaneously that they would meet every year over a mixed grill to soak up the Beaujolais. The 'Men of Arlott', as they became known, sat round a table telling jokes for the unaesthetic chamberpot which was the prize for the best blue story. And there was also the Master's Lunch. John was loath to miss either of these last two events, which took place only a few days apart. Both could be accomplished in one short haul.

One of his rare trips to England was for a Lord's Taverners celebrity romp at Burton-on-Trent in June 1985. John had been one of the earliest members of the Taverners – membership number 19 – and was on the first ever council in the days when they were still unsure of the path they would follow. But it was because he was still chairman of Marcus Robertson's company, who in conjunction with Allied Breweries was helping to mount the event, that he decided to go. Bill Frindall was also there: 'Bill Tidy, the cartoonist, was put on to bowl,' he told me. 'He clean-bowled this chap with his second ball. Arlott, half-watching, seized the public address microphone and said, "That was a perfect cartoonist's dismissal. He drew him forward, crossed him off and rubbed him out." The last words of commentary, John ever gave.'

Another romp in the mid-1980s happened when John sat outside the bar of the sailing club during Alderney Week, giving a commentary on some of the locals attempting to play a game of cricket while standing on inflatable rafts. The familiar Arlott tones wafting across the water amidst the general hilarity caused many a visiting yachtsman to turn his head in wonder.

When a team of Aboriginal cricketers visited Alderney in 1988, John had a line for the occasion. Geoff Rennard was in attendance: 'I got the impression that the main reason they'd come to Alderney was not to play cricket particularly, but to meet John Arlott. His autograph was the thing to have. Before the match, in the garden of Nellie Gray's restaurant where we went for lunch, they made a little presentation to him. Thanking them, he said, "With those green caps, I'd have taken you for Australians, if you weren't so bloody polite." '

As John's health declined and he was less able to move about, boredom set in. I once said to him, semi-seriously, that most of life was boring. 'Yes, it is,' he said, too readily. But his mind was still active, and – though it is not necessarily the same thing – he always had had a low boredom threshold. That revealed itself in his collecting enthusiasms. Whatever the objects – engraved glass, Staffordshire figures, antique bottle-openers – the acquisitive desire was avid and all-embracing. But once he had gone as far as he was likely to go, he was on to the next thing: he needed the stimulation of a new chase.

Illnesses put paid to all that, and brought out the contrary elements in his nature. His son Tim, in his memoir of his father published in 1994, has boldly pulled open the curtains on John's declining years: the scenes in restaurants when he felt he could not get enough air; the demands on Pat and the home nurses, Jane Gaudion and Mandy Kiely, and on relatives and friends; the constant calls for attention; the endless requests for brandy when even wine became an inadequate palliative. Undoubtedly it was a vexed and irksome time for all concerned, particularly Pat, for whom the strain was intense. John's actions were those of a man totally frustrated by infirmity, loathing his vulnerability, and longing for release from the indignities of old age. He had done all he wanted to do, and was fed up with waiting to die.

John's inherent strength made that an almost unbelievably lengthy process. There were so many false alarms. Surely he could not last out? And yet he did, to fight another day. Nobody wanted to see him go. Everybody loved him dearly. But nobody wanted to see him suffer.

Any newspaper headline in the last few years which mentioned the name of Arlott brought apprehension to those who cared for him and knew the state of his health. Once Robert was attacked during an altercation with some local louts when he was driving his father around the island. I caught a glimpse of a fellow strap-hanger's evening paper in the London Underground, and it caused me suspended dismay for a couple of stations.

Another instance was John's falling down his cellar steps in the late 1980s, which resulted in cracked ribs and a splintered spine. Pat was away on a short visit to the mainland, and it was fortunate that John Gatrell was nearby. 'I heard this almighty shout and then a sickening thud. It was a pretty awful mess. He was bleeding profusely and crumpled up in a heap, unconscious. I managed to get him into the recovery position and put my fingers in his mouth to make certain his airway was clear, dialled 999 and fortunately the doctor arrived quickly. The ambulance came shortly afterwards.

'By this time John had come round and was swearing fairly extravagantly. He kept saying to the ambulance men, "Let me die." "Don't be so bloody silly, John," they replied. Just as they got him upstairs and there we all were covered in blood with flashing lights, crises and emergencies and everything, the local builder arrives to talk about the central heating. He took one look and then said, taciturnly, "Well, I think now is probably not the time, is it? I think I better come back."'

John spent much time in various hospitals. At the Radcliffe in Oxford, to the amazement of the nurses, alcohol was fed into his drip-feed on the orders of his physician. Even more amazing to some was the news that his liver was in perfect working order – a great advertisement for wine. 'The Arlott liver processed alcohol in a way that those belonging to other mortals can't do,' laughed David Roper. At hospitals on the south coast, Ian Botham was a regular and devoted visitor. Whenever he was in Alderney, Ian also called in to see his old friend. 'Once John put his head through the bathroom door when he was walking too fast,' said John Gatrell. 'He had developed this slow-medium shuffle and lost his footing.

Ian used to twit him affectionately, "Stop behaving like Linford Christie." '

Perhaps the cruellest blow in all of this battering by the fates was John's virtual loss of his passport to fame. His voice, that God-given instrument, was reduced to a whisper or a gasp. But here again, the spirit of a born fighter refused to give way. He developed a most eloquent facial mime language that would have had Marcel Marceau bowing deferentially. That crinkly face told a story like a relief map, with a grunt being the only concession to audibility. Raising a single eyebrow, or both, or creasing the forehead, or giving an exaggerated wink, all meant different things. When his eyes twinkled, the room smiled.

One longed for the days when he could talk, when, with his head tilted slightly to one side and his eyes looking fractionally upward, he would move his hands in small deprecating gestures, as if he were conducting his words into sentences. There were often long silences, but in those days, when that happened it was because he had nothing to say.

People who did not know John had often found his silences off-putting. But he was never a man for mere polite conversation or easy platitudes. He was a man's man, and enjoyed male company. He disliked talking about himself. He liked some women too, but not in the way that they perhaps expected. Hazel Edelston, the wife of John's close friend and fellow football enthusiast Maurice Edelston, has a view: 'He was not a tactile man. I don't think he thought a lot of women's intellect, either. There were exceptions. He once said to me, "Men will use women just as a physical need, in the same way one needs to have a pee or whatever." Mind you, that was in the 1950s.'

The broadcaster Mavis Nicholson knew John around that time. 'He was certainly more interested in talking to men. Often my feminist toes were curling with annoyance at his attitude, and he would say, "Come on, you Welsh witch, you firebrand, you." He was teasing me out of it.'

Ann Fielden, Christopher's wife, felt that 'He didn't like women who gossiped. They had to listen to him and contribute. He liked women to be straightforward, not ultra-feminine – with frills.' And Debbie Frith, David's wife, was of the opinion that in women's company 'he could sometimes be gauche and awkward'.

The nursery years, with two doting women in tow, a father involuntarily absent and, crucially, no brothers or sisters, meant that John did not have to compete for attention. No doubt that made him sometimes selfish, self-centred and also chauvinistic. Of his generation, he was not alone.

A personal theory, which perhaps does not bear too much analysis, is that his daily proximity to death as a child, witnessing burials from the Cemetery Lodge, sowed the seeds of a melancholic obsession with mortality in his latter years. In 1917, while he was staying in Eastbourne, John had attempted to crawl upstairs to the bedroom where grandfather Clarke's body awaited the undertaker. When he was a little older, he often tried to peer through the keyhole of the mortuary in the cemetery when bodies had arrived. These instances in themselves display no more than the usual morbid curiosity of an adventurous youngster, but decades after, in 1984, he could still become upset when remembering the day his infants' class was told that Violet McLeod and Irene Cornelius, 'the two prettiest girls in the school, had died in the fever hospital up by the old railway bridge near Park Prewett in the murderous post-war scarlatina epidemic'. Or when seven-year-old Reuben Goldstein, 'a gentle, pale, thoughtful creature who lived just off Castens Entry, had taken his own life'. The questions that agonised him then did so still.

As an adult the tragic loss of a cherished son, a dear wife and a baby daughter tipped the balance of his emotional equilibrium. Certainly after Jimmy's death, and even more so after Valerie's, there was a stated death-wish for himself. He had assumed the guilt and burden of what he saw as his own responsibility: a self-made cross. His grief became illogical, as he would occasionally admit. There were, too, elements of self-dramatisation in the display.

It would seem that any belief in God he may have had vanished for a long, long time. Perhaps the divine being was no more than a malevolent mogul? Graeme Wright spoke with John on many subjects other than cricket. 'I think he saw the death of his son as recrimination. You left your wife, I'll take your son. You can have your new happiness, but I'll take one of your happinesses from you – a biblical retribution.'

Mike Brearley also talked with John on the subject. 'There was a certain disillusionment, gloominess and despair about his attitude to life which hit him most strongly with the death of his son. Afterwards, he couldn't really believe there was any real meaning to life. Though possibly he did recognise some sort of theistic being, a divinity that shapes our ends or lies behind things.'

At a late hour, one night in Alderney, I taxed John about his beliefs or lack of them. First he spoke of his father, who was a Congregationalist, and his mother, conventional C. of E. And then of his grandfather, whom he was deputed to take to church in order that he did not go to the pub. And what about him? Simplistic questions draw short answers.

'Do you think there is a God?'

'Well, I say my prayers without question, if that's any answer.'

'That's an easy reply, John.'

(A smile.)

'What do you really think?'

'I do, yes.'

'Have you always thought that?'

'Yes.'

Whether or not his was a kind of popular, community God, towards the end of his life John was always the first down on his knees for prayers in church. In 1991 he received a visit from the Bishop of Basingstoke, the Revd. Michael Manktelow, during which they discussed euthanasia. The bishop gave John a blessing, and thereafter, with rediscovered faith, John would ask Pat to recite the Lord's Prayer every night. A sceptic, ignoring the above testimony, might consider this revival of belief no more than an insurance policy for an imminent journey into eternity.

'Latterly I've become frightened of meeting my maker.'

'Frightened? Why?'

'Because of the unknown. No, not frightened, really. I'm ready to die. I was not really religious until recently . . . No, it's not true. I don't really want to die. Only to avoid the misery of dying.'

'Do you believe in an after-life?'

'I always have.'

'What sort of after-life would you like?'

'I don't really mind. I'll take it as it comes. As long as it's got a wine cellar.'

We said goodbye at the airport. I don't think either of us expected to see each other again. We had been chauffeured through the winding, cobbled streets and the car engine was now silent. John remained quietly in the passenger seat, head bowed. The plane's engines were noisy, ready to leave. I put my arm round his shoulder and kissed him on the forehead. We both mumbled something unintelligible, but words were beyond us. As the Trislander rose in the sky, he was still there.

In fact, we did meet again, but he was too far gone to be remotely his real self. That was really our farewell.

John died at about a quarter past five on the morning of 14 December 1991. A short cough and then he expired, peacefully.

The people gathered in the Island Hall after the funeral felt an entanglement of emotions: happiness, because they had been part of a service that reflected love and triumph; privileged to have known somebody who had enriched their lives; and sad, because they had lost a friend who was a great man in their time.

The tributes to John in the press appeared for days on end: affection, respect, memories of his achievements and generosity being universal chords. Let us settle for a summation from three relatives, two writers, and two cricketers.

Pat: He was very much a family man. A shy man who didn't really flaunt publicity. He certainly didn't use his name like some have done, saying 'Look here, I'm John Arlott, rush around after me.' And he was so kind. Always helping young cricketers and young writers, giving advice if they wanted it. He never thought, 'Well, one day they might take my job.' Peter Walker, Jim Laker if he was still here, and lots of others would say the same thing. People trusted him.

Tim: Aside from being my father, he was the most interesting person I have met in my life. He thought profoundly about the problems everyone experiences and never spoke in cliché. To most people he seemed warm and humorous, but to me, because he was my father, especially so. I share his views on everything – politics, wine, life – and I know I will never meet anybody who will have such a deep effect on me.

Robert: He was immensely perceptive of people – he would attribute that partly to his years in the police. And something Tim admired enormously was his ability to understand an audience, and be sufficiently in control of his thoughts and what he was doing to be able to vary what he was saying in a speech accordingly and very competently. That's a hell of a talent. He was a loyal friend. If you asked a favour, he'd hate to let you down – almost Sicilian, in that respect. He would want to feel that he never let anybody down socially, morally, professionally. 'I'll never let you down' was a phrase in his vocabulary.

Geoffrey Moorhouse: Such a generous man – the outstanding characteristic. Nobody, as far as I know, ever asked in vain for a foreword to a book or a leg-up. There are not many people like that. John never turned anybody down. It affected his own work because he spread himself too thinly. I think he might have been a great writer if he'd worked less hard or not done so many different things. [Kingsley Amis has said exactly the same thing.]

He was anti-establishment. He never forgot his origins and that loyalty, which some working-class hold onto and others, of course, don't. It's very closely linked to sentimentality. I'm tarred with the same brush, too.

He could be strangely insensitive in going on about Valerie in front of Pat. In other ways he was a very sensitive man. I admire Pat, she had a lot to put up with, and as far as I know, she never failed him.

He's a man I wish I'd known earlier than I did, and I wish I'd known him better than I did. He was a very rich man – intellectually, I mean. C.L.R. James put it all in that one phrase, 'What do they know of cricket who only cricket know.' That's why John was so terrific.

Graeme Wright: I was interested in him more as a human being rather than a personality. I'm not sure the personality aspect sat very happily on him. He could perform it, but you almost saw him looking back and thinking, 'How did I get here?' Thinking perhaps that he didn't belong. The autobiography confirmed that a little bit. Maybe using the third person was a device, but it was also an easy device to distance himself from the personality he'd become – as if people accepted him for that, but didn't accept him as the real John Arlott.

I think he saw a lot of himself in Ian Botham – being accepted for your talent and not being accepted for being yourself when your own personality comes out. Certainly John felt that at Lord's. Being offered honorary life membership put him in a quandary. But although his parents would have brought him up to behave in what they saw as a proper manner, he would never have had instilled the middle-class worry about what others thought. Grammar school wouldn't have taught you the things you inherited in a private education.

Players made him privy to their secrets. They trusted him. He was interested in them as people and they knew he would never exploit them.

Mike Brearley: He was extremely generous both in thought and deed, but if you were beyond the pale, you really were beyond the pale. There were certain topics on which you had to have quite a bit of courage to oppose him. There was a tendency to hog a situation, which could have a hypnotic effect, particularly as he got older. But really, he enjoyed people who enjoyed his stories and who would set him going. He was also very interested in what you had to say as well.

He became something of a workaholic as far as cricket was concerned – he didn't often turn down a request to write things. And he certainly would never turn down anything a professional cricketer asked him to do.

Ian Botham: He was very kind, very honest and very straightforward. There were no punches pulled. If John had something to say, he'd say it. We just hit it off and I spent as much time as I could with him. I would have loved to have done a tour with him because I found the man so interesting. He was very warm and a very good friend. I just wish there were more people like John Arlott around in the game of cricket.

G.H. Lewes said: 'It is not by his faults, but by his excellences that we must measure a great man.' So be it of John Arlott. He did everything to the optimum. If his needs were many, his responses were magnificent. In this cynical age, eulogies are suspect. But it is true to say that nobody has ever had a greater capacity to inspire affection from so many, or to give so much pleasure in return. John was a very human human being.

When people die, it is often said that they will never be forgotten. With the best intentions, that is sometimes no more than a wish. Due to modern technology, however, John's voice *will* be with us forever. He cannot be forgotten. He can never die. He will always remain.

On the Christmas Day following John's departure, Ian Botham and his family made a loving gesture in his memory, breaking open a bottle of Beaujolais by the side of his grave. Symbolically, they were saying what so many of the people who knew John, and who have contributed their memories to these pages, would want to put into words. The same words spoken by Jack Donovan as he closed his moving address at the funeral service: 'Rest in peace, John. Goodbye, old friend.'

Prayer for an Immortal Line

Now passes basic metal from my brain,
Slow melting through the deep-banked fires of thought
For spark-flung forging into lengths of chain,
Each link with hammer, sweat and fervour wrought,
Each link then filed with patient, craftsman care
Until the crude and hard-wrought edges show
The humble metal's native greyness bare,
Then polished grimly to a sullen glow.
Yet, while I work, I know these chains must snap
Beneath the tug of time, and, rusted red,
Will pass, rejected, to the age's scrap.
But yet I pray that, when my name is dead,
One age-proof link will still reflect the light,
Its temper fix the smith's endeavour bright.

From *Of Period and Place*, 1944

APPENDIX A

'Death on the Road'

'Death on the Road' first appeared in the Evening News *on 20 October 1952.*

One more commuter has answered his maker,
One more cold motor has gone to the breaker:
One more fatality scored to A3,
One more dark stain on the road to the sea.

With his narrow-brimmed bowler and tight-rolled umbrella,
John Jones was well tailored, an orthodox fella:
If not quite so slim just as pinkily clean
As when he played back for the second fifteen.

They recall at his office the day of his death,
How he rushed through his work – barely pausing for breath –
And his typist will tell, with a well-rehearsed sigh,
How three typing mistakes missed his hurrying eye.

He took lunch at his desk and made no stop for tea,
Signed the post, locked the safe and secreted the key;
Dashed out of the door at a quarter-to-five,
And that was the last time they saw him alive.

He'd parked his new Sheerline directly outside,
His pet acquisition, his Simonized pride.
He 'revved' her and – no hesitation or fuss –
Drove into the Strand and cut in on a bus.

Along through Westminster he bored through the crush
And made Chelsea ahead of the five o'clock rush;
Down the King's Road at forty and taking a chance
On his way to the tennis club's annual dance.

In a devilish hurry to get down through Surrey,
He slashed through the dark in a rain-splashing flurry;
No checking at crossings; the horn – and ahead –
And at two sets of lights he nipped through on the red.

On the road to the South that the maps call A3,
It's a sin to drive slow and a job to ride free;
The traffic swills on like a storm down a drain
And the wide boys stick tight to the right-hand side lane.

At home, in his villa ('own steps to the sea'),
He thought with possessive uxorious glee,
His wife would be waiting as women should be,
For the hum of his motor, the sound of his key.

That his wife was at home was a fair enough guess,
But with no thought of waiting. She couldn't care less.
She was deep in the world – that male arrogance loathes –
Of secrets and envies and schemes about clothes.

Was her precious new dance-frock – so startlingly flared –
Absolutely unique, as Alphonse had declared?
Would the dance-floor reveal – she felt sick with the shame –
Someone else in a copy – exactly the same?

But then she recalled how she needed a mink.
Why he couldn't see it, she just couldn't think.
It was plainly her duty – how dare he protest?
She was doing him credit by looking her best.

They would dine at the 'Royal', then on to the dance
– Here she gave his cold bedroom a cursory glance –
His suit was put out and his studs were put in
And she felt she had earned quite a large double gin.

Meanwhile, taking bends without slackening pace,
Jones on the by-pass was trying to race
A black sixteen Riley and now, at full bore
The speedo' was showing a firm eighty-four.

He drew up with the Riley and then took the lead,
And laughed with the heady excitement of speed.
Now he chased a new Chrysler and, as it pulled wide,
He pressed down his foot and went past it inside.

With his lips curled apart half a snarl, half a grin,
And an ache in his stomach too tensely held in,
He plunged down the cats'-eyes' clear ribbon of light
Through the gulf that his headlights cut out of the night.

As he pushed her on harder and touched eighty-five,
He thought with wild hope of the club's record drive
Now held by Bill Griffith who'd done – so he swore –
A flat eighty minutes from City to door.

(BRITISH ROAD SERVICES, gleamingly red,
Driving to London with ingots of lead;
A full sixteen tons of it loaded behind
And supper the thought in the driver's tired mind.)

Jones had left the wide concrete and come to the tar,
Too narrow a confine for this man and car;
But he wanted that record, he wouldn't be slowed
And he held to his pace on the crown of the road.

The sound of his tyres rose an octave in pitch
And he scared a pedestrian into a ditch.
A road-scout at Fernhurst who saw him go past
Remarked to himself: 'That's a damned sight too fast.'

Just before Midhurst five cars in a line
Slowed our Jones down to a mere twenty-nine.
His attempt on the record had come to an end
Unless he could pass them before that next bend.

He gave her the gun to the very last rev.,
And pulled out to his right past a Ford and a 'Chev',
He overtook four of them – all but the last –
He had come to the corner – and still was not past.

BRITISH ROAD SERVICES, spelt out in white,
Loomed up from Chichester, out of the night.
Twenty-two tons of it, lorry and load –
And it and poor Jones need the same piece of road.

So that was the end of Jones' hurricane ride
For he couldn't pull in and he couldn't pull wide.
He stood on the brake but – as clinical fact –
He was dead in the moment before it could act.

The lorry came on, strong and true as a train,
And the bulb from the dashboard flashed once in his brain.
The high wheels rolled on with no trace of a hitch.
The police found his ribs and his sump in the ditch.

His wife started up at the wheel on the drive
And thought he was late if he'd started at five.
Her eyes were all bright, her complexion was pink,
From the fire and excitement, cosmetics and drink.

The police sergeant gave one short ring on the bell,
Rehearsed his hard message – and hoped he'd do well –
As he heard the sharp cough of high heels on the floor
And saw a bare arm through the glass of the door.

She knew from his carefulness, not what he said,
That the man she had waited at home for was dead.
Her pulse filled her head with a thundering drag
And her face crumpled up like a wet paper bag.

Her stomach went lear, and her dentures were dry:
Her tongue wouldn't swear, and her eyes wouldn't cry:
And the sergeant, whose shift should have ended at three,
Suggested he made her a strong cup of tea.

When the news reached the tennis club dance Jones was dead,
They had two minutes' silence: and plenty was said,
As they formed up again in their groups at the bar
Of the hazards of driving a fast motor car.

Now, the trespasses man carries with him through life
Are not like insurance bequeathed to his wife.
He himself must resolve them as well as he knows,
Or else take them with him wherever he goes.

And, if Jones met his death very far in the wrong,
Well, the time for repentance need never be long.
He paid with his life the stern forfeit he owed
For defying the Highway's definitive Code.

If his hope of salvation seems gloomily dark
– For he wasn't religious – it's well to remark
That in front of his heart at the time of the crash
Was a silver St Christopher nailed to the dash.

And did good St Christopher guard Jones that night
And conduct him along to the throne-room of light?
Or did the old Saint know he came there by chance
As a car-salesman's souvenir brought back from France?

Jones was laden with sin just as all of us are,
And it wasn't his soul that was driving the car,
When the lobes he'd have used if he'd thought about God
Were smashed in a flash by a hot piston-rod.

We may pity Jones less for his death on the road
Than the far too brief time that he had to unload
His burden of mortal and venial sin
As the bonnet went down, and the engine came in.

The subsequent pamphlet which reprinted the poem included drawings by
Margaret Wetherbee. There was also a dedication to John Betjeman, which read:
'This grotesque drive which deplorably – even fatally – failed to allow for the
appreciation of landscape or architecture'. A number of refinements were made
to the text:

On the road to the South that the maps call A3

carried on with:

And which runs down to Portsmouth and Places-on-Sea,
He went headlong and wild as a storm down a drain,
Holding tight as a leech to the overtake lane.

Also, an additional verse added flavour to the wife's 'large double gin':

She looked in the mirror and profiled her bust
And laughed in contempt of all masculine lust.
She inhaled at a Churchman and felt her heart swell
At the thought of the night and a whiff of Chanel.

The other alterations worth noting were minor. The 'black sixteen Riley' became
a 'vintage green Bentley'; 'BRITISH ROAD SERVICES, half-an-hour late' were
'driving to London with maximum freight'; and the police found Jones's 'heart'
and 'hat' in the ditch rather than his 'ribs' and 'sump'.

John Arlott's Publications

A complete bibliography of the writings of John Arlott would take a book in itself, and is likely to be forthcoming eventually from the hands of the assiduous Geoffrey Whitelock. He has already listed many titles, and the results of his initial research appeared in various issues of the *Journal of the Cricket Society* between 1977 and 1980.

The following catalogue, which relies heavily on Whitelock's work, concentrates solely on books and booklets of which John is the author, co-author or editor.

Landmarks: A Book of Topographical Verse for England and Wales
Cambridge University Press, 1943, 236pp Chosen by Sir George Rostrevor Hamilton and John Arlott.
Five Poems by J.A. are included: 'Brighton', 'Southampton', 'Cricket at Worcester, 1938', 'Basingstoke' and 'Isle of Wight'. New edition with many revisions and additions, entitled *The Coloured Counties*, J.M. Dent, 1988, 312pp. Selected and with an introduction by John Arlott

Of Period and Place
Jonathan Cape, 1944, 45pp
Twenty-five poems, including three on cricket: 'On a Great Batsman', 'Cricket at Worcester, 1938' and 'The Old Cricketer'

Clausentum
Jonathan Cape, 1946, 28pp
Twelve sonnets by J.A. Drawings by Michael Ayrton

Indian Summer
Longmans, Green & Co., 1947, 141pp
An account of the Indian tour of England, 1946

From Hambledon to Lord's: The Classics of Cricket
Christopher Johnson, 1948, 143pp
John Nyren, Charles Cowden Clarke, The Revd. James Pycroft, The Revd. John Mitford, Assembled, Edited and Discussed by John Arlott. New edition with preface by J.A. published by Barry Shurlock (Winchester), 1975

Gone to the Cricket
Longmans, Green & Co., 1948, 206pp
An account of the South African tour of England, 1947

How to Watch Cricket
Sporting Handbooks, 1948, 86pp
  Further edition (90pp), 1949, including review of cricket books published in
  1948. Revised edition (111pp), Collins Willow, 1983. Paperback edition,
  Fontana, 1984

First Time in America: A Selection of Poems Never Before Published in the USA
Duell, Sloan & Pearce Inc. (New York), 1948, 199pp
  Collected and introduced by J.A. First American edition. Not published in
  Britain

The Middle Ages of Cricket
Christopher Johnson, 1949, 187pp
  'Being Sketches of the Players by William Denison and "Cricket
  Recollections" from Oxford Memories by James Pycroft. The Whole
  Assembled, Edited and Discussed by John Arlott'

Concerning Cricket: Studies of the Play and Players
Longmans, Green & Co., 1949, 156pp
  A collection of essays, some of which had previously appeared in periodicals.
  Second impression 1950.

The Old Man
Longmans, Green & Co., 1949, 34pp
  Only twelve copies printed. An off-print of pp123–56 of *Concerning Cricket*

Gone to the Test Match
Longmans, Green & Co., 1949, 192pp
  An account of the Australian tour of England, 1948

*Wickets, Tries and Goals: Review of Play and Players in Modern Cricket, Rugby
and Soccer*
Sampson Low, 1949, 236pp
  By John Arlott, Wilfred Wooller and Maurice Edelston

Cricket in the Counties: Studies of First Class Counties in Action
Saturn Press, 1950, 272pp
  By W.E. Bowes, W. Wooller, S.C. Griffith, T.P.B. Smith, John Kay, E.M.
  Wellings, Crawford White and John Arlott. Edited and introduced by John
  Arlott

Gone with the Cricketers
Longmans, Green & Co., 1950, 160pp
  An account of the MCC tour of South Africa, 1948–49, and the New Zealand
  Tour of England, 1949

Cricket: A Reader's Guide
National Book League and Cambridge University Press, 1950, 20pp
  An annotated selective bibliography

The First Test Match: England v. Australia 1877
Phoenix House, 1950, 62pp
  By John Arlott and Stanley Brogden.

Maurice Tate
Phoenix House, 1951, 65pp
  A brief biography

Days at the Cricket
Longmans, 1951, 199pp
  An account of the West Indies tour of England, 1950

The Problem of Infantile Paralysis
Infantile Paralysis Fellowship, c.1951, 8pp
  Three issues with different covers. One of the issues entitled *The Truth about Polio*

Two Summers at the Tests
Sportsman's Book Club, 1952, 320pp
  A composite volume of parts of *Gone to the Cricket* and *Gone to the Test Match*.
  Further edition with new introduction, Pavilion Books, 1986

The Echoing Green: Cricket Studies
Longmans, Green & Co., 1952, 165pp
  A collection of essays, some previously published in periodicals. SBC edition,
  1957

Athol Rowan: A Memoir
R. Clay (Bungay), 1952, 99pp
  Ten copies off-printed from *The Echoing Green*

Concerning Soccer
Longmans, Green & Co., 1952, 186pp
  A collection of essays

Cricket
Burke 'Pleasures of Life' Series, 1953, 278pp
  A dozen essays, with substantial extracts from other authors

The Works of J.C. Clay
Burke, 1953, 24pp
  Three copies off-printed from *Cricket*

British Sporting Stories
News of the World, 1953, 223pp
  An anthology

Death on the Road
James Barrie, 1953, 23pp
  Poem by J.A. Drawings by Margaret Wetherbee

Test Match Diary 1953
James Barrie, 1953, 212pp
  An account of the Test matches between England and Australia, 1953. SBC
  edition, 1954

Theatre of the Empire of Great Britaine (parts 1–4) by John Speed, entitled *John
Speed's England*
Phoenix House, 1953–54
  Edited by J.A. with note

Australian Test Journal
Phoenix House, 1955, 160pp
  An account of the MCC tour of Australia, 1954–55

The Picture of Cricket
Penguin Books, 1955, 32pp
  A delightful essay on the history of cricket illustrations – prints, photographs,
  cartoons, cigarette-cards, postcards. King Penguin Books No. 73

Neville Rogers: An Appreciation
Boscombe Printing Co. (Bournemouth), 1956, 6pp
  Twelve signed copies only

Leo Harrison: An Appreciation
Boscombe Printing Co. (Bournemouth), 1957, 8pp
  Seventy signed copies only

Tetbury Cricket Club: Sam Cook's Benefit Year
No printer or publisher named, 4pp
  An appreciation written for the club. Special benefit match, The Recreation
  Ground: Gloucestershire CCC v. Tetbury CC, Sunday 7 July 1957

Hampshire County Cricket: The Official History of the Hampshire County Cricket Club
Phoenix House, 1957, 240pp
  By H.S. Altham, J.A., E.D.R. Eagar and Roy Webber. J.A. contributed Part
  II, 'Between the Two Wars', pp79–138. SBC edition, 1958

Alletson's Innings
Epworth Press, 1957, 40pp
  First edition limited to 200 signed copies. A study of E.B. Alletson's innings
  of 189 for Notts v. Sussex at Hove in 1911. Second edition 1958. New
  edition (103pp), J.W. McKenzie, Ewell, 1991. Limited to 250 copies plus
  ordinary edition. Includes previously unpublished letters written by E.B.
  Alletson and his contemporaries to J.A., together with additional photographs
  etc. and a new foreword by J.A.

English Cheeses of the South and West
Harrap, 1958, text 26pp

Desmond Eagar: A Memoir on his Retirement from First-Class Cricket
Boscombe Printing Co. (Bournemouth), 1958, 8pp

Derek Shackleton: An Appreciation
Boscombe Printing Co. (Bournemouth), 1958, 8pp
　　Fifty signed copies only.

John Arlott's Cricket Journal
Heinemann, 1958, 255pp
　　An account of the 1958 season, particularly the Tests against New Zealand

V.H.D. Cannings: An Appreciation
Boscombe Printing Co. (Bournemouth), 1958, 8pp
　　Fifty signed copies only

The Boy Collins
Billing & Sons, 1959, 12pp
　　Fifteen signed copies only. A brief Life of A.E.J. Collins

Attention
Newman Neame Take Home Books, 1959, 15pp
　　Pamphlet designed by Dennis Johnson

John Arlott's Cricket Journal No. 2
Heinemann, 1959, 260pp
　　A diary of the 1959 season in England and the Test series v. India

J.R. Gray: A Biographical Note
Boscombe Printing Co. (Bournemouth), 1959, 12pp
　　Fifty signed copies only

Cricket on Trial: John Arlott's Cricket Journal No. 3
Heinemann, 1960, 256pp
　　A journal of the 1960 season, including the Tests v. South Africa

Roy Marshall: A Biographical Note
Boscombe Printing Co. (Bournemouth), 1961, 16pp
　　Fifty signed copies only

Crime and Punishment
Newman Neame Take Home Books, 1961, 16pp
　　Designed by Susan Morton

The Australian Challenge: John Arlott's Cricket Journal No. 4
Heinemann, 1961, 238pp
　　A journal covering the 1961 season, especially the Tests v. Australia. SBC
　　edition, 1963

Colin Ingleby-Mackenzie: A Profile
Boscombe Printing Co. (Bournemouth), 1962, 12pp
  Fifty signed copies only

Hampshire County Cricket Club 1863–1963
(Hampshire v. An England XI) (Southampton, Hampshire CCC, 1963) 4pp
  By H.S. Altham and J.A. An edition of 1550 copies, the first fifty containing
  the aquatints hand-printed by Kenneth New as a contribution to the Hampshire
  CCC Centenary Fund

Arthur Holt: An Appreciation
Boscombe Printing Co. (Bournemouth), 1963, 8pp
  Fifty signed copies only

Mervyn Burden: A Memoir
Boscombe Printing Co. (Bournemouth), 1964, 8pp
  Twenty-five signed copies only

Henry Horton: A Biographical Note
Boscombe Printing Co. (Bournemouth), 1964, 12pp
  Fifty signed copies only

Peter Sainsbury: An Appreciation
Boscombe Printing Co. (Bournemouth), 1965, 10pp
  Fifty signed copies only

Rothman's Jubilee History of Cricket, 1890–1965
Arthur Barker, 1965, 212pp

Vintage Summer: 1947
Eyre & Spottiswoode, 1967, 190pp
  Memoir of a season twenty years earlier

Cricket: The Great Ones. Studies of the Eight Finest Batsmen of Cricket History
Pelham Books, 1967, 188pp
  Includes a preface and 'Jack Hobbs' by J.A. SBC edition, 1968

Lord's and the MCC
Pitkin 'Pride of Britain' Books, 1967, 24pp
  By H.S. Altham and J.A.

Pageantry of Sport from the Age of Chivalry to the Age of Victoria
Paul Elek, 1968, 128pp
  By J.A. and Arthur Daley. Anthology including Pycroft, Pierce Egan and W.J.
  Prowse on cricket, pp72–8. Introduction by J.A. pp13–53

Soccer: The Great Ones. Studies of Eight Great Football Players
Pelham Books, 1968, 160pp
  Preface by J.A. pp5–8. Eight other contributors

Cricket: The Great Bowlers. Studies of Ten Great Bowlers of Cricket History
Pelham Books, 1968, 190pp
  Includes a one-page preface and 'Jim Laker' by J.A. Eight other contributors

Cricket: The Great All-Rounders. Studies of Ten of the Finest All-Rounders of Cricket History
Pelham Books, 1969, 184pp
  Includes preface and 'Keith Miller' by J.A.

David White
Boscombe Printing Co. (Bournemouth), 1969, 8pp
  Twenty-five signed copies only

The Noblest Game: A Book of Fine Cricket Prints
Harrap, 1969, unnumbered pp
  By Sir Neville Cardus and J.A. Also limited signed edition of one hundred
  copies, quarter-bound green morocco. Reissued edition (30 + 129pp) with new
  introduction by J.A., 1986

Jim Laker
Privately printed, c.1969–70, 18pp
  Limited edition of six copies. Off-print pp139–56 of *Cricket: The Great Bowlers*

Cricket: The Greatest Captains. Studies of Eight Great Captains of Cricket
Pelham Books, 1971, 152pp
  Two-page preface by J.A. Eight other contributors

Fred: Portrait of a Fast Bowler
Eyre & Spottiswoode, 1971, 192pp
  Biography of F.S. Trueman. Paperback edition, Coronet, 1974. New edition
  (198pp), Methuen, 1983

The Ashes 1972
Pelham Books, 1972, 182pp
  An account of the England–Australia Tests of 1972

Island Camera: The Isles of Scilly in the Photography of the Gibson Family
David & Charles, 1973, 110pp
  Compiled by J.A. in collaboration with Rex Cowan and Frank Gibson. Second
  edition (112pp) 1983, with note on the edition and fresh reproductions

A Hundred Years of County Cricket
British Post Office, 1973, 24pp
  A souvenir containing three commemorative stamps (3p, 7½p, 9p), drawings
  of W.G. Grace, to celebrate county cricket 1873–1973

The Snuff Shop
Michael Joseph, 1974, 61pp
  A history of Fribourg & Treyer Ltd

My Favourite Cricket Stories
Lutterworth, 1974, 148pp
  An anthology of essays and stories by ten authors. Introduction by J.A.
  pp9–11. SBC edition, 1975. New edition, Peerage, 1986

The Oxford Companion to Sports and Games
Oxford University Press, 1975, 1144pp
  Paperback edition (1010pp), Paladin, 1977

Krug: House of Champagne
Davis-Poynter, 1976, 244pp

Burgundy Vines and Wines
Davis-Poynter, 1976, 268pp
  By J.A. and Christopher Fielden. Paperback edition, Quartet, 1978

The Plain Man's Guide to Wine
Michael Joseph, 1976, 162pp
  By Raymond Postgate. Revised by J.A.

Arlott and Trueman on Cricket
BBC, 1977, 280pp
  Edited by Gilbert Phelps. Includes thirteen chapters by J.A. Also three poems:
  'On a Great Batsman', 'To John Berry Hobbs on his Seventieth Birthday'
  and 'The Old Cricketer', plus an extract from *Fred: Portrait of a Fast Bowler*
  and an anthology of cricket literature

An Eye for Cricket
Hodder & Stoughton, 1979, 208pp
  By Patrick Eagar and J.A.

John Arlott's Book of Cricketers
Lutterworth Press and Angus & Robertson (Australia), 1979, 180pp
  Introduction and twenty-five essays reprinted from various periodicals. Further
  edition, Readers Union, 1982. Paperback edition, Sphere, 1992

The Master: An Appreciation
Privately printed, 1979, 6pp
  Twenty signed copies. Off-print from pp3–9 of *John Arlott's Book of Cricketers*

Jack Hobbs: Profile of the Master
John Murray/Davis-Poynter, 1981, 144pp
  Paperback edition, Penguin, 1982

A Word from Arlott
Pelham Books, 1983, 240pp
  A collection of J.A.'s broadcasts, cricket commentaries and writings, selected
  by David Rayvern Allen

Arlott on Cricket
Collins Willow, 1984, 308pp
 J.A.'s writings on the game, edited by David Rayvern Allen. Paperback edition,
 Fontana, 1985

Wine
Oxford University Press (Small Oxford Books), 1984, 112pp
 Compiled by J.A. 'A pocket anthology of man's celebration of wine in literature
 from the time of the Bible onwards'

Another Word from Arlott
Pelham Books, 1985, 312pp
 A further collection of J.A.'s broadcasts, cricket commentaries and writings,
 selected by David Rayvern Allen

Arlott on Wine
Collins Willow, 1986, 224pp
 Edited by David Rayvern Allen. Paperback edition, Fontana, 1987

John Arlott's 100 Greatest Batsmen
Queen Anne Press, 1986, 280pp
 Revised edition, 1989, with figures for current players updated to end of 1988
 English season

Arlott: In Conversation with Mike Brearley
Hodder & Stoughton, 1986, 143pp
 Based on the Channel Four Television series

The Essential John Arlott: Forty Years of Classic Cricket Writing
Collins Willow, 1989, 320pp
 Edited by David Rayvern Allen. Paperback edition, Fontana, 1991

Basingstoke Boy: The Autobiography
Collins Willow, 1990, 304pp
 Also a de luxe limited edition of 200 signed and numbered copies, Boundary
 Books, Guild Publishing. Paperback edition, Fontana, 1992

Harold Gimblett's Hundred
Richard Walsh Books, 1991, 8pp
 Limited signed edition of 123 copies. The first twenty-five copies bound, and
 signed by J.A. and the five survivors from the match in May 1935 at Frome
 between Somerset and Essex where, on his county debut, Gimblett scored
 123, reaching his century in 63 minutes: H.D. Burrough, R.A. Ingle, T.N.
 Pearce, F. Rist, R. Smith. Reproduction of lyric originally composed to music
 by The Yetties.

Inevitably, in such a long writing career, there were a number of projects that
did not reach fruition: a book on Felix (Nicholas Wanostrocht) and his

nineteenth-century cricketing contemporaries, of which a 111pp typescript draft exists; another on Craig, the Surrey Poet; and one on the philosophy of cricket.

There were undeveloped plans in other fields: a booklet on the churches of Bournemouth following J.A.'s article on the subject in *Hampshire: The County Magazine*; a collaboration with his son Robert on wine labels; a book on Beaujolais; and two ventures with Christopher Fielden, a survey of the wines of Alsace and a celebration of the great Burgundy estate Romanée-Conti.

A Liberal Party leaflet issued during the 1959 election campaign mentions a book on aquatint engraving: this may have been a concept for the old King Penguin series.

Discography

John Arlott's voice has been reproduced many times and in several forms. In impersonation it has enriched the repertoire of stand-up comics and after-dinner speakers. Early on the scene were Jonathan Miller in the revue *Out of the Blue* and Peter Cavanagh as one of Carroll Levis's discoveries; much later came the dramatist's conception in *Underwood's Finest Hour* and *P'tang Yang Kipperbang*. Modern technology found a more durable market for his spoken words, although the singles, 78s and LPs did not escape deletion. The following is a selection of some of the commercially-issued discs in which John was involved.

Highlights of Twenty-One Years of Sports Report, *from 1948 to 1969.* BBC Records 29M, 1969
   J.A. on England v. Australia Test matches, 1948, and Jim Laker's 19 wickets for England, 1956

Cricket: The Lord's Taverners. BBC Records 86M, 1970
   Readings by members of the Lord's Taverners during the tea intervals of the Players' County League 1970 season, televised on BBC–2. Cast: J.A., Alec Bedser, Ian Carmichael, Leslie Crowther, Graham Hill, Donald Houston, Peter May, Mick McManus, Brian Rix, John Snagge and Eric Sykes. Cricket at Worcester, 1938, read by J.A. *Maurice Tate* (by J.A.) read by Alec Bedser. More reflections by J.C. Clay (from *Cricket* by J.A.) read by Donald Houston

Cricket: The Sovran King of Sports. Argo PLP 1182, 1972
   An anthology of poetry and prose read by J.A., Valentine Dyall, Robin Holmes, Russell Napier and Michael Parkinson. J.A.'s contributions: 'The Men of Hambledon' (John Nyren); 'Season's End' (E.V.B. Christian); 'Cricket at Worcester, 1938' (J.A.); 'To John Berry Hobbs on his Seventieth Birthday' (J.A.); 'The Names' (Thomas Moult). Also sleeve note

The World of the Countryside: John Arlott Reads Poetry by John Clare, Robert Bloomfield, Stephen Duck and George Crabbe. Argo SPA 304, 1974
   Interspersed with folk songs performed by The Yetties, Cyril Tawney, Bob Arnold, The Druids, Frankie Armstrong, The Critics, Barry Skinner. Incidental music by The Yetties and Trevor Crozier's Broken Consort.

John Arlott Talks Cricket. Charisma Records CAS 1157, cassette CASMC 1157, 1982. Reissue CD and cassette with three souvenir prints by Ralph Steadman (C.B. Fry, Hobbs and Sutcliffe, Jim Laker), CASCD 1157, CASMX 1157, 1993
   Side One: 'Early Memories', 'May's Bounty' 'Mead/Brown/Tennyson/Strudwick'
   Side Two: 'The Golden Days', 'Laker/Hobbs/Sutcliffe/Fry'

The Lord's Taverners. Best of Test Match Special. BBC Records and Haven Record
Co. Ltd, Haven 1017, 1984
 Featuring Rex Alston, J.A., Trevor Bailey, Henry Blofeld, Farokh Engineer,
Jack Fingleton, Bill Frindall, Brian Johnston, Alan McGilvray, Christopher
Martin-Jenkins and Fred Trueman. Archive material. J.A.'s introduction
recorded at BBC Radio Jersey, 4 April 1984, describing inception and
development of BBC Radio Test cricket commentary and his involvement with
Test Match Special

The Sound of Cricket: John Arlott and The Yetties. The Yetties record/cassette
YETLP 3003, YETC 3003, 1984
 1st Innings: 1 J.A.: Introduction. Song: 'Cricket on the Village Green'. 2 J.A.:
Maker of Bat and Ball. Song: 'John Small'. 3 J.A.: The Cricketers of Hambledon
on Windmill Down, 1789. 4 Song: 'Stonewall Jack'. J.A.: The Old Cricketer. 5
J.A.: Introduction. Song: 'I Keeps it There er Thereabout'. 6 J.A.: Introduction.
Song: 'The Flower Bowler'.
 2nd Innings: 1 J.A.: Fred Grace. Song: 'The High Catch'. 2 J.A.: The Master
Artful Dodgers. Song: 'A Tickle o' me Spinnin' Finger'. 3 J.A.: Introduction.
Song: 'Four Jolly Bowlers'. 4 J.A.: Pride of the County. Song: 'Harold Gimblett's
Hundred'. 5 J.A.: Ian Botham, Somerset CCC.
 Song: 'Somerset/Beefy's Army'. J.A.: Closing.
 All lyrics by J.A. with the exception of 'Cricket on the Village Green' and
'Somerset/Beefy's Army'. Music by The Yetties

Cricket: The Golden Age. BBC Radio Collection, c.1988
 Includes interviews with Charles Kortright and Jack Hobbs

*John Arlott: The Voice of Cricket. Classic commentaries from the Game's Most
Authoritative Voice.* Double cassette, BBC Radio Collection, ISBN 0563 4102 13,
1990
 Side One – The Forties: 4th Test at Headingley 1948, Hutton b. Lindwall
81; 5th Test at The Oval 1948, Bradman's last Test; 1st Test at Durban 1948–
9, last-ball win for England; 5th Test at Port Elizabeth 1948–9, England chase
120 an hour to win
 Side Two – The Fifties: 3rd Test at Trent Bridge 1950, Worrell and Weekes,
Ramadhin and Valentine; 5th Test at The Oval 1951, Hutton out 'obstructing
the field'; 2nd Test at Trent Bridge 1954, Pakistan's first visit, Compton's highest
Test score (278); 4th Test v. Australia at Old Trafford 1956, Laker's 19 wickets;
4th Test v. West Indies at Headingley 1957, Loader's hat-trick
 Side Three – The Sixties: 2nd Test at Lords 1963, Dexter faces Hall and
Griffith; Gillette Cup Final 1963, First one-day final, Sussex v. Worcs; 5th
Test at the Oval 1964, Trueman's 300th Test wicket, Boycott's first 'ton'; 2nd
Test at Trent Bridge 1965, Graeme Pollock's 125
 Side Four – The Seventies and 1980: Prudential World Cup Final at Lord's
1975, Clive Lloyd's match; 2nd Test at Lord's 1975, J.A.'s 'freaker'; Centenary
Test at Melbourne 1977, Randall's heroic 174; 3rd Test at Trent Bridge 1977,
Boycott runs out Randall; 1st Test at Edgbaston 1978, Gower's first Test,
first-ball four; Centenary Test at Lords 1980, J.A.'s last commentary [sic]
 Presented and produced by Peter Baxter

England v. The West Indies, 1950–1976. BBC Radio Collection, ZBBC 1174, 1990
   Double cassette of historic moments down the years, relayed by commentators Rex Alston, J.A., Learie Constantine, Ken Ablack, Roy Lawrence, Alan Gibson, Robert Hudson, Brian Johnston, Tony Cozier, Christopher Martin-Jenkins, Henry Blofeld, Norman Yardley, Freddie Brown, Trevor Bailey, Fred Trueman and Bill Frindall.
   Presented by Peter Baxter and produced by John Stanley

Great Cricket Matches. Commentaries and interviews 1948–1975. BBC Radio Collection, ZBBC 1181, 1990
   Eight of the best Test and one-day internationals from Rex Alston, J.A., Brian Johnston, Tony Cozier and others.
   Presented by Christopher Martin-Jenkins and Peter Baxter

Lord's: The Home of Cricket. BBC Radio Collection, ZBBC 1235, 1991
   Double cassette written and presented by E.W. Swanton. Includes J.A.'s Centenary Test commentary

Video Productions

The Story of Basingstoke from Earliest Times to 1964. The Regional Centre
  Told by John Arlott. Updated and transferred version of Derek Wren's tape/
slide show produced in 1964

Benson and Hedges Golden Great Batsmen. 1983
  Introduced by J.A. Researched and produced by David Frith

John Arlott's Vintage Cricket. A BBC TV Sports Presentation, 1988
  Memorable and historic happenings incorporating original black and white
film and radio commentary. Produced by John Bodnar

The Classic 1920 Silent Movie: Rosebud, the Girl from Casquets. Video Take 1.
Professional video production
  Written by Elizabeth Beresford. Starring J.A. as Sir Arlott Johns, an eccentric
old gentleman. Filmed entirely on Alderney. Produced and directed by Ronnie
Cairnduff.
  Plus *Alderney Memories*

The Classic 1920 Silent Movie: Rosebud and the Godfathers. Video Take 1.
Professional video production
  Written by Elizabeth Beresford. Starring J.A. as the infamous pirate Sir Arlott
Johns. Filmed entirely on Alderney. Produced and directed by Ronnie
Cairnduff.
  Plus *The Shout*: a drama documentary about Alderney's lifeboat and the early
history of the RNLI. Narrated by J.A.

The Classic 1920 Movie: Rosebud and the Murder on the Alderney Express. Apple
Television Ltd
  Written by Elizabeth Beresford. Featuring J.A. as the notorious hanging judge
Sir Arlott Johns. Filmed on location on Alderney. Music composed and
performed by Ian Lynn. Produced and directed by Ronnie Cairnduff.
  Plus *Just Another Day: A Day in the Life of Aurigny Air Services.*

Awards and Trophies

John Arlott kept his own authorship carefully hidden from view in his home. The same was true of the many awards and trophies that came his way. The following is a selection of the unusual and of the prestigious:

Small silver cup with handles. Inscribed 'S.N.B.C. [Probably a Southampton badminton club] L.T.J. Arlott, February 1938.' Possibly presented to J.A. for his feat in drinking fifteen pints of beer in one evening.

•◆•

Small silver pipe on oblong black mount. Silver inscription on side: 'Pipeman of the Year, 1971. Awarded by the Briar Pipe Trading Association: John Arlott.'

•◆•

OBE 1 January 1970

•◆•

University of Southampton. Degree of Master of Arts, *Honoris causa*. Acknowledging the eminent achievements. 13 July 1973

•◆•

The Open University: 'The Honorary Degree of Doctor of the University has been awarded to John Arlott, 6 June 1981.'

•◆•

Somerset CCC Honorary Membership plate

•◆•

British Press Awards: Sports Journalist of the Year, 1979

•◆•

Large silver cup with handle. Inscribed 'John Arlott. Happy Memories from the Sussex County Ground Reporters, 1980.'

•◆•

Silver trophy with two sculptured wavy uprights. Society of Authors: Pye Radio Awards 1980, Sports Personality of the Year.

•◆•

The John Player League: 'John Arlott for your contributions to the John Player League, 7 September 1980.' Left-arm bowler in silver on podium. Green quartz stand.

•◆•

Microphone on mounted stand, inscribed: 'John, from all his friends in Test Match Special.'

•◆•

Television and Radio Industries Club. The ITT Trophy, 1981, Sports Presenter of the Year. Presented by Princess Margaret at Grosvenor House, 2 April 1981

•◆•

Framed parchment certificate: 'Jurat St Emilion, 1981. In nomine Patris et Filii et Spiritus Sancti amen.'

•◆•

Framed parchment certificate: '1884–1984. 28 April 1985. Monsieur John Arlott a apporté son concours en qualité d'expert au Chapitre des Honneurs de la Jurade de Saint-Emilion. Le Premier Jurat, Le Procureur Syndie, Le Marguillier, Le Clerk'

•◆•

Glass trophy, inscribed: 'To the late John Arlott in recognition of his services to the promotion and development of the art of cricket commentary internationally. Accepted by Mrs Pat Arlott from Prime Minister Lester B. Bird on behalf of the Government and cricket-loving people of Antigua and Barbuda. St John's Antigua, 14 April 1994.'

Bibliography

John Arlott's principal publications are listed in Appendix B (p. 357). These titles, and much of the vast corpus of his other written and broadcast work – articles, appreciations, profiles, commentaries, forewords, memoirs, notes, surveys, talks etc. – have been read and listened to by the author over the years, and afresh for this biography. The items bearing John Arlott's name in the list that follows (which repeats some of the titles in Appendix B) are included here because they have provided specific data for this biography.

John Arlott and George Rostrevor Hamilton (eds.), *Landmarks: A Book of Topographical Verse for England Wales*, Cambridge University Press, 1943

John Arlott, *Of Period and Place*, Jonathan Cape, 1944 ('A Second-Hand Bookshop', 'To Andrew Young on Reading his Poems', 'Prayer for an Immortal Line', 'Cricket at Worcester, 1938')

John Arlott, 'Snow Scene', *Semaphore*, 1946

John Arlott (drawings by Michael Ayrton), *Clausentum*, Jonathan Cape, 1946 ('By Night (iii)')

John Arlott, 'Constable' and 'Call Him Tough', *St Martin's Review*, 1946

John Arlott, *Indian Summer*, Longmans, 1947

John Arlott, *Gone to the Cricket*, Longmans, 1948

John Arlott (ed.), *First Time in America: A Selection of Poems Never Before Published in the USA*, Duell, Sloan & Pearce Inc. (New York), 1948

John Arlott, *Gone to the Test Match*, Longmans, Green & Co., 1949

John Arlott, *Concerning Cricket*, Longmans, Green & Co., 1949

John Arlott, *Concerning Soccer*, Longmans, Green & Co., 1952

John Arlott, 'Dylan Thomas and Radio', *Adelphi*, vol. 30, No. 2, 1954

John Arlott, *Attention*, Newman Neame Take Home Books, 1959

John Arlott (ed. David Rayvern Allen), *A Word from Arlott*, Pelham Books, 1983

John Arlott (ed. David Rayvern Allen), *Arlott on Cricket*, Collins Willow, 1984

John Arlott (ed. David Rayvern Allen), *Another Word from Arlott*, Pelham Books, 1985

John Arlott and Mike Brearley, *Arlott: In Conversation with Mike Brearley*, Hodder & Stoughton in association with Channel Four Television, 1986

John Arlott (ed. David Rayvern Allen), *Arlott on Wine*, Collins Willow, 1986

John Arlott (ed.), *The Coloured Counties: Poems of Place in England and Wales*. Selected and introduced by John Arlott, J.M. Dent & Sons Ltd, 1988

John Arlott (ed. David Rayvern Allen), *The Essential John Arlott: Forty Years of Classic Cricket Writing*, Collins Willow, 1989

John Arlott, *Basingstoke Boy: The Autobiography*, Collins Willow, 1990

Annual Register, or a View of the History, Politics and Literature for the Year 1773, printed for J. Dodsley, Pall Mall, London, 1774

Clifford Bax, 'Portrait of Mr. W.S. of "Gulielmo Scespirio"', *New English Review*, 1946

John Betjeman, 'Autumn, 1964', adapted ms

Oswell Blakiston (ed.), *Packing my Cricket Bag: Happy Days and Holidays*, Phoenix House, 1949

Gerald Brodribb (ed.), *The Book of Cricket Verse*, Rupert Hart-Davis, 1953 ('To John Berry Hobbs on his Seventieth Birthday')

James Brough, *The Prince and the Lily*, Hodder & Stoughton, 1975

Peter Cannon-Brookes, *Michael Ayrton: An Illustrated Commentary*, Birmingham Museums and Art Galleries, 1978

John Corin, *Provident and the Story of the Brixham Smacks*, Tops'l Books, 1980

Trevor Evans (ed.), *Willow and Wine: The Great Bohunkus*, W.H. Allen, 1953

Paul Ferris (ed.), *Dylan Thomas: The Collected Letters*, Macmillan, 1985

Margot Fonteyn, *Margot Fonteyn*, W.H. Allen, 1975

Margot Fonteyn, *A Dancer's World*, W.H. Allen, 1978

Forster and Broadcasting: Aspects of E.M. Forster. Essays and Recollections Written for his Ninetieth Birthday, Arnold, 1969

George Glenton, *Last Chronicle of Bouverie Street*, Allen & Unwin, 1963

Justine Hopkins, *Michael Ayrton: A Biography*, André Deutsch, 1994

Richard Hough, *Louis and Victoria: The First Mountbattens*, Hamish Hamilton, 1974

James Pennethorne Hughes, *Thirty-Eight Poems*, John Baker, 1970

Mark Kerr, *Prince Louis of Battenberg*, Longmans

Bernard Knowles, *Southampton: The English Gateway*, 1951

John Marshall, *The Weaving Willow*, Hodder & Stoughton, 1953

C.C.H. Moriarty, *Police Law*, Butterworth & Co, 1st edn 1929

The Pageant of the Streets: Elizabeth Crowned Queen, Odhams Press, 1953

T.G. Rosenthal, 'Michael Ayrton: A Memoir', *Encounter*, May 1976

Arthur Russell (ed.), *The Cool Clear Voice: Ruth Pitter, Homage to a Poet*, Rapp & Whiting, 1969

Richard Shead, *Constant Lambert, 1905–1951*, Simon Publications, 1973

E.B. Stokes and R.C. Crossman, *Queen Mary's School, 1556–1972*, Bird Bros Ltd, Southampton, 1973

Derek Wren, *The Story of Basingstoke from Earliest Times to 1964* (video cassette), The Regional Centre

Noel Whitcomb, *A Particular Kind of Fool*, Quartet Books, 1990

George Woodcock, *Letter to the Past: An Autobiography*, Fitzhenry-Whiteside, Toronto, 1983

Correspondence from Richard Aldington, Rex Alston, Michael Ayrton, Edmund Blunden, E.M. Forster, Dylan Thomas, the Hon. Jeremy Thorpe, T.H. White. Scripts and memoranda: John Arlott collection and BBC Written Archives Centre, Caversham. Tapes, BBC Sound Archives.

Newspapers, magazines and periodicals: *Auckland Weekly News, Basingstoke Gazette, Birmingham Evening Dispatch, Bristol Evening Post, Bristol Evening World, Cape Argus, Cape Times, The Cricketer, Daily Express, Daily Herald, Daily Mail, Daily Mirror, Daily Worker, Durban Daily Dispatch, English Illustrated, Evening News, Evening Standard, Guardian, Herald of Wales, Johannesburg Star, Kent*

Messenger, Liberal News, The Listener, Natal Daily News, Natal Mercury, News Chronicle, North Cheshire Herald, Northampton Chronicle & Echo, Now and Then, Observer, Playfair Cricket Annuals, Pretoria News, Public Opinion, Punch, Radio Times, Rand Daily Mail, Southern Daily Echo, Southern Evening Echo, The Spectator, Spotlight, Sunday Empire News, Sunday Times, Sunday Times (Durban)*, The Times, Wisden Cricket Monthly, Wisden Cricketers' Almanack*